INDECENT EXPOSURE

and the

Court as Custodian of Morals

Australia, New York & Philadelphia
Read-Me.Org Inc.

Library of Congress Control Number: 2024940308

ISBN: 978-0-911577--90-7 (Paper)
ISBN: 978-0-911577-75-4 (Digital)
ISBN: 978-0-911577-76-1 (Hardcover)

Acknowledgments

First, a word about the cover art. This is not a real person. It was the image generated by an early version of Google's Image-FX AI image generator in response to the query "indecent exposure." I was puzzled at first, then realized that her expression captured the essence of modern indecent exposure laws that focus on offense, annoyance, and alarm of the audience. The image also hints at another aspect of modern jurisprudence biased toward detailed management of female nakedness, providing another possible source motivating such a facial expression. The back cover art is also AI-generated. Any resemblance of either image to any person, alive or dead, is purely coincidental.

The technology platforms of Google and Lexis were instrumental in updating and synthesizing fifty years of content into a coherent and well-supported series of observations about the history of the laws and their relationship to the evolution of constitutional interpretation by courts, framing the corollary of custos morum and its relationship with fragmentation of sources of moral authority.

The creation of this book has been a long and largely solitary journey. I credit Graeme Newman, chairman of my dissertation committee, for inspiring an enduring curiosity about crime and deviance, and their role in civil societies. He was also instrumental in reconstituting the committee and leading me through the process of completion of the degree. Many thanks to Graeme and the rest of my dissertation committee, James Acker, Dana Peterson, and Frankie Bailey, for delivering the peer review that I considered a crucial element of closure. Special thanks to Dana for extraordinary support in navigating through the administrative processes necessary to completion of the Ph.D. degree. And thank you, Graeme and Jim, for recommending the dissertation for University Distinguished Dissertation award.

I want to thank my family for encouraging me to complete the work. I owe a debt of gratitude to Michael Boots of the UAlbany Alumni Association for keeping me connected to the School of Criminal Justice and, thus, reminding me of the pressing need for more scholarship to inform policy.

Only a couple of people outside the committee read drafts. Both provided invaluable insights and advice. Kelsey Kofford, former Editor-in-Chief, Hastings International & Comparative Law Review, did a wonderful job of giving feedback on general themes, tone, flow, cultural sensitivities, and technical compliance. Liz Seif, a professional freelance editor and American lawyer and former editor in chief of the Kentucky Law Journal, provided invaluable assistance in technical aspects of preparation of the document.

INDECENT EXPOSURE

and the
Court as Custodian of Morals

BRUCE DAVIS

READ-ME.ORG INC.
OPEN ACCESS PUBLISHERS

Australia, New York & Philadelphia

Table of Contents

Prologue

> The authority of the state, under the Constitution, to enact "morals legislation"—laws reflecting some traditional morality having no authentic social purpose to protect other persons or property—has always been assumed; it has deep roots, and it has seemed obvious and beyond question..[1]

Indecent exposure has been a crime in America since colonial times. Laws governing this crime are a cornerstone of government regulation of morals in America, sharing a common history with the jurisprudence of religion, obscenity, marriage, and sexual relations. The first reported case of indecent exposure in English common law is a widely acknowledged source of American moral jurisprudence that justifies the courts' role as *custos morum*, or custodian of the morals.

The state interests protected by indecent exposure laws are prevention of public behaviors contrary to prevailing moral order, often referred to as evil examples, and protection of the public from offense, annoyance, or alarm caused by such activities. The scope, credibility, and effectiveness of laws prohibiting such evil examples have diminished with changing demographics, the decline of Christianity as the dominant moral authority in America, and the progress of media technology.

These changes have left nuisance as the sole state interest supporting indecent exposure laws in most jurisdictions. This dependence on nuisance theory is evident in audience-focused definitions of the crime in most state statutes. Trends in U.S. Supreme Court doctrine have been weakening this remaining justification, creating questions about the continuing viability of indecent exposure laws as they are currently structured.

Laws governing indecent exposure have been taken for granted academically, politically, and legally, despite their central role in government regulation of morals. Lack of understanding of their history has created confusion, fostering misinterpretation of precedents and reinvention of fundamental concepts that inhibit development of coherent policies for societal management of sexuality and nakedness.

Historical analysis of indecent exposure laws is a heuristic exercise that exposes many insights about the legal management of morality in

America. These insights feed research hypotheses regarding the interplay of civil and religious authorities in managing nakedness in nominally secular societies. The analyses also expose and inform potential constitutional challenges to the laws based on the Establishment Clause, free exercise, free speech, substantive and procedural due process, vagueness, overbreadth, and equal protection claims under the First, Fifth, Ninth, Tenth, and Fourteenth Amendments to the U.S. Constitution.

The history and certain aspects of the recent ruling in *Dobbs v. Jackson Women's Health Organization* (2022).[2] foreshadow obsolescence of the courts' long reign as *custos morum*. The historical analysis highlights potential threats to America's constitutional democracy posed by the degradation of its Christian moral foundation. The findings identify needs for additional research about laws and regulations governing indecent exposure, a crime about which questions are seldom asked or, when asked, are often approached with assumptions influenced by conscious and unconscious biases.

The evolution of these laws in constitutional context indicates a worsening moral crisis as the legal system wrestles with the effects of competing sources of moral authority to guide policy and judicial decision-making. The costs and benefits of potential changes in indecent exposure laws are unclear. Changes in the definition and administration of the laws are likely. The analysis closes with discussion of a legal framework for management of morals consistent with the original meaning of the Constitution that may be better suited to America's demographic trends and political ideals than the status quo or meandering that has characterized *custos morum* for the past half century. Although this approach might mitigate some of the issues in moral jurisprudence, there is much about it to debate and refine.

What is it about public display of nakedness that requires the force of law to buttress the effects of shame, modesty, and clothing in keeping people's "private areas" covered? Fortenberry's literature review of sexual modesty laments the lack of a coherent scientific perspective on its role across multiple domains of expression and experience[3] These implications could be better understood if the law allowed freedom to experiment, assess, and learn. But at what costs?

The first few steps have been taken here by exposing and describing the sources and evolution of the laws and their relation to the U.S. Constitution, hopefully, opening the door to further reflection, reform, experimentation, and study of the ontology of nakedness. The history and analyses uncover numerous important and provocative opportunities for more research and critical thinking.

1. Introduction

> Full nakedness! All joys are due to thee,
> As souls unbodied, bodies unclothed must be, to taste whole joys.
>
> – John Donne[4]

> In women, it deadens the sense of shame and in men it destroys respect for womanhood.
>
> – Hermann Goring[5]

> Render unto Caesar the things that are Caesar's and unto God the things that are God's.
>
> – Jesus Christ[6]

Ever wonder why we all enter the world naked and spend the rest of our lives clothed, encased in shame and modesty, reinforced by law? Who is right, the poet or the fascist? Neither? Is public nakedness a matter for Caesar, God, or both? Indecent exposure law is the arbiter of these perspectives. The first thought of many people when indecent exposure is mentioned is a flasher or pervert masturbating in the shadows. Many other instantiations of the crime and its actors, audiences, and circumstances are subsumed under the concept. The multiplicity of criminal activities, implicated state interests, and interplay of church and state can be beguiling. We will explore these and other weighty matters in legal enforcement of morals.

Indecent exposure has been a crime in America since colonial times. The law adds belt and suspenders to shame and modesty to confine live nakedness to homes and legally managed presentations in nominally private spaces such as bars and strip clubs, sex-segregated facilities, clothes-optional beaches, and sparse communities of secluded nudist camps. Outside these authorized spaces and practices, nakedness Engenders fines, imprisonment, possible registration as a sex offender, and ostracization.

The laws governing this crime, a cornerstone of government regulation of decency in America, share a common history with the jurisprudence of religion, obscenity, marriage, and sexuality. [7] Indecent exposure laws have been justified by state interests in preventing public behaviors contrary to America's Christian moral order, often referred to as evil examples, and protecting the public from offense, annoyance, or alarm caused by such activities. The scope, credibility, and effectiveness of laws prohibiting such evil examples have diminished with changing demographics, the decline of Christianity as the dominant moral authority in America, and the progress of media technology. Reality television and social networks provide compelling evidence of this decline. Series have been created around a wide range of immoral and indecent lifestyles, broadcasting and streaming an endless collage of evil examples. Images of fully nude men and women are readily available on television and the internet, providing easy access to adults and children..[8]

These changes have left nuisance as the sole state interest supporting indecent exposure laws in most jurisdictions. This dependence on nuisance theory is evident in the audience-focused definition of the crime in most state statutes. Trends in U.S. Supreme Court (hereinafter referred to variously as the "Supreme Court" or the "Court") doctrine have been weakening this remaining justification, creating questions about the continuing viability of indecent exposure laws as they are currently structured.

Nakedness is legally managed in all modern societies, not just America. This seminal study of substantive law focuses on the United States. It unearths facts, notes trends and themes, and identifies issues, all as fodder to educate legal analyses and policy discussions in the United States. It is also intended to provoke further research into the role of management of nakedness, clothing, and adornment of bodies in the power relations of civilization. This seminal study of the law lays down first steps on a journey to better understand the role and jurisprudential contours of criminal law in managing morality and maintaining order in civil societies. It addresses critical questions regarding sources of moral authority in a secular society based on a framework of constitutional democracy.

The analysis generates questions about the legitimacy and viability of legacy sources of moral authority and the balance of state interests and individual liberties defined by the crime. Evolving constitutional interpretation regarding this balance and flagging support for moral consensus historically dominated by Christian theology raise serious questions about the continuing validity of such laws and their contributions to maintaining moral order.

The crime is defined by statute in all states. It is also a common-law crime in some jurisdictions. Indecent exposures generally must be intentional, not accidental. Most statutes require evidence of lewd or lascivious intent that offends, annoys, or alarms unwilling audiences in public places, explicitly relying on nuisance theory as the relevant state interest. Lewd and lascivious intent have played an important role in the development of the laws. "Lewd" is derived from Middle English. Its modern meaning is "crude or offensive in a sexual way."[9] "Lascivious" has a similar etymology, meaning "tending to incite lust."[10] Where they differ is that "lewd" is crude and "lascivious" is intended to communicate or provoke sexual desire. Taken together, they describe a crude or offensive effort to incite lust, a clumsy courtship of sorts. Distinctions between the terms "lewd" and "lascivious" are generally ignored by courts and legislatures because they are often used together in statutes and judicial opinions as being synonymous with vulgarity and offensive expressions of sexual intent that annoy or alarm an unwilling audience. Some states have substituted intent to arouse the actor or an unwilling audience. The U.S. Supreme Court employs a similar measure of "prurience" to assess obscenity.

The crux of the crime, when this intent is present, is avoidance of unwanted real or imagined sexual advances. The audience focus of statutes means that the annoyance or alarm that triggers the crime is not always dependent on the intent of the actor. Thus, simple public nakedness may be prosecuted.

The state interest in prevention of evil examples traces to two sources: a seventeenth-century English common-law case involving misdemeanors against the king's peace and a great scandal for Christianity during the reign of King Charles II and American colonial laws prohibiting "unclean carriages."[11] Treatise writer William Blackstone[12] first used the term "evil example" in his *Commentaries*, published in England in 1765. Prevention of evil example focuses on prohibition of public displays of "vicious and debauched"[13] or "lewd and lascivious" behaviors that undermine the moral fabric of society.

Moral crime as a nuisance traces its roots to the same period in English history when brothels were declared public nuisances. The most oft-cited precedent where both these state interests were implicated is *Le Roy v. Sedley* (1663) (hereinafter referred to as *Sedley's Case*), a case that has achieved lasting notoriety.[14]

The nature of the state interest is relevant to characteristics of the actor and audience in indecent exposure. Nuisance law is audience focused. It prevents actions that may offend, annoy, or alarm an unwilling audience. Evil example focuses on the actor's potential long-term effect on the moral foundation of society by prohibiting actions that might have a corrupting influence on audiences. No evidence of actual negative audience reaction is required in either case; it can be presumed. These state interests originally operated in synchronicity. Nuisance focused on reaction of the audience regardless of the intent of the actor. Evil example focused on the intent of the actor regardless of audience. A positive audience reaction to evil example could lead to prosecution of the audience.

These state interests share a common foundation: Christian religious doctrine as the source of moral truth. Indecent exposure laws originated in the seventeenth century in England and the American colonies during a time of rising tension between traditional allies of church and state. The temporal courts in England began to exert their punitive powers as religion and ecclesiastical practices were losing effectiveness due to laxity, corruption, and changes in the public's fear of God and church. On the other hand, there were no ecclesiastical courts in the colonies, which left original jurisdiction over morals to the temporal courts and assemblies. Legal precedent from these times and places melded during the nineteenth century to form the indecent exposure laws of America.

Modern prosecutions focus on public nuisance, with justifications variously characterized as avoiding offense, annoyance, and alarm; protecting audience sensibilities; protecting minors; managing traffic; preserving public spaces as inclusive and safe environments; and, rarely, maintaining good health and hygiene..[15] Most statutes require a reasonable expectation that the audience will be annoyed or alarmed by the exposure. The reasonableness of the audience reaction is generally not assessed. It is implied from a presumed sense of shared morality..[16] This presumption is weakening as the dominance of the Christian religion in America is increasingly challenged by other sources of moral authority. This ambiguity will become evident in the examination of case-law precedent.

Enforcement of morals in general is waning. Most moral offenses of the colonial period are no longer crimes. Indecent exposure has stood the test of time. It has been questioned primarily by constitutional arguments advocating the display of women's breasts for breastfeeding, commercial purposes, and gender equality. Nearly all offenders are men. The penis remains cloaked in shame and the subject of most prosecutions for indecent exposure.

Prologue

> The authority of the state, under the Constitution, to enact "morals legislation"—laws reflecting some traditional morality having no authentic social purpose to protect other persons or property—has always been assumed; it has deep roots, and it has seemed obvious and beyond question..[1]

Indecent exposure has been a crime in America since colonial times. Laws governing this crime are a cornerstone of government regulation of morals in America, sharing a common history with the jurisprudence of religion, obscenity, marriage, and sexual relations. The first reported case of indecent exposure in English common law is a widely acknowledged source of American moral jurisprudence that justifies the courts' role as *custos morum*, or custodian of the morals.

The state interests protected by indecent exposure laws are prevention of public behaviors contrary to prevailing moral order, often referred to as evil examples, and protection of the public from offense, annoyance, or alarm caused by such activities. The scope, credibility, and effectiveness of laws prohibiting such evil examples have diminished with changing demographics, the decline of Christianity as the dominant moral authority in America, and the progress of media technology.

These changes have left nuisance as the sole state interest supporting indecent exposure laws in most jurisdictions. This dependence on nuisance theory is evident in audience-focused definitions of the crime in most state statutes. Trends in U.S. Supreme Court doctrine have been weakening this remaining justification, creating questions about the continuing viability of indecent exposure laws as they are currently structured.

Laws governing indecent exposure have been taken for granted academically, politically, and legally, despite their central role in government regulation of morals. Lack of understanding of their history has created confusion, fostering misinterpretation of precedents and reinvention of fundamental concepts that inhibit development of coherent policies for societal management of sexuality and nakedness.

Historical analysis of indecent exposure laws is a heuristic exercise that exposes many insights about the legal management of morality in

America. These insights feed research hypotheses regarding the interplay of civil and religious authorities in managing nakedness in nominally secular societies. The analyses also expose and inform potential constitutional challenges to the laws based on the Establishment Clause, free exercise, free speech, substantive and procedural due process, vagueness, overbreadth, and equal protection claims under the First, Fifth, Ninth, Tenth, and Fourteenth Amendments to the U.S. Constitution.

The history and certain aspects of the recent ruling in *Dobbs v. Jackson Women's Health Organization* (2022)[2] foreshadow obsolescence of the courts' long reign as *custos morum*. The historical analysis highlights potential threats to America's constitutional democracy posed by the degradation of its Christian moral foundation. The findings identify needs for additional research about laws and regulations governing indecent exposure, a crime about which questions are seldom asked or, when asked, are often approached with assumptions influenced by conscious and unconscious biases.

The evolution of these laws in constitutional context indicates a worsening moral crisis as the legal system wrestles with the effects of competing sources of moral authority to guide policy and judicial decision-making. The costs and benefits of potential changes in indecent exposure laws are unclear. Changes in the definition and administration of the laws are likely. The analysis closes with discussion of a legal framework for management of morals consistent with the original meaning of the Constitution that may be better suited to America's demographic trends and political ideals than the status quo or meandering that has characterized *custos morum* for the past half century. Although this approach might mitigate some of the issues in moral jurisprudence, there is much about it to debate and refine.

What is it about public display of nakedness that requires the force of law to buttress the effects of shame, modesty, and clothing in keeping people's "private areas" covered? Fortenberry's literature review of sexual modesty laments the lack of a coherent scientific perspective on its role across multiple domains of expression and experience[3] These implications could be better understood if the law allowed freedom to experiment, assess, and learn. But at what costs?

The first few steps have been taken here by exposing and describing the sources and evolution of the laws and their relation to the U.S. Constitution, hopefully, opening the door to further reflection, reform, experimentation, and study of the ontology of nakedness. The history and analyses uncover numerous important and provocative opportunities for more research and critical thinking.

1. Introduction

> Full nakedness! All joys are due to thee,
> As souls unbodied, bodies unclothed must be, to taste whole joys.
>
> – John Donne[4]

> In women, it deadens the sense of shame and in men it destroys respect for womanhood.
>
> – Hermann Goring[5]

> Render unto Caesar the things that are Caesar's and unto God the things that are God's.
>
> – Jesus Christ[6]

Ever wonder why we all enter the world naked and spend the rest of our lives clothed, encased in shame and modesty, reinforced by law? Who is right, the poet or the fascist? Neither? Is public nakedness a matter for Caesar, God, or both? Indecent exposure law is the arbiter of these perspectives. The first thought of many people when indecent exposure is mentioned is a flasher or pervert masturbating in the shadows. Many other instantiations of the crime and its actors, audiences, and circumstances are subsumed under the concept. The multiplicity of criminal activities, implicated state interests, and interplay of church and state can be beguiling. We will explore these and other weighty matters in legal enforcement of morals.

Indecent exposure has been a crime in America since colonial times. The law adds belt and suspenders to shame and modesty to confine live nakedness to homes and legally managed presentations in nominally private spaces such as bars and strip clubs, sex-segregated facilities, clothes-optional beaches, and sparse communities of secluded nudist camps. Outside these authorized spaces and practices, nakedness Engenders fines, imprisonment, possible registration as a sex offender, and ostracization.

The laws governing this crime, a cornerstone of government regulation of decency in America, share a common history with the jurisprudence of religion, obscenity, marriage, and sexuality.[7] Indecent exposure laws have been justified by state interests in preventing public behaviors contrary to America's Christian moral order, often referred to as evil examples, and protecting the public from offense, annoyance, or alarm caused by such activities. The scope, credibility, and effectiveness of laws prohibiting such evil examples have diminished with changing demographics, the decline of Christianity as the dominant moral authority in America, and the progress of media technology. Reality television and social networks provide compelling evidence of this decline. Series have been created around a wide range of immoral and indecent lifestyles, broadcasting and streaming an endless collage of evil examples. Images of fully nude men and women are readily available on television and the internet, providing easy access to adults and children.[8]

These changes have left nuisance as the sole state interest supporting indecent exposure laws in most jurisdictions. This dependence on nuisance theory is evident in the audience-focused definition of the crime in most state statutes. Trends in U.S. Supreme Court (hereinafter referred to variously as the "Supreme Court" or the "Court") doctrine have been weakening this remaining justification, creating questions about the continuing viability of indecent exposure laws as they are currently structured.

Nakedness is legally managed in all modern societies, not just America. This seminal study of substantive law focuses on the United States. It unearths facts, notes trends and themes, and identifies issues, all as fodder to educate legal analyses and policy discussions in the United States. It is also intended to provoke further research into the role of management of nakedness, clothing, and adornment of bodies in the power relations of civilization. This seminal study of the law lays down first steps on a journey to better understand the role and jurisprudential contours of criminal law in managing morality and maintaining order in civil societies. It addresses critical questions regarding sources of moral authority in a secular society based on a framework of constitutional democracy.

The analysis generates questions about the legitimacy and viability of legacy sources of moral authority and the balance of state interests and individual liberties defined by the crime. Evolving constitutional interpretation regarding this balance and flagging support for moral consensus historically dominated by Christian theology raise serious questions about the continuing validity of such laws and their contributions to maintaining moral order.

The crime is defined by statute in all states. It is also a common-law crime in some jurisdictions. Indecent exposures generally must be intentional, not accidental. Most statutes require evidence of lewd or lascivious intent that offends, annoys, or alarms unwilling audiences in public places, explicitly relying on nuisance theory as the relevant state interest. Lewd and lascivious intent have played an important role in the development of the laws. "Lewd" is derived from Middle English. Its modern meaning is "crude or offensive in a sexual way."[9] "Lascivious" has a similar etymology, meaning "tending to incite lust."[10] Where they differ is that "lewd" is crude and "lascivious" is intended to communicate or provoke sexual desire. Taken together, they describe a crude or offensive effort to incite lust, a clumsy courtship of sorts. Distinctions between the terms "lewd" and "lascivious" are generally ignored by courts and legislatures because they are often used together in statutes and judicial opinions as being synonymous with vulgarity and offensive expressions of sexual intent that annoy or alarm an unwilling audience. Some states have substituted intent to arouse the actor or an unwilling audience. The U.S. Supreme Court employs a similar measure of "prurience" to assess obscenity.

The crux of the crime, when this intent is present, is avoidance of unwanted real or imagined sexual advances. The audience focus of statutes means that the annoyance or alarm that triggers the crime is not always dependent on the intent of the actor. Thus, simple public nakedness may be prosecuted.

The state interest in prevention of evil examples traces to two sources: a seventeenth-century English common-law case involving misdemeanors against the king's peace and a great scandal for Christianity during the reign of King Charles II and American colonial laws prohibiting "unclean carriages."[11] Treatise writer William Blackstone[12] first used the term "evil example" in his *Commentaries*, published in England in 1765. Prevention of evil example focuses on prohibition of public displays of "vicious and debauched"[13] or "lewd and lascivious" behaviors that undermine the moral fabric of society.

Moral crime as a nuisance traces its roots to the same period in English history when brothels were declared public nuisances. The most oft-cited precedent where both these state interests were implicated is *Le Roy v. Sedley* (1663) (hereinafter referred to as *Sedley's Case*), a case that has achieved lasting notoriety.[14]

The nature of the state interest is relevant to characteristics of the actor and audience in indecent exposure. Nuisance law is audience focused. It prevents actions that may offend, annoy, or alarm an unwilling audience. Evil example focuses on the actor's potential long-term effect on the moral foundation of society by prohibiting actions that might have a corrupting influence on audiences. No evidence of actual negative audience reaction is required in either case; it can be presumed. These state interests originally operated in synchronicity. Nuisance focused on reaction of the audience regardless of the intent of the actor. Evil example focused on the intent of the actor regardless of audience. A positive audience reaction to evil example could lead to prosecution of the audience.

These state interests share a common foundation: Christian religious doctrine as the source of moral truth. Indecent exposure laws originated in the seventeenth century in England and the American colonies during a time of rising tension between traditional allies of church and state. The temporal courts in England began to exert their punitive powers as religion and ecclesiastical practices were losing effectiveness due to laxity, corruption, and changes in the public's fear of God and church. On the other hand, there were no ecclesiastical courts in the colonies, which left original jurisdiction over morals to the temporal courts and assemblies. Legal precedent from these times and places melded during the nineteenth century to form the indecent exposure laws of America.

Modern prosecutions focus on public nuisance, with justifications variously characterized as avoiding offense, annoyance, and alarm; protecting audience sensibilities; protecting minors; managing traffic; preserving public spaces as inclusive and safe environments; and, rarely, maintaining good health and hygiene.[15] Most statutes require a reasonable expectation that the audience will be annoyed or alarmed by the exposure. The reasonableness of the audience reaction is generally not assessed. It is implied from a presumed sense of shared morality.[16] This presumption is weakening as the dominance of the Christian religion in America is increasingly challenged by other sources of moral authority. This ambiguity will become evident in the examination of case-law precedent.

Enforcement of morals in general is waning. Most moral offenses of the colonial period are no longer crimes. Indecent exposure has stood the test of time. It has been questioned primarily by constitutional arguments advocating the display of women's breasts for breastfeeding, commercial purposes, and gender equality. Nearly all offenders are men. The penis remains cloaked in shame and the subject of most prosecutions for indecent exposure.

An enduring exception to the prevention of evil examples emerged in the nineteenth century during development of obscenity law when a privileged space for presentations of naked bodies in media was created, facilitating the development of the adult entertainment industry. In these commercial presentations of primarily female naked bodies, expressions of lewd and lascivious intent are valuable marketing attributes rather than indicia of criminal intent.[17] Permission of the audience and controlled access to the exposure may help to explain the differential treatment from a nuisance perspective. The scale and growth of this industry are signals of decay of the state interest in prevention of evil examples and embody an insidious distortion and channelization of sexuality leading to reciprocal arguments of exploitation.

This study begins with exploration of English common-law and colonial statutory roots of American indecent exposure laws. It first examines in detail the widely acknowledged precedent in English common law, *Sedley's Case* (1663), where the court declared for the first time that it would henceforth be *custos morum*, or custodian of morals. The other cornerstone of American indecent exposure law is the colonial statutes that provided authorities with comprehensive judicial and legislative governance of morals, including indecent exposure. These colonial laws were in place decades before *Sedley's Case* driven by the largely Puritan ethic of early settlers in the New England colonies.

Legal doctrines governing obscenity and pornography in America developed during the nineteenth century to manage channelization of indecent exposure into media technologies, beginning with books, pamphlets, and artwork. The U.S. Supreme Court began deciding a long and tortured series of cases assessing these media derivatives of indecent exposure. As Justice Douglas noted in his concurring opinion in *A Book Named "John Cleland's Memoirs of a Woman of Pleasure v. Attorney General of Massachusetts"* (1966), "[i]t is generally agreed that the first reported case involving obscene conduct is *The King v. Sir Charles Sedley*."[18] *Sedley's Case* (1663) had marked a transition in management of morals from ecclesiastical to common law, serving as the fountainhead for application of *custos morum* (custodian of morals) to indecent exposure, obscenity, pornography, and other matters of public morality.

Justice Douglas lamented that the evolution of obscenity doctrine was fraught with uncertainty: "There is no definition of the term. There is no basis of identification. There is no unity in describing what is obscene literature, or in prosecuting it. There is little more than the ability to smell it."[19] As we will see, his anguish presaged a continuing degradation of what had once been clear images of public indecency in America. This is one of only two mentions of *Sedley's Case* (1663) by the U.S. Supreme Court despite the Court having heartily embraced the role of *custos morum* that the case created. This case is often buried beneath the precedent spawned in the development of the judicial doctrines of public indecency and obscenity. Its role will be exposed and explained.

The U.S. Supreme Court assumed the role of *custos morum* in the late 1800s. It embraced the role with a passion in the second half of the twentieth century, reshaping the moral landscape of America. Beginning in 1957 with *Roth v. United States*,[20] a case involving obscene publications, the Court contributed to (or mirrored) a decline in traditional Christian moral dominance with rulings that decriminalized certain immoral activities in response to constitutional challenges, which primarily related to freedom of speech and privacy. This trend inspired challenges to the constitutionality of laws prohibiting public nakedness, with mixed and often confusing and contradictory results. Evolution of American jurisprudential, social, and political ideals since *Roth* (1957) raise questions about whether indecent exposure laws would survive well-documented constitutional challenges informed by the history presented here.

The Supreme Court has chipped away at traditional rationales for indecent exposure laws—evil example and nuisance—in cases involving hate speech, adult entertainment, political protests, and religious practices. The U.S. Constitution envisioned a limited government where individuals surrender certain natural rights. The Supreme Court later developed a notion "granting" rights. This practice has created considerable confusion and controversy in constitutional interpretation. The Court's posture evokes a balancing of state interests and individual rights that are expressed or implied in the text of the Constitution. A careful study of the original meaning of the Constitution as it relates to moral jurisprudence will shine new light on the Court's performance as *custos morum*.

The prohibition of public nakedness is an increasingly obvious carve-out from growing constitutional protections of life, liberty, and the pursuit of happiness in moral matters. The harm (offense, annoyance, alarm) caused by nakedness has been largely unquestioned despite there being many other activities in public that annoy people that are not criminal. Some of these activities are protected by constitutional rights of free speech and due process. Examination of precedent will expose and explain the factors that courts have employed in relevant constitutional analyses and how the calculus has trended toward greater protection of individual liberties amid the decay of moral consensus. The analysis will show that the Supreme Court's moral jurisprudence has set it on a collision course with laws regulating bodily morality and how this may impact the crime of indecent exposure and legal management of morals in the future.

In modern America, activities that grossly flout community standards but are not crimes, and actors who justify their offenses in constitutional terms, are proliferating. In contrast, claims of constitutional protection for public nakedness have generally failed except in the realm of adult entertainment. A key factor in this limited success is the view that the body has no inherent expression; it serves only as a canvas for expression. This is a strange yet powerful perception. It is presumed to require no explanation. Christian moral doctrine would be an easy answer if not for the commercial exemption. Christian doctrine as the answer would pose problems with the Establishment and Free Expression Clauses of the Bill of Rights. Regardless of the constitutional questions, the moral hegemony of Christianity is crumbling, lessening the persuasiveness of this rationale. If the justification is only to avoid annoying people, that is a weak argument for employing the force of criminal law.

The genesis and evolution of indecent exposure laws, which would have better informed judicial reasoning when assessing such claims, have not been addressed by scholars. The history of indecent exposure laws reveals their foundations. Facing foursquare this source of the laws lends credence to novel constitutional challenges based on the Establishment Clause and equal protection. The research also fuels renewed constitutional challenges based on vagueness, overbreadth, speech, liberty, and privacy.

Moral issues no longer can be resolved simply by reference to authority once provided by the Christian religion. Demographic trends point to continuing significant declines in Christian affiliation. Legacy Christian moral principles are not easily accommodated in government initiatives to embrace secular humanism, polytheism, empiricism, and the internet as America's democracy matures. The growing share of the population selecting "none" as their religion evidences a decreasing consensus on moral judgments based on established religion. Management of morals is likely to be further complicated by the advance of agnosticism based on science, especially computer technology, where a new god is emerging with the development of artificial intelligence. "Moral authority," as used in this work, encompasses all these sources of moral truth. The quest for an acceptable source of moral authority in America is struggling to find its footing. This stress may also be due to the maturation of constitutional democracy as it overcomes a homogeneous morality and replaces it with a more democratic pluralistic morality with local roots, managed by elected officials. Both paths present many issues. Left unresolved, this ambiguity could lead to collapse of America's model of liberal democracy.

Without a political vision, the seemingly inexorable transition to a more pragmatic rule of law regarding regulation of morals is meandering down an intuitive path. It is fundamentally a political change, best guided by elected officials, consistent with the original meaning of the Constitutional. With this in mind, the confusion and contention over morality may be signaling that the time has come for abandonment of the court's role as *custos morum*. Local legislative management of public nakedness is likely to provide a better means of realizing constitutional ideals by allowing more robust experimentation generating data analytics that feed policy decisions about how to adapt the regulation of morals to maintain good order. This thesis deserves more study and support from scholars to inform policy and enforcement decisions. Courts are not equipped to fund, manage, and assess such policy research, nor are they accountable to the electorate.

Lack of understanding of the history of indecent exposure laws has created confusion, fostered reinvention of concepts, and inhibited development of coherent policies for management of sexuality and nakedness. This study is intended to provoke more intellectual and academic focus on indecent exposure laws and their consequences. The crime has not been taken seriously by scholars or the judiciary. Questions are seldom asked and, when asked, they are often framed as presumptions and pursued with conscious and unconscious biases. This inaugural multidisciplinary study touches on many perspectives in describing the crime, exploring its legal history, assessing judicial and statutory precedent to better guide constitutional analyses, theorizing about the role of management of bodies in maintaining order in civil society, and proposing a model for such management better suited to modern American democratic ideals.

Objectives

The objectives of this study are to:

1. Raise awareness of the role of indecent exposure laws in the balance of liberty and order in American society and of the theoretical and practical need for research;
2. Map the structure and history of indecent exposure laws and origins of the court as *custos morum*, custodian of the morals of the people, by
    a. identifying the roots of indecent exposure laws in the seventeenth century in England and the American colonies;
    b. showing the development of case-law and statutory precedents for modern laws; and
    c. describing and explaining variations in the number and nature of elements of the crime in modern common law and in state statutes;
3. Describe explicit and implicit rationales for the laws by
    a. isolating and explaining the forces that created and shaped the laws, including, but not limited to, personal, political, economic, and religious motivations; and
    b. articulating the nature of the governmental, societal, and individual interests affected by the laws;
4. Explore arguments concerning the constitutionality of these laws by
    a. examining modern constitutional doctrine regarding police power and other governmental involvement in the establishment and free exercise of religion and protection of individual liberty, privacy, and freedom of expression as they relate to indecent exposure; and
    b. informing judicial arguments and legislative policies with principled discussion of the degree of concordance between the texts and history of indecent exposure laws, their ostensible purposes, and constitutional limitations on governmental authority as interpreted in contemporary Supreme Court doctrine; and
5. Explore new models for legal management of bodily morality that may be better suited to ongoing changes in sources of moral authority in America's maturing constitutional democracy.

Methodology

This study has two primary components. It begins with a legal history that explores the evolution of indecency exposure laws since the transition of such crimes from ecclesiastical to temporal authorities in the seventeenth century. This history then informs a reevaluation of the relationship of the laws to various constitutional rights.

The historical methodology is similar to Jerome Hall's approach in his book *Theft, Law, and Society*.[21] It includes an in-depth historical study of common-law and state statute development of indecent exposure, identifying its juridical and legislative origins and delineating major paths of diffusion from these starting points. The findings are analyzed using case history and institutional analysis techniques to add depth and meaning to the legal precedents and assess the use of these judgments as precedent in later cases. Municipal codes, which are not systematically examined, are a worthy area for further study.

The legal history is augmented by evidence of religious, political, economic, and social conditions and individual personalities that may have given rise to, or shaped, the laws. Whereas Hall's focus in examining the crime of theft was on economics, the presumptive centers of attention when considering indecent exposure laws are religion and politics. The religious origins of the laws are described in detail. Study of demographic trends tender research hypotheses about effects of population composition and shared morality on the viability of America's constitutional democracy divorced from religion. The discussions of context are more an invitation to further research than rigorous, properly supported arguments. Unlike laws against theft, America's indecent exposure laws raise various substantial constitutional questions.

The study of previous cases with arguably similar facts, known as precedents, is the foundation of common law. It is a fundamental principle of American jurisprudence. The common law develops on a case-by-case basis by applying decisions in reported cases with similar facts to determine just and equitable outcomes.[22] The process is intended to pass down the wisdom of previous generations, foster evenhanded decision-making, and contribute to a perception of integrity in the judicial process. It can, at various times, serve as an anchor impeding accommodation of social change in the pursuit of justice or as an inspiration for orderly evolution of judicial doctrine to support it. It is generally a source of moderation.

The chronological organization of case precedent employed here facilitates an understanding of the development of the laws. Selection of cases is thematic and qualitative. The selections are oft-cited cases that exemplify important elements of precedent in defining modern laws, showing paths of migration, and setting the stage for provocative constitutional analyses regarding the balance of individual rights and community interests and the relationship between the government and established religion in management of morals.

Short summaries of cases add important context for understanding the genesis of indecent exposure law and its role in society. They illustrate the evolution of key elements of the crime: what is exposed and the nature of the actor, audience, place, and relevant state interests. There are frequent quotations to capture the spirit of the times. Careful examination of case-law and statutory precedent exposes threads of progression of core concepts and helps identify political and legal discontinuities.

The U.S. Constitution and attendant Bill of Rights describe basic elements of the structure of a limited government. Their provisions are less a set of rules than a statement of ideals for a constitutional democracy. The Bill of Rights contains the amendments to the Constitution addressing the balance of state interests and individual liberties. These foundational documents are purposely vague, fostering prolonged relevance as society evolves but giving rise to contention about both the substance and methods of interpretation.

The constitutional analyses examine indecent exposure laws from a variety of First, Fifth, Ninth, and Fourteenth Amendment perspectives. The analyses include cases concerning indecent exposure as well as first-order abstractions of obscenity and pornography, classifications that trace their roots to a common ground with indecent exposure in English common law and American colonial statutes, as well as marriage and other aspects of intimate relations.

Interpretation of the Constitution generally employs a theoretical framework in which case law, statutory precedent, and other evidence are assessed using a choice of approaches to assessing the balance of individual and state interests. Courts and other interpreters of the Constitution use the same basic tools of interpretation within these frameworks, although the relative contributions of these choices vary from judge to judge, issue to issue, time to time, and case to case. Some theories of constitutional interpretation are synergistic and others contradictory. These dynamics have given rise to a large body of theoretical literature that will not be covered here.[23]

The most often employed theories are "original public meaning" and "democracy-reinforcing judicial review." The first approach researches evidence of the intent of the framers and ratifiers and the likely common public understanding at the time of ratification. The latter approach engages in a "moral review" akin to *custos morum*.

Claims of infringement of individual liberties are judged using these frameworks and tools. Modern constitutional interpretation by courts is shaped by an initial characterization of the alleged individual right affected as fundamental or ordinary. This is an important step in the process. Fundamental rights warrant *strict scrutiny* of whether there is a *compelling state interest* involved. Ordinary rights are judged using a much lower standard and may be impaired by the government when a *credible rational justification* is shown.

Various intermediate tests have been taking shape since the first such characterization emerged from affirmative action cases. These tests apply to laws that infringe upon, but do not substantially burden, fundamental individual rights, such as content-neutral restrictions on speech. For a challenged law to satisfy intermediate scrutiny, it must be *substantially related to an important governmental interest.*

Discrimination on the basis of race, speech, or religion has generally warranted strict scrutiny. Gender discrimination cases are usually judged by an intermediate level of scrutiny.[24] Sexual orientation, wealth, and age discrimination have been relegated to the lowest tier, where only an arguable rationale need be shown to sustain the law in question. The level of scrutiny is often determinative of the outcome. Likely standards of review in the possible constitutional challenges are identified and their impact on balancing mechanisms is assessed as they relate to indecent exposure laws considering changes in constitutional interpretation and American society.

The most recent Supreme Court moral guidance on interpretation in First Amendment cases is *Kennedy v. Bremerton School District* (2022),[25] in which the Court advised that drawing lines between what is permissible and impermissible in moral matters must accord with history and faithfully reflect the understanding of the Founding Fathers.[26] The Court recently updated and elaborated its preferred modes of interpretation in *Dobbs v. Jackson Women's Health Organization* (2022),[27] in which it engaged in a historical study of abortions and associated legal precedents. These recent pronouncements highlight the importance of detailed historical studies that include both the history of laws and assessment of the likely intent of the framers, ratifiers, and popular public opinion before and at the time of ratification of the Bill of Rights.

The interpretive approach employed in this study is broad ranging, considering the text, history, relevant legal tradition, precedents, purposes or underlying values, and relevant consequences, and mindful of the recent Supreme Court guidance on the subject.[28] The broad approach is meant to provide fodder for more detailed analyses based on choice of interpretive theory. The constitutional analysis will question aspects of the interpretative approach employed in *Dobbs*, with deference to precedents not expressly overruled or disfavored in that opinion, while noting potential implications of the case.[29]

The primary source materials for legal aspects of the analysis are English, colonial, and state statutes and reported judicial opinions in cases of original jurisdiction and on appeal in various forms from various sources depending on the jurisdiction and period under study. There is no concerted effort to extend the study to local ordinances, in which similar principles are usually employed. Brief summaries of the facts in the exemplary cases illustrate the application of theory to circumstances to aid in understanding evolution of the laws. Dates are noted for cases, statutes, and selected publications to place them in historical context. This chronology demonstrates trends and allows readers to speculate about contemporaneous influences on the opinions expressed in the precedents.

Lexis was the primary research tool for identifying and analyzing relevant precedent. Secondary legal materials include yearbooks, treatises, restatements, law reviews, and legislative materials such as debates and committee reports. Sources of data for the historical aspects include both primary materials, such as written records of Puritan sermons and government documents, and secondary materials, such as biographies and histories of religious, social, and economic institutions. Sociological and philosophical inquiries are based primarily on secondary sources, such as published studies and analyses of philosophers and social theorists. The internet, of course, has radically expanded access to such information.

Literature Review

According to Canadian criminologist Richard Schneider, by 1982, indecent exposure had become the largest category of sexual offenses in the western world.[30] Nevertheless, according to British researcher Jennifer Grant, writing in 2021, it is "arguably the most-under-researched of all sexual offences."[31] This literature review illustrates the dearth of scholarship regarding the origins and evolution of indecent exposure laws,[32] the relevance and consequences of the prohibition for offenders and society, and the role of courts as *custos morum,* custodian of morals.[33]

The two leading scholarly books on indecent exposure are Gigeroff's *Sexual Deviations in the Criminal Law* (1968).[34] and MacDonald's *Indecent Exposure* (1973).[35] *Sexual Deviations* has a brief history of the development of criminal law in England as a premise to discussion of reform of Canadian laws regarding sexual offenses. *Indecent Exposure* is a clinical examination of exhibitionism. It contains only brief, descriptive, nonanalytical references to the law.[36] Efforts to characterize and classify offenders have been difficult.[37] Criminological studies of indecent exposure usually begin with the assumption that the actor is engaging in bad behavior due to mental illness or bad judgment.[38] This bias overwhelms opportunities to appreciate alternative realities and obviates attempts to understand why the behavior is "bad."

Grant suggested three primary motivations for indecent exposure based on a review of the literature: demonstration of anger, sexual gratification, and clumsy attempts at sexual interaction.[39] She ultimately concluded that "men who indecently expose themselves are a heterogenous group with varied motivations."[40] Rooth, on the other hand, writing in 1970, found that most offenders were men of "good character and apparently normal personality."[41] This is at least sometimes true. Nudists, for instance, profess the great virtues of public nakedness:

> Anecdotal accounts and the testimony of those who participate in social nudity typically cite such emotional or spiritual rewards as communion with nature, heightened honesty and intimacy and escape from normal routines and mindsets. Subjective social benefits often are claimed as well: increased friendliness between people, absence of class distinctions, less sexism, less homophobia, less racism, and others.[42]

De Vries cited numerous sources of empirical evidence supporting a link between nudism and well-being.[43] Fortenberry notes many implications of sexual modesty across multiple dimensions of epistemology, ontology, and social order in his literature review of research published between 2000 and 2021.[44]

Although many clinical studies of nudism and exhibitionism have been done,[45] the history of the law of indecent exposure has been neglected. The history of substantive law is one of the least studied areas of criminal justice.[46] The neglect may be due less to lack of interest than to lack of competence to undertake the analysis.[47] Historians and other social scientists have been reluctant to scrutinize the law.[48]

The roots of America's laws against public indecency are in judicial decisions of seventeenth-century England and statutes and regulations of colonial New England. Before that, regulation of morality in these jurisdictions had been the exclusive province of religion. The first recorded case of public indecency in English common law occurred in 1663, when England's Court of King's Bench announced in *Sedley's Case*[49] that it would henceforth serve as "*custos morum*," or superintendent of morals, over all the King's subjects. Although *Sedley's Case* will be shown to be a false start as precedent, the doctrine of *custos morum* that it announced became a cornerstone of secular enforcement of morals in England and America. Despite its foundational role in moral jurisprudence in England and America, *Sedley's Case* has been given barely more than a few paragraphs in most criminal law studies.[50] The establishment of the doctrine of *custos morum* in *Sedley's Case* was an epic moment in jurisprudence, yet the assimilation of this concept into early American moral jurisprudence is virtually unexamined. In England, under the authority of *custos morum*, conscience was increasingly managed by fear of prison; before, fear of God had sufficed. The scope of *custos morum* grew over time to encompass a broad range of immoral acts. This authority was embraced with a passion by the U.S. Supreme Court in the second half of the twentieth century.[51]

Assemblies of the "new England" were the other root of indecent exposure laws. They enacted comprehensive statutes governing morals that parroted Scripture, ensuring that plenary legal authority over morality would be established as law as communities were established in New England. Many studies of religious and economic life in the colonies have been published,[52] but few focus on the structure of sexual morality.[53] None examine attitudes and rules regarding public nakedness except indirectly, such as in the study of sumptuary legislation and religious discipline.[54] The textual origins of modern indecent exposure statutes have not previously been mapped to colonial origins.

The declaration of the court as *custos morum* in *Sedley's Case* (1663) justified centuries of judicial management of public morals in America. Commentators and courts alike have cited the case as unquestioned authority for judicial management of morals. Nevertheless, references to it in cases and the academic and legal literature have been anecdotal and presumptuous. An unprecedented, detailed study of this case delves into its historical, social, religious, and legal characteristics. This exercise generates novel and important insights into the origin, evolution, enduring significance, and emerging challenges of the doctrine it created. The underappreciated role of colonial statutes as a source of legal moral authority in America will also be explored and explained. The analysis continues with the story of the melding of these sources of American indecent exposure laws during the nineteenth century and the creation of derivative judicial doctrines of pornography and obscenity.

Seemingly mindless of this history, modern regulation of indecent exposure and other moral crimes is often characterized as a function of the "police power," a right inherent in the states to protect public safety, health, and morals. In his treatise entitled *The Police Power* (1904), Freund posited that the scope of police control of sexual immorality should "set bounds to the indulgence of sexual passion, which is immoral only in so far as society derives no benefit from it."[55] This public nuisance orientation shaped his views. Ignoring the established prevention-of-evil-example rationale, he suggested that private sexual immorality was outside the scope and that open lewdness in front of a consenting audience should be considered private. He suggested that acts involving touching a person could be managed as assault punishable at common law and that exceptions should be made for scientific and artistic exposures.

The term "police power" was coined by Chief Justice Marshall in 1827 in *Brown v. Maryland*.[56] The question of how and when morals came to be protected under the police power has no definitive answer. Three possible explanations have been offered: English common law, natural law theory, and social contract. Historical analysis indicates that the source of police power over morals is a synthesis of English common law and American colonial statutes advancing *custos morum* principles.

Rooth's 1970 four-page note, *Some Historical Notes on Indecent Exposure and Exhibitionism*, is the most extensive previous commentary on the history of the law of indecent exposure.[57] He devoted five paragraphs to *Sedley's Case*, quoting from two diarists' accounts and mentioning a later unprosecuted, naked, late-night frolic with Lord Buckhurst. There was no discussion of the context of and potential motivations for the momentous decision by the court to declare itself *custos morum*—guardian of the morals of the people—a function that had previously been a church responsibility. Rooth went on to discuss how the Vagrancy Act became a tentpole of management of public indecency in the evolution of indecent exposure law in England. The origins of U.S. laws from a synthesis of English common law and colonial statutes were not addressed.

Professors Friedman and Grossman published a journal article entitled *A Private Underworld: The Naked Body in Law and Society* in 2013.[58] The article discussed contemporary statutes and cases of indecent exposure in different contexts. The authors proposed that the common requirement of lewd intent reflects a presumption that men's bodies are dangerous, akin to a "tiger in its cage." The authors linked the origins of indecent exposure laws to vestiges of Victorian prudery,[59] unaware of the laws' seventeenth-century origins and masking the laws' religious origins.

The historical analyses are intended to inform legal and political judgments regarding the nature of a crime and the role of courts in addressing it and related crimes. When jurisprudence of England and the colonies merged in the nineteenth century to form the foundation of laws for the newly independent American nation, the differing traditions yielded a curious concoction. It has been said that "nothing is law that is not reason."[60] Sir Edward Coke called reason the "life of the law" and the "common law nothing else but reason."[61] Yet the reasons for these laws are obscure and problematic. Something more than annoyance is involved. This study follows a meandering path of moral reasoning in the courts to emerging modern jurisprudential and political dilemmas regarding indecent exposure law enforcement.

The details of modern indecent exposure laws were discussed by Narvil in his 1995 comprehensive survey of state statutes.[62] He noted that the laws were characterized by increasing specificity regarding the what, where, why, and how of exposures. What constitutes an offense can vary depending on local cultural norms, societal values, and legal frameworks. We will extend this work to expose and examine the etiology of these statutes. Exemplary cases culled from examination of hundreds of English common-law cases, U.S. state and federal cases, statutes, and legislative histories are employed to illustrate evolutionary changes in statutory definitions of the crime. As to victims, Narvil's literature review reached the same conclusion as others: no empirical research showing that simple nudity is harmful either to the individual practicing it or those who encounter it exists.[63] He pondered alternative explanations for the criminalization of public nakedness: "If a behavior causes no real harm to others or to society, and its continuing prohibition provides no real advantages to society vis-a-vis law enforcement, to what reason may its historical and contemporary prohibition be attributed? Perhaps social, cultural, or religious attitudes best explain the criminalization of public nudity."[64]

The ensuing analysis will put meat on the bones of his rumination. Perhaps the most telling evidence of no intrinsic harm is social nudism. Adherents naturally come to mind when considering indecent exposure laws. In 2018, De Vries published a plea, *The Right to Be Publicly Naked: A Defense of Nudism*,[65] including research indicating that exposure to non-idealized naked bodies can have a positive impact on body image and lifestyle satisfaction and that public nudity has expressive value and is a constitutive element of various spiritual and religious worldviews. He noted that public nudity is frequently used to protest (perceived) social and political evils. Using hypotheticals, Green argued for decriminalization of some forms of exhibitionism in liberal society in a 2018 law review article.[66] His review did not contain meaningful legal history or detailed constitutional analyses.

The twentieth-century nudist movement spawned substantial commentary, mostly written for lay people by proselytizers.[67] The social scientific literature on nudism evidences considerable diversity in disciplines and scope.[68] The subculture has been examined from historical, sociological, psychological, cultural, economic, legal, and geographical perspectives. Findings include detailed accounts of political structures and affiliations, social organization, demographics, religion, and belief structures regarding eugenics, vegetarianism, heliotherapy, body culture, alternative medicine, and fitness. Clothing-optional beaches have provided opportunities for study of experiences that transcend subcultural aspects of the social nudism movement. Nudist society provides an enduring counterpoint to the notion that a public display of a naked body is an evil example. The ramifications of this anomaly are explored and explained. Discussions of legal aspects of nudism offer only sparse and anecdotal accounts of confrontations with the law.[69]

The historical study flows into a constitutional analysis of the ways in which the evolution of indecent exposure laws dovetails with modern American constitutional protections against establishment of religion and in favor of liberty, privacy, and freedom of expression, exposing ambiguities and infirmities created by evolving interpretations of the Constitution.

Constitutional challenges based on freedom of speech and equal protection have engendered scholarly debate. Two law review notes[70] written in the 1970s discussed the constitutionality of indecent exposure laws and reached contradictory conclusions. One concluded that public nakedness was obscene and unworthy of constitutional protection, while the other saw "expressive" public nakedness as important "speech" that should be included in the intercourse of ideas promoting progressive social change. The subject is much more complicated and nuanced than the authors of these law review notes recognized.

A considerable body of literature examines and comments on legal management of women's breasts, mostly in adult-entertainment contexts. Beginning in the second half of the twentieth century, there was considerable debate about public nakedness prohibitions in general.[71] Many constitutional challenges were brought to better describe the crime and to challenge validity based on freedom of religion and speech, equal protection, and due process. None of these challenges have reached the Supreme Court outside commercial contexts.

Professor Kent Greenawalt, a member of the original committee for the dissertation on which this book is based, authored a comprehensive study of methods of constitutional interpretation..[72] He argued that constitutional interpretation differs from statutory interpretation. It requires consideration of text; context and its evolution; subject matter; open-ended concepts; competing interests; difficulties of revision; symbolic significance; primary authors, enactors, and audiences; and allocations of interpretative responsibilities. His advice helped guide analyses of constitutional questions raised by indecent exposure laws in the modern context—analyses that are properly informed by the history of the laws.

The history of indecent exposure laws, viewed through the lens of constitutional interpretation of allegedly immoral activities, provides an informative guide to assessment of the impact and viability of the U.S. Supreme Court's assumption of the role of *custos morum*, a role that may undergo significant change after *Dobbs v. Jackson Women's Health Organization* (2022)..[73] *Dobbs* was a landmark decision of the U.S. Supreme Court reversing *Roe v. Wade* (1973) and holding that the Due Process Clause of the Constitution does not confer a right to abortion.

The Court employed a rational-basis review given the health and safety measures at issue. It concluded that health and welfare laws like those at issue in the case are entitled to a strong presumption of validity that respects legislative judgments about how to best serve legitimate state interests. The standard of review for indecent exposure laws has varied depending on the nature of the constitutional claims advanced.

Dobbs (2022) involved substantive due process under the Fourteenth Amendment. Principles of interpretation articulated by the Court included whether (1) there are explicit references in the text of the Constitution; (2) the claimed right is deeply rooted in the nation's history and tradition and is implicit in the concept of ordered liberty; and (3) there is well-reasoned relevant precedent that can be understood and applied in a consistent and predictable manner.

The precedential power of the case may be limited to due process claims. The Court also cautioned that abortion presents special considerations that may distinguish it from other moral matters. Different standards of review and tests that may be appropriate when considering constitutional issues regarding freedom of speech, establishment of religion, free exercise of religion, substantive due process, and equal protection will be robustly analyzed. Nonetheless, the case's approach will be carefully considered, with deference to precedents not expressly overruled or disfavored in that opinion.

We may be witnessing the passing of the regime of the court as *custos morum*. Should that happen, a better understanding of the role of managing how bodies are displayed in public would be helpful. The management of this crime lies at the foundation of traditional moral structures. The findings can be used to inform development of policies, laws, and processes for a new morality consistent with America's constitutional democracy. There are two primary paths forward. The United States may discern a national morality of the body that transcends Christian doctrine. Or it may more fully embrace basic constitutional principles of representative government and find a path to a workable pluralistic morality focused on the views of communities and local authorities, with the federal government intervening only where legitimate national interests are at stake.

This initial study of the structure, origins, and evolution of laws prohibiting public nakedness is intended to inspire further research and inform public debate and legislative and judicial responses by facilitating principled argument rather than absolutist rhetoric defending or challenging the status quo. Examination of indecent exposure laws according to modern constitutional doctrines regarding governmental involvement with religion and interference with individuals' rights of liberty, privacy, and free expression exposes serious legal and policy questions. The historical analysis begins with a rowdy night at the suitably named Cock Tavern.

2. Emergence of the Court as *Custos Morum* in English Common Law

It was 1663, during the reign of King Charles II, when an epic moment in legal history occurred in *Sedley's Case*: the Court of King's Bench announced it would henceforth be superintendent of the morals of the King's subjects. This case became one of the tentpoles of American public indecency laws. Its influence has persisted into the twenty-first century. This chapter traces American judicial authority over moral affairs to this case.

Little has been published regarding the facts of Sedley's offense, legal theory of the prosecution, and circumstances affecting the Court's view of the offense. The only relatively contemporaneous accounts of the case are brief legal reports, none of which described the legal theory of the prosecution. All that one can discern is that the defendant stood naked on a balcony above a London churchyard and there did and said things that provoked a riot, caused a great scandal, and led to his indictment for several unspecified misdemeanors against the King's peace. Upon a plea of guilty, the defendant was fined and sentenced to prison and bound to good behavior for a period of years. The court justified the punishment of his indecent behavior by asserting for the first time that the Court of King's Bench was *custos morum*, or superintendent of the morals, over all the King's subjects.

Reception provisions in colonial charters granted by the English Crown made English common law the law of the land in the colonies, subject to modification by local legislation..[74] *Sedley's Case* (1663) enjoyed undisputed acceptance as the first case of indecent exposure in English common law. It has been often cited as authority for *custos morum*, a more general judicial involvement in management of public morals.

Sedley's Case was decided by the Court of King's Bench at Westminster in 1663..[75] Despite its wide recognition among legal scholars and historians as the progenitor of modern public indecency laws,.[76] as mentioned previously, little is known of the facts of the defendant's offense or its adjudication. One of the three contemporaneous legal reports was written in an ancient Norman French dialect. Another was written in Latin and buried in the Public Records Office. Neither was translated to English until the latter part of the twentieth century. The third report contained only a summary of the charge and the sentence meted out.[77]

Sedley's Case (1663) has great jurisprudential significance. The doctrine of *custos morum* promulgated by the court in this case became the fountainhead of secular enforcement of morals in Great Britain and one of two identifiable sources of American moral jurisprudence. It is the common-law source of laws regulating all forms of public indecency, including obscenity. With few exceptions, regulation of morality had been a church function in England before *Sedley's Case* (1663). Sedley's trial opened the door to a revolution in legal management of immorality by temporal courts. Under authority of the doctrine, conscience was increasingly reinforced by fear of prison where before, fear of God had to suffice.

Figure 1: Sir Charles Sedley.
Licensed from Alamy.

We will explore in detail the extraordinary circumstances that prompted the court to open a Pandora's box of moral jurisprudence by usurping jurisdiction over crimes against God. The story of *Sedley's Case* begs to be told. It is a tantalizing tale to tell, replete with vagaries, ambiguities, biased and inaccurate descriptions, celebrity, corruption, and political intrigue. In short, it is a lawyer's fright and a mystery reader's delight, hardly the stuff of enduring legal precedent.[78]

There is a whimsical ode to honor Sedley's memory that goes like this:

> Sedley has that prevailing, gentle art, that can with a resistless charm impart the loosest wishes to the chastest heart, raise such a conflict, kindle such a fire Betwixt declining virtue and desire, Till the poor vanquish'd mind dissolves away In dreams all night, in sighs and tears all day.[79]

It is a perfect irony that Sedley, this infamous vilifier of virtue, would indeed "raise such a conflict" as to "kindle such a fire" that would burn more than three hundred years, not to "impart the loosest wishes to the chastest heart" but rather to enlist for virtue's desperate defense the mighty force of law. The defendant was not a commoner. He was Sir Charles Sedley, writer, poet, and confidant of King Charles II (who ruled England from 1660 to 1685).[80] Because Sedley was a man of such significance, his misadventure was worthy of remarks by three diarists whose memoirs have since been published.[81] It would be an easy solution if we found in these the simple truth of Sedley's offense. Unfortunately, none of the diarists witnessed any of the events about which they wrote. One learned of Sedley's crime and appearance before the court in a conversation with a friend.[82] Another received news by way of a letter written to his brother-in-law.[83] And the third did not disclose his source, but it is obvious that his report was based on secondhand information.[84]

A weekly newspaper was published in London at the time,[85] but the possibility of a journalistic account of Sedley's misbehavior was foreclosed by the Licensing Act of 1662, which made it a crime for a person to print "any heretical seditious or offensive Books or Pamphlets . . . which . . . are to the scandal of Religion or the Church or the Government . . . ."[86] One historian suggested that the true purpose of this particular law was to protect the "profligacies of the king, the scandals of the court, and the corruption of the statesmen and the extravagant impudence of the titled courtesans . . . ."[87] Sedley's intimate friendship with the king brought him within the ambit of this Act's protective suppression of publication.

So, there are no firsthand accounts of Sedley's performance on the balcony. Careful study of diaries and legal reports indicates what is likely to have been how the balcony episode was described to the court; in other words, to know the offense as the court knew it. Judicial doctrine does not develop in response to the reality of illegal behavior; rather, it is based on the portrayal of that reality in the courtroom by witnesses and lawyers. To understand what prompted a particular judicial opinion, one must know the portrayal. The aim of evidence rules and judicial procedure is to encourage a high degree of concordance between the portrayal and the real-world event.

A prominent means of excluding unreliable evidence is the hearsay rule, which bars the introduction into evidence of secondhand testimony. However, there was no exclusionary hearsay rule at the time of *Sedley's Case*.[88] (1663), so all manner of tales could have been introduced into evidence. Adversarial confrontation is another means of insuring accuracy, but Sedley chose not to contest the allegations.

Sedley's guilty plea and the absence of a hearsay rule left untested the influence of rumor and prosecutorial bias on the outcome of the trial. The opinion of the court, the descriptions of the court reporters, and at least one of the diarists' accounts were based solely on this evidence. Thus, the composite view of Sedley's offense based on those accounts might overstate the reality of his behavior. The composite, however, would be likely to fairly portray the court's understanding of what took place. Only a few days, at most, intervened between the hearing and the other two accounts of Sedley's offense and prosecution. There is little reason to suspect that any of the accounts differ substantially from the story presented before the justices..[89] This story provided the fertile soil from which the doctrine of *custos morum* would eventually blossom.

Charles II had returned from exile in 1660 following the restoration of the monarchy that ended the Puritan Commonwealth. London society at the time was in a tumbledown state, with streets full of drunken bullies and highway robbers..[90] The repressive Puritanical interlude during a century of widespread immorality and irreverence had ended with restoration of Charles II after eleven years of stifling moral censorship. Society was undergoing radical change. Religion faced a struggle for dominance with both the reason of the Enlightenment and passion freed from repression.

Charles II, a proponent of religious liberty, was a prodigious partier known as the "merry monarch.".[91] Shortly after his return, the Royal Society was founded in London in 1663 with the aim of promoting scientific knowledge. Its motto was *Nullius in verba*, meaning to "take nobody's word for it." This skepticism arose in a Restoration society experiencing an extraordinary outburst of repressed sexual indulgence and vulgarity. The "passions and tastes which, under the rule of the Puritans, had been sternly repressed, . . . broke forth with ungovernable violence as soon as the check was withdrawn" and men "fell into a contrary extreme, of licentiousness . . . ."[92] As a result, little restraint was imposed by public opinion,[93] and encouragement to sin abounded:

> With the restoration of the king a spirit of extravagant joy spread over the nation that brought on with it the throwing off the very profession of virtue and piety: all ended in entertainments and drunkenness, which overrun the kingdom to such a degree, that it very much corrupted all their morals. Under the color of drinking to the king's health, there were great disorders and much riot everywhere; and the pretences of religion, both in those of hypocritical sort, and of the more honest, but no less pernicious enthusiasts, gave great advantages, as well as they furnished much matter to the prophane mockers of true piety.[94]

Public licentiousness and violence observed on the day of Charles's restoration three years before *Sedley's Case* reached such a fever pitch that on the thirteenth of May 1660, the king made a proclamation "against vicious, debauched, and prophane persons" that entreated those "who spend their time in taverns, tipling-houses, and debauches, giving no other evidence of their affection to (the kingdom) but in drinking to (its health), and inveighing against all others who are not of their own dissolute temper" to "cordially renounce all that licentiousness, prophaneness, and impiety with which they have been corrupted, and endeavored to corrupt others, . . . (and to) become examples of sobriety and virtue . . . ."[95] For those who would prove immune to entreaty and example, he purported to fill the void left by lack of conscience with a precursor to *custos morum* by requiring

> all mayors, sheriffs, and justices of peace to be very vigilant and strict in the discovery and prosecution of all dissolute and prophane persons, such as blaspheme the name of God by prophane swearing and cursing, or revile or disturb ministers, and despise the public worship of God . . . .[96]

The King's proclamation urging virtue from the wicked is the first instance of expression of the state interest that would later become known as "prevention of evil example." Ironically, there is reason to doubt that he was acting from good conscience in making this proclamation. It has been suggested that it was done to satisfy the Presbyterian party that had played a key role in his restoration.[97] Evidence of his insincerity quickly arose when he "publicly violated his own order in a few days, at a debauch in the Mulberry-Garden; and more privately at another meeting in the city, where he drank healths to the utmost excess till two in the morning."[98] Indeed, there was no excess that was not encouraged by the ostentatious profligacy of the King and his favorite courtiers. Scarcely any rank or profession escaped the infection of the prevailing immorality. Those persons who made politics their business were perhaps the most corrupt part of the corrupt society. King Charles more than anyone, it seems, deserved the proclamation's reprimand.

Among the most notorious debauchers of the time were a clutch of young literary men known as the Wits, in whose company the raucous restored king spent many or most of his evenings, drinking, celebrating, and carousing.[99] The one who stood higher in the royal notice and favor than any of the other courtiers was Sir Charles Sedley. "The King delighted in him to an excess . . . (and) singl'd him out for the best Genius of the Age."[100] The outrageous antics of the King and his court were an embarrassment for the new government. It was apparent that the King cared more pleasures of the flesh than for the affairs of state.[101] Even those who had been disgusted by the austerity and hypocrisy of the Saints of the Commonwealth began to be still more disgusted by the open profligacy of the Court and the Cavaliers. They began to doubt whether the sullen preciseness of Praise God Barebone might not be preferable to the outrageous profaneness and licentiousness of the Buckinghams and Sedleys.[102]

Tension grew respecting these public exhibitions of vice that negated all appearances of sobriety. Not even dissolute Charles II could have failed to recognize that his court's debauchery was creating greater risks than simple censure, to the point of threatening his newly regained rule. This came to a head on the sixteenth of June 1663.[103] Three of his young courtiers—Sir Charles Sedley;[104] Charles Sackville, then Lord Buckhurst; and Sir Thomas Ogle[105]—met in the notorious Oxford Kate's Cock Tavern in Bow Street near Covent Garden to wine and dine. They were all literary men, two of them members of the Wits. Their probable purpose for being at the Cock was to celebrate completion of arrangements for the staging of *Pompey the Great*, a play translated by Lord Buckhurst and Edmond Waller.[106]

It was a wild affair. "They had six dishes of meat brought in by six naked women."[107] Later, "being inflamed with strong Liquors,"[108] and the tavern no longer sufficient to contain their effusive merriment, they went forth in their shirts[109] into the light of day on the balcony of the tavern, thereby spilling their antics over into the public domain. Antics were not all that spilled over, when the debauchers "putting down their Breeches shit [*sic*] in the Street."[110] Then raising their bottles of wine, they proclaimed, "Ho ever one (that) thirsteth come ye to ye water –Ec." A toast was offered to the "salvation of Judas" and another to the "Babe of Bethlehem." This done, they thought to retire inside to "make laws for ye nation," Buckhurst being then a member of Parliament.[111] Sedley, by now fully in the spirit of the occasion,

> stripped himself naked[112]—acting out all the postures of lust and buggery[113] that could be imagined, and abusing of scripture and as it were from thence preaching a Mountebank sermon from that pulpit, saying that there he hath to sell such a powder as would make all the cunts in town run after him—a thousand[114] people standing underneath to see and hear him. And that being done he took a glass of wine and washed his prick in it and then drank it off; and then took another and drunk to the King's health.[115]

"Whereupon a Riot being raised, the People became very clamorous, and would have forced the door next to the street open, but being hindred, the Preacher and his Company were pelted into their room," returning fire during their retreat by "throwing down bottles (pist in)," as the angry crowd hurled rocks until all the windows were broken.[116]

News of this outrageous "frolick" spread quickly. The recently deposed Fanatical Party (the Puritans) took full advantage of the incident to criticize the new government. It was said that they "aggravated it to the utmost, by making it the most scandalous thing in nature and nothing more reproachful than that . . . ."[117] Summonses were hastily issued.

In one account, the entire ensemble from the balcony scene was summoned to appear before the Court of King's Bench at Westminster Hall.[118] From other reports, it appears that only the foremost participant, Sedley, was charged. In any event, there is no evidence whatsoever that Lord Buckhurst and Sir Thomas Sackville were ever prosecuted. Buckhurst attended Sedley's arraignment, but he did so only as a spectator.

The arraignment was held within days of the offense before the end of the Trinity term on June 19, possibly on that day.[119] Lord Chief Justice Robert Foster, "an old-fashioned high-minded Cavalier of the School of Ormonde and Clarendon,"[120] presided. The Lord Chief Justice "and the rest of the Judges did all of them round give Sedley a most high reproof . . . saying that it was for him, and such wicked wretches as he was, that God's anger and judgements hung over us, calling him 'Sirrah' many times."[121] Having heard that Lord Buckhurst was present, the Lord Chief Justice asked whether it was that Buckhurst that was lately tried for robbery; and when answered "Yes," he asked whether he had so soon forgot his deliverance at that time and said that it would have more become him to have been at his prayers begging God's forgiveness than now running into such courses again.[122]

The charges were then read in open court. They alleged

> several misdemeanors against the king's peace, and which were to the great scandal of Christianity; and the cause was, for that he showed his naked body in a balcony in Covent Garden to a great multitude of people, and there did such things, and spoke such words, etc. (mentioning some particulars of his misbehavior)."[123]

The delicacy of the reporter demonstrated by the parenthetical is unfortunate. All that is certain is that the information contained several counts. Sedley had stripped naked, blasphemed, breached the peace, and caused a great scandal for Christianity, having committed crimes against the state and offenses against God. His entire performance was a satire of church and state. The court had discretion about how to proceed, given that there were offenses against both. The circumstances of Sedley's offense would support either basis for prosecution. The court leaned into the ecclesiastical perspective, asserting that in the past such behavior would have been dealt with by the Court of Star Chamber or the ecclesiastical courts, but it would henceforth constitute a misdemeanor at common law punishable by the temporal courts.

The court asserted that it was "the *custos morum*," or superintendent of morals, "of all the King's subjects; and that it was high time to punish such prophane actions, committed against all modesty, which were as frequent, as if not only Christianity, but morality also had been neglected."[124] The court would exercise its authority and responsibility to protect Christianity and public order and decency from such defilement as that of the Cock Tavern revilers. This was to prove over time to be a game changer in the jurisprudence of public indecency.

Before this pronouncement, enforcement of established religion and sexual morality had been the exclusive province of ecclesiastical courts. The popular view before the Restoration was that natural law was God's law as revealed through Scripture. The emerging common law relied primarily on custom for its rules.[125] Punishment of blasphemy, profanity, procuring prostitution, keeping a bawdy house, tempting or inveigling honest maidens, bigamy, encouraging the return to sin of a repentant, and other similar offenses was the exclusive duty of the clergy.[126] *Sedley's Case* (1663) broke with the prevailing case-by-case development of the precedent-based tradition of the common law. The court's bold assertion was accompanied by expressions of frustration with incorrigibles like

Sedley who did not fear the Lord. Behind the scenes of the public spectacle, there was more to the story.

Structural changes in jurisprudence, a breakdown in civil order, personal motives, and relationships all may have played roles. The incr-easeing competition for authority between canon law and common law may have been a factor. The clergy's monopolistic authority over morality had shown signs of decay well before the decision in *Sedley's Case*.[127] The first significant encroachment was by the Court of Star Chamber, a court created by Henry VII in 1487 to preside over cases of livery, maintenance of private armies, and civil disorder involving nobles.[128] An Act of Parliament expanded this authority, granting Henry VII the right to forbid by proclamation acts that he deemed to be contrary to public policy and making the Star Chamber the instrument for enforcement of such proclamations.[129]

Eventually, the Star Chamber attained virtually unlimited authority as "protector of the public welfare." One might say, on the basis of devel-opments centuries later, that it represented the police power of the state. The Chamber acted, said Hudson, as "the curious eye of the state and the King's council prying into the inconveniences and mischiefs which abound in the Commonwealth."[130] This authority was not constrained by common law or ecclesiastical law. The Star Chamber sought to quash incipient disturbances of the commonwealth:

> By the arm of sovereignty, it punisheth errors creeping into the Commonwealth, which otherwise might prove dangerous and infectious diseases, or it giveth life to the execution of the laws, or the performance of such things as are necessary in the Common-wealth, yea, although no positive law or continued custom of common law giveth warrant to it.[131]

According to Sir Francis Bacon, the Star Chamber had "Censorian power for Offences, under the degree of Capitall."[132] By this he meant to compare the jurisdiction of the court to that of the Roman Censor, an appointed officer of the Empire who "exercised a moral jurisdiction and superintendence which extended itself in time over the whole public and private life of the citizens."[133] The aptness of the comparison is borne out by reports of prosecutions in the Star Chamber for prostitution, gambling, inveigling of young gentlemen into contracts of marriage, and sorcery.[134] In time, the plenary authority of the Star Chamber[135] made it vulnerable to corruption. It developed such a reputation as an instrument of royal caprice that it was abolished by Parliament in 1641 in answer to a bill introduced by Sir Edward Hyde, the same man who later became Lord

Chancellor under Charlies II and played a key behind-the-scenes role in *Sedley's Case*.[136] The influence of ecclesiastical law was also rapidly declining due to dislike of ecclesiastical courts having coercive authority over lay people and the increasing control of the common-law courts over legal matters.[137]

The Court of King's Bench itself had sometimes punished moral offenses as misdemeanors at common law during the tenure of the Star Chamber before the Puritan interregnum. One such instance was a prosecution of a man in the 1618 case *Rex v. Atwood*,[138] for uttering these blasphemous words: "That the religion now professed was a new religion within fifty years, Preaching was but prating, and hearing of Service more edifying than two hours Preaching."[139] His words were deemed by the Court to be "seditious statements against the state of our Church and against the peace of the realm, and as they are spiritual words, again he betrays a temporal consequence, namely disturbance of the peace."[140] The blasphemy was seditious because the King was not only the Chief of State but also head of the Anglican Church, so words spoken in derogation of the church were, in effect, an attack on the authority of the King.

Words and deeds questioning the authority of the King were believed to naturally tend to social disruption and breach of the King's peace. There is no evidence that the blasphemer's words provoked an actual breach of the peace. His words were punishable because they questioned religious authority, which put into question royal authority, thus weakening the political order. In this sense, blasphemy alone constituted a constructive breach of the peace regardless of its effect on the audience. The threat to political order posed by this religious criticism justified the temporal court's intrusion into the realm of spiritual jurisdiction.

The political theory on which this legal theory was based had been prevalent for years before the decision in *Atwood* (1618). According to Professor Holdsworth, by this time its roots were centuries deep:

> During the Tudor period, as in the medieval period, Church and State were regarded from many points of view as a single society which had many common objects, and the two members of that single society were still regarded as bound to give one another assistance in carrying out those common objects. The Church must help the State to maintain its authority, and the State must help the Church to punish nonconformists and infidels. The Church was the Church of the State, and membership in it was therefore a condition precedent for full rights in the State. The King was supreme head of both Church and State, and the law of the Church was the King's

> ecclesiastical law. But if the Church is thus regarded as an integral part of the State, if the Church's law is as much the King's law as the law of the State, a fortiori Christianity must be regarded as part of the law of the land.[141]

Statements in *Atwood* (1618) that words alone could constitute a breach of the peace and that an attack on the established religion was equivalent to rebellion against the government had no immediate juridical consequences because publication of the case was delayed for more than forty years and because of concurrent jurisdiction over such matters by ecclesiastical courts, Parliament, and the Star Chamber, none of which administered the common law. The first publication of *Atwood's Case* (1618) was in 1658,[142] five years before *Sedley's Case*.

William Blackstone cited another early incursion by the King's Bench into moral matters in 1627 in what he termed a prosecution for frequenting a house of ill fame.[143] However, examination of the report of the case that he cited[144] shows that the defendant was indicted and convicted at Sessions not only for frequenting a house suspected of being a bawdy house but also for being a common nightwalker; that is, a person who prowls about at night and exhibits a suspicious appearance or suspicious behavior. Several objections were made on appeal contesting the validity of the part of the indictment relating to frequenting the bawdy house. The court gave no opinion regarding these objections, having decided that because there was no question that the Justice of the Peace had authority to arrest a common nightwalker, the indictment should not be quashed even if the objections were valid. Thus, the holding in the case did not legitimize arrests for frequenting bawdy houses as Blackstone asserted.[145] However, nothing in the language of the case suggests that such arrests were uncommon.

The discussion of this case was in Blackstone's chapter "Offences Against God and Religion" (1765) in a section concerning "public wrongs" describing offenses "against religion and morality," including "grossly scandalous and public indecency." He explained that the licentiousness of the post-Restoration society had given rise to such hypocrisy that the "feeble coercion of the spiritual court" would not be effective.[146] This passage ascribes the source of temporal court authority over morals to *Atwood* (1618). *Sedley's Case* (1663) gained enduring notoriety when it coined the expression "*custos morum*" as it declared that henceforth the temporal courts would serve as custodian of morals over the people. Both cases were inspired by the collapse of ecclesiastical courts and religious influence before and after the Puritan interlude (1642 to 1660).

Regardless of whether one could be punished under common law for frequenting brothels and bawdy houses, keeping them was an indictable offense. In 1644, Edward Coke explained why:

> (K)eeping of them is against the law of God, on which the common law of England is based; . . . although adultery and fornication be punishable by the Ecclesiastical Law, yet the keeping of Bawdie or Stewes, or Brothel-house, being as it were a common nuisance, is punishable by the Common Law, and is the cause of many mischiefs, not only to the overthrow of the bodies, and wasting of their livelihoods, but to the endangering of their souls.[147]

Here, once again, the temporal courts found authority for punishment of a spiritual offense due to its temporal consequences as a common nuisance. Whereas in *Atwood* (1618) sedition was the imagined concern, here the presumed nuisance of leading to ill consequences sufficed to bring penal force to bear on the reformation of morals and manners and maintenance of Christian traditions. We see in the legal management of bawdy houses an early instantiation of a doctrine known as secondary effects employed in modern First Amendment cases to justify regulation of adult entertainment venues.[148]

Two public addresses made during the time between sessions after Sedley's arraignment point toward the Star Chamber rather than the common law of *Atwood's Case* (1618) as the historical source for the idea of *custos morum* authority. Just a few days after the arraignment, on the twenty-third of June, Lord Chancellor Edward Hyde, the Earl of Clarendon, urged the court to take on the additional authority and responsibility of being *custos morum* over the people.[149] In a speech made upon the occasion of the elevation of Sir John Kelyng to the bench, the Lord Chancellor asserted that King's Bench was "the highest Court, and, therefore, the one wherein the manners of men may be best reformed." He addressed the justices as "the King's inquisitors whose duty it is to punish all horrid misdemeanors such as duels, debauchery, etc.," but admitted that he had been reproached by the King for this attitude. He cautioned justices that "such crimes may be gotten into great company, too hard for the jurisdiction of this Court," perhaps in reference to the recent arraignment of Sir Charles Sedley, but was quick to add that "the King hath specially commanded me to tell you, he will assist you with his authority to punish such transgressors."

Justice Thomas Twisden, in his charge to the Grand Jury of Middlesex three days later, reiterated the Lord Chancellor's suggestion.[150] After discussing the offenses of treason, felony murder, and robbery,

Twisden turned his attention to other offenses "that like gangrenes, if in time not prevented, will soon overturn the State." He instructed the jurors that "this is a court which is to correct ill manners; and therefore you that are the eyes of the Kingdom that must search and find all debaucheries, which are now done in the face of the sun," referring specifically to child stealing, buggery, libel, battery, corruption in the courts and other public offices; perjury, subordination, forgery, fraud and other deceits; nuisances on the highways; disturbances in alehouses; gaming houses; blasphemy; violation of the Sabbath; and being a Quaker. This proposition was further reinforced shortly after the trial, on August 22, 1663, when King Charles reissued the earlier proclamation against vicious and debauched persons and directed that it be read in all churches once a month for six months.[151] We see here the origins of prevention of evil example as a rationale for common-law prosecution of immoral acts.

The correspondence of Twisden's remarks to Hudson's characterization of the Star Chamber described above may be more than coincidental. Hudson, in a treatise written around 1635, had called the Star Chamber "[t]he curious eye of the state" whose duty it was to "punisheth errors creeping into the Commonwealth, which otherwise might prove dangerous and infectious diseases."[152] Twisden told the Grand Jury that they were "the eyes of the Kingdom" who must, by indictment, authorize the King's Bench to punish offenses "that like gangrenes, if in time not prevented, will soon overturn the State." The impression is unmistakable that even if his words were not a paraphrase of Hudson's, his intention was to resuscitate the suppressive power of the Star Chamber and make it an element of the authority of the King's Bench to punish moral misdemeanors at common law.

There is no way to tell for sure to what extent the court in *Sedley's Case* (1663) derived the idea of *custos morum* from the earlier cases or simply thought to assimilate the authority of the Star Chamber. The Court made no mention of the temporal consequences of Sedley's misbehavior, although nuisance would have certainly been an apt characterization of the balcony antics. Because of the coincidence of the motives of King's Bench and the Star Chamber for exercising jurisdiction over moral matters, our inability to make that distinction is not crucial. Both of them supported maintenance of good public order through defense of church and state.

Christian ethics were the recognized foundation of civil society at the time of *Sedley's Case* (1663). The King was head of the church as well as the state. Thus, violation of established religion inevitably had temporal—

that is, political—consequences. Upholding the religion of the Church of England was a mainstay of civil order. The ecclesiastical courts had been stripped of their punitive powers long before *Sedley's Case*. Their ultimate sanction was excommunication,[153] a punishment that would have been ineffectual against disbelievers and libertines like Sedley. The Star Chamber and the King's Bench stepped in to fill the punishment void, satisfying a practical need for consequences for actions by infidels undermining religious order.

Sedley's guilty plea prevented a fuller exposition of the Court's intention in promulgating the doctrine of *custos morum*. During the Michaelmas term following Sedley's arraignment, the court required him to take his trial at bar, "but being advised, he submitted himself to the Court, and confessed the indictment."[154] Siderfin reported that, this being done, the Court considered what judgment to give, and

> inasmuch as he was a gentlemen, bearing arms for the King, from a very ancient family (residing in the County of Kent), and his estate was encumbered (not intending his ruin, but his reformation) they fined him 2,000 marks,[155] imprisoned him for a week without bail, and ordered him to provide sureties for his good behavior for 3 years.[156]

Sir Robert Hyde, first cousin of the Lord Chancellor, presided at Sedley's trial because Lord Chief Justice Foster had died between terms.[157] Upon receiving sentence, Sedley "made answer, that he thought he was the first Man that paid for shiting." In reply, Lord Chief Justice Hyde asked whether he had "ever read the Book called The Compleat Gentleman, &c. to which Sir. Ch. Made Answer, that set aside from his Lordship, (no one) had read more books than himself."[158] This concluded the court proceedings, but for Sir Charles, the matter was not yet settled.

"The day for payment being appointed, Sir Charles, seeking to use his favored status with King Charles II, desired Mr. Henry Killigrew," a former page to the King who was at the time a groom of the Bedchamber of the Duke of York and who would years hence be appointed by King William to the novel role of Court Jester,[159] "and another Gent. To apply themselves to his Majesty to get it off; but instead of that, they beg'd the said sum of his Majesty, and would not abate Sir Charles two pence of the Money."[160]

Having failed in this attempt to escape the fine, Sedley paid the fine, but that was still not the end of it.[161] It appears that the King may have found a way to surreptitiously reduce the fine. A note in the state papers indicates that the sum was paid in July 1664 and was disbursed from the

King's Privy Purse to George Hamilton, Esq., Sedley's good friend and Anthony à Wood's brother.[162]

As to the week in prison, if Sedley did serve it, in the opinion of one historian it "could certainly have involved no great hardship. In those days, if a prisoner had sufficient money to pay the rent of a room and the perquisites of the gaolers, he could live in far greater comfort than the miserable wretches who herded on the 'common side.'"[163]

Historical accounts of Sedley's performance on the balcony may seem incredibly wild. There is no means of ensuring that these accounts were fair portrayals. Although there are no firsthand reports, there is inferential support for the outrageousness of his antics. The indictment charged "several misdemeanors against the King's peace." The misdemeanors were not described in detail because of Sedley's decision to confess to the indictment, but the nonlegal accounts referred the offenses as "riot"[164] and "debauchery."[165] This is consistent with one legal reporter's description based on observations in court on the day judgment was rendered and is reconcilable with the remaining legal report. Both legal accounts mentioned Sedley's nakedness; both alluded to other actions, one specifically mentioning a breach of the peace and the other describing the offense only in general terms. Only that last report mentioned speech. The rolls of the court do not show that speech was part of the offense alleged against him. There is no way to determine whether failure to mention speech on the roll necessarily means that it formed no part of the offense.

The observations in the diaries and legal reports differ only in emphasis and degree of specificity. The court reporters mentioned nakedness, exposure of private parts, breach of the peace, and "such things." The diarists wrote of debauchery and riot. That one of the court reporters excised the particulars of Sedley's misbehavior and emphasized the omission by the insertion of a parenthetical is a clue that the court reporters understated the behaviors constituting the offense. Surely if throwing down bottles was all there was in addition to public nakedness, the reporter would not have hesitated to specify the misconduct. Another wrote of a "great scandal for Christianity," while the other reporter characterized the offense as a "Scandall of Government." Though a breach of the peace by members of the court during a drunken frolic might form the substance of the latter, it would hardly be a great scandal for Christianity. Sedley's quip in the courtroom after sentencing further reinforces the likelihood that the accounts of outrageous antics attributed to the trio were fairly rendered.

Armed with all available facts of *Sedley's Case* (1663) and a grounding in legal precedent, it is time to tackle the greatest mystery of *Sedley's Case*: the decision of the court to seize upon it as the moment to announce that, henceforth, it would be *custos morum* over all the King's subjects. Sedley had abused Scripture, derided the King, and caused a riot, leading to substantial public disorder, breach of the peace, and damage to property. Rather than innovate, the Court could have proceeded against him for the traditional offenses of breach of the peace,[166] riot,[167] or sedition,[168] or, at least, inciting to breach of the peace or riot.[169] Virtually any public misbehavior was sufficient cause to bind an offender to good behavior.[170] The court did not have to elevate itself to *custos morum* over the people in violation of basic principles of common law to proceed against Sedley.

The relationship of the King and judiciary to a central figure in Restoration politics, Edward Hyde, Earl of Clarendon and Lord Chancellor, may help explain the court's radical departure. Edward Hyde had enjoyed the utmost confidence of Charles II's father before that monarch's dethronement. On March 3, 1643, Hyde had been granted life tenure as chancellor and sub-treasurer of the Exchequer by Charles I. He was privy to the most secret affairs of the state and composed many of the most important state papers. Frequently, he supplied answers to various declarations of the parliament that the King copied in his own hand to disguise the true author's identity. So great was Charles I's trust in Hyde that he chose him to accompany his son Prince Charles when political discord became so serious that it was thought wise to exile the young prince to ensure his safety. Shortly thereafter, King Charles was overthrown and executed. Immediately after the death of King Charles, Hyde was sworn to the new King's privy council. He continued to serve as his majesty's chief advisor during exile. In 1658, he was entrusted with the Great Seal, its corresponding obligations, and the title of Lord Chancellor.[171]

Hyde accompanied thirty-year-old King Charles II upon the Restoration in 1660 and immediately began reconstruction of the government. Hyde managed all the important business of the state. Although not so titled, he was in effect prime minister.[172] Meanwhile, the youthful monarch

> grew more disposed to leave all things to their natural course, and God's providence; and by degrees unbent his mind from the knotty and ungrateful part of his business, grew more remiss in his application to it, and indulged to his youth and appetite that license and satisfaction, that it desired, and for which he had opportunity enough . . . .[173]

One of Hyde's prerogatives was to make appointments to the Courts of Justice in Westminster Hall.[174] The primary political criterion for selection was, of course, loyalty to the monarchy, but beyond this Hyde based his decisions on personal concerns of ideological conformity and loyalty.[175] The Chief Justice at the hearing on the indictment in *Sedley's Case* (1663) was Robert Foster; the other justices were Thomas Twisden and Wadham Wyndam. During the period between Sedley's hearing and the adjudication four months later, Chief Justice Foster died and was replaced by Robert Hyde, and John Kelyng was elevated to the bench.[176] Robert Hyde, the replacement for Foster, the "old-fashioned, high-minded Cavalier of the School of Ormonde and Clarendon,"[177] was a first cousin of Edward Hyde and an undistinguished lawyer whose most salient qualification for the post was his relation to the Lord Chancellor.[178] Edward Hyde, no doubt, had considerable influence with the other justices, whose appointments to the bench he had secured.

The interplay of Charles's propensity to vice and the Lord Chancellor's concern for the affairs of the state may reconcile several paradoxes of *Sedley's Case* (1663). Clarendon sometimes chastised Charles II for immorality openly practiced and encouraged at court. For a time, the youthful king acknowledged these fatherly remonstrances with promises of cooperation. Recall the 1660 proclamation against vicious and debauched persons that Charles himself publicly violated only a few days after its issuance and that was reissued in August 1663, followed shortly thereafter by Charles's surreptitious attempt to pay Sedley's fine. During the early years of Restoration, Charles at least would pay this lip service to the advice of his Lord Chancellor. However, Hyde's efforts to save the soul of the wayward King faced determined resistance by Charles's licentious courtiers. The prosecution of Sir Charles Sedley may have been an outgrowth of this confrontation in which Hyde summoned the Court of King's Bench to aid in his efforts to manage the King's behavior.

It appears that *Sedley's Case* (1663) was a showdown between the Lord Chancellor and Charles' courtiers. Henceforth, Hyde would control their encroachments on the loyalty and temperament of the King through the legal authority of the Court of King's Bench as *custos morum*. His victory, however, proved to be a shallow one. The admission in his speech to the King's Bench between Sedley's arraignment and sentencing that he had been reproached by the King for his view of the court as superintendent of the morals presaged hard times for Clarendon. His assertion that the king had promised to aid the court in the punishment of moral transgressors was hardly true, as evidenced by Charles's attempt to nullify Sedley's fine by taking from the Treasury the very amount the malefactor had been ordered to pay into it.

Sedley's Case (1663) marked a significant downturn in the King's appreciation and tolerance of Hyde. The Lord Chancellor's favor with the King soon turned into loathing.[179] Charles had "patiently submitted to the remonstrances Hyde sometimes ventured to offer against the immorality so openly practised and encouraged at Court. But at length the panders to those practices obtained the mastery."[180]

The King tired of Hyde's reproachful lectures, administered, as the Chancellor acknowledged, with unadvised earnestness. Hyde's enemies at court were increasingly jealous of his influence. Hyde all along had been obnoxious to Presbyterians and Roman Catholics. The common people, taught to attribute to his mismanagement the miscarriages of the state, were strongly prejudiced against him as well. The way was paved for the intrigue of his removal, in which the chief actors were the Duke of Buckingham, Lord Arlington, and Sir William Coventry, urged on and aided by the Duchess of Cleveland, the King's shameless mistress. Clarendon, conscious of innocence, refused to resign, and the Great Seal was taken from him on August 30, 1667.[181]

Four years after the decision in *Sedley's Case* (1663), the career of the great statesman Edward Hyde ended with an Act of Parliament banishing him from the kingdom. He fled to France, where he remained until his death in 1674 at the age of sixty-six.[182] After the banishment of Hyde, Charles ensured that there would be no further interference from the Court of King's Bench by making appointments to the bench to serve at his pleasure in place of the tenure during good behavior granted by Clarendon.[183]

If Edward Hyde instigated and orchestrated the prosecution of Sir Charles Sedley, one would expect that with the Lord Chancellor discredited and banished and the King himself now filling vacancies on the bench, there would be no further assertions of *custos morum* authority against the immorality of the King's companions. The evidence is strikingly confirmatory. Not only was the doctrine of *Sedley's Case* (1663) never used against the courtiers, but it seems to have been forgotten altogether during the remaining years of the reign of Charles II. None of the treatises and abridgments written during the period even mentions the historic case.[184] The Wits continued their "frolics" unabated. Lord Rochester, a member of the Wits, is said to have asserted that he and his friends "in their frolics would have chosen sometimes to have gone naked, if they had not feared the people."[185] Nevertheless, it appears that he overcame this fear on at least one occasion when he and a companion performed the "beastly prank" of "running along Woodstock Park naked."[186] When freed from Clarendon's moralizing, the Wits' penchant for naked and licentious exploits flourished. Their exploits included Sir George Etherage's naked dancing in his chamber with two young women[187] and Harry Saville's clothes-less romp "around Rosamund's Fair Fountain."[188]

The Wits' freedom from moral and legal censure was extraordinary. Wilson reported that at least two "frolics" of the Wits resulted in deaths, yet none of these episodes are known to have led to arrest or prosecution.[189] Even our own Sir Charles and Lord Buckhurst forcefully demonstrated the legal impunity of the King's courtiers during the year following the Lord Chancellor's banishment by "running up and down all night with their arses bare through the streets."[190] Eventually, they became involved in fighting, whereupon a constable arrested them both and locked them up for the night. The constable's unexpected reward for conscientious maintenance of the King's peace was a turnabout that freed the malefactors and landed him behind bars in their place. Under the King's direction, "Lord Chief Keeling . . . laid the constable by the heels [an allusion to stocks] to answer it next session."[191] This intervention was not at all extraordinary. Charles habitually interfered with both the enforcement[192] and adjudication[193] of the law regarding such misbehaviors.

Further evidence that the Earl of Clarendon was the prime mover in *Sedley's Case* (1663) is the fact that the Wits' licentious, disruptive, and sometimes violent antics seem to have had no deleterious impact on their careers. The three young men on the balcony later went on to distinguished careers in public service. Lord Buckhurst was at the time of the indictment a member of Parliament. He became the Earl of Dorset and Middlesex, Lord Chamberlain, and a Fellow of the Royal Society. Sir Thomas Ogle, Knight of Pinchbeck, Lincolnshire, was later Governor of Chelsea College.[194] The most egregious offender, Sedley, was chosen to fill a vacancy in Parliament in 1668, shortly after Hyde's banishment, and was reelected three times in the remaining years of the reign of Charles II.[195] It was said that "his speeches display[ed] ripe judgment and sound common sense."[196]

The Court of King's Bench did once more during the reign of Charles II exercise authority over an offense against the established religion, but then only at the urging of Parliament and without mentioning *Sedley's Case* (1663). The defendant[197] in *Rex v. Taylor* (1675)[198] had been committed to prison on the order of a country justice for saying that

"Religion is a Cheat," among other things, in derogation of the established religion. Notice of his confinement reached the House of Lords. He was summoned and admitted blasphemy. His derangement led the House to order confinement for bread, water, and bodily correction. When this treatment failed to stem his blasphemous tide, the House of Lords ordered the Court to determine how to properly proceed against his crime. The justices replied that he could be prosecuted in the ecclesiastical courts or by indictment or information in the temporal courts. The local Ecclesiastical courts were overburdened and ineffective, leaving the temporal courts as the sole remedy.[199]

Seemingly unaware of *Sedley's Case* (1663), the court found that his offense was not simply one against

> God and Religion; but a crime against the laws, state, and government, and therefore punishable in this Court. For to say, Religion is a Cheat, is to dissolve all those obligations whereby Civil Societies are preferred, and that Christianity is parcel of the laws of England; and therefore, to reproach the Christian Religion, is to speak in subversion of the Law.

The accused was convicted and sentenced to pillory, fined one thousand marks, and imprisoned until he found sureties for his good behavior for life. The case quickly became the leading authority for temporal court authority to suppress unorthodox religious opinions.[200]

The theory supporting prosecution of Taylor's offense at common law was the same as in *Atwood's Case* (1618) sixty years earlier: contravention of Christian principles subverted the order of civil society. Others have argued that Chief Justice Hale was relying on defamation as the secular basis for prosecution and that his remarks about the relationship about Christianity and law were dicta.[201] In any event, the remark that Christianity was part and parcel of the laws of England was nothing radical, being little more than a parallel or paraphrase of Coke's justification for condemning brothel houses, and it was obviously true.

The reign of Charles II ended in 1685. He was succeeded by James II, who was quickly deposed in favor of King William III and Queen Anne. The moral laxity of Charles's period was still common. Rather than firm precedent, *Sedley's Case* (1663) had been an aberration. Later, we will note parallels between this period of moral laxity and the current ambiguous and chaotic state of American morality. What came next is instructive.

A royal proclamation issued in 1691 ordered enforcement of laws against immorality, noting that they had been grossly neglected.[202] A Society for the Reformation of Manners was formed in 1692 to present a counterforce against the prevailing tide of immorality.[203] More than a century before the reign of Victoria, we see in these acts the seeds of a transformation of English society from the seventeenth century's openly licentious behavior to the closeted lust and public prudery of Victorian morality.

Development of a concerted legal framework for suppression of public immorality began at the turn of the century with a campaign against obscene literature. The first major prosecution was *Rex v. Hill*[204] in 1698. Hill was indicted for printing obscene poems written by Lord Rochester that were characterized as tending to the corruption of youth. He absconded from the country before trial and was outlawed.

In the next major prosecution for the publication of an obscene libel, *Sedley's Case* (1663) was resurrected from forty years of desuetude when it was offered as a precedent to establish jurisdiction in support of the indictment in *Regina v. Read* (1707),[205] a prosecution for the printing and publishing of a "lascivious and obscene libel entitled 'The Fifteen Plagues of Maidenhead.'" Lord Chief Justice Holt, in considering a motion in arrest of judgment, demanded: "Shew me any precedent."[206] *Sedley's Case* (1663), offered in reply, was rejected. According to Justice Powell, "there was something more in that case, than shewing his naked body in the balcony, for that case was quod vi & armis[207] he piss'd down upon the people's heads,"[208] quoting Keble's report of the case. He added, in reference to the libel, "There's no law—I wish there were: It indeed tends to the corruption of good manners, but that is not sufficient for us to punish."[209] A judgment for the defendant was entered.

Chief Justice Holt viewed the case as one for the ecclesiastical courts, which still had jurisdiction over kindred moral offenses such as adultery, whoredom, drunkenness, blasphemy, and failure to attend church.[210] Their authority had been usurped before the Commonwealth by the Star Chamber, but restoration of the monarchy had been accompanied by a replenishment of ecclesiastical jurisdiction despite the short-lived competition evident in *Sedley's Case* (1663).[211] The Chief Justice did not agree that the King's Bench in *Sedley's Case* (1663) had intended to take for itself some of what the Star Chamber previously had taken from the ecclesiastical courts.

The justices in *Read* (1707) believed that had there been no violence, no actual breach of peace, the Court of King's Bench would have abdicated responsibility for the adjudication of *Sedley's Case* (1663) to the nominal authority of the ecclesiastical courts. This was the last reported case that did not interpret the ruling as establishing *custos morum*. There were no reported obscenity prosecutions for twenty years following *Read* (1707).[212]

The first treatment of *Sedley's Case* (1663) by a treatise writer significantly departed from the *Read* (1707) court's interpretation. Writing in 1716, William Hawkins took *Sedley's Case* (1663) to stand for the proposition that all "open lewdness, grossly scandalous, such as was that of those persons who exposed themselves naked to the people in a balcony in Covent-garden with most abominable circumstances," is punishable at common law.[213]

Open lewdness was one of five classes of offenses treated under the heading "Offences Against God not Capital at Common Law." The others were blasphemy, profane scoffing at scripture or exposing it to contempt or ridicule, impostures in religion, and seditious words in derogation of the established religion. All were temporal offenses because they "tend to subvert all Religion or Morality, which are the Foundation of Government . . . ."[214] Therefore, they should be "punishable by Temporal Judges with Fine and Imprisonment."[215] Hawkins specifically restated the theory of *Atwood's Case* (1618) and *Taylor's Case* (1675) as "Seditious Words in Derogation of Established Religion are indictable, as tending to a Breach of the Peace."[216] The breach of the peace referred to need not be an actual breach of the peace. As those cases showed, derogation alone could constitute a constructive breach because of its tendency to disrupt the religious foundation of civil society. Hawkins's treatise (1716) was widely read. His statement of the rule of the case substantially influenced the view that derogation of religion and morality were, in themselves, breaches of the peace. Open lewdness was an offense against God but punishable at common law.

A case eleven years later struggled with the competing interpretations of actual versus constructive breach as explanations for *Sedley's Case* (1663). The issue in *Rex v. Curl* (1727)[217] was whether to punish publication of an obscene book as a libel in the temporal courts or to recognize the exclusive jurisdiction of the ecclesiastical courts over such matters. The attorney general, Sir Philip Yorke, argued in the fashion of Hawkins (1716) that the publication was a common-law offense because it tended to corrupt the morals of the King's subjects and was against the King's peace. The concept of peace meant good order and government, which could be disrupted without actual force, as in the case of seditious and blasphemous words and writings, or by immoral behavior. Immoral behavior was an offense against the peace of the government because "government is no more than public order, which is morality."[218] He disclaimed an intention to hold every immoral act to be indictable, "but if it is destructive of morality in general, if it does, or may, affect all the King's subjects, it is then an offence of a public nature."[219] It is the public-private distinction, he insisted, that distinguishes temporal court jurisdiction from the province of the ecclesiastical court, which had traditionally managed private moral offenses such as adultery and fornication.

Chief Justice Robert Raymond agreed that if the writing "reflects on religion, virtue, or morality, if it tends to disturb the civil order of society, . . . it is a temporal offence," thereby disapproving the view of the court in *Regina v. Read* (1707). Justice Fortescue dissented, adhering to the *Read* view that there must be an actual breach of the peace. A third justice emphasized Sedley's nakedness: "[T]his is surely worse than Sir Charles *Sedley's Case* (1663), who only exposed himself to the people then present, who might choose whether they would look upon him or not, whereas this book goes all over the kingdom." A fourth justice accepted the prosecution's argument without referring to *Sedley's Case*.

Curl was bound over until the succeeding term, when Justice Page replaced the lone dissenter, Fortescue, permitting the court to reach a unanimous conclusion that the libel was punishable. The new justice summarized the opinion of the reconstituted court by writing that "it was plain the force used in *Sedley's Case* (1663) was but a small ingredient in the judgment of the court," for if "force was all they went upon, there was no occasion to talk of the court's being censor morum [*sic*] of the king's subjects." Curl was set in the pillory as punishment. Samuel Richard wrote in 1741, in reference to *Curl* (1727), that the time had come when it was a moral duty to "decry such Novels and Romances, as having a tendency to inflame and corrupt."[220] "Given this atmosphere, it would have taken more than legal precedents, or the lack of them, to save Edmund Curl."[221]

The opinion in *Curl* was an important step in the evolution of moral jurisprudence of temporal courts because it reaffirmed the theory of *Atwood* (1618) and *Taylor* (1675) that no actual breach of the peace needed to occur for public defamation of religion and morals to be punishable at common law. Because public order is morality, immorality was a per se offense against the peace of the government. The *Curl* (1727) opinion illustrates the beginning of a process of secularization of rhetoric. In *Atwood* and *Taylor*, Christianity was the admitted foundation of civil society. Sedley's offense was recognized as against Christianity and morality, but in *Curl*, concern for Christ had gone underground. The reaffirmation in *Curl* of public immorality as a temporal offense raised the issue of boundaries of the offense. What kinds of immorality would be included? Attorney general Yorke proposed one definition: only those acts that were of a public nature should be indictable.

Yorke proposed to limit the jurisdiction of temporal courts to matters affecting civil order and public morality. He believed that jurisdiction over private morality should remain in the ecclesiastical courts. This public-private distinction was to become the most significant and enduring limitation on *custos morum* authority. It kindled debates that endured into modern times. It provided a rein against which judicial authorities tugged and a wall against which defense attorneys backed up to fight for the next three hundred years. The limitation that it provided was not secure—in England because the division between ecclesiastical and temporal jurisdiction lost significance as the reality of the ecclesiastical court diminished and eventually disappeared, and in America because ecclesiastical courts were never established in the colonies. Several themes from this period of English common law permeate constitutional interpretation by the U.S. Supreme Court during modern times, such as the question of whether erosion of morality is an offense against the peace of government and the public/private distinction as a jurisdictional limit and definition of rights of privacy.

The scope of substantive behavior governed by *custos morum* authority remained unclear and evolving as years passed. Not every immoral act or breach of good manners committed in public was cognizable as a temporal offense. Legal scholars and judges have long puzzled over the curious substantive exception recognized in the next reported judicial opinion citing *Sedley's Case* (1663). The full text of *Rex v. Gallard* (1733),[222] as reported by William Kelynge, was as follows:

> Indictment contra bonos mores [against good morals], for running in the common Way naked down to the waist, the Defendant being a Woman. S. moved to quash because the Fact is not indictable. S. cont': "indictments will lie contra bonos mores, as against Curle for publishing an obscene book. 1 Sid. 168. Sir Charles Sidley's Case. 1 Keb. 620. Quia immodeste & irreverenter behaved himself in Church." Another Indictment was for printing Rochester's Poems fed per Cur,' the Indictment must be quashed, for nothing appears immodest or unlawful.[223]

The "S." referred to as speaker was Sir John Strange, attorney for the defendant. Not only did the court come to the surprising conclusion that there is nothing immodest or unlawful in a woman running naked to the waist in a public common, but Strange, counsel for the defendant, appeared to offer up the precedents most damning to his client. How could this be? How could an attorney argue the law against his client only to have the court render a judgment contrary to the attorney's argument and in favor of the attorney's client? The solution to the paradox of *Rex v. Gallard* (1733) lies in the report of the case rather than the case itself.

There was another, heretofore undiscovered, report of the case by Thomas Barnardiston. This account of the case was lost in historical records when it was published under the name of *Rex v. Tallard*.[224] In *Tallard*,

> the defendant was indicted for encouraging Hacon to run naked from his waist upwards, in Chapel Field in the City of Norwich, which Hacon did accordingly. Mr. Strange submitted that this was no offence indictable; accordingly moved that the indictment might be quashed. And the court made a rule for that purpose.

The argument of precedents attributed to "S." in Kelynge's account was given by Mr. Filmer, attorney for the prosecution, in reply to the court's preliminary ruling on a motion to quash.

> Mr. Strange argued on the other side and said that a man's being stripped from the middle upwards could be no indecent sight. If it were so, the Legislature would not have ordered that men shall be whipped in that manner; as they have done by several Acts of Parliament.

The court agreed and made the rule absolute.

The report of the trial at Sessions of *Rex v. Gallard* (1733).[225] confirms that Tallard is Gallard. In that action, the defendant was indicted for the "abetting, assisting, and encouraging of one Thomas Hacon to run naked, except for garters and stockings, in . . . Chapel Field, on the 9th day of May," etc. Gallard was not a girl but a boy. With this realization, the case makes sense and is unremarkable.

As mid-century approached, the clash of sin and morality intensified. Henry Fielding[226] captured the spirit of the times when, in his charge to the grand jury at Middlesex on June 29, 1749, he decried a "fury after licentiousness and luxurious pleasures . . . grown to so enormous a height, that it may be called the characteristic of the present age."[227] He urged the men of the grand jury to act as "censors of this nation" who with "the rod of the law . . . must restrain those within the bounds of decency and sobriety, who are deaf to the voice of reason, and superior to the fear of shame." He instructed them that, although moral offenses were generally ecclesiastical concerns, there were two species of moral offenses punishable by common law. First, there was the "open act of lewdness and indecency in public, to the scandal of good manners," as in *Sedley's Case* (1663), referencing Siderfin's Report. The second was keeping a brothel or bawdy house, which could be punished as a kind of common nuisance.[228]

By this time, the authority of the Court of King's Bench as *custos morum* had expanded to open lewdness and indecency, obscene books and prints, and the moral nuisances of brothels and bawdy houses. This authority was limited to punishment of public immorality, but in 1763, a century after *Taylor's Case* (1676), in *Rex v. Delaval*,[229] the remaining authority of the ecclesiastical court that had not yet been specifically appropriated was subsumed into *custos morum*. In *Delaval*, Sir Francis Blake Delaval, his attorney John Fraine, and a musician named William Bates were charged with conspiring to remove a woman, eighteen years of age, from Bates, to whom she was bound as an apprentice, and place her in the service of Delaval for prostitution in exchange for a sum of money. Although the girl was "notoriously kept" by Delaval, the court did not address the issue of publicity in defending its jurisdiction. The Court was determined to punish this immoral conspiracy. Lord Mansfield referenced a case in the Court of Chancery where a man had "formerly assigned his wife over to another man" and the court found that to be a transaction "notoriously and grossly against public decency and good manners." Ignoring the question of publicity, Mansfield admitted that many

> Offences of the incontinent kind fall properly under the jurisdiction of the Ecclesiastical Court and are appropriated by it. But, if you except those appropriated cases, this court is *custos morum* of the people, and has the superintendency of offences contra bonos mores [against good morals]: and upon this ground, both Sir Charles Sedley and Curl, who had been guilty of offences against good manners, were prosecuted here.[230]

Weakening the precedential value of the case, the court asserted an alternative basis for establishing jurisdiction in finding that there was a conspiracy and confederacy among the defendants.

A few years after *Delaval* (1763), in the first edition of his famous *Commentaries*, Blackstone reiterated Fielding's 1749 public-private distinction in what moral offenses were cognizable by temporal courts. He closed his chapter "Of Offences Against God and Religion" by describing the indictable offense of "open and notorious lewdness: either by frequenting houses of ill fame . . . ,[231] or by some grossly scandalous and public indecency," citing *Sedley's Case* (1663).

In the introduction to that chapter, Blackstone offered an alternative rationale of prevention of evil example as the limitation of *custos morum* authority to public acts:

> [P]rivate vices, or the breach of mere absolute duties, which man is bound to perform considered only as an individual, are not, [and] cannot be, the object of any municipal law; any farther than as by their evil example, or other pernicious effects, they may prejudice the community, and thereby become a species of public crimes.[232]

"[B]oth public and private vices are subject to the vengeance of eternal justice; and public vices are besides liable to the temporal punishments of human tribunals."[233] The rule of temporal justice, thus stated, was that liberty of conscience and associated private behaviors were tolerable, but creation of public knowledge of such behaviors by word or example could be enjoined and punished by courts of law. Blackstone's reference to *Sedley's Case* (1663) in the treatise and a similar reference in Hawkins's 1716 treatise publicized *Sedley's Case* and its doctrine of *custos morum* throughout England and the American colonies, exerting a profound influence on the development of indecent exposure laws. The publicity requirement continued to be generally recognized. In an anonymous tract entitled *Laws Respecting Women* published in 1777, the writer instructed that

> [l]ewdness of all kinds, or an illicit commerce between the sexes, is properly cognizable and punishable by the ecclesiastical law courts. But when such practices affect the good order and decorum of society, they become crimes properly cognizable by the civil magistrate. Upon the same principle open and scandalous lewdness of every kind may be punished on indictment at common law . . . .[234]

At the turn of the century, Edward East published this summary of *custos morum* authority:

> In like manner, all malicious revilings, in public derogation and contempt of established religion, are punishable by the common law, inasmuch as they tend to breach the peace. Similar to these are all scandalous and open breaches of morality exhibited in the face of the people, such as was the conduct of one who exposed himself naked to the public view from a balcony in Covent Garden. Offences of this kind sap public morals, the necessary foundation of good government; and are therefore properly cognizable by the temporal magistrates . . . .[235]

With the public/private distinction reasonably well settled, courts turned their attention in the early 1800s to an exploration of the nature of the act and intention of actors. The first reported conviction at common law for simple public nakedness was Rex v. Crunden (1809).235F236 The defendant had undressed on a beach to bathe in the sea. To his misfortune, there were inhabited houses nearby. The indictment was not set out in the report of the case, but Joseph Chitty described the facts of the case in considerable detail in his *A Practical Treatise on the Criminal Law* published in 1816. The indictment charged that

> John Crunden, the younger, late of Brighton in the county of Sussex, tailor, being a person of a wicked, depraved, and abandoned mind and disposition, and wholly lost to a due sense of decency and morality, and intending as much as in him lay to vitiate and corrupt the morals of his Majesty's liege subjects on, &c. with force and arms at, &c. aforesaid, unlawfully, wickedly, deliberately, and wilfully, did expose and exhibit himself naked, and in an indecent posture and situation near to, and in front of divers houses of the liege subjects of our said lord the king, situate at, &c. aforesaid, and also near to a certain, public, and common, king's highway, there and also in the presence of divers liege subjects of our said lord the king, both male and female, with intent to vitiate and corrupt the morals of his Majesty's liege subjects, to the great scandal and subversion of decency, religion, and good order, to the great corruption of the morals and manners of his majesty's liege subjects, to the evil example, &c. and against the peace, &c.[237]

Crunden was convicted even though there was "no evidence of . . . any wanton indecency, or having exposed his person beyond what was necessary for the purpose of bathing,"[238] and despite testimony by defense counsel that nude bathing had taken place at the location for many years and, at Millbank, since "time immemorial,"[239] fully exposed to the public view. Crunden had simply bathed in the sea opposite East Cliff at Brighton on a Sunday afternoon in July, undressing and dressing on the beach. Marryat, for the defendant, was willing to admit that the conduct amounted to a "breach of delicacy and good manners,"[240] but he insisted that it did not amount to an indictable offense because the defendant had no criminal intent. His objective was to procure health and enjoy a favorite recreation, not to outrage decency or corrupt public morals. Furthermore, to declare Crunden's act an offense would, in effect, prohibit the poor from bathing on any part of the southern coast, in the Thames, and in all other navigable rivers, where people are constantly passing and repassing. In any event, if Crunden's swim was a public nuisance, the complainants were barred by having come to it by building their houses on the cliffs overlooking this traditional bathing area.

Marryat's arguments were not well received. Chief Justice M'Donald's opinion rippled with indignation:

> I can entertain no doubt that the defendant by exposing his naked person . . . was guilty . . . . The law will not tolerate such an exhibition. Whatever his intention might be, the necessary tendency of his conduct was to outrage decency, and to corrupt morals. Nor is it any justification that bathing at this spot might a few years ago be innocent. For anything I know, a man might a few years ago have harmlessly danced naked in the fields beyond Montague house but it will scarcely [be said] . . . that anyone might now do so with impunity in Russell Square. Whatever place becomes the habitation of civilized men, here the laws of decency must be enforced.[241]

The intent of the actor was unimportant. Treatise writers Hawkins, Blackstone, and East cited this case, alongside *Sedley's Case* (1663), as an example of the "established principle, that whatever openly outrages decency, and is injurious to public morals, is a misdemeanor at common law."[242]

Recall that Sedley demonstrated plenty of immoral intent in his misbehavior. The argument in *Crunden* (1809) about the defendant's intent introduced a significant new element into the discourse of moral jurisprudence. The court's conclusion that criminal intent was not a prerequisite to prosecution would support prosecutions for both prevention of evil example and nuisance. The court's outrage suggests that evil example may have been top of mind. If the necessary tendency of conduct were to outrage decency or corrupt morals, an offense has been committed.

Sir William Russell adopted this as an "established principle" in his treatise on the criminal law published in 1819.[243] Russell's publication and Chitty's inclusion of the form of the indictment from *Crunden* in his treatise, published in 1816, ensured that the opinion would get wide publicity. Both works were prominent sources of authority in England and America during the nineteenth century. Lawyers in both nations were by now becoming well-schooled in the doctrine of *custos morum* and its purpose to prevent subversion of religion, decency, and good order through prevention of evil example.

The secular philosophy of the Enlightenment continued to degrade ecclesiastical authority over moral matters in England, creating a void. Parliament stepped in during such times to add more secular penal force to management of morals. These efforts were memorialized in the eighteenth and nineteenth centuries in statutes such as the Proclamation for the Discouragement of Vice (1787), Vagrancy Acts of 1822 and 1824, and Obscene Publications Act 1857. Prosecutions for indecent exposure were generally based on section six of the Vagrancy Act of 1824, section 28 of the Town Police Clauses Act of 1847, and local acts and bylaws.[244]

Codification of indecent exposure in England began when Parliament passed the first statute prohibiting indecent exposure as a provision of the Vagrancy Act of 1822. The Act focused on the public nuisance aspect of the crime. It deemed to be "rogues and vagabonds" "all persons openly exposing or exhibiting in any Street, Road, Public Place, or Highway any indecent Exhibition, or openly and indecently exposing their Persons."[245] The legislation was motivated by the numbers of people being forced to live on the streets due to the conclusion of the Napoleonic Wars, the social effects of the Industrial Revolution, and the Enclosure Acts.[246] When the Vagrancy Act was substantially reenacted in 1824, the provision was modified to include

> every Person willfully exposing to view, in any street, road highway, or public place, an obscene print, picture, or other indecent exhibition, (and) every person wilfully, openly, lewdly, and obscenely exposing his person in any street, road, or public highway, or in view thereof, or in any place of public resort, with intent to insult any female.[247]

The 1824 revisions broadened the scope of the Act by adding places of public resort and places in view of streets, roads, and highways, but limited its application to cases in which the exposure was made with the intent to insult a female. Committee records indicate that the change was made because it "had been stated by the magistrates, that the offence was so frequent, and it was so difficult to prevail upon females to overcome their natural delicacy, and prosecute the offender in a court of justice, that some summary punishment was almost indispensable."[248] The revision may have been enacted to protect the modesty of decent ladies during their travels from intrusions by the inadequately dressed and ill-mannered country peasants being drawn to the cities by the Industrial Revolution. It was focused on the effect on the audience, with a goal of mitigating public nuisances for these ladies; however, at least nominally, it required a showing of bad intent. This statute was complementary to common law, addressing specific concerns about the safety and comfort of ladies traveling on highways.

The first reported case involving a conviction under the statute was in 1831, in *Rex v. Justices of the Town and Country of Newcastle-upon-*

Tyne.[249] John Booteman had been convicted of exposing his person in a butcher market with the intent to insult a female and was sentenced to two months at hard labor. The focus of the case on appeal was a procedural matter resolved in favor of the defendant. The case's relevance lies in its proposition that to obtain a conviction under the statute, the prosecution had to prove three elements: (a) an obscene exhibition of the person, (b) in a certain specified place, (c) done with the requisite intent.

At common law, proof of criminal intent or a specific intent to insult a female was not required. For this reason, the intent requirement in the statute had little impact on the development of the law of indecent exposure. In any cases where the intent was not present and could not be presumed, the courts proceeded against the offender at common law by information. The principal advantage of the statute was that it promoted judicial economy and efficiency because it was a summary offense that could be managed by local authorities and in answer to which defendants had no right to a jury.

Common law continued to evolve alongside statutory developments. The publicity requirement was refined in *Rex v. Rouverard*,[250] a case tried at Yorkshire in 1830. A French master was indicted for exposing his person in a window of his house to excite a servant girl on the second floor of a house on the opposite side of the street. The jury was instructed to determine whether there was sufficient publicity to his act; that is, "whether those in the street could have seen him or not (not whether they did see him)," exposure to the servant girl alone not being sufficient, in the opinion of Parke B., who considered indecent exposure to be a public offense. The defendant was convicted. Exposure to one person was not sufficient to make the offense public and therefore indictable, but the exposure need not be seen by more than one person. It is enough that it was capable of being seen by others.

An attempt to extend *custos morum* authority to include male same-sex sexual behaviors failed in *Regina v. Rowed* (1842) due to the indictment's vagueness.[251] Two men were charged with having met in Kensington Gardens

> for the purpose and with the intent of committing and perpetrating with each other, openly, lewdly and indecently, in said public place, divers nasty, wicked, filthy, lewd, and indecently, in said public place divers nasty, wicked, filthy, lewd, beastly, unnatural and sodomitical practices; and . . did commit these acts "in sight and view of divers of the liege subjects . . . to the great scandal and

disgrace of mankind, in contempt, &c. to the evil example, &c. and against the peace, &c.

Defendants had been tried and found guilty. A motion in arrest of judgment on the ground that the indictment was not sufficiently certain and precise to allow the defendants to prepare an adequate defense was granted. Chief Justice Lord Denman commented that there was no authority for the form of indictment presented. Justice Patterson noted that the indictment "may have a certainty in common parlance, but it wants legal certainty." Indecent exposure was well known and understood. The indictment did not have sufficient preciseness to enable the defendants to know whether what they had done was an "offence known to law" because the acts done had not been alleged with proper certainty. The delicacy of the court records that had resulted in a lack of specificity about the acts charged in *Sedley's Case* (1663) two centuries earlier was no longer tolerable.

Three years later, in *Regina v. Bunyan* (1844),[252] an allegation that the defendants "unlawfully and wickedly did meet together, . . . with the intent . . . of committing . . . diverse natural and sodomitical acts and practices, . . . in sight and view of one C.S. and divers other liege subjects, and did divers lewd and beastly acts" was not questioned as to certainty and precision, thus opening the door for the addition of same-sex sexual practices to the class of moral offenses cognizable by temporal courts.[253] The issue in *Bunyan* was whether there was sufficient publicity attending the alleged acts. The defendants had been observed behind the closed doors of a parlor in a public house by a female servant, who summoned a police officer and another witness. Counsel for the defendants argued that the proper standard was whether the defendants were reckless of the probability of being overlooked. The court took a stricter view and instructed the jury to acquit them only if they believed them to be in "such a situation that there was no reasonable probability of their being so discovered." The defendants were convicted. *Rouverard* (1830) had propounded a publicity test based on the probability that the immoral act would be seen by others. *Bunyan* (1844) rejected the standard of whether the defendants had been reckless of the chance of being seen in favor of retaining the *Rouverard* test of mere capability of being seen by the public.

Regina v. Watson (1847).[254] confirmed that exposure to a single person was not considered "public." *Watson* was a case before the Court of Queen's Bench for indecent exposure by a man in Paddington Churchyard in the presence and view of a twelve-year-old girl. Counsel for the defendant argued that exposure to one person only is not indictable.

The Court agreed, stating the general rule "that a nuisance must be public, that is, to the injury or offence of several." The court noted that the offense would be summarily punishable under the Vagrancy Act, which required only one person, a woman, to be present if the exposure were in one of the enumerated places.

The reluctance of courts to punish indecent exposure to only one person appears to have been a consequence of a theoretical shift in common-law cases from the concern evidenced in earlier cases about the contagious effect of immorality on public order to a view of indecency as a public nuisance. No matter what its effect on the victim, an indecent exposure to an individual was not a public nuisance but a private annoyance. The doctrine of *custos morum* that sprang from the vague and ambiguous circumstances of *Sedley's Case* (1663) supported this view. One might argue, though, that the number-of-witnesses limitation made no sense where the person who saw the indecent exposure was unwilling, particularly in cases like *Watson* (1847) involving a gross sexual exhibition before a presumably innocent child of tender years.

It did not take long for the single-victim exemption to be challenged and overcome. It was statutorily overruled with passage of the Town Police Clauses Act in 1847.[255] Section 28 of that Act provided for the fine or imprisonment of "[e]very person who in any Street, to the Obstruction, Annoyance, or Danger of the Residents or Passengers, . . . willfully and indecently exposes his Person." The Vagrancy Act requirement that the exposure be done with the intent to insult a female was not carried over. However, once again, this statute's reach was more limited than the common law in that the offense had to occur in a "street." Yet, in another sense it was arguably broader than the common law in prohibiting exposures that annoyed residents or passersby without an explicit publicity requirement or any actual audience. Like the Vagrancy Act, it offered the advantage of summary disposition before local authorities.

The Court of Queen's Bench reconsidered the common-law publicity requirement during argument on an indictment involving male, same-sex sexual acts in *Regina v. Orchard* (1848).[256] The defendants were alleged to have met in a public urinal in Carrington Market and exhibited and exposed their persons and private parts to each other, laid hands on each other, and committed divers sodomitical acts. Their defense was that under the rule of *Watson* (1847), the indictment must allege that the exposure was within sight of several persons. The prosecutor replied that if passers-by can see in, it is sufficiently public. Justice Creswell, speaking for the court, agreed with the defense, adding that the urinal is not a public place because "[e]very man must expose his person who goes there for a proper purpose,"[257] meaning that an exposure in such a place is not indecent. Creswell skirted the central issue in this case, which was not the simple fact of exposure but the way it was done and the acts of which it was part and parcel.

During the next year, the Exchequer reaffirmed the rule that exposure to a single person was not a common-law offense in *Regina v. Webb* (1848).[258] The court applied the *Watson* (1847) rule that exposure to an individual is not indictable. The woman was tending bar at the time of the incident. Webb took out and exposed his penis, whereupon she ran off and told her husband, who summoned the police. Only the woman witnessed the exhibition. The defense was that a passageway to the bar of a public house is not a sufficiently public place or, alternatively, that there must be more than one person present—citing East's treatise (1803),[259] *Rex v. Crunden* (1809), and *Sedley's Case* (1663)—unless the act was done with intent to insult the barmaid, in which case the act would be punishable under the Vagrancy Act. The court engaged defense counsel in an extended colloquy.[260] The court recounted *Rex v. Rouverard* (1830), the case of the French tutor and servant girl. Clarkson, for the defendant, rejoined with a quote from *Burn's Justice* that only an exposure "to public view" is indictable, as in the *Watson* (1847) case. He went on to say that the indictment was defective on its face in that it alleged that the exposure took place "in the presence of" the victim without alleging that it was within the sight of anyone.

The court replied that the indictment alleged it occurred in a public place. Clarkson disagreed that the passageway to the alehouse was a "public place." To this, the prosecutor rejoined that a public place was simply "a place to which all persons have a right to go." The court did not find it necessary to settle the issue. In a unanimous opinion, the court found nothing more than exposure to a single person had been proven, so, under *Watson* (1847), the conviction must be reversed. In particular, the public-place issue need not be resolved because the indictment had not alleged a common nuisance but only the private nuisance of one woman. There was no mention of the purpose of the law being to prevent evil example.

Five years later the publicity requirement was reaffirmed in the context of printed materials. In *Dugdale v. The Queen* (1853),[261] the court held that mere possession of obscene and indecent prints and pictures did not constitute an indictable offense. Mere possession was a private vice, not a public wrong.

Regina v. Holmes (1853).[262] was decided during the same term. In *Holmes,* the court upheld the conviction of a man who had exposed himself in the presence of several females on a public bus. In overruling objections to the sufficiency of the indictment, the court relied on the Criminal Procedure Act 1851, which empowered courts to sustain indictments containing incidental defects. The statute also empowered courts to amend defective pleadings..[263] Chief Justice Campbell answered a defense objection that a common nuisance had not been alleged. Breaking with the prevailing view, he reasserted the seemingly forgotten purpose of the law to prevent subversion of religion, decency, and good order by stating, "This is an offense against public decency, rather than a common nuisance.".[264] He went on to say, "It would be a disgrace to the law if we had any doubt that the indictment is good. The defendant exposed himself in a public omnibus in the New Road, in the presence of several women and this country would not be fit to live in if this were not an offence.".[265] The conviction was affirmed by a unanimous court.

Eight years later, the Court of Queen's Bench reexamined the *Rouverard* (1830) rule that an act may be punished even though witnessed by only one person if it was capable of being seen by others. In *Regina v. Elliot* (1861),.[266] the court considered an appeal from conviction of a man and a woman for copulating on Wordsworth Common within view of a public highway. At trial, the judge charged the jury that if their acts "could be seen without difficulty by other persons on such public place and on such public footway or bridge," the defendants should be convicted, and they were. The Queen's Bench voted 3–2 to sustain the conviction, but the chief judge refused to uphold the conviction on such a narrow split and ordered a rehearing. In the following term, the court decided that the issue did not merit reconsideration, so the defendants, who had been freed pending rehearing, went unpunished.

Two years later, in *Regina v. Thallman* (1863),.[267] Chief Justice Earl, who was not on the court when *Elliot* (1861) was decided, ruled that the publicity requirement did not limit place to those traditionally considered to be "public places," such as markets, churches, depots, highways, and the like. He remarked that "'[p]ublic place' does not mean a public highway. We are all of the opinion that here there was abundant publicity" where the defendant, a servant in a house on Albemarle Street in Piccadilly, repeatedly crossed over the roofs of several houses almost entirely naked to present himself before the window of the sleeping quarters of a group of female servants. The meaning of "public" expanded from physical places to state of mind and intention of the actor. The rooftops became public because Thallman used them to present himself to the unwilling audience.

Five years later, *Regina v. Hicklin* (1868),[268] a case brought under the Obscene Publications Act 1857,[269] established the definition of obscenity that would become the first definition used by lower courts in the United States and later, famously, the generally accepted judicial source for identifying violations of the Comstock Law, which made it illegal to send "obscene, lewd or lascivious," "immoral," or "indecent" publications through the mail.[270] Notably, the "obscene" publication in *Hicklin* was a pamphlet consisting of extracts taken from the writings of theologians on the doctrine and discipline of the Romish Church. It was found to be obscene because it was "calculated to produce a pernicious effect in depraving and debauching the minds of the persons into whose hands it might come." There was no mention of *Sedley's Case* (1663). The *Hicklin* test defined material as obscene if it tended "to deprave or corrupt those whose minds are open to such immoral influences, and into whose hands a publication of this sort may fall." This test prevailed until *Roth v. United States* (1957),[271] which held that the *Hicklin* test was inappropriate. *Thallman* (1863) and *Hicklin* (1868) were the last British common-law cases to play any part in the development of American public indecency laws.[272]

The doctrine of *custos morum* originated in a seventeenth-century political struggle between an elder statesman and a band of licentious courtiers for the loyalty of a king referred to by historians as the "merry monarch." Society had recently been freed by revolution from a religiously repressive government. Intervention of temporal courts into the moral affairs of citizens was confined to a single case during the reign of Charles II, one in which religion and morals were affirmed as cornerstones of public order. The doctrine, expressed there as *custos morum*, explicitly fused prevailing religious tradition with the temporal concept of good order. As the court in *Taylor's Case* (1675) put it, "Christianity is parcel of the laws of England; and therefore, to reproach the Christian Religion, is to speak in subversion of the Law." In later, more secularly minded times, the semantic abstractions of decency and morality were substituted for Christianity. Nevertheless, the principles of sexual morality that the law enforced remained those of the Christian faith.[273]

From its common-law roots in Sedley's wild and riotous behavior, drunkenness, profanity, blasphemy, mockery of the Crown, public nakedness, and utterly crude mockery of sexuality, the law of public indecency grew to encompass blasphemy, publication of obscene books, conspiracy to promote prostitution, sodomy and buggery, exhibitionism, and nude bathing.

No one questioned the legitimacy of the state interests involved. Prevention of evil example and public nuisance formed the bedrock of prosecution. There was no need for actual breach of the peace or any expectation of reprisals or other forms of violence. Immorality per se constituted a constructive breach of the peace. The most persistent limitation on *custos morum* authority was the requirement of publicity. Only public immorality was punishable. Courts expressed expansive views of the meaning of "public," over time stretching the commonsense notion of traditional public places like streets, stores, and transit stations to any location in which the exposure was capable of being seen by more than one unwilling viewer. Under the common law, indecent exposure before a single person was no offense. No proof of criminal intent was necessary; it could be presumed from the circumstances of the activity. Benevolent motives were no excuse.

Statutes forbidding indecent exposure that were passed in the nineteenth century offered the advantage of summary adjudication of offenses occurring in places of public convenience. However, they provided only limited penalties, and, unlike under the common law, intent was a material element of the crime. The first two statutes enacted included one that required a showing of intent to insult a female; another, a showing of willful and indecent exposure.

These jurisprudential threads formed one leg of the foundation of modern American indecent exposure laws. The second source was the comprehensive statutory management of bodily morality enacted in colonial America.

3. Moral Jurisprudence and Biblical Hegemony in American Colonies

All seventeenth-century colonial statutory frameworks contained extensive lists of moral crimes that were seen as challenges to maintaining civil order in the New World.[274] Most colonists who settled in North America were Protestants from England, Scotland, and Germany. It is estimated that eighty to ninety percent of colonists were Christian.[275] The power elite of the New England colonies was dominated by the faithful. Many statutes concerning morality in these colonies contained explicit references to Scripture. The law of God was the law of the new settlements except to the extent that English common law was required by charter.[276]

Most early settlers migrated from England to gain freedom to practice their religion. Among them, Puritans in particular felt that the reformation within the Church of England had not gone far enough with establishment of the state church—that it had left vestiges of Roman Catholicism. This dissatisfaction put the Puritans at odds with the English governing class. The Puritans who settled New England were principally yeomen, tradesmen, and artisans from England's cities.[277] They left England to escape imposition of the doctrine of the Church of England, popish heresy, religion-based economic sanctions, and increasingly widespread licentious conduct.[278] The Puritan migration mainly comprised entire families. The way of life they established in the colonies was marked by intense devotion to the family. Leaders among the earliest settlers were utopians who came to the new land to establish a "Bible Commonwealth."[279] The laws they created provided a foundation upon which their utopian ideals would be realized. While they were driven from England because of their religious beliefs, they did not advocate freedom of worship for others.[280]

These emigrants who left England to form a "New" England in the New World played a significant role in the creation and evolution of indecent exposure laws in America. A significant share of cases in the colonial superior courts during the formative years before 1660 involved lewd behavior, filthy dalliance, unclean carriage,[281] and lascivious conduct.[282] As Bradley Chapin, author of *Criminal Justice in Colonial*

America, 1606-1660 noted: "The England [the colonialists] had left was perceived as disorderly, immoral, and crime ridden. As participants or observers, they had seen there an archaic, inefficient, and capricious judicial system attempting unsuccessfully to stem the tide of vice and crime."[283] Seven jurisdictions were established in colonial America before 1660, populated mainly by Christians.[284] Not all settlers were Puritan. There were Quakers, Baptists, Unitarians, Deists, Dutch Reformed Church members, and other denominations.[285] They shared a basic Christian faith and tolerated sectarian differences to enable political unity.

Some colonies had official state churches, while others allowed religious freedom and diversity. No ecclesiastical courts were formed. Religion was an obviously powerful influence in the development of legal structures created to govern the new England.[286] God's presence was pervasive and formidable. The letters patent establishing the first official settlement in the New World, the Colony of Virginia, praised the noble venture of the settlers in propagating the Christian religion to the savages, who "as yet live in darkness and miserable ignorance of the true knowledge and worship of God, and [the settlers] may in time bring the infidels and savages, living in those parts, to human civility, and to a settled and quiet government. . . ."[287] Notice juxtaposition of the concepts of knowledge and worship of God, human civility, and settled and quiet government. These were enduring core themes of moral jurisprudence until the moral upheaval in America that began in the 1960s.

More colonies and settlements were established in the wilderness along the eastern shore of America later in the seventeenth century. They were all, like the Virginia colony, consecrated in God's guiding light. For example, when the first government of the New Haven Colony took form in a plantation covenant, the settlers agreed upon the Scriptures not only as a religious framework but as a civil code. The new government was based on the proposition that the Scriptures provided "the perfect rule for the government of all mankind,"[288] wherein the "word of God shall be the only rule to be attended unto in ordering the affayres of Government. . . ."[289] The Puritans in New England sought to create a "godly society . . . [that] would serve as a shining example to the rest of the world."[290]

Seventeenth-century colonial law was an amalgam of English common law, biblical law, and indigenous influences; "indigenous" meaning driven by efforts to remove personal conduct from church courts and reform English criminal law. Chapin's statistical study of the origins of substantive criminal law found that "in four of the five jurisdictions where radical Protestantism was to prevail, the Bible furnished obvious and transcendent precedents for criminal law."[291] Chapin concluded that English law was the source of seventy-seven percent of the criminal law before 1660.[292] Eighteen percent came from the Bible. The remaining twenty-five percent was indigenous.

The percentage of law of biblical origin ranged from one percent in Rhode Island to forty-three percent in New Haven. The three Puritan colonies were most reliant on the Bible; however, "the Bible or ecclesiastical precedents [had] considerable impact on definitions of sexual offenses everywhere."[293] Chapin observed that the Bible was explicitly referenced in twenty-one to forty-three percent of the criminal statutes involving sexual morality. Crimes like buggery and sodomy were viewed as crimes against both God and nature. Public masturbation was punishable by death in some jurisdictions.

There were common-law cases as well. They accounted for more than one-half of prosecutions. As Priestley noted, the

> laws of a country are necessarily connected with everything belonging to the people of it; so that a thorough knowledge of them, and their progress would inform us of everything that was most useful to be known about them; and one of the greatest imperfections of historians in general, is owing to their ignorance of the law.[294]

It is equally true that to know the laws of a country, we must also understand everything belonging to the people of it, especially their sources of moral authority.

One cannot help but be struck by the dominance of theology in the development of the first laws in the New England colonies. Noted historian Perry Miller advised that "without some understanding of Puritanism, it may safely be said, there is no understanding of America."[295] Daniel Boorstin noted that for Puritans, "the doctrines of the Fall of Man, of Sin, of Salvation, Predestination, Election, and Conversion were their meat & drink. Yet what really distinguished them in their day was that they were less interested in theology itself, than in the application of theology."[296] As further analysis will show, religious principles of the Puritan theocracy are still evident in modern laws regarding indecency.[297] Puritan religious conceptions have informed both the substance and administration of these laws.[298]

There was substantial unanimity among the early Puritan settlers that the "State's first duty was the maintenance and support of religion."[299] In statutes, judicial decisions, and other recorded legal activities, the people of the Puritan colonies recognized the word of God, as declared in the Holy Scriptures, as the irrefutable authority in temporal as well as spiritual affairs.[300] The Puritans considered the Bible to be the revealed word of God and, as such, to constitute "a complete body of laws, an absolute code in everything it touched upon," and they "extended Scripture to cover the whole of existence."[301] Notably, Puritans in England before the time of migration to North America had recommended abolition of the common law and substitution of the law of Moses.[302] In one such proposal, a postscript to a statement of principal grounds for law among Christians contained the assertion that "all wantonness, lasciviousness, and filthy acts of uncleanness, are to be severely punished by the civil magistrates," citing Scripture.[303] Sexuality was seen as explicitly competing with faith. "Husband and wives were often directed by ministers to save their greatest love, not for each other, but for God, while single persons were advised to substitute love of God for forbidden lusts of the flesh."[304]

Calvin's *Institutes of the Christian Religion* was the Puritans' chief religious and political authority.[305] The Puritans also relied heavily for theological guidance on Martin Luther. Luther launched his reforms with an essay entitled "Commentary on Galatians" that posited an ideal of Christian freedom that would liberate men from the old law of works to the freedom of the law of faith.[306] Most colonial governments, not just the Puritan settlements, "recognized the word of God, as declared in the Holy Scriptures, as a guide, as an authority, as a law in temporal as well as spiritual affairs."[307]

According to Professor Lawrence Friedman in his *Crime and Punishment in American History*,

> it would be hard to overemphasize the influence of religion—the beliefs of magistrates and leaders—in shaping the criminal codes, in framing modes of enforcement, and generally, in creating a distinctive legal culture. The criminal justice system was in many ways another arm of religious orthodoxy. This was true everywhere in the colonies, but most strikingly perhaps, in the Puritan north.[308]

Unlike in England, there was never any doubt in the American colonies that the temporal courts had the authority to punish immorality. Within a few years after the settlement of Jamestown and fifty years before *Sedley's Case* (1663), secular legal codes regulating both public and private morality were enacted in the New World. Colonial codes often lumped together offenses against religion and government, along with other breaches of respect for authority and civil and ecclesiastical order. The earliest printed code of laws (though more a set of military rules and regulations than civil law), the *Lawes Divine, Morall and Martiall, &c.*[309] for the Colony of Virginia published in 1612, alternated between secular and profane in its list of felonies: fidelity to government, derogation of the Holy Trinity, blasphemy, traitorous words, and derogation of religion. Sodomy, adultery, and ravishment were capital crimes.

One prohibition, primarily aimed at protection of public health, provided incidental control of public nakedness as well. It was forbidden that anyone should "within less than a quarter of one mile from the Pallizadoes, dare to doe the necessities of nature, since by these unmanly, slothful, and loathsome immodesties, the whole Fort may be choked, and poisoned with ill aires."[310] Furthermore, it was ordered that

> [n]o man shall have given any disgraceful words, or comit any act to the disgrace of any person in this Colonie, or any part thereof, upon pain of being tied head and feet together, upon the guard every night for the space of one month, besides to be publicly disgraced himself, and be made incapable ever after to possess any place, or execute any office in this employment.[311]

The first New England settlers arrived at Plymouth eight years later in 1620. By 1623, the four towns of New Hampshire, Maine, Plymouth, and Massachusetts Bay were established. In 1638, the first printing press in New England began operation. Before that, written laws had been read on appointed days to assemblies in the towns.[312]

Religion was front and center in the earliest laws of the colonies. Criminal provisions of these early laws[313] addressed public and private morality and personal appearance in public. As early as 1630, in Massachusetts Bay, the General Court passed an act "prohibiting short sleeves, and requiring garments to be lengthened so as to cover the arms to the wrists, and gowns to the shoe buckles; [and banning] immoderate great breaches, knots of ribbon, broad shoulder bands, and . . ., silkroses, double ruffs and cuffs."[314] During the next year, a law was promulgated making adultery punishable by death.[315] Courtship more generally was carefully regulated under the threat of corporal punishment and fines.[316]

The first compilation of criminal laws in New England was published in New Plymouth Colony in 1636. It contained provisions outlawing adultery, drunkenness, idleness, swearing, and cursing and required advance parental consent to courtship. "Fornication and other unclean carriages" were to be punished at the discretion of magistrates.[317] The expression "other unclean carriages"[318] appears to have been intended to vest broad powers in local magistrates to deal with immorality, both public and private.[319] There is evidence of prosecution for lascivious carriage involving flagrant displays of sexual intentions between a man and woman not married to each other in the 1650s.[320] Capital offenses included treason and rebellion, willful murder, witchcraft, arson, sodomy, rape, buggery, and adultery.[321] Each of these provisions in the compilation was preceded by a citation to an appropriate passage from Scripture. The pervasive influence of the teachings of Calvin in the Plymouth laws led a commentator to characterize them as "Genevese rather than English."[322]

Massachusetts Bay leaders tried to operate the colony without written laws, relying on magistrates to interpret God's laws. Concern about abuse of discretion led to creation of the first body of written laws in the colony.[323] In 1641, in Massachusetts Bay, John Cotton and the Reverand Nathaniel Ward were commissioned by the government to propose a set of laws whereby the colony should be governed. Each man submitted a proposal. Ward's proposal[324] was enacted. Cotton's *Abstract of the Lawes of New England*, also known as *Moses His Judicials*, attracted considerable publicity and was adopted in New Haven, printed in England, and widely distributed.[325]

Cotton's code described as capital crimes the offenses of blasphemy, idolatry, witchcraft, consulting with witches, heresy, false worship, scandalous living (i.e., cohabitation), reviling of religion, perjury, Sabbath-breaking, treason, being an unreverend magistrate, reviling of magistrates, rebellion, being a rebellious child, murder, adultery, incest, sodomy, buggery, polluting a woman known to be in her flowers (i.e., having intercourse during menstruation), whoredom, man-stealing, and false witness. The crimes deserving corporal punishment or fine were swearing and cursing, drunkenness, rape of a maiden, fornication, mayhem, theft of a beast, burglary, and slander.[326]

Rev. Ward's *Body of Liberties* contained only half the number of capital crimes: idolatry, witchcraft, blasphemy, murder, manslaughter, poisoning, bestiality, sodomy, adultery, man-stealing, false witness, conspiracy, and rebellion.[327] Published in 1641, it cited Scripture in its "Capitall Laws"[328] prescribing death for worshipping false gods, witchcraft, and blasphemy. Cotton concluded his code with an homage to the Lord from Isaiah: "The Lord is our Judge, The Lord is our Law-giver, The Lord is our King. He will save us."[329]

At that time in Virginia, the clergy were bound to temporal jurisdiction over moral affairs by a statute calling for yearly meetings of ministers and church wardens, at which they were to report certain offenses, such as swearing, profaning, showing contempt for religion, adultery, whoredom, fornication, and drunkenness to commanders and commissioners of the county courts.[330] Neglect of this duty was punishable by fine.[331]

The prohibition of "unclean carriages" was formalized, in an act by the General Court of New Haven Colony in December 1642, as an expression of approbation of the conviction of Nicholas Olmstead two years earlier at a session of the Particular Court for "lascivious carriage." The term "carriage" referred to the way people conducted their behavior in public. "Lascivious" referred to carriage that was considered lewd, lustful, or inclined toward sexual indulgence. The term applied to behaviors that were deemed improper or offensive according to prevailing social norms. It encompassed a range of activities that were considered sexually suggestive with someone who was not a spouse, such as overt flirting, promiscuous behavior, or public displays of affection.

The prohibition of "lascivious carriage" was aimed at maintaining public decency and upholding moral standards within the community in support of families as sources of stability and accountability. Colonial societies placed great importance on maintaining strict moral codes. Behaviors deemed lascivious were often condemned and subjected to social censure or legal consequences. The New Haven Act empowered and directed the Particular Courts to punish "lascivious carriage and behavior."[332] It supplemented the discretionary authority of the Particular Courts to punish unchaste and wanton behavior, often by whipping at the tail of a cart, fines, and compulsory marriage (authority they had possessed before passage of the Code of 1642.).[333]

Although Nicholas Olmstead[334] was not as colorful a character as Sedley, and not nearly as much has been written about him, it is interesting to observe that he, like Sedley, went on to become a respected, even distinguished, citizen. Olmstead was convicted of "lascivious carriage & foul misdemeanors at sundry times with Mary Brunson," for which he was sentenced to the pillory at Hartford and fined £20.[335] Three months after the trial, Olmstead married Sarah Loomis of Windsor, Connecticut, who bore him his first child, Sarah, within a year.[336] After serving as a soldier in the Pequot War, Olmstead was chosen a deputy of the General Court in 1672.[337] He died on August 31, 1684, at the age of 72.

The distinguished later careers of Sedley and Olmstead illustrate the modernity of the conception of immorality as an enduring personality trait. In their cases, immoral and rambunctious behavior appears to have been (or have been considered) episodic, a frivolity of youth that gave way to stability, respectability, and a conservative lifestyle in later years. Nowadays, such misbehavior can lead to lifelong designation as a sex offender or other enduring damage to reputation and employment.[338]

These early compilations of laws that served as models for legal codes in most of the American colonies, and later in new settlements in the frontier, were little more than codifications of Scripture. Citation to Scripture in civil law codes of New England colonies was commonplace.[339] The Bible was the principal source of law for the New England colonies.[340] Morality was regulated by law and enforced with threats of corporal punishment, fine, imprisonment, and death. I have found no documentation of secular justifications for these laws. When *Governor Eaton's Code for the New Haven Colony* was published in 1656, it contained on its title page a quotation from Romans chapter 13, which it described as the "basic source of Puritan civil authority."[341] Verses 1 and 2 of that chapter read: "Let every Soul be subject unto the Higher Powers: for there is no Power but of God, the Powers that be are Ordained of God. Whosoever therefore resisteth the Power resisteth the Ordinance of God: and they that resist, shall receive to themselves Damnation."

The Second New Plymouth Compilation of Laws, published in 1658, likewise opened with a succinct summary of the Puritan philosophy of law, stating that "the only true law was the law of God as revealed in His Holy Scriptures, and that laws made by man must be derived from them and conformable to them in all respects."[342]

The early laws evidenced a concern for enforcement. For the laws to be effective, there had to be a means of promulgating rules, rooting out immorality, and bringing it to the attention of the authorities. The family was a primary mechanism for implementation.[343] As an important source of surveillance and discipline, the family was closely guarded and strongly reinforced by the laws that it served. Single persons were disfavored. Laws were enacted to bring them within the control of families or banish them.

In 1656, the New Haven Colony passed an ordinance to "prevent or suppress inconvenience and disorder in the course and carriage of sundry single persons who live not in service, nor in any family relation," by requiring that they reside either "with some allowed relation, or in some approved family licensed thereunto by the Court," to be watched by the head of such family and reported for any misbehavior, idleness, or irreligiousness.[344] Colonial laws regulating sexuality channeled it into its proper setting and purpose: marriage and procreation.[345] These practical benefits gave the laws secular purposes that did not need to be articulated given the general acceptance of ecclesiastical authority. This channelization of sexual behavior into the family enhanced productivity, education, and civil order, and it mitigated the need for care of illegitimate children and provided protection against single, unaffiliated men and women. Single people were viewed as potentially disruptive forces. Concern about them became a crusade across the colonies. Ordinances regulating the place of residence of single persons, like the law passed in 1656 in New Haven, were also enacted in Massachusetts and New Plymouth colonies.[346]

In 1659, an act was passed in New Haven Colony providing for the transportation back to England of single people not preparing the way for their families or merely passing through. Otherwise, "they are exposed to great temptations, and some of them live under suspicion of uncleanness, if they do not fall into lewd and sinful courses . . . ."[347] An act concerning vagabonds promulgated in Massachusetts Bay three years later authorized summary arrest and corporal punishment. The preamble read:

> This Court being sensible of the increase of prophaneness and irreligious-ness, by reason of the vagrant and vagabond life of sundry persons, as well inhabitants as foreigners, that wander from their families, relations and dwelling places, from town to town, thereby drawing away children, servants, and other persons, both younger and elder, from their lawful callings and employments, and hardening the hearts of one another against all subjection to the rules of God's Holy Word, and the established laws of this Colony. . . .[348]

Ungodly excess in dress was also regulated. Sumptuary laws were reenacted in the same year to curb "an excess in apparel . . . unbecoming a wilderness condition, and the profession of the Gospel, whereby the rising generation are in danger to be corrupted and effeminated; which practices are witnessed against by the law of God, and sundry civil and Christian nations."[349]

The earliest identifiable law prohibiting indecent exposure as that term is used in modern American laws was enacted in 1656 in the New Haven Colony. It outlawed public masturbation, sodomy, child molestation, and adultery:

> [I]f any man shall act upon himself, and in sight of others pour out his seed, by example, or counsel, or both, corrupting or tempting others to do the like, which tends to the sin of Sodomy, (Gen. 38:9,24) if it be not one kind of it; or shall defile or corrupt himself and others, by any other kind of sinful filthiness, he shall be punished according to the nature of the offence. . . .[350]

All these developments antedated *Sedley's Case* (1663). By the time of *Sedley's Case*, legal control of morality in America was comprehensive and commonplace, embodied in criminal laws anchored in Scripture. Unlike in England, management of morality transcended place. The lack of ecclesiastical courts justified the expansive jurisdiction of the temporal courts. Family attachments and the fear of God were the wellsprings of civil order. Those untouched by these sources of control were hemmed in by the law. Most notably, single persons were confined under the watchful eyes of chosen families or banished. Suppression of public indecency was assured by a multitude of public acts. Examples include a Virginia law forbidding disgraceful words and acts, a New Plymouth Colony Act empowering magistrates to punish "unclean carriages," and the New Haven Colony provision for the punishment of "lascivious carriages and behavior."

As the Court of King's Bench of England readied for its bold assertion that it was "*custos morum*" over the people, the colonial judiciary was already an authoritarian regime armed with plenary power to prevent and punish immorality and vice in the service of God.[351] In both England and America, bans against public nakedness arose from pious notions and concern about good order and productivity of civil society. In both countries, the connections to established religion were often explicit and undeniable. The preeminence of Christianity in England began to be challenged by new ideas about morality in the Enlightenment, also known as the Age of Reason, that advocated critical thinking, skepticism, and freedom of conscience; however, the sexual morality of its natural-law theories largely parroted established ecclesiastical doctrine due to concern about indolence of the body. The Enlightenment contributed to the long process of subversive secularization of the language of indecency in the law and society.

By the end of the seventeenth century, Pennsylvania and Rhode Island had expressly rejected biblical models for their legal systems. Legal regulation of morals in the colonies was becoming more reliant on English common law. As the common law was synthesized into colonial governance in the early decades of the eighteenth century before the American Revolution, further fragmentation of religion, dissipation of civil moral authority, and concomitant loosening of public morals were evident.[352] Prosecutions for moral offenses dropped precipitously throughout the eighteenth century in many colonies, while the numbers of property and violent crimes increased.[353]

The precedential effect of colonial law is evident in the reenactment in Connecticut in 1733 of the 1642 Act for punishing lascivious carriages. This reaffirmation was an important vehicle for migration of moral jurisprudence from the acts of colonial assemblies into statutes that would govern the newly formed United States and provide historical context for the drafting of the Declaration of Independence and U.S. Constitution later in the eighteenth century. The prohibition appeared in the following form:

> For the preventing of lascivious carriages and practices, against which (in regard of the variety of circumstances) particular and express laws cannot suddenly be suited and made.
>
> It is enacted, &c., that several and respective county courts within this Colony shall be, and are hereby, empowered to proceed against and punish such offenders, either by fine, committing to the House of Correction, or by corporal punishment, according to their discretion; that such seasonable and exemplary executions may be done upon offenders in that kind that others may hear and fear.[354]

The preamble to the Act evidenced an intention to encompass within its proscription all manner of immoral behaviors not prohibited by specific laws, such as those providing for punishment of adultery, fornication, incest, sodomy, and bestiality. Because all these specific offenses involved consummated sexual intercourse, the statute appears to have been directed at incipient sexual activities; that is, those that fell short of carnal connection.

As early American conceptions of indecent exposure evolved in the interleaving of precedents from colonial statutes and English common law, explicit biblical references became less common. Indicia of the laws' religious origins faded into the background.[355] There were three primary sources in English common law for the semantic concepts expressed in nineteenth-century codifications of public indecency laws:

- *Sedley's Case* (1663), the most common source of statutory language;[356]
- Hawkins's (1716) characterization of the offense in that case as "open lewdness grossly scandalous;" and
- Blackstone's (England 1765; America 1772) characterization of Sedley's crime as "grossly scandalous and public indecency."

These were the cornerstones of statutory definitions of indecent exposure in the late eighteenth and early nineteenth centuries. There was little attribution to early laws of the colonies.

Treatise writers were instrumental in shaping the merger of English common law and colonial laws in eighteenth-century statutory developments. In 1773, one hundred and ten years after *Sedley's Case* (1663), *Burn's Abridgement*,[357] also known as *The American Justice*, was published in Boston. It contained a quotation from *Hawkins Pleas of the Crown* (1716) that "in general, all open lewdness, grossly scandalous, is indictable, as tending to subvert religion and morality." [358] The most influential early statute embracing this legal theory was a 1784 Massachusetts statute forbidding "open gross lewdness and lascivious behavior." The statute's semantic ancestors appear to be the 1733 Connecticut law against "lascivious carriages and behavior" and Blackstone's and Hawkins's characterizations of Sedley's offense as "open lewdness grossly scandalous." The statute provided:

> If any man and woman, not being married to each other, shall lewdly and lasciviously associate and cohabit together, or if any man or woman, married or unmarried, shall be guilty of open gross lewdness, and lascivious behavior, they shall be set in the pillory, whipped, fined, imprisoned, bound to good behavior, or all or any of these according to the gravity of the offense.[359]

The Connecticut law had proscribed private as well as public immorality. The expression "open gross lewdness and lascivious behavior" in the Massachusetts statute is a curious synthesis of precedent. One aspect had roots in mid-seventeenth-century colonial statutes; the other, in English common law. The latter aspect is evident in the expression "open gross lewdness," which closely resembles Hawkins's interpretation of *Sedley's Case* (1663) that "[a]ll open lewdness grossly scandalous" is punishable at common law.[360] Hawkins's treatise was published in England in 1716 and quoted in the edition of *Burn's Justice* published there in 1755.[361] Blackstone paraphrased Hawkins in his *Commentaries*, published in England in 1765 and in America in 1772.[362]

The Massachusetts statute was a clumsy merger of common-law and colonial statutory concepts. The "open gross lewdness" clause prohibited a course of conduct whose natural consequence would be to create the appearance of adultery or fornication without requiring proof of performance of specific sexual acts. It may have been the earliest infusion into American jurisprudence of semantic conceptions of public indecency from *Sedley's Case* (1663). The second clause created ambiguity. It prohibited certain vaguely defined behaviors, identified as "lascivious behavior," an expression that had first appeared in the 1642 New Haven statute, where it was intended to address activities that were considered lewd, lustful, or inclined toward sexual indulgence. Coincident use of these overlapping expressions became commonplace in American statutory and case law.

Whereas "open gross lewdness" cautiously emerged from an encroachment of temporal jurisdiction on the traditional domain of the ecclesiastical courts of England in *Sedley's Case* (1663), "lascivious behavior" arose in a context in which the law of God, as revealed in the Scriptures, was the law of the land in the American colonies, where church and state were synonymous. The synthesis of these concepts provided comprehensive coverage for both established rationales for enforcement of indecent exposure: public nuisance and prevention of evil example.

Whereas no showing of immoral intent was necessary to prove and suppress a nuisance, prevention of the evil example of lascivious conduct focused on wanton and willful disregard of societal standards, as in *Sedley's Case* (1663). In jurisdictions where these threads were not woven together, the source of precedent could have significant consequences. The key distinction was the relevance of intent and place. Intent had a double-edged significance in the common law: both the intent of the actor and the intent of the audience could be relevant. Courts and assemblies continued to wrestle with the boundaries of the meaning of "public."

Laws similar to the 1784 Massachusetts statute were enacted in New Hampshire (1791), Maine (1821), Michigan (1838), Missouri (1838), Wisconsin (1838), Vermont (1845), Virginia (1847), and Minnesota (1866) and were eventually enacted in nearly all New England states and the Northwest territory. The "lascivious carriage and behavior" of Olmstead and "open and notorious lewdness" language of Blackstone's (1765) description of *Sparrow v. Sherwood* (1627) combined with Hawkins's and Blackstone's conceptualizations of *Sedley's Case* (1663) to inform drafting of these transitory statutory composites that traversed early American states and territories.

By the time the Massachusetts statute was enacted, the only reported successful prosecutions in England under the doctrine of *Sedley's Case* (1663) were for blasphemy and publication of obscene libels. Routine and widespread citation to *Sedley's Case* (1663) as a judicial precedent in England did not begin until 1809 in *Rex v. Crunden*.[363] Adultery, fornication, and sodomy were not yet justiciable in the temporal courts of England. American courts were fully equipped to manage sexual morality. They were not constrained by disputes about ecclesiastical jurisdiction or any denial of the divine inspiration for the laws.

The juxtaposition of English and colonial legal principles in the expression "open gross lewdness and lascivious behavior" created ambiguity, one that prophetically fed the ambivalence of nineteenth-century courts beholden to English common law by reception statutes.[364]

while being imbued with moral jurisprudence of the American Colonial era.[365]

A new nation was formed in the last decades of the eighteenth century. This was followed by an early-nineteenth-century moral resurgence during which Victorian moral perspectives and the English tradition of *custos morum* were imported and fused with remnants of American Colonial laws and customs. The nation building began with several declarations regarding civil rights and representative democracy. The Declaration of Independence, adopted by the Continental Congress on July 4, 1776, stated reasons for separating from England and expressed ideals of civil society and justification for separating from Great Britain,[366] one of which was the following:

> We hold these truths to be self-evident, that all men are created equal, that they are endowed by their Creator with certain unalienable Rights, that among these are Life, Liberty and the pursuit of Happiness. That to secure these rights, Governments are instituted among Men, deriving their just powers from the consent of the governed. . . .

The U.S. Constitution was drafted at the Constitutional Convention in Philadelphia in 1787.[367] The Declaration and Constitution have influenced each other and informed interpretation of the rights and responsibilities of America's government and people for the last 250 years. The Constitution, providing a framework for representative democracy, established a system of checks and balances, federalism, separation of powers, and representation to form an enduring, more perfect union. The Bill of Rights, introduced in 1789 and ratified in 1791, added explicit protections of individual liberties and states' rights to the Constitution, such as freedom of speech, religion, press, assembly, and petition; trial by jury; and due process of law. These documents influenced the drafting of constitutions for the newly formed states. They channeled and synthesized doctrines from colonial statutes and English common law into fundamental legal principles of the newly formed constitutional democracy. The basic concepts of the new nation included a limited government and explicit recognition of the natural rights of its people. This marked the beginning of a centuries-long reconciliation of legal management of public indecency and constitutional principles of separation of church and state, freedom of speech, and due process of law.

4. Fusion of Colonial Ideology and English Common-Law Tradition in Nineteenth-Century America

The American Revolution (1775–1783), Declaration of Independence (1776), and Constitution (1787) marked an embrace of principles of natural rights, social contract, popular sovereignty, separation of church and state, and freedom of worship. These developments were correlated with declines in formal religious affiliation and increases in religious diversity and pluralism in the colonies. By the end of the eighteenth century, the percentage of Christians in the population had declined from the high nineties to seventy-five to eighty-five percent, and the number of religiously unaffiliated or "nones" was growing. Enlightenment ideas about other potential sources of natural law circulated among civic leaders and played a role in advancing key concepts in the Bill of Rights and the federal and state constitutions of the newly formed United States. There was a substantial amount of contentious debate about religion. Nevertheless, Enlightenment notions of natural rights and social contract, and denominational religious contention, had little effect on indecent exposure laws and the original public meaning of the Constitution and Bill of Rights insofar as those documents related to management of sexual morality. The moral sentiments of the framers, ratifiers, and general population remained grounded in Christian religious doctrine.

Christian religion struggled with sectarian rifts, funding issues, and diminished participation in the late 1700s and early 1800s. This led to a series of religious revivals known as the First Great Awakening (1730s–1740s) and the Second Great Awakening (1790s–1840s) to counter the decline in religiosity and inspire renewed interest in Christianity.[368] It has been estimated that before the Second Awakening, only ten percent of Americans were regular churchgoers.[369] These movements were accompanied by advocacy for social reforms, including abolition, temperance, women's rights, and access to education, each of which enjoyed a measure of success. The percentage of Christians among the population increased during this period to around eighty-five to ninety percent, with increases in the numbers of evangelical Protestants, Methodists, Baptists, Mormons, Adventists, and Pentecostals. Legal enforcement of morality also experienced a renaissance, providing context for understanding how the intent of the framers and the original public meaning of the formation documents for the new nation related to legal management of morality.

Study of the melding of English common-law and colonial statutory moral jurisprudence in the eighteenth and nineteenth centuries will provide important insights into America's legal management of indecent exposure and morality more generally. During this period, judges and legislatures refined the definition of the crime and largely took for granted traditional state-interest rationales. They sought greater clarity regarding critical elements of the crime—what was exposed, states of mind of actors and audiences, and place—while employing precedent with a casual confidence, reassured by eminent legal scholars of the time. New terminologies and rhetoric during the nineteenth century further obscured religious aspects of the crime's history—for example, by incorporating enlightenment jargon about natural laws and social contracts and by reference to police power. Management of morality was becoming a political force without attribution. Throughout the nineteenth century, the court's role as *custos morum* was unquestioned.

This chapter reviews and analyzes significant cases and statutes for exemplary fact patterns, juridical theories, and social and political factors forming precedent for modern indecent exposure laws. These nineteenth-century precedents dovetailed with social, scientific, and political trends toward labeling and compartmentalizing sexuality, including the legal and sociological characterizations in America of homosexuality,[370] pornography, and obscenity as species of indecent exposure.

No American common-law cases of indecent exposure were reported before 1800 because the colonies had no indigenous common law addressing the subject. Prosecutions relied instead on English common law and acts of colonial assemblies. Under the guidance of reception statutes directing the adoption of English common law, courts and legislatures focused on accommodating these laws in social and religious norms and structures of the new nation. The result was a fusion of English common law and American colonial ideology. Remnants of colonial statutes have persisted into the present in many state statutes.

The synthesis of English common law and colonial laws and culture, and the process of accommodation whereby these forces were integrated in the development of nineteenth-century common law and fundamental statutory enactments, are discussed in this chapter. Judicial views regarding characteristics of actors, audiences, and places are explored in the context of traditional objectives of prevention of evil example and avoidance of public nuisances. Concern about the publicity element of the crime caused considerable debate. Courts often turned to English common law when interpretating statutes to address these issues. The courts seldom cited colonial laws, so attribution to these sources faded into the background. Nevertheless, the colonial influences in the evolution of relevant statutes and strident rhetoric of judges and justices in some cases are apparent.

The functional role of the common law was growing as notions of the law's religious origins receded into the shadows. Colonial magistrates continued to enforce morality but, by the middle of the eighteenth century, most such enforcement outside of New England had broken down, with prosecutions declining even in the old Puritan colonies. Prosecutions shifted away from distinctly religious offenses (e.g., blasphemy and Sabbath violations), which had long made up the bulk of prosecutions, to sexual offenses such as adultery, fornication, and bastardy.[371] Lawyers were increasingly turning to Enlightenment thinkers such as John Locke rather than the Bible for concepts of right and wrong. Following the break from England, a majority of states enacted provisions in their new constitutions incorporating the common law as the law of the land.

The first reported case of indecent exposure in the 1800s in America examined the publicity requirement of "open gross lewdness and lascivious behavior" in the 1784 Massachusetts statute discussed in the previous chapter. In *Commonwealth v. Catlin* (1804),[372] the defendant was charged with violation of the statute for (1) being in bed with a woman who was not his wife, (2) lewdly and lasciviously putting his arms around her, and (3) performing similar acts on another occasion. Defense argued that only "secret acts" had been proven. A unanimous court construed the word "open" in the statute as modifying both lewdness and lascivious behavior and dismissed the indictment, agreeing that only "secret or private lewdness" had been shown. No precedents or other authority were cited. Only isolated acts were alleged, and the defendant was not charged under the cohabitation provision of the statute.

The Supreme Judicial Court of Massachusetts later examined the cohabitation clause of the statute in *Commonwealth v. Calef* (1813),[373] a prosecution under the clause for a single act of sexual intercourse between unmarried people. The court dismissed the conviction, having determined that by "cohabiting must be understood a dwelling or living together, not a transient and single unlawful interview. The design of this particular provision of the statute was directed at prevention evil and indecent examples, tending to corrupt the public morals." The charge was insufficient in not alleging a course of conduct.

Catlin (1804) and *Calef* (1813) involved consensual sex. *Fowler v. State* (1811).[374] considered the effect of an unwilling audience in another case of arguably private indecent exposure. The court was charged with construing the meaning of "preventing lascivious carriages and practices" in the 1733 Connecticut statute. The defendant in *Fowler* had been convicted for entering the home of Jeremiah Parker at a time when only Parker's unmarried daughter and her twelve-year-old sister were present. After sending the younger girl away, Fowler pursued and repeatedly propositioned the young woman and then unbuttoned his pants and forcibly tried to push her hand into them. She resisted and was saved from further advances by the arrival of her father.

Defense counsel argued that the offense, as stated, was not in the statute. Justice Baldwin disagreed. The offense of lascivious carriages and practices could be committed by "one person only, exhibiting his lascivious carriage, to another unconsenting person, of a different sex." Justice Baldwin's construction was based on the statute's preamble, which expressed the legislature's intent to include and suppress "all those wanton acts, between persons of different sexes, flowing from the exercise of lustful passions, which are grossly indecent and unchaste; and which are not otherwise punished as crimes against chastity and public indecency." There was no mention in the case of prosecution for rape or assault, despite the alleged attempt to force the unwilling victim to engage in sexual activity, perhaps because there was only nominal force and no consummation of the intended effect.

Recall that the court in *Catlin* (1804) considered similar circumstances when only one person was present in addressing a prosecution under the Massachusetts statute that prohibited "open gross lewdness and lascivious behavior." The text of the statute was ambiguous as to whether the adjectives "open" and "gross" were intended to modify both "lewdness" and "lascivious behavior." The court in *Catlin* (1804) did not specify whether the publicity requirement applied only to the lewdness prohibition or whether the presence of more than one person in the audience would make the offense "public." The *Fowler* court construed the prohibition against "lascivious carriages and practices" in the Connecticut statute as covering a single, incipient, immoral sexual act done in a private home. Justice Baldwin admitted that he presumed the actions alleged did not constitute an offense in English common law.

Fowler's (1811) construction of the ancestral Connecticut statute forbidding lascivious carriages as encompassing both public and private immorality contrasted with the opinions in *Calef* (1813) and *Catlin* (1804) interpreting a similar Massachusetts provision as criminalizing only acts destructive of morality in general through prevention of evil example. The Massachusetts court opinions embodied concern for the moral well-being of the populace rather than protection of the public from nuisances or of individuals from unwanted sexual advances. These cases debated early instantiations of what would become modern concepts of protection of privacy in the home as an exception to the prevention-of-evil-example rationale for indecent exposure. As we saw in nineteenth-century English cases and will observe in coincidental American cases, the publicity requirement for indecent exposure was not limited to what are generally considered public places.

Catlin (1804), *Fowler* (1811), and *Calef* (1813) were cases of statutory interpretation involving single acts done in private versus courses of conduct. The first reported nineteenth-century common-law case of *Knowles v. State* (1808).[375] involved a number of critical elements of the crime, including the nature of the act, the state of mind of the audience, and the interplay of these characteristics with the state interest served by the prohibition. In this Connecticut case, the defendant had been charged, under a statute for the suppression of mountebanks,[376] for hanging up a sign on a street corner containing a picture of a "human monster" to be exhibited at a local public house, and thereafter, exhibiting the thing pictured to the public for a fee. On appeal, the court held that the alleged offense was not one within the scope of the statute.

The "monster," a deformed human fetus, was alleged to be highly indecent, terrifying, and annoying; therefore, displaying it publicly was a violation of the statute and action against the peace. Knowles was convicted and fined. The exhibition itself, not the advertisement for it, was the crime. This being so, because the audience exclusively comprised persons who voluntarily, and for a fee, sought to witness the fetus, the theory of the prosecution was limited to prevention of evil example.

In considering whether the conviction could be sustained at common law, which at this time meant the English common law, the court concluded that "[e]very public show and exhibition, which outrages decency, shocks humanity, or is contrary to good morals, is punishable at common law" but that the information on which the prosecution had been based was too vague to support a conviction under this theory. Though only dicta, such statements became archetypes of the American common law of public indecency. Repeatedly during the next hundred years, similar statements justified judicial suppression of immorality. Indecent exposure was not limited to naked bodies. The essence of such crimes was public demonstration of immorality. This basic theme enjoyed unquestioned loyalty by the judiciary until well into the twentieth century, when doubt began to arise as to application of indecent exposure laws to matters other than naked bodies.[377]

As in *Calef* (1813) and *Catlin* (1814), there was no public nuisance because there was a willing audience in private. The governmental interest at stake in *Knowles* (1808) was control of morbid curiosity and suppression of public fascination with this "unnatural" creature. The evil example in this case was not one related to sexual activity, nor was it one that was likely to cause immediate disruption of the social order. If the exhibition posed a threat, it was that permitting such an exhibition would open the door to broader audiences and exhibitions of other deviant activities. It needed to be suppressed because of its potential for piercing the cloak of Christian morality that buoyed convention by restraining curiosity about something outside the norm of pious everyday life. The case presaged the paradox of an eventual exemption for adult entertainment as constitutionally protected speech under the First Amendment.

Circumstances similar to those in *Knowles* (1808) were considered as a matter of common law in the Pennsylvania case of *Commonwealth v. Sharpless* (1815),[378] in which the prevention-of-evil-example rationale was challenged, and the public-place requirement was debated. In *Sharpless*, six men appealed from convictions for having shown, for money in a private house, a painting that depicted a man and woman in an indecent posture "to the manifest corruption and subversion of youth." Appellants argued, alternatively, that the alleged acts constituted no offense at common law, that the indictment was insufficient in failing to charge that the acts were done publicly or to the common nuisance of all citizens, and that the description of the painting was too vague. The prosecution and the defense presented lengthy arguments on relevant English precedents.

Chief Justice Tilighman disposed of the first objection—that the act did not constitute an offense at common law—by citing *Rex v. Curl*

(1727),[379] in which a conviction for the publication of an obscene book had been sustained. Justice Tilighman then confronted the argument that there was no offense because the act had not been done publicly. In his view, the public/private distinction in English common law had emerged as a boundary between the jurisdictions of ecclesiastical and temporal courts. Tilighman reasoned that because there were no ecclesiastical courts in the United States, there was no ground for recognizing the public-private distinction. He was reluctant, however, to abandon the common law, which he felt legally bound to enforce. To escape this dilemma, he looked first to acts of assembly and statutes by which states had filled the ecclesiastical void, but the offense charged had not yet been embodied in a statute in Pennsylvania.

Determined to sustain the conviction, he proceeded by analogy to the key English precedents of *Sedley* (1663), *Curl* (1727), and *Delaval* (1763), which, in his opinion, had established the principle that "an offense may be punishable, if in its nature and by its example, it tends to the corruption of morals; although it be not committed in public." Morals may be corrupted in private places by making indecent materials "public." There was no doubt that Sedley's offense was public. Tilighman reasoned that just as the sale of a book in *Curl* (1727) was sufficient publication, so was the showing of a picture. Even though the book in *Curl* had enjoyed wide distribution, the location of the exhibition was not dispositive. "If the privacy of the room was a protection, all the youth of the city might be corrupted by taking them one by one into a chamber, and there inflaming their passions by the exhibition of lascivious pictures."[380] This implied an answer to the third objection—that no common nuisance had been averred: "It is not an indictment for nuisance, but for an action of evil example, tending to the corruption of youth, and other citizens of the commonwealth, and against the peace, etc."[381]

The liberal definition of publicity in *Sharpless* (1815) was extended, in *Grisham v. State* (1831), beyond purposeful publication of private acts to a willing audience to indirect or presumptive disclosure.[382] The court construed the term "notorious," as used by Blackstone (1765) in commenting on the expression "open and notorious lewdness" to describe the English common law, to mean "done in such a manner, or under such circumstances as necessarily to become public, or generally known in the neighborhood."[383]

Grisham (1831) involved an appeal from a conviction at common law of a man and woman for living together under an invalid oral contract of marriage. No public sexual acts were alleged or proven. The Tennessee

Supreme Court applied English common-law precedent to emerging American common law to establish cohabitation as a crime. It had been exclusively a statutory offense in America until this time. As in *Sharpless* (1815), the reasonableness of having any publicity requirement at all was questioned. The *Grisham* court responded similarly that limited temporal jurisdiction in England over immoral acts was due to contemporaneous jurisdiction of ecclesiastical courts over certain moral crimes, such as adultery. Given that there were no such courts in America, temporal courts' common-law *custos morum* authority should extend to all immoral acts. The court reasoned that immoral acts not cognizable in English temporal courts were "not thereby legalized, or rendered dispunishable, as not being offences."[384] In the absence of ecclesiastical courts, the moral jurisdiction of American temporal courts should not be limited to public acts constituting a nuisance. In other words, the jurisdiction of county courts of pleas and quarter sessions should encompass not only the common law of England but the canon law as well insofar as their jurisdiction was not "repugnant to our [state] constitution and form of government."[385]

Tilighman, in *Sharpless* (1815), had expressly referenced colonial law precedent, noting that authorities in the colonies abrogated English common-law limitations through the promulgation of various acts by legislative assemblies that provided for secular enforcement of religious principles. The court in *Grisham* (1831) recognized that an equally logical approach would be to simply disregard the publicity requirement. The *Sharpless* court, citing *Delaval* (1763), *Sedley* (1663), and *Curl* (1727), concluded that an immoral act is sufficiently "notorious" if done in such a manner or circumstance that it would necessarily become public or generally known in the neighborhood.

Although most early-1800s cases focused on prevention of evil example, there were some notable nuisance prosecutions. As in England and colonial America, public acts of indecent character, being offensive, degrading, and contrary to prevailing religious views, were considered nuisances to modest and moral citizens who might be unwittingly or unwillingly exposed.[386] The earliest reported common-law case in America expressly relying on the nuisance theory was *Nolin v. Mayor of Franklin* (1833).[387] The town of Franklin, Tennessee, had a municipal ordinance assessing a five-dollar penalty for the exhibition of a stud horse in town. In this case, the ordinance was upheld on appeal as a valid regulation of a public nuisance, a crime akin to the showing of a deformed fetus in *Knowles* (1808); but it was a nuisance rather than an evil example because of the exposure to an unwilling audience.

The nature of the audience requirement for a nuisance prosecution was considered in the North Carolina case of *State v. Roper* (1835).[388] Roper had been convicted for exposing his private parts to public view on a highway. The conviction was questioned for failure to allege in the indictment that more than one person had been present. The conviction was affirmed. The court considered it "a clear proposition . . . that whatever openly outrages decency, and is injurious to public morals, is a misdemeanor at common law," quoting *Rex v. Crunden* (1809).[389] As in *Crunden*, nothing more than simple nakedness was alleged, yet Justice Gaston, writing for a unanimous court, termed the exhibition "among the most offensive of those outrages on decency and public morality." Regarding the publicity requirement, the court determined that it was not necessary that the "disgusting exhibition should have actually seen by the public; it is enough that it be probable that it would be publicly seen, thereby endangering a shock to modest feeling, and manifesting a contempt for the laws of decency."[390] *Roper* (1835) was the first appellate court consideration in America of simple public nakedness.

The first statutory prohibition of simple public nakedness was enacted two years later in 1837. An Arkansas statute on obscenity contained a provision that "[e]very person who shall appear in public placed naked, or partly so, with the intent of making a public exhibition of his nakedness, or who shall make an obscene exhibition of his person, shall be deemed guilty of a misdemeanor."[391] Notice that the statute described two distinct offenses, one involving a person making an intentional exhibition of his nakedness in a public place and another involving a person making an obscene exhibition of his person, apparently regardless of place, audience, or intent. Looked at this way, the first clause was essentially a restatement of *Roper* (1835), and the second prohibited "unclean carriages" in the fashion of the 1642 New Haven Colony Act.[392] The broad scope of this law granted a moral jurisdiction coextensive with Old Testament jurisprudence of the early colonial period and greater than the contemporaneous *custos morum* authority of English temporal courts.

An attempt to use the publicity requirement to limit jurisdiction failed in *State v. Cagle* (1841).[393] The defendants were convicted under the common law for "open and notorious lewdness."[394] The indictment alleged that they did "openly and publicly live, dwell, and cohabit" together.[395] The judgment was arrested on the ground that the indictment did not allege sufficient notoriety. The state appealed, and the decision of the circuit court was reversed; "openly and publicly" was deemed a sufficient allegation of notoriety under the rule of *Grisham* (1831).

Britain v. State (1842).[396] was the first reported case in America where female nudity was addressed. In this case, the Tennessee Supreme Court affirmed the conviction of a slave owner for "open and notorious lewdness" for having not kept his female slave properly clothed and her "organs of generation" concealed from public view. She had been seen on several occasions "almost entirely destitute of clothing, with some tattered rags hanging upon her." The issue in the case was not whether the facts as alleged constituted lewdness, but only whether there was sufficient reason to believe that her conduct was not voluntary but rather caused or permitted by the owner so that he could be held responsible for her nakedness.

The legal condemnation of simple public nakedness evidenced by *Roper* (1835), *Britain* (1842), and the Arkansas statute (1837) gained ground in 1842 with the passage of an Act by the New Hampshire legislature ordering that "[n]o person shall within the view of any dwelling house or of any public road, street, or wharf, in the daytime, bathe or swim without necessity, or expose his person indecently in dressing or undressing for the purpose of swimming or bathing, or otherwise, without necessity.".[397]

This law captured the spirit of the English case *Rex v. Crunden* (1803). It even gave an answer, in the necessity defense, to the objection of defense counsel in that case that a conviction would take from the poor all opportunity to bathe in rivers and the sea. The statute demanded discretion: it suggested bathing and swimming at night or in secluded areas. It was an eminently civilized and reasonable rule if one assumes that public exposure of a naked body should properly be suppressed. This statute, though, was one of a panoply of New Hampshire laws regulating morality. Adultery, fornication, incest, blasphemy, swearing, and open, gross lewdness or lascivious behavior laws remained in effect. The bathing rule ensured jurisdiction over public nakedness done so innocently as to arguably avoid prosecution under the traditional rubrics. It was an early instantiation of narrowly tailored, time, place, and manner restrictions that government may be allowed to impose on otherwise protected speech.[398]

William Russell published his *A Treatise on Crimes and Misdemeanors*.[399] in 1845. Russell cited *Sedley's Case* (1663) for the proposition that it was an established principle that "whatever openly outrages decency, and is injurious to public morals, is a misdemeanor at common law.".[400]

Later in his treatise, he rephrased the crime as "[i]n general all open lewdness grossly scandalous is punishable by indictment at common law. . . ."[401] Authorities he cited for the definition included *Hawkins' Pleas of the Crown, Burn's Justice* (on lewdness), *Blackstone's Commentaries*, and the cases of *Rex v. Crunden* (1809) (nude bathing), *Sedley's Case* (1663) (appearing naked on a pub balcony), and *Harring v. Walrond*[402] (displaying a deformed fetus for money).

In 1846, the Michigan legislature amended its statutory prohibition against lewd and lascivious behavior by adding a clause providing that no one "shall designedly make any open and indecent exposure of his or her person, or the person of another." Iowa (1851) and Wisconsin (1858) followed suit. Texas (1856) and Louisiana (1875) forbade such exposures as part of obscenity statutes outlawing publication or printing of any "indecent or obscene print, picture, or written composition, manifestly designed to corrupt the morals of youth." The latter part of these statutes outlawing the showing of the person of another appears to have been a codification of *Sharpless*, the 1815 Pennsylvania case discussed earlier that involved prosecution for showing a painting that depicted a man and woman in an indecent posture.

The Vermont Supreme Court, in *State v. Millard* (1846), considered an indictment for "open and gross lewdness and lascivious behavior" involving facts similar to those in *Fowler* (1811).[403] The defendant was convicted for having gone to the house of a married woman, Polly Parker, when she was alone with her infant. He pursued her in and out of the house, urging her to have intercourse with him, and repeatedly exposed himself. On appeal, defense counsel argued that the purpose of the statute was to safeguard public morals, not prevent private nuisance, and that the statute codified the common law (of England), wherein there was no offense of this sort. The state's attorney argued that "whenever there is an indecent exposure to one, or more, without a manifest intention of prudent concealment, in other words, when such exposure is voluntary, it should be deemed open and gross."

The court agreed with the prosecutor and leveled the following broadside at immoral conduct:

> No particular definition is given, by the statute, of what constitutes [open and gross lewdness and lascivious behavior]. The indelicacy of the subject forbids it . . . . The common sense of the community, as well as the sense of decency, propriety, and morality which most people entertain, is sufficient to apply the statute to each case and point out what particular conduct is rendered criminal by it.

> That the conduct of the respondent . . . was lewd and lascivious is beyond question. A public exposure of himself to, a female, in the manner this respondent did, with a view to excite unchaste feelings and passions in her and to induce her to yield to his wishes, is lewd, is gross lewdness, calculated to outrage the feelings of the person . . ., and to show, that all sense of decency, chastity, or propriety of conduct was wanting in him, and that he was a proper subject for jurisprudence.[404]

"Open" under the statute was interpreted to mean "undisguised, not concealed, and opposite to private, concealed, and unseen." The crime did not depend on the place of exhibition, the number of persons who viewed the exposure, or the audience's reaction. The actor's intent was key. The indictment in *Millard* did not allege a nuisance. The defendant was charged with an intent "to excite . . . lewd and unchaste desires and inclinations" tending to the corruption of the manners and morals of the audience. The publicity requirement could be met by a showing of intent to "publicize" the act to this unwilling audience of one.

Miller v. People (1849) also considered the publicity requirement, this time where no lewd intent was proven.[405] Convictions of a pair of elderly bachelors for indecent exposure were reversed. The prosecution had been instigated by an elderly and unfriendly female neighbor, one Mrs. Deere. The gentlemen had appeared naked or partly clad in their own backyard early one morning, unaware that Mrs. Deere was peering over a five-foot fence that surrounded the yard. In ordering a new trial at which the jury would decide whether the behavior of these old gentlemen was an "intentional, wanton, and indecent exposure . . . in such a manner, as to offend against public decency," the court concluded that the exposure had not been shown to be indecent and that there was insufficient evidence that exposure of these "inoffensive laboring men, of fair moral character" was the result of impure motives. Their intent was a necessary element of proof and a question of fact for the jury.

If the exposure were accidental, the purpose of the law to prevent corruption of good morals and manners would not be furthered by punishment. But what of the nuisance rationale? This theory was neither argued before the court nor addressed by it. The court seemed to be influenced by the fact that the complainant had observed the exposure only because she spied on the defendants in their own backyard, which was surrounded by a fence and more than a quarter of a mile from the nearest house, save that of Mrs. Deere. A willing audience and an innocent exposure meant there was no offense.

Suppose Mrs. Deere had accidentally witnessed the exposures of her bachelor neighbors. Such a situation involving innocent actors and an unwilling audience is perhaps the most difficult case a nineteenth-century court might face. A prosecution for nuisance could be justified by the shock and annoyance caused to Mrs. Deere, but one of the fundamental principles of criminal law, mens rea (guilty mind), would be lacking. Discretion whether to prosecute and convict in such a case would traverse two dimensions: the tolerance to be expected of the audience when subjected to such an exhibition and the actors' concern for the well-being of the audience.

Each of these dimensions was assessed according to the circumstances surrounding the exposure. As the court in *Miller* (1849) pointed out, the yard was surrounded by a high fence and was distant from neighboring houses, save one. The inhabitants could have reasonably concluded that they might appear in a state of undress in that yard without offending others. Had the other houses been closer or the wall shorter, the reasonableness of their behavior would have diminished, so that unintentional exposure might have been considered evidence of reckless or callous disregard for others' feelings. To be fair, this obligation might be balanced by a requirement that the audience come upon such a display by accident. As later cases would hold, there might not be an offense where the audience could have averted their glance.

These hypothetical parameters of the interaction describe the rules of decency in nineteenth-century moral jurisprudence. Exposure of the naked body was confined to certain designated private places. If the audience deliberately or recklessly pried into the containment, they generally could not complain. They also could be found guilty of an invasion of privacy, such as in the case of a Peeping Tom.

What if Mrs. Deere had voluntarily witnessed the exposure and the old bachelors had intentionally exhibited their private parts for her amusement? Under the rules established in earlier nineteenth-century cases—*Knowles* (1808), *Sharpless* (1815), and *Bixby* (1875)—both Mrs. Deere and her neighbors could be prosecuted to suppress their evil example. In *Knowles* and *Bixby*, the criminality of the person causing the exhibition was the central concern, while in *Sharpless*, the audience that had solicited an indecent exhibition was punished.

The culpability of the audience is not solely dependent on its willingness to view the indecent exposure. Exceptions would be appropriate, for instance, for those who ferret out evil examples or administer medical diagnosis and treatment. Audiences should be punished only when they seek out an indecent exhibition for pleasure or curiosity, not when the purpose is to condemn it. Courtship of husband and wife should be outside the scope. The same might not be true for consensual courtship of persons not married to one another.

Miller (1849) was remanded for retrial on the issue of the actors' intent because if the gentlemen had intentionally exposed their private parts to Mrs. Deere, then they ought to be punished.[406] Presumably, although the Miller court addressed this point only indirectly, if the defendants had exposed themselves recklessly, they likewise ought to be punished or at least reprimanded and made to promise to be more careful.

The *Miller* (1849) requirement of specific intent formed a basis for appeal in the Massachusetts case of *Commonwealth v. Haynes* (1854). Haynes was charged with having appeared naked in a public building at Sherbourne within the sight and view of several persons.[407] He objected to the charge on the grounds that it contained no allegation of intent or common nuisance, and it was altogether vague and uncertain. His objections were overruled.

Sufficient intent had been alleged in the *Hayes* indictment with the words "devising and intending" and "unlawfully, scandalously and wantonly." The vagueness and uncertainty objections were overruled by reference to traditional practice and the authority of Chitty's[408] and Archbold's[409] suggested forms. As for vagueness, the prosecution in *Miller* (1849) had used allegations that were in every respect identical to those made in the present case. Haynes's appeal on this point appears to have been ill-advised. If Haynes had been convicted at trial rather than entering a plea and had objected that the alleged intent had not been shown, he would have properly invoked the authority of *Miller* (1849). Nevertheless, Haynes's exposure was alleged to have occurred in a public building within the sight and view of several persons, allowing for an inference of the requisite intent or at least recklessness worthy of legal condemnation.

These legal challenges to the publicity requirement refined its contours. Its continuing role as a critical element of the crime was demonstrated in the Tennessee case of *State v. Moore* (1851).[410] There, Justice Totten dismissed an indictment for cohabitation, adultery, and fornication that failed to allege notoriety. He distinguished *Cagle* (1841)[411] on the basis that notoriety had been alleged therein but ignored the broad language of *Grisham* (1831) in responding to a prevention-of-evil-example argument by the Attorney General that adulterous cohabitation is a "direct attack upon the marriage institution" whose results are "most injurious" to society. With few exceptions, the public/private distinction withstood efforts at transcendence. Rather than fail altogether, the concept was stretched to its logical limits.

The courts in *Sharpless* (1815) and *Grisham* (1831) properly pointed out that the absence of ecclesiastical jurisdiction in America left a void in enforcement of morals that they could fill. Reception statutes requiring fidelity to English common law and a natural limitation of state interest to prevention of evil example impeded expansion of common-law doctrine. Statutes largely respected the boundary in their definition of crimes. It remains a bedrock principle of legal management of morals in modern times.

By mid-century, the common law of public indecency had been extended by analogy to include obscene words used in public in the Tennessee case of *Bell v. State* (1851).[412] The court justified the extension by citing *Grisham* (1831)[413] and, once again, as in *Grisham* (1831), the *Rex v. Crunden* (1809) footnote that "it appears to be an established principle, that whatever openly outrages decency, and is injurious to public morals, is a misdemeanor." Rather than adopt the *Grisham* (1831) dictum that the American courts are not limited to the temporal jurisdiction of English courts, Justice McKinney asked this rhetorical question:

> [A]re the outrageously vulgar and obscene words found in this record, if uttered in the ear of the public, less likely to shock anyone's sense of decency, and to corrupt the morals of society—not to speak of their inevitable tendency to provoke violence and bloodshed, than other offenses traditionally cognizable at common law?[414]

The court did not cite *Sharpless* (1815), but one year after *Bell* (1851), a Pennsylvania court reached the same conclusion based on that earlier case.[415] In 1857, the Missouri Supreme Court reached the same result.[416] Such cases inspired the development of "hate speech" doctrine in First Amendment challenges a hundred years later.[417] Indecent words ultimately found protection in the First Amendment.

Francis Wharton summarized the state of public indecency law in 1855 in his *Treatise on the Criminal Law of the United States*[418] as follows:

> Intentional or negligent indecent exposure of the person to public view is a nuisance at common law.
>
> Mere exposure of the naked person down to the waist is not enough;

> the private parts must be exposed; or at least as much as is usually hidden, and the exposure of which tends to scandalize, or to excite lascivious desires.
>
> The exposure is in a public place, where it can be seen by persons having the opportunity of access to such a place.
>
> It might not be necessary to aver that the exposure was "in the sight of divers persons."
>
> Places found to qualify in cases included public buildings, a highway, a urinal in a marketplace, a public foot path, the inside of a bus, a beach, a rooftop; and in a room or a booth where people paid for admission.
>
> Intent may be a material ingredient and may be inferred from recklessness.
>
> Exposure to one person only is not indecent exposure, although it may be assault.
>
> An indecent exhibition is an offense against decency under common law. When done in public in a way that can be viewed by bystanders, passersby, or neighbors, then it is a nuisance.

In Wharton's view, the crime had become personal, foreshadowing the general structure of modern indecent exposure statutes, with a focus on the intent of the actor and the audience. The list did not include indecent exposure of subject matter other than naked bodies, such as deformed fetuses or stud horses, nor did it address the notion of deriving "publicity" from intent in otherwise private places or expressly address topless women. His summary focused on nuisance theory, even though many case-law precedents had wrestled with the implications of prevention of evil example. This may have been prescient, as a sign of abatement of the omnibus moral jurisdiction of American courts to prevent evil example appeared soon thereafter in *McJunkins v. State* (1858).[419]

The Supreme Court of Indiana considered an appeal from convictions of six persons for "singing indecent and vulgar songs and using vulgar and indecent language" in the presence and hearing of a man and his family.

The record did not show any arraignment or plea. The court sustained an objection based on this omission and then went on to consider an alleged error by the lower court in overruling a motion in arrest of judgment. Several reasons were urged; the first was that the information did not charge a public offense. The defendants had been charged with the statutory offense of "notorious lewdness, or other public indecency."

The court considered several definitions of indecency in general and legal dictionaries and concluded that

> the term public indecency has no fixed legal meaning—is vague and indefinite and cannot itself imply a definite offense. And that the Courts, by a kind of judicial legislation, in England and the United States, usually limited operation of the term to public displays of a naked person [citing Sedley's Case (1663)], obscene books [citing Curl (1727)],or the exhibition of a monster [citing Knowles (1808)]—acts which had a direct bearing on public morals, and affect the body of society.[420]

This was the first time a court in England or America expressed doubt about the definition of "public indecency," foreshadowing an agonizing decades-long struggle to define obscenity in the twentieth century. The court was concerned that a statute "prescribing so severe a penalty as the deprivation of liberty by imprisonment, ought to be clearly worded, so as to leave no doubt or ambiguity about its meaning."[421] The expression of community standards through the judgment of the jury would not cure the defect. If the legislature intended to punish vulgar, obscene language, "a very few words could have made that intention manifest." This aspect of the opinion presaged elaboration and specification of elements of the offense that characterized later statutes and case law.

When describing the common law of public indecency, the *Mc-Junkins* (1858) court ignored a contrary line of recent cases—*Bell* (1851), *Barker* (1852), and *Appling* (1857)—and explicitly rejected the community standard for curing vague statutes espoused in *State v. Millard* (1846). By requiring specification of the prohibited acts, this decision represented a dramatic first step toward narrowing the reach of the criminal law over moral matters and the *custos morum* authority of the courts.

One year later, the Arkansas Supreme Court similarly scrutinized the applicable statute in ruling against a motion to quash by a woman charged with indecent exposure for appearing in public partly clad. In *State v. Hazle* (1859),[422] the court turned to a dictionary to define "obscene," a word whose meaning had never been questioned in the dozens of cases in which it had appeared.

In *State v. Hansen* (1859),[423] a Texas court similarly sustained an exception to a conviction under the statute for an obscene publication, ruling that "the composition, or print, should have been set out, or such description given of it, as that the court could judge of its character, in reference to the alleged indecency and obscenity." Without this, the defendant would not be expected to be able to prepare an adequate defense.

These holdings contradicted the opinion of Chief Justice Tilghman in *Sharpless* (1815) justifying withholding details to order to preserve the chastity of court records and trust in the judgment of the jury. The real basis for the requirement in *Hansen* (1859) may have been mistrust of the jury, because setting out the composition or print in the record or carefully describing it would contribute little to the ability of the accused to identify which of the class of offenses included in the statute he was charged with; simply naming the object forming the basis of the indictment would have been sufficient.

This mid-century onslaught of criticism for vagueness continued when the Indiana Supreme Court declared the term "public indecency" void of legal meaning in the 1861 case of *Jennings v. State*.[424] The defendant appealed from a conviction for public indecency. Indiana had no common law of crimes; all offenses were described by statute. An earlier case had held "common nuisance" too vague to constitute an offense. The court determined that the expression "public indecency" was no more descriptive than "common nuisance." It noted that there was no statutory definition of the term and no enumeration of the constituent elements or acts. "Without a definition of the offense, the acts which constitute it must vary with the different phases of society; depending on the fastidious, refined, or primitive views of the community in which they happen to occur." The trial court's decision was reversed, and the case was remanded for further proceedings.

In 1856, the Texas legislature enacted a concise and conservative characterization of the current state of the law of obscenity, declaring it to be an offense "[i]f any person shall make, publish or print, any indecent and obscene print, picture or written composition, manifestly designed to corrupt the morals of youth, or shall designedly make any obscene and indecent exhibition of his own or the person of another, in public. . . ."[425] The clause relating to obscene prints, pictures, and writings appears to have been adapted from the form of indictments used in prosecutions of that sort in English common law. The second clause is from an 1851 Iowa

Code definition of "lewdness."[426] The statute was narrow in that it required criminal intent and did not outlaw public indecent words.

Ohio enacted a similarly narrow statute in 1862 that provided for a fine and incarceration for

> any person, of the age of fourteen years and upward, [who] shall willfully make any indecent exposure of his or her person in any street, lane, alley, or other place, in any city, town, village, or country, or shall utter, speak or use any obscene or lascivious language or words in the presence or hearing of any female . . . .[427]

The age limitation and designation of a female audience in the obscene language provision had little influence on the development of laws in other jurisdictions. The latter specification bears a resemblance to the English Vagrancy Act of 1822 provision repealed in 1824, and the enumeration of places in the first clause likewise mirrors that provision.[428] There is no documentary evidence to support an inference from general textual similarity.

In 1864, renowned law reformer David Dudley Field proposed a code provision on indecency and obscenity[429] that eschewed American colonial and common law and was, instead, a distillation of four English cases: *Watson* (1847) (exposure to one person not sufficient),[430] *Webb* (1848) (reaffirmed *Watson* holding),[431] *Orchard* (1848) (urinal in open market not a "public place"),[432] and *Holmes* (1853) (defining "public place").[433] Field's proposal provided for punishment of "[e]very person who, willfully and lewdly . . . exposes his person, or the private parts thereof, in any public place, or in any place where there are present other persons to be offended or annoyed thereby."[434] The provision was not included in "crimes against religion and conscience."[435] Rather, it was characterized as a crime "against the person and public decency and good morals." Other crimes in that title included rape, abandonment and neglect of children, abortion and concealing death of an infant, child stealing; bigamy, incest, and crimes against nature; violating sepulture and the remains of the dead; obscene exhibitions, books and prints; disorderly houses; lotteries; gaming; and pawnbrokers. This category of offenses encompassed regulation of sexuality, broadly speaking, along with other activities that would undermine good moral order.

Field made no reference to statutory development in America from biblical roots, nor did he recognize the ecclesiastical roots of English common-law precedent. His code proposal divorced the jurisprudence of bodily morality from its religious foundations. Nuisance theory and prevention of evil example had been the dominant themes of American jurisprudence until then. Field focused lawmakers on preservation of the morals and manners of the people without explaining how such morals and manners were established or how state interests were served. Field's proposal was immediately enacted in Oregon[436] but never enacted into law in New York, where it was first proposed. It was the model for legislation in most states west of the Mississippi River, particularly after its adoption in California in 1874.[437]

The statute's application was limited by requirements that the exhibition be made willfully and with lewd intent in a public place or other place in which there was an audience who would be offended or annoyed thereby. The annoyance or offense of the audience was not sufficient to sustain a conviction if the perpetrator lacked lewd intent.[438] Private exhibitions like those in *Knowles* (1808) and *Sharpless* (1815) would have fallen outside the ambit of this prohibition. The Field Code proposal contained a separate and specific provision forbidding "model artist exhibitions" and obscene publications.

By 1866 the Massachusetts Supreme Court had come round to the view that lewdness included "illicit sexual intercourse, and the irregular indulgence of lust, whether public or private."[439] This expansive view was justified by reference to *Fowler* (1811) and *Millard* (1846). The statute broadened the common-law meaning of "lewdness." "Open" could be inferred from intent. It need not be a public place. The number of persons present was not dispositive. "Open" was used as opposed to "secret." Thus, the conviction of a man for exposure of his genitals to an unwilling eleven-year-old girl was sustained in *Commonwealth v. Wardell* (1880)[440] even though no one else was present. The Wisconsin Supreme Court in *State v. Juneau* (1894),[441] likewise, condemned an indecent exposure by a man before a five-year-old girl. The court explained that

> "open" has no reference to place at all, nor to number of people. It was used simply to define a quality of the act of lewdness. . . . It is "open lewdness" as opposed to "secret" lewdness. The offense could be committed by the intentional act of exposing one's person indecently in the presence of one person, to whom it is offensive, as well as, in the presence of many persons.

Open, then, became a quality of the audience reaction, being considered indecent; that is, unconventional or unwanted. The generality of the offense described by the statute was such that at least one court held it was insufficient to charge in the words of the statute. To adequately apprise the accused of the specific charge that he would defend against, it was necessary to describe the lewdness or lasciviousness with a greater degree of certainty.[442]

As the New York Supreme Court put it in *People ex rel. Lee v. Bixby* (1875),[443] a similar case in which six prostitutes had exposed themselves to five men in a parlor for money, "any place may be made public by a temporary assemblage." An objection was also made to the vagueness of the indictment. The court concluded that the vagueness was justified by a concern for "the chastity of our records."

Sharpless (1815), *Knowles* (1808), and *Bixby* (1875) all arose in commercial contexts. Entrepreneurs seeking to exploit the public desire for sexual stimulation and forbidden knowledge were confronted by the charge that their ventures would undermine the moral foundation of society if allowed to persist. Voluntariness of the audiences' exposure was no defense. The seeds of disruption spread in secret posed threats worthy of penal condemnation. Rather than disregard the temporal/ecclesiastical division of jurisdiction in the English common law that did not fit within the traditional moral jurisprudence of their jurisdictions, the courts in each of these cases, feeling compelled by reception statutes to take the chaff of English law with the wheat, tugged on the common meaning of "public" to expand the publicity constraint to bring these limited-access exposures within legal control.

New York enacted a statute in 1881 that retained the Field Code proposal's requirement that the act be done willfully and with lewd intent but did not require that the persons present be offended or annoyed by it. The 1881 law was so broad that if literally construed, it would have authorized conviction of a husband for making romantic overtures toward his wife in the privacy of their bedroom. Despite this overbroad literal inclusiveness, analogous statutes were adopted in Minnesota and Mississippi.[444]

That recklessness could constitute sufficient culpability to justify punishment was confirmed in *Van Houten v. State* (1884).[445] Van Houton admitted urinating in a yard overlooked by residences of three families. The trial court had instructed the jury under both the nuisance and evil-example theories by instructing that the

> law defines [indecent exposure] to be any such intentional exhibition in a public place of the named human body, or the exposure of the private member, as is calculated to shock the feelings of chastity in those who witness it, or to corrupt their morals; . . . [and] [i]ntent may be inferred from recklessness.

State v. Walter (1895).[446] was instructive on the interplay of the actor's intent and publicity. A boy met a woman on a public highway and started toward her with his "member exposed." She screamed and ran away. He did not follow. At the boy's trial, the judge instructed the jury that if one person saw the exposure and others could have seen it, there was sufficient publicity. It was not alone sufficient that he intentionally made an exhibition to the unwilling woman. There must have been at least an opportunity for others to have seen the exposure.

Virtually all offended parties in cases throughout history after *Sedley's Case* (1663) were women. Special statutory dispositions toward protection of women in the language of statutes were rare. The courts also tended to refrain from characterizing public indecency laws only as a means of protecting women. Both traditional rationales for the laws would be served by a broader definition of audiences.

Nineteenth-century American courts wrestled with the proper disposition of cases in which a man or boy exposed himself to a lone woman or girl. The conceptual difficulty with such situations is their similarity to courtship rituals, which distinguishes such situations from cases like *Sharpless* (1815) where the intentional exhibition was made purely for pecuniary gain. Recall that in *Sharpless*, the intentional exhibition of an indecent painting in a private room to a willing audience was held to constitute public indecency. To foreclose an obvious circumvention of the law's purpose to prevent evil example, the intent of the actor to make the painting known to the public was held to satisfy the requirement of publicity.

As we have seen, it is also often difficult to draw a meaningful distinction between public and private. Simply counting the number of persons in the audience would leave outside the reach of the law annoying and alarming "private nuisances" like the exposure in *Walter* (1895). Two solutions evolved. One was to create fictitious others—those who "could have seen" the exhibition. The other was to consider exposure to an unwilling audience to be an attempt to publicize. The first theory was limited by physical location and was tied into the public-nuisance theory. The latter approach was broad enough to encompass all nonconsensual exposures. The theoretical basis was prevention of the evil example of overzealous courtship. As a practical matter, the latter theory would keep the pants on men in the presence of women unless and until the women give permission for them to be removed. This provided a legal means to deter conduct short of rape and attempted rape that might provoke fear of the more serious intrusions in the woman and desire to engage in them in the man.[447]

McJunkins (1858), *Hazle* (1859), *Hansen* (1859), *Jennings* (1861), and the Field Code (1864).[448]—all dissents from the traditional view of public indecency—followed closely upon one another after two hundred years of legal hegemony over moral affairs. Compare the opinion expressed in *Jennings* (1861) with the preamble to the 1733 Connecticut Act for the prevention of lascivious carriages, which based its comprehensive reach on the "variety of the circumstances for which particular and express laws cannot be easily suited and made."

The social and political contexts of the evolution of indecent exposure laws during the nineteenth century warrant further scholarly attention. At an elevated level, a survey of studies of the period show that it was characterized by political movements to transform sexual morality. There were reform movements and campaigns against prostitution and pornography. Abolitionists exposed the sexual exploitation of enslaved women. Feminists challenged the legal and social subordination of women. Free lovers advocated voluntary unions based on love and equality. Spiritualists explored alternative forms of sexuality and gender. Utopians experimented with communal living and sexual arrangements. Birth control advocates disseminated information and devices to limit reproduction. Doctors asserted their authority over sexual matters.[449] The atmosphere was similar to that of the sexual revolution of the 1960s and 1970s inspired by introduction of "the pill." Judicial opinions regarding indecent exposure in both eras appear to have been influenced by cultural change.

Nineteenth-century courts tended to liberally construe the definition of publicity without wholly abandoning it. Some of them refused to abandon the requirement despite explicit recognition that the sole articulated rationale for the public/private distinction was inapplicable to the United States. Rather than abandon the requirement, they broadened the concept of "public" to encompass arguably private acts that communicated the message of a sexually deviant experience to an unwilling audience of one or more people. The thin rationale for the extension into arguably private experiences was that the exposures tended to corrupt the audience by evil example. In a sense, then, there was a convergence of the two principal rationales of moral jurisprudence: public nuisance softened, and prevention of evil example was extended and strengthened to cover what in other contexts would be considered private acts. In the twentieth century, the polarity reversed under the weight of constitutional claims based on the Bill of Rights.

Whether a particular jurisdiction followed the evil-example theory or nuisance theory was significant. Most obviously important was the relevance of intent as an element of the offense. No showing of bad intent by the actor was necessary to prove and suppress a nuisance. On the other hand, prevention of evil example focused on wanton and willful flouting of societal standards. No evidence of annoying or alarming an unwilling audience was required to prevent an evil example.

The themes of nature of the act, intent of actor and audience, and place where the acts occurred dominated development of the law. They swirled around a theme of maintenance of Christian morals and concomitant concepts of civil order. Throughout the first two centuries after *Sedley's Case* (1663), the greatest concern of the law had been with prevention of evil example and the preservation of morals as a foundation of civil society. The controlling myths of society were a synthesis of religion and civility. Indecent exposure laws protected society against public assaults on the dominant morality and incipient threats from evil examples. Clothing the body, except in well-established courtship rituals and the privacy of the home, was a universal mandate: "Despite historical talk of tolerance, cities of eros, Victorian compromises, or a wholesale paradigm shift from morals to property, the regulation of public morality continued to play an absolutely central role in nineteenth-century American life. Morals police remained one of the matter-of-fact obligations of government in a well-regulated society."[450]

The Fourteenth Amendment was ratified in 1868 as part of efforts to remedy racial discrimination after the Civil War. Over time, the Supreme Court interpreted it as applying portions of the Bill of Rights to state laws. This had little effect on indecent exposure and related crimes until after the end of the nineteenth century. The twentieth century would bring a great deal of complexity to what had been relatively settled law concerning many elements of these crimes and the state interests served. The definition of "lewd and lascivious behavior" was reasonably well understood based on shared conceptions of morality. The justifications for the laws—prevention of evil example and avoidance of public nuisances—were largely unchallenged. Diminishment and fragmentation of the sense of decency in the twentieth century would become evident as legislatures and courts focused on increasing the specificity of elements of the crime and a presumptuousness regarding their justification. Over time, prevention of evil example would fade into desuetude under the weight of cultural change and expansion of concepts of individual liberty in the moral realm. Nuisance theory would follow suit in late-twentieth-century constitutional interpretation by the U.S. Supreme Court. These changes may create pressure for changes in the definition of the crime or, even, its obsolescence.

5. Taboo, Nonexistence, and Silence; the Structure of Modern Laws Forbidding Public Nakedness

At the outset of the twentieth century, significant waves of immigration from Europe and Asia brought millions of new arrivals to the United States. By 1920, immigrants constituted more than ten percent of the population. This influx was religiously diverse, contributing to continuing decline of the hegemony of Christian Protestant morality.[451] The percentage of Christians among the population declined to around seventy-five to eighty percent. The latter half of the twentieth century witnessed a watershed of forces accelerating a weakening of the historical model of moral consensus. Urbanization, industrialization, modernization, globalization, science, technology, war, depression, recession, civil rights, feminism, counterculture, consumerism, media, and entertainment contributed to, or exemplified, an onslaught of challenges to the traditional role and authority of the Christian religion in American society.

Constitutional interpretation changed radically in post-war America. The Warren Court marked a turning point in moral jurisprudence for the U.S. Supreme Court. Earl Warren served as Chief Justice of the Court from 1953 to 1969. He presided over several landmark decisions that expanded the concept of civil rights, including *Brown v. Board of Education* (1954) (overturning the "separate-but-equal" doctrine),[452] *Reynolds v. Sims* (1963) (establishing the principle of "one person, one vote"),[453] *Miranda v. Arizona* (1966)[454] (holding that criminal suspects must be informed of their right to remain silent),[455] and *Loving v. Virginia* (1967) (affirming a right to interracial marriage).[456] The Court's role as champion of civil rights continued in the decades that followed, chipping away steadily at civil authority based on Christian principles, until the *Dobbs* decision in 2022. The question of indecent exposure, *per se*, was not before the Court during this period.

The modern state of the law was thoroughly examined by the California Court of Appeal in 1966 when it considered a claim that a California statute containing traditional language criminalizing "wilfully and wrongfully" committing any act "which openly outrages public decency" was unconstitutionally vague. The court in *In re Davis* (1966) engaged in an extensive review of laws prohibiting public indecency before agreeing with petitioners, noting that it did not have to reach the question of whether display of a woman's breasts in a fashion show constituted protected speech.[457] It lamented:

> 1. Nothing we have said intimates that the Legislature, in a properly drawn statute, cannot prohibit the conduct for which petitioners were convicted; 2. by the same token we have given no consideration whatever to any constitutional problems which would arise if the Legislature did so attempt; and 3. we are not taking judicial notice—as we have been urged to do—nor do we hold, based upon our own experience—as we have also been urged to do—that petitioners' conduct is today's norm and that the decisions of the trial judge and of the judges in the appellate department indicate that they adhered to a standard of conduct or morality which is outmoded.[458]

"Public indecency"? What previously had been well understood and accepted was now a minefield of statutory construction and constitutional ambiguity. The court's research in the *Davis* (1966) case indicated that the traditional principles of indecent exposure were no longer sufficient to provide fair warning of what is prohibited as required by due process.[459]

The ambiguity has worsened. Is immorality still indecent? Many instances of immorality in the colonial period are no longer crimes. For instance, Cotton's code, adopted in New Haven in 1641 and widely distributed, included among capital crimes blasphemy, idolatry, witchcraft, consulting with witches, heresy, false worship, scandalous living (i.e., cohabitation), reviling of religion, perjury, Sabbath-breaking, treason, being an unreverend magistrate, reviling of magistrates, rebellion, being a rebellious child, murder, adultery, incest, sodomy, buggery, polluting a woman known to be in her flowers (i.e., having intercourse during menstruation), whoredom, man-stealing, and false witness. Lesser crimes, deserving corporal punishment or fine, were swearing and cursing, drunkenness, rape of a maiden, fornication, mayhem, theft of a beast, burglary, and slander.[460]

Blasphemy, idolatry, witchcraft, consulting with witches, heresy, false worship, scandalous living, reviling of religion, perjury, Sabbath-breaking, being an unreverend magistrate, reviling of magistrates, rebellion, being a rebellious child, sodomy, buggery, polluting a woman known to be in her flowers, and fornication are no longer crimes. Many of the former crimes are now constitutionally protected rights. Unclean carriages and adultery[461] are the last vestiges of this moral regime.

Like indecent exposure, adultery is a crime rooted in Christian dogma. It has been decriminalized in most states and has largely devolved to a contract dispute, providing grounds for divorce. Indecent exposure laws have persisted—increasingly secularized, without meaningful substantive changes, and with their origins obfuscated through semantics and ignorance or mischaracterization of history. Originally a crime against God and religion, indecent exposure became an unquestioned exercise of police power. Virtually no early twentieth-century cases and statutory amendments questioned the validity of the laws, focusing instead on refinement of parameters of the crime, including specification of body parts, the public/private distinction, and the intent of the actor and audience.

Much has changed in the past sixty years since *Davis*. Statutes continued to evolve based on nuances from case-law and statutory precedent in the nineteenth century discussed previously, as courts and legislatures blended concepts from English common law and colonial statutes into increasingly specific definitions of elements of the crime. Common-law precedent and principles continued to influence drafting and interpreting modern laws.[462]

Indecent exposure is a crime in every state today as a statutory or common-law violation.[463] The most common terms refer to exposure of the genitals and intent to arouse, making the typical target a demonstration of anger, sexual gratification, or a clumsy, annoying courtship effort such as observed by Grant in her investigation.[464] At the time of the *Davis* (1966) case, modern state statutes had largely adopted common-law requirements with few additions and modifications. Most modifications focused on specificity of prohibited acts to provide adequate notice of what constitutes criminal conduct. Some specified body parts. Others referred to private parts, intimate parts, or "the body" or one's "person." Most states now have more than one statute under which prosecution may be brought for exposing genitalia and other private parts in the presence of an unwilling audience that is offended, annoyed, or alarmed by the exposure.

The most common and least interesting offense is the pervert masturbating in the shadows. Simple public nudity is the most difficult to justify. There are many nuances in between. Factors considered in arrest and prosecution generally include what is exposed, how it is exposed, location, distance from victims, gender of the parties, duration of exposure, intent and reaction of the audience, and number of actual, potential, or virtual witnesses. The typical statute outlaws willful exposure of "private parts" in a public place in the presence of an unwilling audience that may be annoyed or alarmed by the exposure. These elements are not independent. In Narvil's 1995 survey of indecent exposure statutes,[465] he noted variations in standards of exposure, intent, and circumstances from state to state, reflecting local cultural norms, societal values, and legal frameworks. The specific prohibited acts, penalties, and definitions varied by state and locality as well. More consistency has developed in the years since then.

Despite widespread agreement on broad principles, courts continue to wrestle with the precision and clarity of statutory language and precedent and with the balance of individual and governmental interests. Specific regulations and penalties for public nakedness vary depending on local laws and cultural norms. Providing adequate warning to potential offenders is the ostensible prime driver for increasing specificity. The growing need for specification also is evidence of the decay of moral consensus. The complexity of these laws and questions about application of precedent tends to intimidate actors around the fringes, broadening the effective reach of moral prohibition. The trend toward greater specificity is understandable but inadequate to accommodate the paradigm shift in governing morals that is underway.

Most indecent exposure violations are misdemeanors, but some states escalate to felonies for repeat offenses. Penalties range from fines to jail time, depending on the state and the number of offenses. Indecent exposure is also a crime on federal lands[466] and in the military.[467]

The text of state indecent exposure laws, classification of offenses, and penalties are available from Findlaw.[468] The most common elements of indecent exposure that must be proven are described below.

Actors: What, Who, and Why?

Actor, audience, exposure, intent, and place form a complicated web of enforcement. Simple public nakedness is a crime in some jurisdictions. Specific prohibited exhibitions include terms like "penis," "pubic hair," "genitals," "perineum," "anus," "buttocks," "breasts," "areola," and "sex organs." Many statutes still refer to "private parts" or "person." In most state statutes, the scope of the crime is limited to sexual misbehaviors in showing these body parts. The most common provision prohibits exposure of the penis with intent to arouse the actor or an unwilling audience.

Gender matters except in cases involving political protests, social nudism, and clothing-optional beaches. Men account for most of the arrests and prosecutions. Cases involving simple public nudity by men are rare. Three well-known instances involved Andrew Martinez, U.C. Berkeley's "naked guy;"[469] Great Britain's Vincent Bethell, founder of Freedom to Be Yourself; and Stephen Gough, the "naked rambler."[470] Naked Guy's lifestyle led Berkeley to adopt an ordinance banning simple public nudity. He was convicted under the ordinance and his life ended in tragedy, as he died in jail. None of these protests ended well.

The situation for women is quite different. Legal management of women's breasts is a cacophony of conflicting images and hypotheses. Cases of indecent exposure by women have generally involved breast-feeding, political protest, adult entertainment, and other forms of entertainment. Cases involving women are more complicated and contentious than those involving men, accounting for most political and constitutional challenges to indecent exposure laws. This has led to exemptions and accommodations. All states now allow discreet breastfeeding. Some jurisdictions allow women to go topless without fear of prosecution. Most of them permit women to get naked in front of mostly male paying customers.

Laws in thirty-four states permit public female toplessness without restrictions.[471] The primary argument for general exemption is that women's breasts are akin to men's breasts and not sufficiently inherently erogenous to justify legal discrimination or support an adequate state interest in their being covered.

Statutes in a dozen states regulate exposure of female breasts and nipples. In states that do not allow female toplessness, courts have generally upheld the prohibitions. For instance, a recent ruling upheld a Maryland city ordinance that prohibited women from going topless on city beaches, finding that "protecting the public sensibilities from the public display of areas of the body traditionally viewed as erogenous zones—including female, but not male, breasts—is an important government objective."[472]

For those jurisdictions that have not embraced a more general toplessness exception for both men and women, the sexual nature of the breast has been the centerpiece of litigation. Topless women in commercial and artistic exhibitions are often exempted from criminal prosecution or subject to time, place, and manner restrictions.

Such exhibitions and political protests have been subject to regulation but also enjoy First Amendment protection that will be explored in the next chapter. An entire industry has been built around the erogenous nature of the breast. The exposures in that industry are considered constitutionally protected "speech." The core commercial messaging is erotic. Breast-feeding is an exception in all states[473] as a convenience with presumptively minimal "lewdness or lasciviousness."

Intent is not always required and may be an excuse. Absent a rare confession, the presence and nature of the intent may be inferred from the circumstances.[474] Six states disregard evidence of intent, banning public nudity absent attenuating circumstances. The remaining state statutes require that the exposure be willful and intentional.[475] Intent to arouse the actor or audience, known historically as lasciviousness, is the most common measure of intent. Many states still use the expressions "lewd" and "lascivious" to characterize this intent. In states where lewd and lascivious behavior or intent to arouse is required, there may be local ordinances that extend the scope of the prohibition. For instance, California requires a showing of intent but expressly recognizes that local authorities may ban public nudity where there is no such intent without running afoul of principles of preemption.

When a showing of intent is required, context often determines whether a particular act constitutes a crime. Simple nude images, which would otherwise be legally shown, can be transformed into crime by evidence of lewd intent, as shown in *State v. Watts* (2021),[476] a Supreme Court of Utah case concerning a sting operation where the defendant sent nude images to someone he thought was a thirteen-year-old girl. The court held that the Utah obscenity code's requirement of prurient interest[477] was satisfied by defendant's coincident sexually explicit message and that such a requirement did not violate the First Amendment. The defendant argued that the images were protected speech because they showed only nude women's breasts and did not depict sexual activity. The court affirmed his conviction, finding that nudity without sexual depiction may be obscene under such circumstances and that the First Amendment does not prohibit laws abridging obscene speech.

Audience

Audience is intertwined with actor in definition of the crime. There is no requirement that the audience actually see the actor's private parts, nor is actual display of private body parts always necessary where the requisite intent is found. No particular negative reaction is required. The audience does not always need to be shocked or offended by the exposure.[478]

Intentional observation outside commercial contexts can lead to prosecution of the audience for voyeurism, depending on the intent of the actor. Age and gender of the actor and audience are important. Prosecutions are rare where the actor and audience are the same gender. Many statutes exempt actors below the age of maturity. Special statutes in most states target indecent exposures to children.[479]

There has been an important shift in state interests since the 1600s as they relate to audience. In the colonial period, public indecency was not limited to naked bodies and sex. Audience presence or reaction really didn't matter. Place was more important. The sensibilities of the audience were subjugated to fidelity to biblical teachings, concern about productivity, and support for legitimate births within the family as a pillar of civil society. In England, *Sedley's Case* (1663) arose out of frustration with a breakdown in moral order after the restoration of Charles II. Sedley's appearance in public naked and his outrageous, profane antics led the prosecution to focus more on prevention of evil example than on any particular concern for the audience that witnessed the escapade. Although *Sedley's Case* was not cited as precedent until long after the end of the reign of Charles II, it rose to prominence in the nineteenth century as a means to address obscene publications and maintain decorum in public places.

Despite the secondary role of the audience in *Sedley's Case* (1663), it became more important during this period. Justification of indecent exposure laws shifted almost entirely to avoiding offending, annoying, or alarming an unwilling audience. This shift was coincident with increasing deference to the extension of the application of the Bill of Rights to state laws, expansion of concepts of individual liberties, constitutional protection of access to media portrayals of nakedness and deviant sex, and a general breakdown of decency and decorum in society. Secularization of the state interest has effectively eliminated the prevention-of-evil-example rationale from legal discourse, leaving the lone justification of preventing annoyance and alarm—or "just because" that is the way it has always been, despite a radical general diminution in the scope of crimes of sexual morality and higher expectations of tolerance of offensive behaviors in public.

Public Place

Definitions of "public place" differ by state but generally include locations open to public view where people are present who may be offended or alarmed. Private premises visible to the public may also qualify. Some states have exceptions for places designated for nudity or "clothing-optional" venues. According to common law, "public place" may be defined circumstantially by characteristics of the act, actor, and audience, not just the physical location. As evidenced in the analysis of nineteenth-century precedents, even a private home can be a public place.[480] It is not necessary to show that more than one person witnessed the exposure if the place is public.[481] There may not need to be any audience at all in these circumstances.[482] Some places are more sensitive than others with regard to the nature, extent, and intent of the exposure—say, a church or commercial flight versus a beach.

The public/private distinction continues to inspire lively debate. Whether the goal is prevention of evil example or public nuisance affects the contours of the publicity element of the crime. Generally, nakedness among consenting adults in private homes, commercial entertainment clubs, and sex-segregated facilities is not criminal. Elsewhere, public nakedness engenders fines, imprisonment, and ostracization. In determining whether a particular place is public within the meaning of a statute or ordinance prohibiting indecency or lewdness in a public place, the courts have examined statutory definitions of the term "public place" and applied judicially created tests and definitions of the term that often focus on reasonable foreseeability and potential witnessing by unwilling members of the public. Courts have stressed that the surrounding facts and circumstances must be considered in each case.

The legislative purpose of the statute is often considered when assessing the public place requirement. Avoidance of public nuisance justifies prohibition of exposures in public places and places where audiences could or would be subjected to unwanted indecent exposures. Some courts have found a relatively narrow legislative purpose, for example, to protect unsuspecting, unwilling, nonconsenting, innocent, surprised, or likely-to-be offended or corrupted types of viewers.

Where broader purposes are posited—for example, that the state has the inherent police power to enact laws to promote the safety, health, morals, and general welfare of society[483]—creation of virtual public places can be justified, as in *Abbott v. State* (1931),[484] in which the court affirmed a conviction for common lewdness when the defendant had bragged about a Christmas gift he gave to an unsuspecting woman containing sexually explicit tree ornaments.[485] The package had been opened privately. His bragging in public was sufficient to support the conviction. The court cited *Grisham* (1831) for the proposition that causing it to be known in the neighborhood was sufficient notoriety.[486]

Case law is mixed on whether exposure in nudist camps that are screened from public view and populated with a consenting audience is criminal.[487] Communities sometimes create special exemptions for festivals and celebrations such as Mardi Gras, the World Naked Bike Ride, and gay pride events. It has been hypothesized that "the licensed and controlled nature of the public nudity that occurs within these events effectively channels, contains and defuses any challenge this could pose to the system of dress regulations, revealing how this permitted transgression ultimately affirms rather than undermines the limits placed on public nudity."[488] Local authorities also sometimes designate special spaces for nudity, typically beach areas.

Defenses

Consent of the audience is generally a valid defense, indicating the diminished role of prevention of evil example as a legitimate state interest. The consent implies the absence of annoyance or alarm that creates a nuisance.

An offense may be avoided if the audience could have averted their gaze. For instance, in the 2023 case of *State v. Thompson*,[489] the Court of Appeals of Washington rejected an appeal alleging vagueness under the Fourteenth Amendment. Thompson had been seen by young girls standing at his sliding glass door near a playground making stroking motions on what appeared to be an erect penis under his clothing. The Washington statute defined indecent exposure as "any open and obscene exposure of his or her person knowing that the conduct is likely to cause reasonable affront or alarm." Thompson argued that the statute requires a showing of actual nudity. The court disagreed, characterizing "obscene exposure" as a legal term of art. *Woodlands Pride*,[490] discussed in the freedom-of-speech analysis in chapter seven, provides a potential counterpoint.[491]

A reasonable expectation of privacy may be a good defense.[492] A reckless exposure may result in prosecution.[493] Accidental or inadvertent exposures are generally not criminal.[494] The availability of any particular defenses depends on the specific facts of the case and the applicable statute or common-law precedent in the jurisdiction. A few defenses are generally recognized, such as consent of the audience; lack of lewd or lascivious intent; no actual exposure; medical care; participating in a play, show, exhibition, or other entertainment; and performing an excretory function.[495] The value of the exposure to the perpetrator is generally not considered relevant. Consideration of the intent of the actor focuses on whether the intent is lewd, lascivious, or intended to create sexual arousal. Many jurisdictions have a minimum age for culpability.

Legitimate State Interests

Indecent exposure laws prohibit offensive public displays of nudity that violate standards of decency, judged by some conception of community norms. The primary goal is to protect unwilling audiences from offense, affront, or alarm. Nuisance and prevention of evil example had been unquestioned tentpoles of maintenance of good moral order in society for centuries. They continue to support prosecutions, albeit with different jargon. State interests are variously described as follows:

- *Prevention of evil example.* The purpose is to maintain established norms and standards of public behavior, including expectations of modesty and clothing in public spaces.
- *Breach of the peace.* Public nudity may cause public disturbances, discomfort, or distractions. For instance, it could lead to accidents or traffic hazards if people become distracted by nudity while driving or walking in public spaces.
- *Protection of audience sensibilities.* The goal is to prevent the intentional exposure of genitals or other intimate body parts in a way that is likely to offend or distress others. Indecent exposure laws aim to protect individuals from unwanted and offensive sexual conduct in public.
- *Preserving public spaces as inclusive and safe environments.* The purpose is to ensure that people of all ages and backgrounds can use and enjoy public spaces without feeling uncomfortable or threatened.
- *Protecting minors.* The interest is in protecting minors from exposure to sexual content, including naked bodies, in public spaces. Children are presumed to not have the emotional or cognitive capacity to understand or consent to such exposure.
- *Hygiene and health concerns.* Public nakedness might contribute to the spread of disease or create unsanitary conditions, although these concerns could be addressed with time, place, and manner restrictions.

All but the last of these justifications focus on audiences.[496] Maintenance of a shared morality as a means of promoting order in civil society has given way to protection of audience sensibilities. Despite the waning of the credibility of prevention of evil example, the harm (annoyance or alarm) caused by nakedness that must be punished is still largely unquestioned despite there being other moral annoyances that are not criminal or that are protected as free speech or privacy (bodily autonomy). The prohibition of public nakedness is an anomaly among expanding constitutional protections of life, liberty, and the pursuit of happiness supported by archaic notions of prevention of evil example and public nuisance, now characterized as protection of sensibilities loosely defined and disputed.

The history of indecent exposure laws illuminated how two basic rationales for suppression of indecent exposure emerged from the fusion of English common law and American colonial statutes focused on the intent and willingness of actors and audiences. These theories would not always command the same result for a given factual pattern. Most state statutes require that the actor be shown to have an "intent to arouse" and/or knowledge that the exposure is likely to annoy or alarm an unwilling audience. The interplay of mental states of actor and audience determines whether a crime has been committed.[497] The actor's intent can be inferred, the audience can be real or hypothetical, and the act must be done in place or manner that is construed as public.[498] The nakedness need not be complete or even necessary. Exposure of the genitals, anus, or women's breasts[499] (the "private parts") usually suffices.

	INTENT/EFFECT		**CRIME**	
	Actor	**Audience**	**Actor**	**Audience**
I	innocent	enjoyment	none[500]	none
II	innocent[501]	annoyance	nuisance	none
III	immoral	enjoyment[502]	evil example	evil example?[503]
IV	immoral	annoyance[504]	nuisance	none[505]

The use of hypothetical community standards is casual and often displaced by intuitive judgments. The reasonableness of the annoyance of an unwilling audience is seldom questioned. The community standards, if considered, flow from the Christian religion as a foundation of civil society and its necessary cohort of government. In modern America, many activities that are not crimes grossly flout community moral standards and offend Christian doctrine. Legitimacy of the distinction of public nakedness in this regard is presumed and unexplained. The historical support for these laws is often presumed, ignored,[506] or mischaracterized.[507]

An important difference from other evil examples and nuisances is the non sequitur that the body has no expression. Even when the crime requires a showing of intent, the positioning or motion of the body is deemed to be the expression. The body is just a tool for effectuating the message. This is odd and anomalous. The selection of specific areas of the body would seem to indicate that those areas have special meaning. Suppose those areas are not used to convey lewd intent? What exactly is it that is an evil example or nuisance that is not an expression in such situations? How can there be a crime where its essence is audience reaction, but no expression has been communicated? What is the audience reacting to that is not communication? The law today has it both ways: it is a crime and there is no expression. This conundrum regarding the body is confounded by something profound that does not need to be, or cannot be, explained. The key here, explored in later chapters, is the nature of the expression. The law deems it unworthy of constitutional protection, although it is often characterized as nonexistent. This is known as a viewpoint restriction, one grounded in Christian theology. In other situations where the actor intends to communicate (lewd or lascivious intent) that the audience perceives as annoying or alarming, communication has occurred, yet again it is deemed unworthy of First Amendment protection.

Naked Bodies and Public Decency

Public indecencies such as blasphemy, mockery, foul language, deformed fetuses, and stud horses are no longer crimes. Prevention of evil example is moribund: plenty of evil examples are readily available on television and the internet and in bars, strip clubs, and adult entertainment stores. That leaves public nuisance to carry the weight of state interest. The definition of the crime has narrowed in most state statutes to acts that are distinctly sexual. This lascivious character distinguishes the crime from other offensive behaviors, for instance, shouting, drunkenness, and threatening suicide. Unlike these noncriminal annoying or alarming acts, the act of indecent exposure itself is often defined by audience attitudes and behavior. Not all indecent exposures involve sexual intent. Arrests and prosecutions where such intent is not involved continue, premised on local regulations where not covered by state statute.

Indecent exposure statutes have generally withstood state and federal constitutional challenges of vagueness and overbreadth.[508] Concern about understanding traditional terms such as "private parts," "lewd and lascivious," and "indecent" may be evidence of the decline in consensus moral truth. The constitutional balancing of interests of the individual (actor) and community has been shifting toward the individual actor and the offense, annoyance, or alarm of the immediate audience, leaving the community as a background check on reasonableness of the actual or presumed reaction of the actual or implied audience. Where there is no audience or an unidentified audience, judges often favor their own assumptions about community sentiment over statistical or panel research.

The U.S. Supreme Court has not expressly considered the constitutionality of indecent exposure laws. Most lower-court challenges to indecent exposure laws have focused on freedom of expression and equal protection for public exposure of women's breasts. Most of these challenges have been unsuccessful.

Judicial decisions should be grounded in analysis of text, history, precedent, and social and political contexts.[509] This study provides a wealth of history behind relevant common law and statutes, delving into details of language, circumstance, and precedent and mapping a thread from the inception of laws prohibiting public nakedness to modern proscriptions. The entanglement of religion is undeniable. The notion of the body not being expressive unless its existence is combined with established means of expression like dance is questionable and subversive. Content and viewpoint restrictions are implicated.

The evolution of moral jurisprudence explored in later chapters raises questions about whether these laws can continue to survive constitutional challenges. Moreover, indecent exposure gave rise to the centuries-old regime of the court as *custos morum*, but careful study of historical and legal precedent indicates a seemingly inexorable weakening of this judicial doctrine. It is important to illuminate this trend and develop a strategy that will support improvements in America's constitutional democracy. The analyses provide important context to inform well-reasoned discussion of policy about effective political and legal approaches to managing bodies for maintenance of civil order.

In the early 1970s, in a moment of luxurious liberality, Chief Justice Burger announced in *Miller v. California* (1973) that the "'sexual revolution' of recent years may have had useful byproducts in striking layers of prudery from a subject long irrationally kept from needed ventilation."[510]

In an earlier case, *Labine v. Vincent* (1971), while dissenting from a majority opinion upholding a state law excluding from intestate succession illegitimate children whose fathers had publicly acknowledged them, Justice Brennan accused the majority of legitimizing an "untenable and discredited prejudice of bygone centuries."[511]

Years before either case, scholar Benjamin Cardozo, in describing the "paradoxes of legal science," remarked that law curiously "accepts as the pattern of its justice the morality of the community whose conduct it assumes to regulate."[512] Legal precedent generally serves as a source of moderation; it is at once master and servant of the people. *Custos morum* in America has not been a voice of moderation, nor has it embraced the morality of America. It has been more a sword than a shield, addressing prejudices and prudery according to philosophies of the Justices. Regardless of your view of wisdom of the changes, this has been moral tyranny by nine Justices who are lawyers, not politicians, sociologists, or philosophers.

When there is consensus or little linear temporal variation in the moral views of the citizens, courts acting as *custos morum* is uncontroversial and insignificant. Problems arise during paradigm shifts in controlling myths of civil society. Christian religion has governed morals in America since its inception. Supreme Court Justices seem a poor choice of high priests of the yet-undefined new source of moral authority for America.

Long ago, the Supreme Court of Virginia reluctantly sustained a demurrer in a case where a slave owner savagely beat his slave and was indicted for a common-law crime against the peace and dignity of the Commonwealth. Noting that the unbridled exercise of *custos morum* authority would "erect a power truly inquisitorial" and that there are times when the danger is greatest, the court wrote:

> It is said to be the boast of the common law, that it continually conforms itself to the ever-changing condition of society. But this conformity keeps on pari passu with those changes. Like them it is slow and imperceptible: so that society may easily conform itself to the law. When great changes take place in the social order, a stronger hand, that of the Legislature, must be applied.[513]

The findings in this study provide fuel for unprecedented constitutional arguments and challenges and for better-informed arguments in more familiar circumstances. The origin of indecent exposure laws is indisputably religious. This provides grounds for a novel challenge under the Establishment Clause of the criminalization of simple public nakedness as indecent exposure. As the body is found to have expression, then

Free Speech is implicated. If there is no harm, then the Fifth and Fourteenth Amendments should provide relief. Differential treatment of commercial nakedness accompanied by lewd intent provides fodder for Equal Protection arguments. Social nudists and libertines suffer from content and viewpoint restrictions.

Indecent exposure is already a hornet's nest of modern constitutional interpretation. It is about to move up a level in intensity and complexity. Why not liberate the body? These are the challenges facing the U.S. Supreme Court in the twilight of its role as *custos morum*. How will it decide? Is legal repression of the body good or bad for the progress of society and the realization of America's constitutional goals? The effect on society of loosening restrictions on public nakedness would shine a light on the significance of its role in the maintenance of civil order. On the other hand, it might let the genie out of the bottle. Questions concerning the effects of indecent exposure laws on society and individuals have not been addressed by scholars and warrant significant research. In the meantime, the historical study of the laws provides insights and suggestions about how this will play out.

The progress of rational philosophies in the twentieth century, driven by broadening appreciation for the scientific method and the advent of digital technologies, is forming a new mythos of morality that is not yet entrenched or even understood. This calls for a new jurisprudential model along the lines discussed later. The right to display one's body in public has been managed since the beginning of time in civil society. Indecent exposure jurisprudence in America is looking less favorably on protection of the majority when there are differences of opinion on moral matters, demonstrating a bias toward individual rights regarding matters of conscience, expression, and lifestyle.

The founders did not understand rights as we do. The Constitution was designed to protect local government from federal interference. Local families, judges, and magistrates were to manage morality and social order. Acting through these institutions protected communities from outsiders, including federal judges. Creation of social policies resided in local legislatures—the voice of the people—managed by periodic voting. The Supreme Court embraced *custos morum* in a model inspired by common-law and colonial jurisprudence to create rights not expressed in the Constitution and to expand the reach of rights set forth in the Bill of Rights. It chose to do this rather than enforce the notion of limited government imposed upon the natural rights of the country's people. What then is the proper role of the courts in management of morality? Numerous constitutional challenges to indecent exposure laws will be examined in depth, including the following:

- Establishment Clause issues relating to the religious origins of indecency laws
- free-exercise claims arising from precedent defining "religion"
- First Amendment issues regarding public nakedness as potential protected speech
- due-process arguments concerning vagueness, overbreadth, and personal liberty
- the balance between government interests in regulating morality and individual rights to free expression and privacy
- equal-protection arguments related to gender, exceptions for adult entertainment, and the treatment of social movements and philosophies with long histories such as nudism and libertinism

6. Secular State or Christian Nation? Legal Enforcement of Christian Moral Principles

1963:

The authority of the state, under the Constitution, to enact 'morals legislation'—laws reflecting some traditional morality having no authentic social purpose to protect other persons or property—has always been assumed; it has deep roots, and it has seemed obvious and beyond question.

Louis Henkin, constitutional scholar.[514]

1964:

Title VII of the Civil Rights Act's national prohibition on discrimination based on "race, color, religion, sex or national origin" defines religion as concerning personal beliefs on the "ultimate ideas" of "life, purpose, and death."

U.S. Congress.[515]

2003:

[T]he fact that the governing majority in a State has traditionally viewed a particular practice as immoral is not a sufficient reason for upholding a law prohibiting the practice; neither history nor tradition could save a law prohibiting miscegenation from Constitutional attack.

U.S. Supreme Court.[516]

2022:

The Constitution does not grant the nine unelected Members of this Court the unilateral authority to rewrite the Constitution to create new rights and liberties based on our own moral or policy views.

U.S. Supreme Court.[517]

The First Amendment commands that "Congress shall make no law respecting an establishment of religion, or prohibiting the free exercise thereof." The history presented in earlier chapters raises important questions regarding the role of religion in the law of indecent exposure. It illustrates that America's "community standards in respect of nakedness in public" that indecent exposure laws protect are Christian moral principles. No meaningful secular justifications have been offered other than to prevent offending, annoying, or alarming unwilling audiences. If there is no secular justification, do the laws force acceptance of Christian beliefs in violation of the Establishment Clause of the Constitution? Does legal enforcement of moral principles regarding these acts, which have no material consequences, imply that America is a de facto Christian nation? Is social nudism a religion?[518] Is the nudist's nakedness a free exercise of that religion?

If the motives for suppression of public nakedness are religious, then does it follow that criminalizing acts of people who do not embrace this conception is prohibiting free exercise of religion, as religion is defined in modern constitutional interpretation? If the rationale is to avoid annoying unwilling audiences on the basis of their religious views, can this survive modern constitutional challenges on establishment, free-exercise, or free-speech grounds? These circumstances ripened through the development of judicial doctrine concerning separation of church and state and protection of individual liberties. This comprehensive history of indecent exposure laws sheds new light on these questions.

During the colonial period in America, virtually everyone was Christian.[519] In the nineteenth century, the notion that the United States was a Christian nation became controversial. A recent Pew Research poll found a resurgence of interest in Christian nationalism, with forty-five percent of Americans in favor, although one-half of those polled said they had never heard of the expression "Christian nation."[520] The poll did not uncover whether this meant that the respondents believe that the country should be guided by Christian values, recognize Christianity as the nation's official religion, or declare the country a Christian nation.

The Christian-nation controversy that was once the subject of lively debate was not resolved but merely submerged in a new rhetoric as it relates to indecent exposure. As the years passed, Christian moral principles regarding public displays of the body continued to be enforced as before, but without reference to God or Christ, despite the introduction and evolution of constitutional guarantees of religious liberty. The history of indecent exposure laws viewed through the lens of modern constitutional doctrine raises serious doubts about the legitimacy of this prohibition and the courts' role as *custos morum*. The next several chapters examine these issues from a variety of perspectives, weaving together the text of statutes; history of statutory prohibitions and common-law cases;

and theories, traditions, and precedents of constitutional analysis. The merits of facial and applied challenges on establishment and free-exercise grounds will be addressed.[521]

The general structure of indecent exposure statutory provisions, the history of statutes and the common law, and the progression of precedents have been presented. Various rationales for state interests supporting indecent exposure laws have been discussed. A connection between prohibition of public nakedness and good order in society is presumed but not supported by empirical evidence. The defense of Christian dogma implicit in the laws is sub-rosa. The consequences of the prohibition[522] for actors and audiences are complex and not well understood. This study has elucidated how Christian moral principles, subsumed under the police power rubric, have assumed the character of secular absolutes in America. This rhetoric obfuscates the true religious character of the relationship between legally enforced moral principles and individual autonomy. The religious foundation of indecent exposure laws has been obscured by blind acceptance of protection of "morals" as if the morals emerged spontaneously from society. The constitutionality of the court as *custos morum* was not seriously questioned until recently.[523]

Judges across the nation are educated to use the same basic interpretive tools. Where statutes or constitutions are involved, the judicial process begins with the text of the document. Given that indecent exposure is most often defined by statute, these principles apply to interpretation of relevant provisions of both the statute and the Constitution. In constitutional analyses, the facts of the case and applicable law generally are assessed against the constitutional clause's history, including evidence of the original intent of framers and ratifiers, original public meaning, relevant legal tradition, precedents, purposes, underlying values, and likely consequences of the decision.[524] Case-law precedent plays an important but not determinative role.

The classic paradigm for deciding whether a particular law is constitutional depends on the specific language of the law as well as the circumstances surrounding its enforcement. Indecent exposure laws are typically justified as a means of protecting public morality and preventing offensive behavior in public spaces. Constitutional challenges have been made for vagueness and overbreadth and for violations of freedom-of-speech and equal-protection rights. The free-speech claims have generally involved adult entertainment and resulted in regulation of the time, place, and manner of the exposures. Vagueness, overbreadth, and equal-protection claims have fostered statutory refinements in elements of the crime and an exception for breastfeeding in public. Before addressing such constitutional arguments in more detail in later chapters, we will explore the implications of enforcing Christian moral principles in the context of modern trends in constitutional interpretation.

The constitutionality of indecent exposure laws has not been challenged on Establishment Clause grounds despite the crime's indisputable foundation in Christian morality. The First Amendment to the Constitution states that "Congress shall make no law respecting an establishment of religion, or prohibiting the free exercise thereof . . . ." These clauses have engendered a great deal of litigation and impassioned debate. Historical evidence will be presented that these provisions originally reflected a compromise intended to minimize social and political conflicts from religious differences in American colonies and to protect local communities from imposition of an overarching religion by the federal government that was being formed.[525]

First Amendment protections did not apply to state laws until years after the Fourteenth Amendment was ratified in 1868 as part of the Reconstruction Amendments following the Civil War. The application of First Amendment judicial doctrine to the states began with *Cantwell v. Connecticut* (1940), in which the U.S. Supreme Court declared that guarantees of First Amendment liberties applied to the states via the Fourteenth Amendment. The Court declared, with respect to the Religion Clauses, that this

> constitutional inhibition of legislation about religion has a dual significance. On the one hand, it forestalls compulsion by law of acceptance of any creed or practice of any form of worship. Freedom of conscience and freedom to adhere to such religious organization or form of worship as the individual may choose cannot be restricted by law. It also safeguards free exercise of one's chosen form of religion. Thus, the Amendment embraces two concepts—freedom to believe and freedom to act. The first is absolute; but, in civil society, the second cannot be. Conduct remains subject to regulation for the protection of society.[526]

Judges and commentators most often have begun their search for the clause's meaning by attempting to discern the intention of the framers. Traditional sources include debates at the First Congress and writings of James Madison and Thomas Jefferson, who were leading influences in formulating the clause. Whereas previous historical inquiries regarding the meaning of the Establishment Clause focused on state aid to education, the analysis of their relationship with indecent exposure laws benefits from reevaluation of these sources to discern the extent to which, if at all, the framers intended to divest government of its power to enforce Christian moral principles.

> The Constitution, as ratified, mentioned religion only once—in the Article VI clause prohibiting religious tests for national office. The delegates to the Philadelphia Convention thought that, since they were creating a government of limited powers, with no authority to act on matters relating to religion, no further protection was necessary.[527]

There were appeals at several ratifying conventions for explicit protection for religious freedom. James Madison reworked various state proposals to suggest the following two amendments:

> The Civil Rights of none shall be abridged on account of religious Belief or worship, nor shall any national religion be established, nor shall the full and equal rights of conscience be in any manner, nor on any pretext infringed.[528]
>
> No state shall violate the equal rights of conscience or the freedom of the press, or the trial by jury in criminal cases.[529]

Madison's proposals would prohibit both state and federal governments from infringing on rights of conscience but would restrain only the federal government from establishing a religion. The proposals were sent to a committee for consideration. The committee version of the Establishment Clause that was submitted for plenary consideration was revised to read:

> No religion shall be established by law, nor shall the equal rights of conscience be infringed.[530]

The word "national" before "religion" had been omitted, thus proposing the extend the establishment prohibition to states.

When debate on the Bill of Rights opened on August 15, Peter Sylvester objected to the broad language of the amendment, which he feared "might be thought to have a tendency to abolish religion altogether."[531] Madison explained that the more limited purpose of the amendment was to quiet the fears of convention delegates in the states that

> the clause of the Constitution, which gave power to Congress to make all the laws necessary and proper to carry into execution the Constitution, and the laws made under it, enabled them to make laws of such a nature as might infringe the rights of conscience, and establish a national religion.[532]

Believing that the "people feared one sect might obtain a pre-eminence, or two combine together, and establish a religion to which they would compel others to conform,"[533] he suggested reinsertion of the word "national" to better indicate the intended purpose of the amendment. Anti-Federalist concern over the symbolic significance of putting the word "national" in a fundamental legal document caused Madison to withdraw the suggestion.[534] The clause proposed by the committee was voted down. A few days later, Fisher Ames of Massachusetts suggested that the language be changed to

> Congress shall make no law establishing religion, or to prevent the free exercise thereof, or to infringe the rights of conscience.[535]

The House accepted Ames's version and sent it to the Senate where debates were held in secret. After considerable debate of unknown content, the Senate sent a modified proposal back to the House:

> Congress shall make no law establishing articles of faith or a mode of worship, or prohibiting the free exercise of religion.[536]

The House rejected it and asked that a conference committee convene.[537] The committee worked out the final version. By choosing the words "an establishment" over "the establishment," the framers seem to have intended to forbid "only those activities that tended to promote the interests of one or another particular sect,"[538] not to deny the government the opportunity to prefer religion over irreligion.[539] This intention was confirmed later in the year when Congress reenacted the Northwest Ordinance of 1787, which set aside federal lands for schools in the territory. The ordinance had a clause that read, "Religion, morality, and knowledge, being necessary to good government and the happiness of mankind, schools, and the means of learning shall be forever encouraged."[540]

According to the general understanding of the framers and ratifiers at the first Congress, the purpose of the First Amendment was not so much to sever the connection between religion and government as it was to prohibit the federal government from interfering with the religious establishments of the states. Federalism, not the politicization of religion, was the dominant concern of the Congress.[541] Few, if any, of the members of the first Congress were likely to have doubted the divine truth of Christianity. Most of them were good Christian men who presumably conceived of the United States as a Christian nation, one nation under God. That the first Congress felt free to promote religion was shown in the Northwest Ordinance of 1787, as noted above. The government's support for Christianity was further evidenced by its efforts to convert American Indians and establish Christianity as their religion well into the nineteenth century.[542]

While this consensus would be likely to lead to encouragement of the Christian religion generally, it would not necessarily imply that the force of law should be brought to bear against those who strayed from its religious truth. The statesmen were all too aware of the consequences of such tyranny. Liberty of conscience was a great virtue to be protected. To restrain the government from using force to spread Christian principles, the First Amendment included, in addition to the Establishment Clause, a clause forbidding Congress from making laws prohibiting the free exercise of religion.

The original meaning of the free-exercise clause is not settled. As with the Establishment Clause, the intention of the framers is a fair starting place. There was little debate about the Free Exercise Clause during the first Congress. It had been suggested by Fisher Ames of Massachusetts on August 20. He proposed this language:

> Congress shall make no law establishing religion, or to prevent the free exercise of thereof, or to infringe the rights of conscience.[543]

Malbin has pointed out that Ames's proposal raises a host of questions: What was the relationship between the "free exercise" and "rights of conscience" clauses? Were they redundant? Was the phrase "free exercise" meant to suggest that something more than rights of conscience or belief ought to be protected? If so, what did the word "exercise" mean? Since Madison used the word "worship" in his first version of the Religion Clauses, did "exercise" refer to the utterance and expression of belief through worship? If so, was the idea of worship understood to be limited to traditional modes of public congregational prayer, or were other forms of expressive activities and/or religiously motivated behaviors to be protected as well?.[544] The absence of meaningful congressional debate on this element of free exercise has led historical analysts to turn to an earlier controversy for clues to the meaning of the clause.

In 1785, the Virginia General Assembly passed "An act for establishing religious freedom," which was written by Thomas Jefferson and sponsored by James Madison.[545] Jefferson's bill was presented in opposition to a "Bill for Establishing Support for Teachers of the Christian Religion" offered by Patrick Henry that would have named Christianity as the official religion of Virginia.[546] The expression "free exercise" first appeared in proposals to the first Congress by the Virginia state convention, so, by implication, the meaning of the expression that can be discerned from debates and writings about the Virginia controversy has been taken to approximate the intent of Ames in proposing the First

Amendment Clause or, at least, the understanding of representatives who assented to it. Malbin wisely suggested that because the Virginia bill was the most liberal law respecting religious tolerance enacted before the first Congress, the meaning of the expression for Ames and the other representatives was not likely to have been more liberal than the meaning attached by the most liberal Virginia reform advocates: James Madison and Thomas Jefferson.

Madison originally suggested a legal right to "free exercise" of religion in a clause on religious liberty for the Virginia constitution in 1776 that provided:

> That religion, or the duty we owe our Creator, and the manner of discharging it, being under the direction of reason and conviction only, not of violence, or compulsion, all men are entitled to the full and free exercise of it according to the dictates of conscience, and therefore that no man or class of men ought on account of religion to be invested with particular emoluments or privileges nor subjected to any penalties or disabilities, unless under color of religion the preservation of equal liberty, and the existence of the State be manifestly endangered.[547]

According to this proposal, religious activity would be protected unless it threatened equal liberty or the very existence of the state; however, it proved to be too radical and was rejected by the delegation.[548] The clause that was adopted read as follows:

> That religion, or the duty we owe to our Creator, and the manner of discharging it, can be directed only by reason and conviction, not by force or violence, and therefore all men are equally entitled to the free exercise of religion, according to the dictates of conscience; and that it is the mutual duty of all to practice Christian forbearance, love, and charity toward each other.[549]

Notice the theories embodied in the clause: true religion results only from reason and conviction, not violence, and forbearance from violence is a Christian duty.

Madison[550] was instrumental nine years later in the controversy between Jefferson and Henry over whether Christianity should be declared the established religion of Virginia. Madison championed Jefferson's cause in his famous Memorial and Remonstrance of July 1785 and his speech against assessments in support of religion made before the Virginia General Assembly. In his notes to that speech, he wrote that "religion is not within the purview of civil authority," that experience shows how religion is corrupted by establishment, and that the civil magistrate is incompetent to judge religious belief.[551] The declarations of his Memorial and Remonstrance elaborated on these points. Madison differentiated between the legitimacy of professing and promoting religion and the coercion of nonbelievers:

> Whilst we assert for ourselves a freedom to embrace, to profess and to observe the Religion which we believe to be of divine origin, we cannot deny an equal freedom to those whose minds have not yielded to the evidence which has convinced us. If this freedom is abused, it is an offence against God, not against man . . . .[552]

To Madison, Henry's suggestion that Christianity be named the official religion of the state implied "either that the Civil Magistrate is a competent Judge of religious truth; or that he may employ Religion as an engine of Civil policy."[553] Both implications were objectionable: "The first is an arrogant pretension falsified by the contradictory opinions of Rules in all ages, and throughout the world: The second, an unhallowed perversion of the means of salvation."[554] History provided ample testimony that the establishment of Christianity inevitably led to "pride and indolence in the Clergy; ignorance and servility in the laity, [and] in both, superstition, bigotry and persecution."[555]

Madison's ideal that true religion was inspired by reason and conviction only and cannot be compelled, that rights of citizens should not be enlarged or diminished based on their religious principles, and that civil magistrates are incompetent judges of religious beliefs can be traced to John Locke's *Letter Concerning Toleration* (1689). Madison's first writing on religious freedom, the proposed clause for the *Virginia Declaration of Rights* in 1776, purported to grant the free exercise of religious belief unless such acts "manifestly endangered" the existence of the state. His *Memorial and Remonstrance* nine years later did not similarly define the limits of free exercise.

Locke's extensive discussion of religious toleration facilitates an understanding of the relationship between Madison's views on free exercise of religion and the state's authority to suppress immorality. Locke supported the notion of *custos morum*. He also believed that the authority of the Civil Magistrate encompassed a right to punish certain immoral acts. In observing with chagrin that the zeal with which unorthodox sects were persecuted did not carry over into the punishment of immorality, Locke disclosed a Christian ascetic justification for the discouragement of immoral acts:

> [A]dultery, fornication, uncleanliness, lasciviousness, idolatry, and such like things, cannot be denied to be the works of the flesh, concerning which the apostle Paul has expressly declared that they who do them shall not inherit the kingdom of God. Gal. v. Whosoever, therefore, is sincerely solicitous about the kingdom of God, and thinks it his duty to endeavor the enlargement of it amongst men, ought to apply himself with no less care and industry to the rooting out of these immoralities than to the extirpation of sects.[556]

Based on the general principles for separation of ecclesiastical and civil affairs that he propounded in *A Letter Concerning Toleration*, one would suppose that, although these acts should be discouraged, he would not sanction suppression by the civil authorities. Foremost among Locke's principles was that the duty of the civil magistrate is to secure the people in their possession of "civil interests." Such interests include "life, liberty, health, and indolency of body, and the possession of outward things, such as money, lands, houses, furniture, and the like."[557] This was to be the whole jurisdiction of the magistrate. It "neither can nor ought in any manner to be extended to the salvation of souls."[558] The magistrate might attempt to persuade wayward souls to walk the path of righteousness with argumentation but never with threats or penalties.[559] The power of the legislature, likewise, should go only to providing for the "security of each man's private possessions, for the peace, riches, and public commodities of the whole people, and, as much possible, for the increase of their inward strength against foreign invasions."[560]

> [P]olitical society is instituted for no other end, but only to secure every man's possession of the things of this life. The care of each man's soul, and of the things of heaven, which neither does belong to the commonwealth nor can be subjected to it, is left entirely to every man's self.[561]
>
> [T]he magistrate cannot take away these worldly things . . . for a cause that has no relation to the end of civil government . . . ."[562]

Despite this elaborate and coherent contention that civil authority should be limited to protection of person and property from injury by others, Locke nonetheless asserted that moral matters were the concern of both church and state—even though he recognized that this conjoint authority led to a "great danger, lest one of these jurisdictions entrench upon one another and discord arise between the keeper of the public peace and the overseers of souls."[563] With regard to this danger, Locke insisted that "all difficulty in this matter" could be removed by considering his general principles concerning separation of ecclesiastical and civil matters set forth above.

Those principles limited civil authority to immorality in commercial dealings and those acts that physically intrude upon an unwilling citizen. However, Locke would not so limit the jurisdiction of civil authority: in anticipation of criticism of his stand that the civil magistrate may not interfere with the rites and ceremonies of any church, Locke wrote:

> You will say, by this rule, if some congregations should have a mind to sacrifice infants, or (as the primitive Christians were falsely accused) lustfully pollute themselves in promiscuous uncleanliness, or practice any other such heinous enormities, is the magistrate obliged to tolerate them because they are committed in a religious assembly? I answer, No.[564]

Certainly, the sacrifice of an infant must not be tolerated. This comports with his general principle regarding the protection of life. But on what basis could society punish "promiscuous uncleanliness"? In saying that such acts need not be tolerated because they are committed in a religious assembly, Locke overlooked the fundamental question: what principle could justify civil authority jurisdiction over such practices? There is nothing in Locke's general principles offered in support unless his inclusion of "indolency of body"[565] among the civil interests was intended to imply that it is the business of the state to encourage study and reflection and that it may do so indirectly by suppressing the competition presented by temptations of the flesh. This view finds support in Locke's statement that a "good life, in which consists not the least part of religion and true piety, concerns also the civil government,"[566] but he contradicts this position repeatedly elsewhere in the essay. For instance, when addressing idolatry, Locke wrote:

> [I]t does not follow that because it is a sin it ought to be punished by the magistrate. For it does not belong unto the magistrate to make use of his sword in punishing everything, indifferently, that he takes to be a sin against God. Covetousness, uncharitableness, idleness, and many other things are sins, by the consent of men, which yet no man ever said were to be punished by the magistrate. The reason is because they are not prejudicial to other men's rights, nor do they break the public peace of society.[567]

The encouragement of study and reflection as a basis for civil authority over licentiousness would seem to be ruled out. In cases in which there is no actual breach of the peace, how would licentiousness prejudice other men's rights? One can see, for instance, how adultery might directly prejudice the property interest of one spouse in the other if one subscribed to this view of marriage. Although Locke twice specifically called for the punishment of adultery, it does not appear that he would limit the punishment of sexual immorality to this class of offense. Locke distrusted atheists because he supposed that promises, covenants, and oaths have no hold upon them.[568] One need not question this assumption because doing so does not solve the puzzle either. Recall that Locke would punish promiscuous uncleanliness even if committed in a religious assembly; therefore, it was not any supposed connection to atheism that convinced Locke of the need to punish immorality. In addition, he advocated civil equality for Jews, Mahometans, and even pagans.[569] One of the traditional purposes of moral jurisprudence—to prevent evil example—does not seem to have been his basis for punishment of immorality either:

> The care . . . of every man's soul belongs unto himself, and is to be left unto himself. But what if he neglect the care of his soul? I answer: What if he neglect the care of his health or of his estate, which things are nearer related to the government of the magistrate than the other? Will the magistrate provide by an express law that such a one shall not become poor or sick? Laws provide, as much as is possible, that the goods and health of subjects be not injured by the fraud and violence of others; they do not guard them from the negligence of ill-husbandry of the possessors themselves. No man can be forced to be rich or healthful. . . .[570]

But he can be forced to be sexually virtuous, chaste, and ashamed of his body? If society cannot be protected from the disturbing, distasteful, and degenerate vice of neglect of one's health and estate, how can civil authority be brought to bear against the pleasures of the flesh? Locke would draw the line against expression of opinions "contrary to human society, or to those moral rules which are necessary to the preservation of civil society."[571] Holding such opinions would be so outrageous, in Locke's opinion, that he was hard-pressed to offer examples. He would punish and suppress expressions of opinion that men are not obliged to keep their promises, that princes may be dethroned by those who differ from them in religion, or that the dominion of all things belongs only to those who hold such opinions.[572] These are matters, once again, of property, person, and politics—all legitimate civil interests according to Locke's general principles. The only way, it seems, to conform his desire to punish sexual immorality to his general principles is to assert that the rules of sexual morality violated by such acts are essential to the presser-vation of society.[573] Although Locke makes this premise nowhere explicit, a brief allusion in the very paragraph wherein he condemned promiscuous uncleanliness performed in religious assemblies may supply the key to understanding what is, from all other perspectives, anomalous. That allusion is to "Gal. v." It refers to chapter five of the Epistle of apostle Paul to the Galatians in the New Testament.

In Galatians, Paul, the fountainhead of Christian ascetic philosophy, crucified the flesh. He admonished the Galatians to "use not liberty for an occasion to the flesh,"[574] nor to "fulfil the lust of the flesh;"[575] but to "walk in the Spirit," for only in this way would they be able to "love they neighbor as thyself." "For the flesh lusteth against the Spirit, and the Spirit against the flesh . . . ."[576] Works of the flesh include adultery, fornication, uncleanness, and lasciviousness, as well as "idolatry, witchcraft, hatred, variance, emulations, wrath, strife, seditions, heresies, envyings, murders, drunkenness, revellings, and such life." "They that do such things shall not inherit the kingdom of God. But the fruit of the Spirit is love, joy, peace, longsuffering, gentleness, goodness, faith, meekness, temperance."[577] For Apostle Paul, flesh was a wellspring of evil. Conveniently, Paul also advocated that every person obey governing authorities.[578]

This may be the source of Locke's theory of the civil punishment of sexual immorality. No other source of inspiration is evident, yet even this approach does not resolve theoretical inconsistencies in Locke's essay. His views appear conflicted and unsettled. Without acknowledging it, Locke would in this instance allow civil authority to enforce a religious truth, an action that he expressly disapproved of because of the fallibility of human judgment in the affairs of religion. Furthermore, in doing so he would violate the principles of "Christian warfare" taught by Jesus, the Prince of Peace, which he cited with approval:

> [It was he] who sent out His soldiers to the subduing of nations, and gathering some of them into His church, not armed with the sword or other instruments of force, but prepared with the Gospel of peace and with the exemplary holiness of their conversation. This was His method. Though infidels were to be converted by force, if those that are blind or obstinate were to be drawn off from their errors by armed soldiers, we know very well that it was much more easy [*sic*] for Him to do it with heavenly legions that for any son of the church, how potent soever, with all his dragoons.[579]

Locke may have eschewed Christ's great lesson under the pretense of public good, perhaps due to doubts about the effectiveness of civil authorities. If the immoralists err, force need not be brought to bear, for, in Locke's own words, "truth certainly would do well enough if she were once left to shift for herself."[580] "[I]f truth makes not her way into the understanding by her own light, she will be but the weaker for any borrowed force violence can add to her."[581] Are we thus left to conclude that by advocating legal suppression of immorality, Locke admitted the falsity of Christian sexual morals? If crucifixion of the flesh was grounded in moral truth, then Locke should rest content that truth alone would prevail.

Locke's interest in preservation of good order appears to be based on a theory akin to that which gave rise to the emergence of the court as *custos morum* in seventeenth-century England. Despite Locke's general predilection for toleration of various religions, he would limit the manner of discourse and substance of moral criticism to reason and words, according to Christian ascetic principles. The effect of such a limitation is to immunize the traditions of modesty, shame, and legal repression of the flesh from meaningful critical inquiry. Locke's approach paralleled the theory of early English blasphemy prosecutions like *Atwood* (1618) and *Taylor* (1675): that to impugn religion would dissolve all obligations whereby civil societies are preferred. Equality of civil rights belonged only to "those whose doctrine is peaceable, and whose manners are pure and blameless . . . ."[582]

The teachings of the Apostle Paul in his *Epistle to the Galatians* are an obvious source of inspiration for these principles. No empirical basis for Locke's rule appeared anywhere. The contradictions in his views on orality are logically irreconcilable but understandable. During Locke's youth, his family was sympathetic to Puritans yet remained members of the Church of England. He was well-schooled in classics. His upbringing and experience led him to believe that society was based on a social contract that gave the government permission to exact necessary compliance for good order. Labels like "natural law" and "social contract" inspired Locke and later Enlightenment thinkers but changed nothing about Locke's Pauline predisposition against passion and lust. His distrust of the natural state of man caused him to believe that repression of the body was a legitimate exercise of governmental power to encourage study and reflection and resist temptations of the flesh. Apostle Paul wrote of the duty of Christians to obey civil authorities in Romans 13:1-7.[583] One of his reasons was practical: civil authorities had the power to punish those who did not fear God. This idea is reminiscent of the 1660 Proclamation by Charles II against vicious and debauched person and subsequent arrest of Charles Sedley, where civil authorities might act as an enforcement mechanism against infidels. The ultimate authority in defining the crime in both cases would still emanate from God. Locke's unconscious subterfuge and Paul's homage to civil authorities presaged the usurpation and secularization of religious dogma by legal authorities in America.

Like Madison, Thomas Jefferson heavily relied on Locke for theory to support his preference for religious liberty. The influence of Locke's *Letter Concerning Toleration* on Jefferson's *Bill for Establishing Religious Freedom* as well as the *Declaration of Independence* is well known. However, Jefferson explicitly rejected the proposition, implicit in Locke's position regarding punishment of immorality by civil authorities, that Christianity formed any part of the common law. Jefferson may not have been aware of *Sedley's Case* (1663) when he wrote in his *Commonplace Book* in 1814 that "we may safely affirm (tho' contradicted by all the judges and writers on earth) that Christianity neither is, nor ever was a part of the Common law."[584]

Locke presumed the truth of Christianity and tolerated religious differences out of a spirit of Christian charity and concern about the fallibility of human judgment regarding details of belief and worship and to ameliorate civil strife. Jefferson was prepared to admit even the possibility of no God. As he advised in a letter written in 1787 to his nephew, Peter Carr:

> Shake off all the fears and servile prejudices under which weak minds are couched. Fix reason firmly in her seat, and call to her tribunal every fact, every opinion. Question with boldness even the existence of God; because, if there be one, he must approve of the homage of reason, than that of blind-folded fear.
>
> Do not be frightened from this enquiry by any fear of its consequences. If it ends in the belief that there is no God you will find incitements to virtue in the comfort and pleasantness you feel in its exercise, and the love of Others which it will procure you.[585]

In the last sentence of the passage quoted above, Jefferson showed that he did not share Locke's distrust of atheists. There would be practical inducements to virtue to substitute for the absence of faith in, and fear of, God. Jefferson did not share Locke's Pauline assumption of the natural depravity of man as expressed in Epistle to the Galatians either. He believed "that morality, compassion, [and] generosity are innate elements of the human constitution."[586] This distinction is important in that Jefferson would not necessarily assume, as Galatians taught, that the appearance of the flesh inevitably heralded a domino-like onslaught of depravities. Therefore, he would not feel the same urgency to suppress the show of flesh that Locke believed provided adequate justification to override his general principle that civil authority is limited to protection of person and property.

The first section of Jefferson's *Bill for Establishing Religious Freedom* contained an emphatic restatement of Locke's general principles. In the second section, the authority of the civil magistrate was expressly limited to "overt acts against peace and good order." "[T]o suffer the civil magistrate to intrude his powers into the field of opinion and to restrain the profession or propagation of principles on supposition of their ill tendency is a dangerous tendency, is a dangerous fallacy, which at once destroys all religious liberty . . . ."[587] Coupling Jefferson's denial that Christianity was part of the common law with this further rejection of the "ill tendency" standard for civil intervention might imply rejection of the doctrine of *custos morum*, for *custos morum* is based on the supposition that religious principles governing morality are part and parcel of the foundation of civil society and properly administered by magistrates. At a minimum it denigrated the prevention of example rationale for indecency laws.

Strict adherence to Locke's general principles would limit the concept of "good order" to regulation of the manner of conducting commerce and to suppression of violence. Jefferson's Notes on Virginia contained the statement, "The legitimate powers of government extend to such acts only as are injurious to others."[588] Extending "good order" to regulation of acts such as public nakedness that have no immediate material consequences for the sake of conformity to traditional practices would violate those general principles. Jefferson was aware of the tremendous costs of regulation intended to produce religious uniformity:

> Millions of innocent men, women, and children, since the introduction of Christianity, have been burnt, tortured, fined, imprisoned; yet we have not advanced one inch towards uniformity. What has been the effect of coercion? To make one half of the world fools, and the other half hypocrites.[589]

Jefferson disagreed with Locke's view that toleration should be denied to those who entertain opinions contrary to the "moral rules necessary for the preservation of society," whatever those rules may encompass.[590] Despite reference by Jefferson to "homage to reason" in the passage quoted above, he would not limit the manner of critical discourse so as to exclude irrational expression: "Nothing but free argument, raillery and even ridicule will preserve the purity of religion."[591] Jefferson maintained that use of force leads only to persecution and hypocrisy and is contrary to the teachings of Christ. The civil authorities are justified in acting only against overt acts threatening the public peace and good order.

Thus, prevention of evil example should not be sanctioned.

Jefferson was a self-styled "rational Christian;" in his words, he was a real Christian, that is to say, a disciple of the doctrines of Jesus.[592] His interpretation of those doctrines did not wholly conform to any recognized religion. He had the impression that "I am of a sect by myself as far as I know."[593] Jefferson's rational individualistic approach to religion would naturally support a liberal interpretation of principles of religious liberty to protect necessary opportunities for experimentation from foreclosure by prevailing religious views. His empiricism was opposed to a priori legal enforcement of religious principles.

Madison's position on the suppression of immorality by civil authorities is more difficult to discern. In a proposed clause on religious liberty for the Virginia constitution, he suggested that free exercise could be inhibited only when "the preservation of equal liberty, and the existence of the State be manifestly endangered"—a paraphrase of Locke's general principles. It is not clear whether Madison agreed with Locke's theological applications within those principles. With no specific reference to bodily morality, we are left to speculate as to whether he subscribed to Locke's view of the matter or adhered to a more restrictive opinion of governmental authority to regulate individual conduct. As for Jefferson, there is considerable reason to believe that he might have taken the position that government should leave matters of the flesh to the dictates of conscience unless the acts were "injurious to others;" that is, threatened violence to their person or property.

Such were the views of the three major intellectual forces in the development of the concept of religious freedom embodied in the First Amendment. All three men were Christians, all three were united in opposition to the establishment of a religion by the government, and all believed that religious opinion ought to be free from governmental control. With respect to the free exercise of religion, Locke appears to have had the most restrictive view. He would allow suppression of mere opinions contrary to the moral rules necessary for the preservation of society even when they were not acted upon. In his estimation, the essential moral rules included not only those relating to commerce and the protection of human life but also those relating to bodily immorality, such as prohibitions against adultery and promiscuous uncleanliness. Such acts, even if performed in religious assemblies, could and should be prohibited. The link between bodily morality and the preservation of society in Locke's moral jurisprudence appears to have been the Pauline conception of the degeneracy of the flesh.

The theoretical problem posed by Locke's allowance for punishment of immorality by civil authorities is that the thesis that crucifixion of the flesh is necessary for the preservation of society, unless substantiated by empirical evidence, would seem to violate the literal meanings of both the Establishment Clause and the Free Exercise Clause. It establishes a particular religious doctrine as a fundamental principle of civil society and sanctions suppression of the free exercise (expression, reduction to practice) of competing moral (or immoral, if one prefers) doctrines. Limitation of moral discourse to reason and words, thereby excluding passion and symbolic actions, is an insidious foreclosure of effective criticism against the prevailing Christian moral order.

The framers never explicitly addressed such concerns. The primary issue for these early advocates of religious freedom was the degree of toleration that should be accorded to differences of opinion within the Judeo-Christian tradition. Virtually all colonists and citizens of the United States during the eighteenth and early nineteenth centuries were Christians. Jews shared the Pauline conception of the flesh. Indigenous Americans, enslaved people, and the few Caucasian infidels were more objects of ridicule and pity than sources of legitimate criticism of the Christian nation. Christian moral principles ruled unchallenged. Locke's contradictions, Madison's silence, and Jefferson's sketchy remarks regarding legal enforcement of Christian morality are not surprising in this context. The very sanctity of long-standing taboos surrounding public display of the body removed them from serious scrutiny. The great depth of centuries of institutionalized repression of the body prevented these Christian men from recognizing the incongruities of their views on management of decency as they advocated religious freedom.

When trying to discern the original meaning of the Religion Clauses of the Constitution, the mindset of the ratifiers and general public meaning should also be considered. Whereas there might be ambiguity regarding aspects of the framers' intent, there is no doubt about the common understanding of the role of religion among leaders of the newly formed states. A blinding sanctification is observable in provisions of early state constitutions. Evidence of Locke's influence abounds in constitutional provisions on religious liberty expressly recognizing the intra-faith nature of the religious controversy that was to be tolerated. For instance, the Connecticut constitution of 1776 forbade the showing of a preference to any "Christian sect."[594] The first Maryland constitution assured equal rights to "all persons, professing the Christian religion."[595] Religious differences among the various sects did not focus on morality. A consensus regarding moral issues made it possible to frame the guarantees of religious liberty in such a way that implicitly exempted morality from criticism. Early obscenity and blasphemy prosecutions evidenced that even rational, verbal criticism of the dominant morality was for a long time outlawed.[596] A few state constitutions expressly declared piety, religion, and morality to be essential to the preservation of civil government.[597] Others, to the same effect, traced Locke more closely in limiting "liberty of conscience" to not "excuse acts of licentiousness."[598]

There was a telling debate at the New York Constitutional Convention of 1821 on a proposal to add to the constitution a provision that the judiciary should not declare any particular religion to be the law of the land.[599] Erastus Root made the proposal as a follow-up to a conviction for blasphemy ten years earlier in the New York Supreme Court in *People v. Ruggles* (1811), which had featured Chancellor Kent repeatedly acknowledging the ultimate truth and moral supremacy of the Christian religion.[600] Kent, who was present at the convention, denied that the decision meant that Christianity was a religion established by law. Blasphemy was a crime not because "Christianity was established by law, but because Christianity was in fact the religion of this country, the rule of our faith and practice, and the basis of the public morals."[601] If blasphemy were to be countenanced by the courts, it "would shock the moral sense of the community, and degrade our character as a Christian people."[602] "The authors of the constitution . . . meant to preserve, so far as it came within their cognizance, the morals of the country, which rested on Christianity as the foundation."[603] Kent had accepted the argument of the prosecutor against reversal of the conviction on appeal that "(w)hile the constitution . . . allowed a free and fair discussion of all points of controversy among religious sects, it has left the principle engrafted on the body of our common law, that Christianity is part of the laws of the state, untouched and unimpaired."[604] The constitutional convention then voted in alignment with the *Ruggles* holding and Chief Justice Kent's reasoning.

People v. Ruggles (1811) was the first reported prosecution for blasphemy in New York and the first test of the meaning of religious freedom as guaranteed by the New York constitution. The defendant was indicted for saying "Jesus Christ was a bastard, and his mother must be a whore." He was convicted and sentenced to three months in prison and fined $500. On appeal, defense counsel argued that although Christianity was a part of the common law of England because in that country there was an established church, in this country establishment was forbidden by a provision in the New York constitution allowing "free toleration to all religions and all kinds of worship," and the verbal attack was against only Christ, not religion in general or morality. "For aught that appears the prisoner may have been a Jew, a Mahometan, or a Socinian; and if so, he had a right, by the constitution, to declare his opinions."[605] Justice Kent, speaking for a unanimous court, thought this last objection was preposterous. The court could not be bound by the constitution,

> as some have strangely supposed, either not to punish at all, or to punish indiscriminately the like attacks upon the religion of Mahomet or of the grand Lama; and for this plain reason, that the case assumes we are a Christian people, and the morality of the country is ingrafted upon Christianity, and act upon the doctrines or worship of those imposters.[606]

In other words, the English common law of *custos morum* was not abrogated by provisions for religious liberty in the state constitution. Learned debate over doctrinal differences could be tolerated. The right to "free and decent discussions on any religious subject, is granted and secured; but to revile, with malicious and blasphemous contempt, the religion professed by almost the whole community, is an abuse of that right" and "a gross violation of decency and good order" because "it tends to corrupt the morals of the people, and to destroy good order."[607] Moral discipline and principles of virtue bind society together. Christianity is the foundation of morals, so "whatever strikes at the root of Christianity tends manifestly to the dissolution of civil government."[608]

Root's antiestablishment proposal went down to defeat by a vote of 74 to 41 in the face of Chancellor Kent's overtly Christian notion of civil and moral order. This debate and its resolution have several noteworthy aspects. First, the ultimate truth of Christian moral principles was presumed. The principle that religion and morality are essential to the preservation of civil society meant, in practical effect, that Christianity was the foundation of civil society. Second, certain forms of criticism—those that were indecent or contrary to good order—were not allowed because of their tendency to corrupt morals and destroy good order. Criticism would be tolerated only if presented in the form of decent, rational debate.

The preservationist circularity in this rhetoric—the Catch-22 it describes—is but one early example of the encapsulation of morality that protects it from meaningful criticism. Indecent criticism of decency and disorderly criticism of the good order are forbidden; decent criticism, that which does not disrupt the good order or "corrupt" morals, is the only legitimate method of moral disputation. "Decent" criticism is dispassionate, verbal, rational, a Christian ascetic ideal.[609] As one convention delegate put it, "[i]f a man were to go naked in the streets, he might claim a right to do so, by the law of nature; but every man who had a suitable regard for decency or morals, would rejoice in bringing him to punishment."[610]

Most state court opinions after *Ruggles* (1811) adopted one of two basic solutions to the Christian-nation problem. Some held that Christianity was obviously a part of the law of the land. Others denied that Christianity or any other system of religion could, consistent with the U.S. Constitution, constitute any part of the law except in a limited sense where, as the dominant religion, it could be protected against blasphemous reviling and scoffing and no more.[611] In one such case, *Commonwealth v. Kneeland* (1838),[612] the Supreme Court of Massachusetts addressed Establishment Clause and free-speech defenses advanced by a newspaper that, because it questioned the existence of God, was prosecuted under the statute of 1782 prohibiting blasphemy. The statute was explicit:

> It is the right, as well as the duty, of all men in society, publicly, and at stated seasons, to worship the Supreme Being, the great creator and preserver of the universe. And no subject shall be hurt, molested, or restrained, in his person, liberty, or estate, for worshipping God in the manner and reason most agreeable to the dictates of his own conscience; or for his religious profession or sentiments; provided he doth not disturb the public peace, or obstruct others in their religious worship."[613]

Freedom of the press provided a general right of publication but did not excuse any crimes committed by use of language therein. The establishment and free-exercise claims were dismissed on the basis that the statute was intended not to prevent or restrain opinions but to punish acts that disturb the peace.

The Christian-nation concept gave rise to great controversies during the first hundred years after passage of the First Amendment. Some people believed that religious freedom meant liberty of opinion and worship within the Christian faith. To these people, Christianity was the only true religion, so, by definition, religious freedom did not protect the beliefs and practices of infidels and atheists. As the nineteenth century wore on, Christian ascendancy in the moral realm diminished, allowing for serious "decent" debate. The controversy continued until late in the nineteenth century, when the courts came upon an ingenious semantic device for divorcing legal enforcement of moral principles from its theocratic foundation.

The necessity of going through the abstraction that bodily morality is essential to the preservation of civil society to legally enforce Christian moral principles seemed to Christian politicians to be a needless and troublesome formality. The states of the United States were obviously united not only economically and politically but also in belief in the ultimate truth of Holy Scripture. This led to proposals to amend the Constitution to unambiguously proclaim the United States a Christian nation. All such proposals failed. The first attempt was in 1863, when eleven Protestant denominations combined into a National Reformation Association to

> secure such an amendment to the Constitution of the United States as will declare the nation's allegiance to Jesus Christ and its acceptance of the moral laws of the Christian religion, and so indicate this is a Christian nation, and place all the Christian laws, institutions, and usages of our government on an undeniably legal basis in the fundamental law of the land.[614]

In 1864, the association proposed that the Preamble to the Constitution be amended to read as follows:

> We the people of the United States, humbly acknowledging Almighty God as the source of all authority and power in civil government, the Lord Jesus Christ as the Ruler among the nations, His revealed will as the supreme law of the land, in order to Constitute a Christian government, and in order to form a more perfect union . . . .[615]

The proposal was considered by the House Judiciary Committee in 1874 and rejected as contrary to the intention of the framers of the Constitution. This nation was to be the "home of the oppressed of all nations of the earth, whether Christian or pagan."[616] Similar proposals were introduced in Congress in 1951, 1953, and 1959, possibly in reaction to the perceived Communist menace. None of the proposals were reported out of committee.[617]

The conclusion of the House Committee in 1874 regarding the intention of the framers is certainly debatable, but the issue had little practical importance for the development of moral jurisprudence. The doctrine of *custos morum*, which by then had been fully assimilated into American jurisprudence from the English common law, assured the legal enforcement of Christian moral principles, albeit under a secular rubric. However, as recent global political developments have demonstrated, the controversy over moral codes is no longer "largely theoretical,"[618] as noted First Amendment scholar Leo Pfeffer described it.[619]

The matter has no practical import only so long as the moral predominance of the Christian religion in the United States is undisputed and the courts abide by the common-law theory of *custos morum* without demanding empirical support. Both these premises have been increasingly questioned and implicated in major policy debates and judicial rulings in recent years. Whether America is a Christian nation or a home for the oppressed of all nations has become an issue of considerable significance.[620] A Christian nation could certainly be a home for the oppressed of the world without abandoning its conception of morality. However, nearly one-half of Americans think America should be a Christian nation.[621] Christianity has been the dominant faith since colonial times. It continues to be the professed religion of the majority of American citizens and has profoundly influenced the nation's culture and traditions. These facts do not belie the issue of whether the apparatus of the state can, should, or may be used to impose Christian principles on people who do not accept them.

The government has been reluctant to admit that the United States was a Christian nation when it operated in the sphere of international trade and politics. For instance, in 1797, while negotiating a treaty with Tripoli, this concern led to an outright denial. The treaty contained this clause:

> As the government of the United States is not, in any sense, founded on the Christian religion; as it has in itself no character of enmity against the laws, religion or tranquility of Musselmen[622] . . . it is declared . . . that no pretext arising from religious opinion shall ever produce an interruption of the harmony existing between the two countries.[623]

When a more extensive superseding treaty was entered into eight years later, the words "is not, in any sense, founded on the Christian religion" were omitted.[624] The assertion was obviously false. The promise not to allow any pretext of religious opinion to interfere with relations between the countries was retained.

Fifty years later, the United States Supreme Court adopted a position contrary to the treaty with Tripoli in *Vidal v. Girard's Executors* (1844).[625] In this case, the Court brazenly asserted that Christianity was a part of the laws of the United States and turned to *custos morum* theory to support its decision. Girard's heirs had contested a will in which he had bequeathed a substantial sum of money for the establishment of a school on the condition that no religious officials or missionaries ever be allowed on its premises. Daniel Webster, arguing for the heirs, called the plan "derogatory to the Christian religion, tending to weaken men's respect for it and their conviction of its importance. It subverts the only foundation of public morals, and therefore is mischievous and not desirable."[626] Justice Story upheld the will, despite his recognition that "the Christian religion is a part of the common law of Pennsylvania," because Christianity was part of the law only in the qualified sense "[t]hat its divine origin and truth are admitted, and therefore it is not to be maliciously and openly reviled and blasphemed against," and Girard had neither impugned nor repudiated Christianity nor barred the teaching of it.[627]

The relation of church and state has a long and contentious history. Modern Supreme Court doctrine on the matter originated in *Reynolds v. United States* (1879),[628] an appeal of a bigamy conviction involving a Mormon man. This was the first church/state case because the First Amendment applied only to the federal government at that time. Jurisdiction was based on Reynolds living in Utah, a federal territory that was not yet a state. Founder of the LDS church Joseph Smith's 1843 revelation espoused polygamy. Reynolds's sincere belief in this doctrine was not challenged.

Chief Justice Waite rejected a defense based on the free exercise of religion. With no precedent to rely on regarding the Establishment and Free Exercise Clauses, he asked a neighbor who was writing a history of the Constitution for a lead. The neighbor suggested he consider the writings of a "leading American statesman," Thomas Jefferson. It appears that Waite later skimmed an index of Jefferson's collected works, where he found a letter to a group of Baptists in Danbury, Connecticut. In it, Jefferson had referenced "a wall of separation between church and state." The Court accepted this "almost as an authoritative disposition" of the matter, unaware that Jefferson was not involved in drafting the Bill of Rights and was out of the country, serving as Minister to France, at the time of its adoption.[629] This letter and the gift of cheese that inspired it have been the subjects of many analyses.[630] It serves as a case study in the dangers of casual historical analysis. The importance that this dictum garnered as precedent far exceeded what was warranted by its substance, circumstances, and irrelevance to the disposition of the case.[631] Had Waite not been guided by his neighbor to Jefferson, he might have turned to Justice Story's *Commentaries on the Constitution of the United States*,[632] published in 1833, and reached a quite different conclusion.

Reynolds's conviction was upheld despite the Court's findings regarding separation of church and state. The Court noted that Virginia had banned polygamy even after enacting a religious-freedom statute promoted by Jefferson.[633] Waite addressed the Establishment Clause objection by saying, "Marriage, while from its very nature a sacred obligation, is nevertheless, in most civilized nations, a civil contract, and usually regulated by law"[634]—an argument one might be tempted to make regarding indecent exposure laws. This, however, restated the question rather than answering it. Government regulation of a religious practice does not magically transform it into a secular one. The question that Justice Waite ignored is whether, in doing so, the state violated the principles of the First Amendment. No one would question that the government could not, consistent with the Constitution, forbid marriage altogether. Why, then, was it acceptable for the government to limit the number of wives to one? Chief Justice Waite offered a secular justification: polygamy "leads to the patriarchal principle."[635] Yet, if patriarchy is bad, why not discourage it more fully by allowing polyandry or polyamory?[636] One is left to suppose Justice Waite's opinion to be that the union of one man and one woman for life is exactly right: not too much patriarchy, not too little. In fact, this was precisely the theory of another Supreme Court Justice fifty years later in *Murphy v. Ramsey* (1884), a case upholding a statute that excluded polygamists from voting or holding office.[637] Justice Matthews wrote:

> Certainly no legislation can be supposed more wholesome and necessary in the founding of a free, self-governing commonwealth . . . than that which seeks to establish it on the basis of the idea of the family, as consisting in and springing from the union for life of one man and one woman in the holy estate of matrimony; the sure foundation of all that is stable and noble in our civilization; the best guaranty of that reverent morality which is the source of all beneficent progress in social and political improvement.[638]

Whose "idea of the family"? Christianity's, of course. As Justices Field and Bradley put it in two other cases of the period in which the legality of polygamy was considered, the practice was a crime "by the laws of all civilized and Christian countries"[639] and "contrary to the spirit of Christianity and the civilization which Christianity has produced in the Western world."[640] To allow polygamy to subsist would sanction "a return to barbarism,"[641] "destroy the purity of the marriage relation, . . . disturb the peace of families, . . . degrade woman and . . . debase man."[642] Justice Field, in *Davis v. Beason* (1890), characterized labeling advocacy of polygamy as a tenet of religion to be an offense to the "common sense of mankind." He expressly defended Christianity as the source of marriage and a legitimate state interest:

> Probably never before in the history of this country has it been seriously contended that the whold [*sic*] punitive power of the government for acts, recognized by the general consent of the Christian world in modern times as proper matters for prohibitory legislation, must be suspended in order that the tenets of a religious sect encouraging crime may be carried out without hindrance.[643]

What is most remarkable about these opinions maintaining the sanctity of monogamy in the face of establishment and free exercise claims is that the Mormons themselves were Christians, members of the Church of Latter-day Saints. The Supreme Court rejected their arguments, defending Christian orthodoxy against the challenge of this unconventional Christian sect. As Pfeffer pointed out, this was "not a conflict between morality and unmorality [*sic*], but between Christian and Biblical concepts of family life. It is both unfair and inaccurate to designate the Mormons as immoral; in many respects they were and are more Puritanical than almost any other element of our population."[644]

At the time, Mormons were a deeply religious and strongly self-disciplined subculture. Amid claims that it was protecting morality, the Court ignored the obvious empirical evidence of the moral and social stability of polygamists to arbitrarily enforce a cardinal principle of orthodox Christianity. Although there is doubt regarding the intentions of the framers and ratifiers on more radical propositions, it is clear that the First Amendment was intended to remove doctrinal controversies within the Christian faith from secular control. Despite the clarity of the general principles on this issue, had someone posed the question to the framers whether polygamy should be permitted, they, too, might well have balked at allowing violation of such a fundamental and widely held general Christian principle. However, nowhere in the Constitution was provision made for conservation of strongly held Christian beliefs by civil authorities.

The Supreme Court in these cases sought to limit the application of the First Amendment guarantees of religious liberty through another approach. Even though the government could not interfere with religious opinions and beliefs per se, it could justify intervention when these were transformed into overt actions threatening public peace and good order.[645] For instance, no one would expect the government to tolerate human sacrifice done for religious reasons. This example is consistent with the principles of Locke, Madison, and Jefferson that the sole purpose for which civil authority may act is to secure the person and property of its citizens from invasion.

Does this theory justify the state's assertion of an exclusive legal preference for monogamy? Unlike killing or expropriating property, the internal structure of the family has no direct material consequences. It does not pose an immediate threat to the person or property of citizens with different views, nor does it disrupt the flow of commerce or discourage study and reflection. In fact, considering the empirical evidence provided by Mormon society, differences of opinion and practice regarding the number of wives were quite independent of moral judgments concerning the preservation of life and property, appreciation for study and reflection, and modes of commerce.

In a crucial step in the development of American moral jurisprudence, Justice Field, in *Davis v. Beason* (1890), traversed the treacherous issue of the connection between bodily morality and social order by adding the preservation of morals to Locke's enumeration of the legitimate interests of civil society. According to Justice Field,

> [i]t was never intended or supposed that the amendment could be invoked as a protection against legislation for the punishment of acts inimical to the peace, good order, and morals of society.
>
> . . . [N]o interference can be permitted, provided always the laws of society, designed to secure its peace, prosperity, and the morals of its people, are not interfered with.[646]

By a subtle semantic manipulation, Field contentedly transferred morality "recognized by the general consent of the Christian world" to the protective custody of civil jurisdiction. These matters on which there could be no real debate were now secular absolutes. This pronouncement was not so radical or deceptive as it may seem when considered out of context, for it dovetailed neatly with a developing conception of the "police power" as a right inherent in the state to protect public safety, health, and morals. The ideal of police power gave civil authorities a source of the power to regulate morality as an end in itself.

The police power traces its origin to the English common law of moral jurisprudence described earlier. There it was shown that the original justification for legal control of morality was that immorality was contrary to Christianity. Christianity was considered the foundation of civil society in England, where church and state were one. Thus, violations of religious precepts were deemed constructive breaches of the peace regardless of their immediate temporal consequences. Historian Christopher Tiedeman argued that the source of police power over morals and the moral jurisprudence that formed the traditional basis for legal suppression of public indecency were the same when he wrote in his *Limitations of Police Power in the United States*:

> A high morality is inconsistent with a state of chronic irreligiousness. Anything, therefore, that is calculated to diminish the people's religious inclinations is detrimental to the public welfare, and may therefore be prohibited. Public contumely and ridicule of a prevalent religion not only offend against the sensibilities of the believers, but likewise threaten the public peace and order by diminishing the power of moral precepts. Inasmuch, therefore, as Christianity is essentially the religion of the country, any defamation of its founder or of its institutions, as well as all malicious irreverence towards Diety, must and can be prohibited.[647]

The Christian view of human nature supporting this theory was a familiar notion of innate depravity of the flesh. It was the duty of every person to wage "Christian Warfare," that is, "to strive against the flesh . . ., to resist and to hate the ungodly motions thereof, and with grief to think them burthenous and troublesome."[648] "The warriors, are the temptor, and the Christian Soldier."[649]

> The temptor is the Prince, or his helpers. The Prince is Satan and his angels . . . . His helpers are the flesh and the world. The Conflict of these all, is temptation, whereby man is provided to commit such wickedness, as is hurtful to the salvation of his soul. Dearly beloved, I beseech you, as strangers and pilgrims abstaine from fleshly lusts, which fight against the soule."[650]

Blackstone influenced formulation of the American conception of the police power.[651] Jurists and legislators turned to his *Commentaries* (1765) for guidance. There, Blackstone described the duty of the law to ensure "due regulation and domestic order; . . . whereby the individuals of the state, like members of a well-governed family, are bound to conform their general behaviour to the rules of propriety, good neighborhood, and good manners; and to be dent, industrious, and inoffensive in their respective stations."[652]

The first explicit reference to the police power by the United States Supreme Court was in an 1842 case in which the Court declared unconstitutional a state statute that punished the owner of a runaway slave for seizing and removing the slave.[653] According to Justice Story—the justice who asserted that Christianity was a part of the law in *Vidal v. Girard's Executors*—the police power belonged to the state by virtue of its general sovereignty. It provided state governments with "full jurisdiction to arrest and restrain runaway slaves, and remove them from their borders, and otherwise to secure themselves against their depredations and evil example, as they certainly may do in cases of idlers, vagabonds, and paupers."[654] This rather inauspicious introduction foreshadowed rapid development of gargantuan authority over public morals during the late nineteenth century in the name of the police power.

By the end of that century, the police power was "universally conceded to include everything essential to the public safety, health, and morals, and to justify the destruction or abatement, by summary proceedings, of whatever may be regarded as a public nuisance."[655]

Public nuisances were not only conditions injurious to the health, safety, and physical comfort of the citizens; those things that damaged the public morals, such as gambling houses and lottery tickets, were suppressed as well.[656]

Chief Justice Waite, who wrote the opinion in the first polygamy case to reach the Supreme Court, was no stranger to the developing police-power doctrine. In a case that came to the Court one year after *Reynolds* (1879), he went so far as to say that the government had an absolute and inalienable obligation to supervise public morals. In his view,

> [n]o legislature can bargain away the public health or the public morals. The people themselves cannot do it, much less their public servants. The supervision of both these subjects of governmental power continues in its nature, and they are dealt with as the special exigencies of the moment may require. Government is organized with a view to their preservation and cannot divest itself of the power to provide for them.[657]

Waite would sanctify morals, elevate them to an absolute, and immunize them from criticism and change.[658]

The police power has never been limited to immoral acts having immediate material consequences such as violence or the disruption of commerce. In *Winters v. New York* (1948), the Court found that a statute regulating publication of crime stories was unconstitutionally vague: "When a legislative body concludes that the mores of a community call for an extension of the impermissible limits, an enactment aimed at the evil is plainly within its power, if it does not transgress the boundaries fixed by the Constitution for freedom of expression."[659] The only limits are constitutional.[660] The law must have a legitimate aim, be sufficiently specific to provide adequate notice, and employ means that are reasonably calculated to secure that objective without unnecessarily impinging upon any freedoms guaranteed by the Constitution. The enforcement of morals *per se* was considered a legitimate aim that did not impinge on constitutional guarantees and needed no explanation or justification.

The advantage of reliance on the police power to justify legal control of morals as compared to the earlier line of cases in the American tradition of moral jurisprudence was that the legacy of the police power contained no explicit references to Christianity. Justice Story described the power as one inherent in the concept of sovereignty. Enforcement of morals was not maintenance of a bridge between Christianity and civil society; it was an end in itself. The defense of religious liberty, even the thought of such a defense, were muted. After losing repeatedly in open battle for constitutional amendment, we see here how Christianity ceded nominal authority to secular authorities through semantics, with no substantive changes in the laws. The cardinal principles of Christian asceticism, now referred to by the secular equivalent "morals," could be enforced as ends in themselves without invocation of Christ or the Bible and without changes to the Constitution.

In 1892, the Supreme Court found that a federal statute prohibiting importation of foreigners under contracts of labor was inapplicable to a contract with an English clergyman migrating to become rector and pastor of a congregation because "no purpose of action against religion can be imputed to any legislation, state or national, because this is a religious people."[661] The Court cited as precedent Chancellor Kent's opinion in *Ruggles* (1811) and Justice Story's statements in *Vidal* (1844). The transformation to a secular premise for enforcement of morals in Supreme Court doctrine lay fallow and unchallenged for decades until *Everson v. Board of Education* in 1947, in which Justice Waite's allusion in *Reynolds* (1879) to the "wall of separation" got a boost as precedent.

Everson (1947) was a case in which the Court, by a 5-to-4 vote, found that reimbursement of expenses for transporting children to private religious schools did not violate the First Amendment, as it supported the secular goal of facilitating school attendance in general.[662] The Court, referencing *Reynolds* (1879), perpetuated the myth of Jeffersonian authority in interpreting the First Amendment by erroneously stating that Jefferson played a leading role in the drafting and adoption of the amendment.[663] Justice Black then extended the *Reynolds* dictum with his own dictum, writing that neither the state nor federal government "can pass laws which aid one religion, aid all religions, or prefer one religion over another."[664] These "precedents" of *Reynolds* and *Everson* dominated constitutional interpretation of the Religion Clauses for much of the twentieth century.

In the 1960s and '70s, there was a transcendental loosening of moral restrictions on lifestyles amid the increasing reach and power of television, Vietnam war protests, racial unrest, improved contraception, and the rise of feminism. Judicial perspectives on certain aspects of Christian morality changed concomitantly. Notions of expanded definitions of liberty, privacy, and freedom of expression were the workhorses of the Sexual Revolution in the 1960s and 1970s.[665] The Religion Clauses played a prominent role in military draft cases, where the definition of religion expanded beyond traditional boundaries.

A better understanding of the original meaning of the Establishment and Free Exercise Clauses, coupled with the expansive characterizations of religion from these cases, supports a credible constitutional challenge to indecent exposure laws on establishment and free-exercise grounds. Given the nature of the interests involved, the Court should apply strict scrutiny and require a compelling state interest. Constitutional text, history, and tradition—all areas explored thus far—frame this unprecedented claim.

Lemon v. Kurtzman (1971)[666] and *Kennedy v. Bremerton School District* (2022)[667] are important precedents for interpretation of the Establishment and Free Exercise Clauses. The construction of the religion-clause challenge begins with these cases, with comments where appropriate about potential impacts of the *Dobbs* (2022) abortion case, followed by analysis of the military draft cases. The Court in *Dobbs* did not cite any of these cases. No establishment or free-exercise claims were advanced by parties in the case. Much of the Court's opinion in *Dobbs* focused on means to identify unenumerated rights in substantive-due-process claims.

The Court in *Lemon* (1971) found that a Rhode Island statute that provided financial support for private schools that had been given to church-related institutions was unconstitutional because it fostered entanglement between government and religion. It described a three-part "cumulative criteria" test for judging constitutional objections to laws based on the Establishment Clause. This test provided guidance as precedent for the next fifty years. A law does not violate the Establishment Clause only if three conditions are satisfied. The law must

- have a secular legislative purpose;
- have a principle or primary effect that neither advances or inhibits religion;[668] and
- not foster an excessive government entanglement with religion.[669]

This test was rejected, but not overruled, in *Kennedy* (2022), a case that featured a high school football coach who lost his job because he knelt and prayed at mid-field after games. He appealed to the Supreme Court, alleging violation of his constitutional rights to free speech and free exercise of religion. The Court found that his actions were protected by these First Amendment rights in that his "speech" was private, not government, speech; the district failed to act pursuant to a neutral and generally applicable rule; and the school district did not show that its actions were essential to avoid a violation of the Establishment Clause.

In *Kennedy* (2022), the Court was faced with a straightforward, orthodox prayer in the free-exercise challenge. It proposed that the Establishment Clause must be interpreted with "reference to historical practices and understandings," including evidence of the framers' intent, applying strict scrutiny. Justice Gorsuch, writing for the majority, opened his remarks by noting that "[t]he Constitution and the best of our traditions counsel mutual respect and tolerance, not censorship and suppression, for religious and nonreligious views alike." He proposed that the juxtaposition of Establishment, Free Exercise, and Free Speech Clauses in the same amendment suggests that they should be read as having complementary purposes. He went on to say, referencing the writings of James Madison, that the Free Exercise and Free Speech Clauses provide overlapping protection for religious exercises.

> The Clause protects not only the right to harbor religious beliefs inwardly and secretly. It does perhaps its most important work by protecting the ability of those who hold religious beliefs of all kinds to live out their faiths in daily life through "the performance of (or abstention from) physical acts."[670]

The district fired the appellant because it perceived it was in a vise between the Establishment and Exercise Clauses because it could be viewed as endorsing his religious beliefs and practice. It had relied on *Lemon* (1971) to justify the termination of employment. The Court went on a tirade against *Lemon*'s "ambitious, abstract, and ahistorical approach" to interpretation. The Court instructed that proper analysis should focus on historical practices and understanding, including evidence of the intent of the framers. It did not expressly overrule *Lemon* despite the heavy criticism. It also did not engage in any meaningful historical analysis that it deemed essential to a proper disposition.

Three justices dissented, accusing the majority of misrepresenting the facts and noting that the appellant had done more than engage in private prayer during lulls in his duties. They lamented what they referred to as overruling *Lemon* (1971), calling into question decades of subsequent precedents. The opinion in *Kennedy* (2022) involved a balancing of fear that the district's continued employment of the appellant might be found to be a violation of the Establishment Clause versus an unconstitutional limitation on Kennedy's free-exercise and free-speech rights.

Kennedy (2022) is an important signal of a shift in constitutional interpretation from doctrine to original intent and precedent, foreshadowing the opinion in *Dobbs* (2022). Given the recency of the opinion, its failure to expressly overrule *Lemon*, and the vast "offshoot" precedents over the last fifty years, our analysis will continue with both approaches in mind. Similarities and differences in likely outcomes will be identified and assessed, and the potential impact of *Dobbs* will be noted where appropriate.

Justice Gorsuch recently reiterated disfavor for *Lemon*, asserting that establishment claims should be measured against the Constitution's original and historical meaning, not a hypothetical reasonable observer.[671] This has already been explored in detail. The following analysis will yield additional doubts about the constitutionality of indecent exposure laws. Application of *Lemon* (1971) criteria to the crime of indecent exposure, mindful of *Kennedy* and *Dobbs*, indicates the following:

Secular Legislative Purpose

One of my goals is to improve the understanding of the roles of the law of God and the law of reason in defining the crime of indecent exposure and associated state interests. Scholars have pondered the respective influences since the inception of the common law of England. Writing in the early sixteenth century, amid rising tension between Tudor England and the papacy, Christopher St. Germain characterized the law of man

> as derived from reason, as a thing which is necessary, and probably following the law of reason, and of the law of God [and] therefore in every law positive well made, is somewhat of the law of reason, and of the law of God; and to discern the law of God and the law of reason from the law positive, is very hard. And though it be hard, yet it is much necessary in every moral doctrine and in all laws made for the commonwealth. And that the law of man be just and rightwise [*sic*], two things be necessary and that is to say wisdom and authority.[672]

This tension between church and state ebbed and flowed in England and America over the centuries before succumbing to constitutional democracy pressures to enshrine dominance of the state in America. Constitutional democracy is inclined to reason and a search for secular justifications for its laws. The history of laws forbidding public nakedness leans in the direction of God, with only two explicit justifications: prevention of evil example and suppression of public nuisances. Management of health risks has been mentioned but not argued. The evil example that is prohibited is contravention of a basic tenet of the historically dominant religious establishment. The doctrine of the Fall and crucifixion of the flesh are the principles insulated by law from such behavior. No significant effort has been made to substantiate any effect on public peace and good order of failing to banish "private parts" of bodies to "private" places, leaving offense, annoyance, or alarm of an unwilling audience as the only credible justification. When accompanied by express or implied threats of sexual violence, the conduct can be managed through other laws.

The question of defense of religious doctrine was considered in *Epperson v. Arkansas* (1968).[673] There the Court struck down a state statute forbidding teaching of the Darwinian theory of evolution in public schools, concluding that the government "may not aid, foster, or promote one religion or religious theory against another or even against the militant opposite."[674] The Darwin case provides answers to the argument one might be tempted to make: that even if failure to prohibit public nakedness did not immediately disrupt the peace and good order, the long-term effect would be to diminish moral sentiments forming the basis of civil society. The principles of Darwinian evolution wrought significant social consequences in competition with the biblical explanation of the origin of man and woman. If legislatures are not free to conserve an existing social order based on the particular religious doctrine at issue in *Epperson*, what justifies their support for the religious premise of shame and modesty that supports indecent exposure? Surely, many people were offended, annoyed, and alarmed by theories of evolution.

In a passage quoted by Justice Fortas, respected scholar Robert Leflar made the incisive observation that

> the same ideological considerations underlie the anti-evolution enactment" as underlie the typical blasphemy statute. . . . [T]he purpose of these statutes is an "ideological" one which "involves an effort to prevent (by censorship) or punish the presentation of intellectually significant matter which contradicts accepted social, moral, or religious ideas.[675]

The forerunner of the statute in question, which was declared unconstitutional in the famous "Scopes Monkey Trial," contained an explicit reference to the Bible.[676] The modern statute had different language but the same substance. The cosmetic change did not fool the Court. "Plainly, the law is contrary to the mandate of the First, and in violation of the Fourteenth, Amendment to the Constitution."[677] Why isn't it just as plain that indecent exposure laws, cloaked in secular rhetoric, are unconstitutional?

The public nuisance theory does not rescue the laws from constitutional infirmity. In *Burstyn v. Wilson* (1952), where the Court lifted a ban on the sacrilegious film *The Miracle*, the Court opined that "the State has no legitimate interest in protecting any or all religions from views distasteful to them . . . . It is not the business of the government in our nation to suppress real or imagined attacks upon a particular religious doctrine . . . ."[678] Both religion and government fare better when intermeddling is forbidden. Enforcement of religious principles is not a secular purpose.

A contra argument can be derived from *McGowan v. Maryland* (1961),[679] a case in which the Supreme Court upheld Sunday closing laws, despite their undeniable religious origins, in response to nonreligious arguments for their perpetuation, such as provision for a uniform day of rest, that had emerged in the nineteenth century. The majority of the Court turned away an argument that a one-day-in-seven rule would suffice to meet the secular objectives without sanctioning the Christian preference for Sunday closings over the Jewish preference for Saturday closings or any other preference. They refused to invalidate the ban on Sunday sales because its "reason or effect merely happens to coincide or harmonize with the tenets of some or all religions."[680] This reasoning would not apply to indecent exposure laws because the history of the laws indicates that their connection to religion was not just coincidental.

Unlike with Sunday closing laws, no secular justifications for indecent exposure laws have been proffered. The only obvious purposes are to insulate religious dogma from critical inquiry informed by experiential data and to protect those who accept this dogma from exposure to heretical exhibitions. Neither purpose is within the province of civil authority as constrained by constitutional guarantees of religious liberty. That there is historical precedent for these laws and that public nakedness in most circumstances is punishable in all jurisdictions should not cure the constitutional defect, as might be suggested as an implication of *Dobbs* (2022) reasoning regarding the value of tradition.[681]

One need not look far for enduring, time-tested opposition to indecent exposure laws.

The nudist movement is instructive. It emerged in America in the late 1920s.[682] and grew into a persistent yet subdued challenge to indecent exposure laws. Realizing the enormous and unyielding Christian control over the machinery of punitive regulation in this country, nudists settled for the opportunity to liberate the flesh in specially adapted, secluded areas rather than engage in open war with the Christian faith..[683] Their persistence and ability to adapt to the prevailing social order is evidence contrary to the theological conception of the depravity of the flesh that is the source of legal repression of the body via indecent exposure laws. Nudist retreats are not hotbeds of depravity. They maintain good order through common understanding and acceptance of published rules of engagement. Their beliefs are sincere and enduring and have the character of religious conviction. Hundreds of social nudity enclaves exist in North America..[684]

Advances or Inhibits Religion

Torcaso v. Watkins (1961) was a clash between believers and non-believers. An atheist appointed to public office refused to take an oath. The Supreme Court asserted that all religious tests for public office were unconstitutional because civil authority may not use its coercive powers against any individual to advance the cause of any religion, or of religion in general. In the words of Justice Black,

> [w]e repeat and again reaffirm that neither a State nor the Federal Government can constitutionally force a person "to profess a belief or disbelief in any religion." Neither can constitutionally pass laws or impose requirements which aid all religions as against non-believers, and neither can aid those religions based on a belief in the existence of God as against these religions based on different beliefs..[685]

The last sentence of the passage expressly disapproved of Locke's position that atheists do not deserve tolerance. It comports well with the Jeffersonian view that there must be separation of church and state so that religious matters are left to the dictates of individual reason and conscience, and that if this leads to a belief that there is no God, the value of oaths will not necessarily be diminished but will derive its force from practical rather than theological sources. The word "profess" means not only to affirm through speech but to "practice as one's profession" and "to accept into a religious order."[686] Every prosecution and threat to prosecute for indecent exposure forces the citizen at whom it is aimed to practice as his or her profession a Christian conception of the body as temptation and distraction, an ally of the Prince of Darkness. Notably, Islam, another of the world's dominant religions, even more rigorously prescribes covering bodies in public, especially for women. Both religions advocate modest dress.[687] Women in many countries report being harassed for wearing clothing that is too modest or too secular.[688] More than sixty countries have government regulations regarding head coverings for women.[689] Christianity and Islam do not agree on the style and degree of concealment of bodies in public.

The Supreme Court has long held the view that the Constitution does not require it to enforce a "religion of secularism." The Court expressly disavowed such an intention when it banned the reading of the Bible for theological purposes in public schools in the case of *Abington School District v. Schempp* (1963).[690] The Constitution requires that the government maintain a position of neutrality regarding theological matters.[691] The *Abington* opinion cast doubt on the continued viability of Justice Douglas's opinion in *Zorach v. Clausen* (1952) upholding the constitutionality of release time from public schools for religious instruction. To justify the decision in *Zorach*, Douglas quoted the nineteenth-century *Church of Holy Trinity* (1892)[692] opinion that "[w]e are a religious people whose institutions presuppose a Supreme Being." To "guarantee the freedom to worship as one chooses," the government must accommodate "the public service to their spiritual needs;" otherwise, in his opinion, the government "would be preferring those who believe in no religion to those who do."[693] Quixotically, he had stated in a previous paragraph that so far as free exercise and establishment were concerned, separation must be complete and "unequivocal." He then immediately equivocated and wrote that "common sense" implied that the separation is not so complete in "every and all respects." Among the examples of the impossibility of complete separation, he mentioned Thanksgiving Day as a national holiday (without realizing that both Madison and Jefferson had steadfastly refused repeated efforts by the clergy to achieve that declaration);[694] the provision of fire protection (which is easily justifiable under Locke's principle of protection of person and property owed to all citizens and groups of citizens); and mention of God in certain government mottos (hardly a necessity).

Although references to God in government mottos have not been expunged, the Supreme Court in the early sixties refused to enlarge the permissible role of religion in government speech by declaring unconstitutional the composition of a nondenominational prayer to be read each day in public schools, although students would not be required to recite. The case was *Engel v. Vitale* (1962).[695] Justice Black's majority opinion explained the theory of the framers that union of church and state destroys government and degrades religion, and that religion loses respect if it must rely on special favors from the government to survive. People truly find God only through faith and reason, not fear of the police. The latter begets only hypocrisy, persecution, and hatred of both religion and government (with this, Black was parroting Jefferson's notes on Locke).

A government that is truly neutral regarding religion would not facilitate religion. It would studiously ignore it, treating all individuals and organizations alike regardless of theological orientation. Ignoring the theological dimension does not demonstrate hostility toward religion or a preference for atheism; it demonstrates indifference, which is precisely what well-informed judicial interpretations of the language and spirit of the Constitution require.

Religious instruction would not disappear without release time; it would simply be rescheduled for after school hours and on weekends. Even if one were to accept Douglas's predilection for facilitation of religion as a reasonable interpretation of the First Amendment, the allowance for release time is distinguishable from punishment of indecent exposure. The distinction is between facilitation and compulsion. Although one could argue that the First Amendment was not intended to prohibit nonsectarian aid to religion, no one could seriously claim that it allows compulsion of citizens to accept any particular creed. Douglas admonished that the government "may not thrust any sect on any person."[696]

Harris v. McRae (1980)[697] is a head scratcher. The Court found that the Hyde Amendment, an amendment to the Medicaid Act that denied funding for medically necessary abortions, did not violate the Establishment Clause. Citing *McGowan v. Maryland* (1961) (Sunday closing laws), the Court noted that the fact that the funding restrictions coincided with Catholic religious doctrine was not enough. The Court concluded that the Hyde Amendment was "as much a reflection of 'traditionalist' values towards abortion, as it is an embodiment of the views of any particular religion."[698] It did not dig any further into the history of the "tradition" to determine whether it was rooted in religion. As has been shown, indecent exposure's relation with religion is more than mere coincidence, leaving the relevance of this precedent in limbo for lack of a coincidental legitimate secular state interest.

Excessive Government Entanglement with Religion

The Supreme Court's holding in *Zorach* (1952) forces the government to judge the truth of religious belief. The very concept of release time for religious instruction necessitates a determination of what is "religious" instruction. In practice, the privilege of release time was limited to students affiliated with traditional, institutionalized religions. This preference for traditional, primarily Christian, religion is an insidious violation of government neutrality regarding religion. Making an exception from secular routines for religion involves the government in defining religion, with inevitable judgments about religious truth being made by public officials.

This entanglement of secular and sacred authority in *Zorach* (1952) led to religious lobbies in Congress and religious determinations by civil authorities, actions contrary to the concept of separation of church and state. The First Amendment contemplates

> a state without religion, and a Church without politics—that is to say, . . . one should never be used as an engine for any purpose of the other . . . . Our [founding] fathers seem to have been perfectly sincere in their belief that the members of the Church would be more patriotic, and the citizens of the State more religious, by keeping their respective functions separate. For that reason they built up a wall of complete separation and perfect partition between the two.[699]

Despite the *Abington* (1963) and *Vitale* (1962) opinions, Chief Justice Burger stoked the coals of *Zorach* (1952) in *Lemon* (1971) by saying,

> Our prior holdings do not call for total separation between church and state; total separation is not possible in an absolute sense. Some relationship between government and religious organizations is inevitable. According to Black, judicial caveats against entanglements must recognize that the line of separation, far from being a "wall," is a blurred, indistinct, and variable barrier depending on all circumstances of a particular relationship.[700]

Although relationships between religious organizations and government are inevitable, this does not justify preferential relationships between a particular class of religious organizations and the government. The government cannot constitutionally afford special privileges and protections to such organizations or their constituents. The necessity for fire safety inspections and building and zoning regulation of property owned by religious groups does not blur the wall of separation of church and state, as Chief Justice Burger seemed to believe. All organizations, regardless of their purpose, are subject to these regulations. The wall of separation is maintained by government neutrality; that is, by treating all religious organizations and belief structures alike without reference to their dogma or creed.

Enforcement of indecent exposure laws puts the imprimatur of government on a particular religious practice. American law prescribes the Christian ascetic view of proper public appearance as the exclusive public demeanor. It establishes this religious doctrine as a rule of civil society and implicitly denies the truth of contrary views, religious or otherwise, that the body is not dangerous or dead flesh but a temple of God, or of Woman or Man, an object of beauty and a subject of love, not a source of disgust and damnation. Hearken back to the poetic verses of Donne and Whitman. Indecent exposure laws are, in effect, laws respecting an establishment of religious doctrine, forcing everyone into outward conformity to an ascetic ideal regardless of the dictates of conscience. The entanglement of religion and government around the cardinal principle of repression of the body is so thorough that it takes an extraordinary effort to even recognize the issue, never mind bring it to a resolution.

Inhibit the Free Exercise of Religion

Display of the naked human body, without more, poses no threat to the person or property of others. It may offend, annoy, or alarm some Americans. It is also true that enforced covering of most of the body, particularly that of women, offends many Americans. These differences in custom have clear religious antecedents. Enforced covering of the body denies individuals the right to self-determination according to their religious inclinations.

The Court has developed an expansive view of the definition of religion worthy of protection in First Amendment cases that assists in analyzing free-exercise claims. The primary source of the Supreme Court's definition of religion in these cases is *United States v. Seeger* (1965) and its progeny. The issue in *Seeger* concerned the applicability of a statutory exemption from military combat service for conscientious objection to war based on "religious training and belief" of men not associated with any orthodox religious sect. Justice Clark delivered the opinion of a unanimous Court,[701] an opinion that deserves extended discussion. Although ostensibly a case of statutory interpretation, commentators and courts generally agree that *Seeger* (1965) laid down an important constitutional principle regarding the Religion Clauses.[702]

The earliest statutory version of the conscientious-objector exemption excused only members of established religions whose articles of faith forbade participation in war. A later military conscription statute excused conscientious objectors who were affiliated with a "well-recognized religious sect or organization." A constitutional challenge to this exemption based on First Amendment guarantees of religious liberty was peremptorily rejected as preposterous. The unanimous Court felt that the "unsoundness" of the challenge was "too apparent" to require discussion.[703] The statute was later broadened to include those whose objections were based on "religious training and belief." "Religious training and belief" was statutorily defined as "an individual's belief in a relation to a Supreme Being involving duties superior to those arising from any human relation, but [not including] essentially political, sociological, or philosophical views or a merely personal moral code."[704]

The "narrow" question the *Seeger* (1965) opinion purported to address was whether the term "Supreme Being" in the exemption was limited to "the orthodox god or the broader concept of a power or being, or a faith, 'to which all else is subordinate or upon which all else is ultimately dependent.'"[705] To answer that narrow inquiry, Justice Clark cited a variety of civil authorities and then proceeded to quote from Christian theologian Paul Tillich, the bishop of Woolwich; John A.T. Robinson, the Schema of the Ecumenical Council; and a leader in the Ethical Culture Movement—all the while oblivious to the intertwining threads of secular and religious authority in his analysis. Seeger won his exemption after passing the "threshold question of sincerity" and a determination that his belief was not "merely personal." The evidence in his favor:

> He was a product of a devout Roman Catholic home; he was a close student of Quaker beliefs from which he said "much of (his) thought is derived;" he approved of their opposition to war in any form; he devoted his spare hours to the American Friends Service Committee. . . .[706]

He did not disavow any belief in a "Supreme Being." The court set out the following test for exemption: "A sincere and meaningful belief which occupies in the life of its possessor a place parallel to that filled by the God of those admittedly qualifying for the exemption comes within the statutory definition."[707]

Five years later, a man named Welsh brought his case to the Supreme

Court,[708] claiming that denial of conscientious-objector status for his "deep conscientious scruples" against war either violated the Establishment Clause or was the result of too narrow a view of the test propounded in *Seeger* (1965). Justices Black, Douglas, Brennan, and Marshall decided for Welsh on the basis that the Court in *Seeger* (1965) "made it clear that . . . sincere and meaningful beliefs that prompt the registrant's objecttion to all wars need not be confined in either source or content to traditional or parochial concepts of religion."[709] Welsh had stricken the words "my religious training and" from his application for conscientious-objector status and also had written that he could not definitely affirm or deny that he believed in a "Supreme Being." He characterized his beliefs as the products of "reading in the fields of history and sociology."[710] The Justices were not deterred by Welsh's explicit disavowal of a religious basis for his beliefs.

The Court boldly declared it would be arbiter of the secular-theological distinction for Welsh, noting that "accordingly a registrant's statement that his beliefs are nonreligious is a highly unreliable guide for those charged with administering the exemption."[711] An astonishing assertion: the Court claimed to know the conscience of a man better than the man himself did. This was a blatant transgression of the principle that civil authorities are not competent judges in matters of conscience. Can it be true that the Supreme Court has supreme competence in such matters? The Court's benevolent intent was unnecessary, for it could have reached the same result while staying within its recognized competence as guardian of constitutional values, as described below.

The Justices chose the tortuous path of nullification of the unconstitutional provision by interposing a grossly distorted interpretation of the language rather than face the problem squarely. Justice Harlan, who had reluctantly gone along with the majority in *Seeger* (1965), stepped back from the plurality's journey into the absurd in *Welsh* (1970) to declare the theistic exemption that Congress obviously intended was a violation of the Establishment Clause of the First Amendment. Justice Harlan ably pointed out that "Congress, of course, could, entirely consistently with the requirements of the Constitution, eliminate all exemptions for conscientious objectors. Such a course would be wholly 'neutral' and, in my view, would not offend the Free Exercise Clause . . . ."[712]

In his opinion, a law that has a sufficiently strong secular purpose is not unconstitutional because it may incidentally interfere with religious beliefs. The state need not create an exception for persons with contrary religious beliefs from a law enacted for a legitimate secular purpose. But, if the government creates an exemption, "it cannot draw the line between theistic and nontheistic religious beliefs on the one hand and secular beliefs on the other. Any such distinctions are not . . . compatible with the establishment clause of the First Amendment."[713]

As Justice Harlan had commented in an earlier case, "[n]eutrality and voluntarism stand as barriers against the most egregious and hence divisive kinds of state involvement in religious matters."[714]

One year later, with Justice Harlan no longer on the bench, in the case of *Wisconsin v. Yoder* (1971), the Supreme Court, led by Chief Justice Burger, ignored Harlan's admonition that the First Amendment requires government neutrality regarding theological concerns as it sustained an objection by Amish families to compulsory school attendance laws. The Amish parents had refused to permit their children to continue in public schools beyond the eighth grade because the values taught in public schools

> are in marked variance with Amish values and Amish way of life; they view secondary school education as an impermissible exposure of their children to a "worldly" influence in conflict with their beliefs. The high school tends to emphasize intellectual and scientific accomplishments, self-distinction, competitiveness, worldly success, and social life with other students. Amish society emphasizes informal learning through doing; a life of "goodness" rather than a life of intellect; wisdom rather than technical knowledge, community welfare, rather than competition; and separation from, rather than integration with, contemporary worldly society.[715]

Principles of Amish society were allowed to override the state interest in promoting education because they were grounded in theological doctrine.

The Court was careful to limit its holding, noting that a "way of life, however virtuous and admirable, may not be interposed as a barrier to reasonable state regulation of education if it is based on purely secular considerations. . . ."[716] But by what standards are "religious beliefs" to be distinguished from "secular considerations?" First, the Court admitted that it is "a most delicate question," one which called in question the "very concept of ordered liberty." Among the relevant factors identified by the Court were the organized structure of the Amish and their strictly enforced social code, static lifestyle, and belief in the absolute truth of the Epistle of Paul to the Romans. (What a coincidence and telling paradox to find the Apostle Paul held up as a source of religious liberty, stagnation, control, and organization—are these the proper criteria of religious liberty?) The Court went further and pointed to "Thoreau's choice[, which] was philosophical and personal rather than religious." Such a "belief does not rise to the demands of the Religion Clauses."[717] What of the concept of liberty of conscience? Can one find God only through affiliation with a traditional form of worship? Have faith and reason, the means suggested by Jefferson, been purged and replaced by a modern institutional ideal? And what of human fallibility of the civil magistrate? The judges in *Yoder* (1972) set themselves above this admonition. The Religion Clauses establish a preference for reposing errors concerning religious belief in the individual, not the government. As the framers cautioned, when the government errs in determining true religion, there is tyranny; when the individual errs, only his soul suffers and no one else is worse for his misjudgment. The *Yoder* court fell back on institutional criteria precisely because the relation of men and women to the supernatural is unfathomable and indefinable. Any limiting definition is necessarily reactionary.

A pattern of abuse of religious liberty emerged in the lower federal courts because of the Supreme Court's meddling in theological definitions in *Seeger* (1965), *Welsh* (1970), and *Yoder* (1972). The Fifth Circuit and the Southern District of Florida later defined religious belief worthy of constitutional protection as belief that had an "institutional quality about it"[718] or "is shared by an organized group."[719] These judicial decisions sanctioned usurpation of individual conscience by herd consciousness.

The natural tendency of the institutional criterion is to reinforce existing faiths. This means, in effect, the defense of Christianity and its progeny. The power to define is the power to control. The disparate criteria of *Yoder* (1972) on the one hand and the unhinged views of *Seeger* (1965) and *Welsh* (1970) on the other provided means to expand or contract the definition of religion according to the predilections of judges. Witness Judge Ainsworth of the Fifth Circuit, in *Theriault v. Carlson* (1974), who would exclude from constitutional protection "so-called religions which tend to mock established institutions and are obviously shams and absurdities and whose members are patently devoid of religious sincerity."[720]

Without judicial pontiffs like Judge Ainsworth to protect true religion against "obvious shams and absurdities," when "forbearance toward religious objection is combined with the new permissiveness in defining religion dissidents of all kinds—nudists, LSD users, racists, utopians, and groups as yet imagined—can be expected to present claims for religious freedom."[721] Such challenges indeed have been made, with mixed results.

In the racists' claim, the Fifth Circuit in *Brown v. Dade Christian Schools, Inc.* (1977) denied constitutional protection to an allegedly religious policy of exclusive, white, private school admissions because the basis of the policy was determined to be social or political rather than religious.[722] In *United States v. Kuch* (1968), an LSD user's claim was judged "false" by the District Court for the District of Columbia.[723] Marijuana use for allegedly religious reasons was denied constitutional protection in *United States v. Kuch* (1968), despite resort to the famous decision by the California Supreme Court in the case of *People v. Woody* (1964)[724] that exempted use of peyote by members of the Native American Church from prosecution. The decision in *Woody* was later administratively approved on the federal level when the Commissioner of Food and Drugs inserted a special exemption to the same effect in analogous federal statutes.[725] The main distinctions between these contrary decisions appear to have been a longer period of establishment of the Native American Church and the "irreverence" of the LSD-using Neo-American church, whose motto was "Victory Over Horseshit." The court found this latter factor "helpful in declining to rule that the Church is a religion within the meaning of the First Amendment."[726]

As an alternative basis for denying the LSD and marijuana users' claims of religious liberty, the district court purported to apply the balancing test of *Sherbert v. Verner* (1963),[727] in which the Supreme Court held unconstitutional, as applied, a state statute under which a Seventh Day Adventist was denied unemployment compensation because of her refusal to work on Saturday contrary to her religious beliefs. In the opinion of the court, the state had not shown that the incidental impact on her free exercise of religion was justified by a "compelling state interest in the regulation of a subject within the State's constitutional power to regulate."[728]

The Court noted that legitimate regulation of religious conduct was invariably due to "some substantial threat to public safety, peace or order."[729] LSD and marijuana use for religious reasons apparently were not sanctioned because the court determined that such use posed health hazards, promoted non-drug crimes, and precipitated antisocial behavior and psychotic episodes. The legitimate state concern about these consequences outweighed the defendant's right, if any, of free exercise.

In denying these practices outright, the Court chose not to assess application of time, place, and manner restrictions as suggested in *Jones v. Opelika* (1942).[730] Such restrictions would be preferable to outright prohibition of activities involving religion when those restrictions are sufficient to accomplish the legitimate state aims. The Court found no substance in the defendant's claims in any event, so there was no right to be protected by application of less drastic measures.

The Supreme Court revisited use of peyote in religious ceremonies in *Employment Division v. Smith* (1990), finding that Oregon's prohibition of peyote use in religious ceremonies did not violate the Free Exercise Clause.[731] The Court applied the least stringent rational-basis review in finding that the law was a neutral law of general applicability and not aimed at promoting or restricting any particular religious belief.[732] Congress disagreed with the choice of standard for review and enacted the Religious Freedom Restoration Act of 1993 (RFRA)[733] by a nearly unanimous vote of both houses of Congress.[734]

The RFRA requires application of strict scrutiny to any law that burdens religious freedom and provides that such laws can be justified only if they impose the least restrictive means of pursuing a compelling state interest. The law reinstated the *Sherbert* (1963) and *Yoder* (1972) tests for conducting such analyses.[735] The Supreme Court declared application of the RFRA to states unconstitutional in *City of Boerne v. Flores* (1997).[736] Since then, twenty-one states have passed laws mirroring the RFRA for state and municipal governments.[737]

The claims of those who do not accept the nakedness prohibition should not be disposed of as were the defenses of the racists, LSD users, and marijuana users without even scrutinizing the questionable reasoning and findings of "fact" in those cases. Nakedness does not involve significant threats to health, welfare, property, or person such as those posed by illegal drugs. The broad definition of religious belief in *Welsh* (1970), including all beliefs that "stem from . . . moral, ethical, or religious beliefs about what is right and wrong . . . that . . . [are] held with the strength of traditional religious convictions," would encompass the attitudes of many or most of those who deny the validity of the pervasive clothes prescription.[738] On the other hand, even the narrow definition of *Yoder* (1972) arguably encompasses affiliates or followers of the tenets of social nudism and members of the Garden of Eden Church[739] founded by Christian naturists in 2010.

Lee v. Weisman (1992) provides another argument supporting a claim of violation of the Establishment Clause.[740] This case pioneered use of the "coercion test" in evaluating school prayer. In *Lee,* the Court addressed the question of whether a nonsectarian prayer given by a member of the clergy at a middle school graduation ceremony violated the Establishment

Clause. The district court had applied the *Lemon* (1971) test and concluded that the prayer session violated the clause. The Supreme Court agreed with the decision but chose not to apply the *Lemon* (1971) formula. Rather, it simply noted that coercion of participation in a religious experience, even indirectly, is a violation. So, if the requirement of wearing clothes in public is merely Christian orthodoxy, indecent exposure laws coerce non-believers to embrace its dogma. As a case in point, consider the plight of social nudists.

Social nudism has ancient roots.[741] It is an organized worldwide movement with hundreds of thousands of members.[742] Its modern beginnings were around the turn of the twentieth century in Germany. Nudist societies formed in most European nations, Canada, and the United States.[743] Many societies published documents explaining the basic tenets and aims of social nudism. The Credo of the American League for Physical Culture is representative:

> Our goal is the healthy mind and the healthy body. Sun, light, and air are vital conditions of human well-being. We believe that these elements are insufficiently used in present day life, to the detriment of physical and moral health. For the purpose of health and recreation and for the condition of man to his world we offer a new social practice, based on the known wholesome value of exposure to these elements and in the spirit of naturalness, cheerfulness, and cleanness of body and mind that they symbolize. We aim to make the fullest possible use of sun, light, and air by a program of exercise and life in the open in such a way as will result in the maximum physical and mental benefit.
>
> We believe in the essential wholesomeness of the human body and all its functions. We therefore regard the body neither as an object of shame nor as a subject for levity or erotic exploitation. Any attitude or behavior inconsistent with this view is contrary to the whole spirit of the society and has no place among us.
>
> The practice of our physical culture tends toward simplicity and integrity in all ways.
>
> We counsel for our members the sane and hygienic life. We reserve the right to impose abstinence from stimulants and intoxicants at our meetings and on our grounds.[744]

Yoder (1971) presented three criteria for constitutional protection: (1) the practice must not be merely a matter of personal preference, but one of deep religious convictions, and it must be (2) shared by an organized group and (3) intimately related to daily living.[745] The first criterion is more a restatement of the issue than a clue to its resolution. One way to put flesh on it is to treat it as a summary of the tests set forth in *Torcaso* (1961), *Seeger* (1965), and *Welsh* (1970). The core principles of the American League for Physical Culture include concern for moral health, the relationship of people to their world, cleanness of body and mind, wholesomeness, and "simplicity and integrity in all ways," principles in some ways strikingly like those espoused by the Amish, although the two groups pursue these aims through different means. Public nakedness is not only intimately related to daily life but also the very crux of the nudist credo.

The institutional character of social nudism is beyond question. The movement has withstood the test of time and political and legal opposition. Its adherents were forced by law to retreat to secluded "nudist camps" usually far removed from the rest of society and often surrounded by high walls and fences..[746] Membership in these camps is often subject to various restrictions regarding age, sex, and marital status. There are operating rules governing acceptable behaviors that are usually more specific and restrictive than those of open society.

Nudists do not share the Christian ascetic view of the flesh that made the ubiquitous covering of the body a rule of law. Because of their beliefs, they were forced into these enclaves without secular justification. The state interests at risk were classic public nuisance and prevention of evil example. No one would suggest that the nudists presented a "threat to public safety, peace or order." No harm to person or property or disruptions to commerce or other material consequences from their practices have been alleged. No secular purpose has been required or articulated.

Nudists work earnestly to divorce nudity from sexuality..[747] Some authorities would say they have a religious conviction about this. A "Declaration of Body Independence" in Emily Coleman and Betty Edward's book *Body Liberation* (1977).[748] espoused the religious nature of the nakedness prohibition, the feelings that oppose it, and the theocratic tyranny that flows from it. Here is their statement, in full:

> When in the course of human events, it becomes necessary for a people to dissolve the customs, laws, and beliefs that have kept them from being connected with their bodies and to assert their right to liberate their bodies in the manner which the laws of nature and nature's God have intended, a decent respect to the opinions of mankind requires that they should declare these causes which impel them to the separation.
>
> We hold these truths to be self-evident—that all bodies are created equal, not equal in looks and inherent abilities, but equally

worthwhile in the eyes of God, the law, and other men; that our bodies are endowed by our Creator with certain unalienable rights, that among these are the rights of our bodies to sufficient physical, emotional, and intellectual nourishment to develop to their full potential; the right of our bodies to discover and follow their own destiny without being told by any other body—be it the state, a corporation, or a mate when to work, play, make love, or die; and the right of our bodies to experience pleasure.

We also believe that when any customs, laws, or beliefs, instituted among men, become destructive of these body rights it is the obligation of the people to alter or abolish them. Such customs, laws, and beliefs, long established, shall not be cast off lightly but when they seem about to create an absolute despotism, it is our right, it is our duty, to get rid of them. The history of the body abuses to which we have been subjected for centuries is a history of repeated injuries and usurpations all having as their object the establishment of an absolute tyranny over our bodies. To prove this, let facts be submitted to a candid world.

Body tyrants have divided us by letting us believe that the color of some bodies is superior to the color of other bodies and that young bodies are superior to old bodies.

Body tyrants have blinded us to the awesome beauty of the human body by making us afraid to look at and proudly acknowledge our entire naked bodies.

Body tyrants have starved us for comforting and loving human touch by limiting the number of others we are allowed to touch and be cruelly rationing the occasions on which we may touch.

Body tyrants have robbed us of our full and joyous humanity by tricking us into believing our bodies are like machines and that, like machines, they are only valuable for what they can do.

Body tyrants have cheated us of the opportunity to explore the untapped potential of our bodies by teaching us our bodies aren't worth studying.

Body tyrants have imprisoned our tears and anger and grief within our bodies by telling us that some emotions are not acceptable.

Body tyrants have deafened us so that we can no longer listen to the wisdom of our own bodies—eat now, defecate now, create now, play now, make love now, die now.

We, therefore, solemnly publish and declare that our bodies are, and ought to be, free and independent entities and that all connections with the body tyrants of the past are, and ought to be, totally dissolved. As free and independent bodies we each have the full power and right—but not the obligation—to seek body liberation.

> And to make the principles stated in this declaration a reality, we do mutually pledge to each other all of the aid and support we can give for this purpose.[749]

This is a much more eloquent and powerful statement of belief than that expressed in *Seeger* (1965) or *Welsh* (1970). If the only purpose of indecent exposure laws is to punish nonconformance to community standards that are nothing more than Christian moral principles, then such laws are laws respecting an establishment of religion and are forbidden by the First Amendment to the Constitution.

The companion protection against interference with free exercise may be more difficult to comprehend. How is the decision to go naked in public an exercise of religious freedom? Religious establishments are generally fairly easy to recognize. They usually have names, organizational structures, memberships, literature, and other concrete evidence of their existence. What is definable is the "establishments" of religious establishments; that is, their institutional qualities. Religion, and particularly individual religious sentiment, traditionally has been defined in the Western world as the relationship of the individual to God. However, over time, the concept has expanded to include Supreme Beings known by other names and, finally, to encompass a person's conception of his or her place in the universe.

The Supreme Court has attempted to meet the constitutional requirement of protection of the free exercise of religion by expanding definitions, but without a God or Supreme Being to focus on, there seems to be little left to the definitional task that does not lead inexorably to a form of "state-authorized orthodoxy."[750] Social nudism has all the qualities of religion, including a conception of adherents' place in the universe. They have a well-defined nonconformist moral code and a long history and civilized manner of social discourse, except for the lack of clothing.

The Court's tortured logic is naturally devolving to recognition that religious belief is indefinable through the paradoxical practice of expanding its definition to the same effect. Justice Jackson, in *West Virginia State Board of Education v. Barnette* (1943),[751] suggested a better line of inquiry in establishment and free-exercise cases. Jehovah's Witnesses had challenged a school requirement that pupils salute the flag. Their refusal to salute was no doubt offensive. This "non-action" was deemed a protected right under the First Amendment.

Justice Jackson offered noteworthy observations regarding semiotics:

> [T]here is no doubt that, in connection with the pledges, the flag salute is a form of utterance. Symbolism is a primitive but effective way of communicating ideas. The use of an emblem or flag to symbolize some system, idea, institution, or personality, is a short cut from mind to mind. Causes and nations, political parties, lodges, and ecclesiastical groups seek to knit the loyalty of their followings to a flag or banner, a color or design. The State announces rank, function, and authority through crowns and maces, uniforms, and black robes; the church speaks through the Cross, the Crucifix, the altar and shrine, and clerical raiment. Symbols of State often convey political ideas just as religious symbols come to convey theological ones. Associated with many of these symbols are appropriate gestures of acceptance or respect: a salute, a bowed or bared head, a bended knee. A person gets from a symbol the meaning he puts into it, and what is one man's comfort and inspiration is another's jest and scorn.[752]

This court grasped the importance of symbols in power relations, noting that even non-action can be expressive, and that clothing is a common medium of expression of authority. The prescribed salutes violated the children's fundamental beliefs, and national unity was not a sufficient state interest to overcome those beliefs even while the nation was at war with the Nazis.

The opinion addressed First Amendment rights without specifying or elaborating on free exercise or free speech. In striking down the requirement, Justice Jackson broadened the issue from freedom of religion to general freedom from unnecessary state compulsion:

> [The issue does not] turn on one's possession of particular religious views or the sincerity which they are held. While religion supplies appellees' motive of enduring the discomforts of making the issue in this case, many citizens who do not share these religious views hold such a compulsory rite to infringe Constitutional liberty of the individual. It is not necessary to inquire whether non-conformist beliefs will exempt from the duty to salute unless we first find the power to make the salute a legal duty.[753]
>
> . . .
>
> One's right to life, liberty, and property, to free speech, a free press, freedom of worship and assembly, and other fundamental rights may not be submitted to a vote, they depend on the outcome of no elections.[754]
>
> . . .

> [These rights] are susceptible of restriction only to prevent grave and immediate danger to interests which the State may lawfully protect . . . .[755]

Justice Jackson here expressed a historically grounded view of religious rights, reflecting what is known of the intent of the framers, ratifiers, and general public view at the time of drafting of the Constitution regarding the general concept of limited government. Modern trends in constitutional interpretation are turning in this direction, yet justices still find it hard to resist defining religion and parsing out rights already belonging to individuals. As this migration to original principles continues, precedent indicates that a sincere belief anywhere along the spectrum of conscience may prove adequate. Conscientious belief, liberty, privacy—whatever rubric one chooses, these freedoms should be encroached upon only when justified by reasonable measures used to secure legitimate state aims. The only legitimate state aims are those proposed by Locke: protection of life and property. The Court should follow either Locke's reason or his religion and either eschew guardianship of America as a Christian nation or openly affirm it.

The history of indecent exposure laws illuminates a two-hundred-fifty-year-long secularization of the rhetoric of moral authority. This leads to a split in the road at some point: affirm America is a Christian nation or develop a moral jurisprudence based on another source of moral authority. There is substantial evidence that the framers and ratifiers of the Constitution, and the general population at the time, understood the country to be a Christian nation. America could embrace this identity and still accommodate alternative philosophies through charitable ideals. It would probably require a constitutional amendment. Such an amendment is very unlikely to pass. If it did, it would likely lead to continuing social unrest. Alternative models will be discussed in the final chapter after an assessment of other potential constitutional claims relating to indecent exposure laws.

The claims discussed in this chapter based on the Establishment and Free Exercise Clauses are novel, yet they go to the heart of the prohibition of public nakedness. There is something mysterious, metaphysical, and profound about the controls that these laws impose. Sure, it is easy to understand the need to prohibit incipient sexual advances against unwilling audiences, but what is so threatening about allowing a choice of simple public nakedness? The lack of honest comprehensive history, the selection of anecdotes motivated by desired outcomes, and the conscious and unconscious denial of the interests that are protected by the laws impede the progress of jurisprudence.

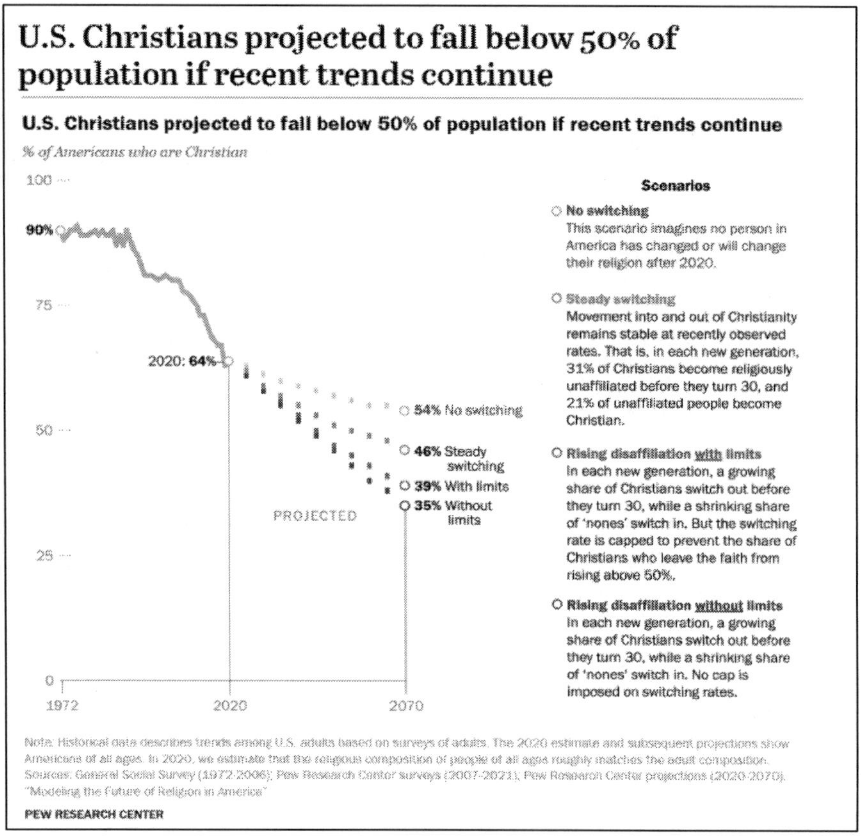

Figure 2: Pew Research on Religious Affiliation.[1]

The percentage of Americans identifying as Christians has declined materially since inception of the nation. As stated earlier, it has been estimated that eighty to ninety percent of colonists were Christian.[756] The last two decades witnessed a precipitous decline of Christian affiliation.

America may now be the most religiously diverse country in history.[757] This gives rise to unprecedented moral challenges. The percentage of Christians among the population has fallen to around sixty-three to seventy percent. There have been large increases in "nones"—those identified as religiously unaffiliated or of no religion in population surveys.

Notable correlated or coincident social changes have been observed, including political polarization, moral relativism, individualism, and secularization. The decline of Christianity's role in America's moral order is expected to continue, with "nones" approaching a majority of the population by 2070, leaving the country that has been guided by Christian theology in moral matters rudderless and fragmented regarding legal enforcement of moral truth. A new and convincing rationale or as-yet-unidentified process of accommodation of moral diversity is needed.

Broad-ranging evidence in law, society, technology, and demographics indicates that the trend toward a polytheistic/secular gestalt will continue to eat away at the Christian roots of these laws. The most problematic aspects of the new religious movements are the internet and AI, which add to the complexity. They will present novel challenges as sources of moral truth. The new "religion" they represent lacks consensus, fostering fragmentation, divisiveness, and extremism. They do not support the ideals of "good order" contemplated in the Constitution. The substantial decline of Christian moral authority fosters uncertainty about sources of ultimate truth in moral matters, creating ambiguity with broad-ranging negative implications.

The Constitution has an uneasy peace with religion. America's current moral crisis is exacerbated by failure to recognize and acknowledge or abandon the prevalence of Christian moral principles,[758] expressly accommodate different religions with which some of its moral principles may not be compatible, or defend legacy Christian moral authority to the growing share of religiously unaffiliated. American democracy is struggling to establish a new source of moral authority to support its constitutional ideals.[759] Most U.S. adults believe that America was founded as a Christian nation and that it remains one today.[760] Explicit recognition of Christianity as the source of moral truth over other religions would tend to alienate believers in other religions and ring hollow with non-affiliates. Retrenchment as a means of mitigation seems unlikely given population trends, technological change, and conflicting views about the Establishment Clause. Where, then, is this truth to be found?

Karl Marx theorized that religion is an invention of the elite for control of the masses. For the regime to be effective, it must be credible and coherent. America's indecent exposure laws enforce Christian moral principles in criminalization of public nakedness without credible secular justification. Prohibition of public nakedness is consistent with other well-established religions, including Judaism and Islam.

> Abrahamic religions . . . recount the legend of the Garden of Eden, found in the Hebrew Bible, in which Adam and Eve are unaware of their nakedness until they eat the forbidden fruit of the Tree of Knowledge of Good and Evil. After this, they feel ashamed and try to cover themselves with fig leaves. Genesis 3:74. Each of these religions has its own unique understanding of what is meant to be taught with the recounting of the story of Adam and Eve..[761]

Their common ground is covering private areas in public. The extent of the coverage varies. The controlling myths of each religion proscribe exposure of various "private parts" in public. This divine knowledge is unchallenged by adherents. Thus, religion alone is likely to keep most people clothed in public. There are also many obvious benefits to clothing.

Shame is presumed or imposed in indecent exposure. Display of the private areas of the body is banished from public view except when channeled for artistic or commercial purposes or presented abstractly via media. Protected displays are often unnatural, characterized by lewd and lascivious intent, and presented in commercial contexts. The natural self is invisible, proscribed by law.

There are signs that even Christians are softening their views on indolence of the body. Catholics represent about twenty percent of the U.S. population. In 1981, the leader of the Catholic Church, Pope John Paul II, recommended a more sensitive view regarding nakedness in *Love and Responsibility*:

> The human body can remain nude and uncovered and preserve intact its splendour and its beauty . . . . Nakedness as such is not to be equated with physical shamelessness. . . . Immodesty is present only when nakedness plays a negative role with regard to the value of the person . . . . The human body is not in itself shameful . . . . Shamelessness (just like shame and modesty) is a function of the interior of a person..[762]

American government purports to accommodate the views and practices of multiple religions worshipping different singular or multiple deities, as well as the increasing share of "nones," who may be agnostic, atheistic, or plain uncertain, despite obvious and irreconcilable differences. The waning of Christian moral dominance is leaving a gulf of chaos with no obvious replacement. This may be little more than effects of maturation of America's particular form of constitutional democracy.

Mindful of the folktale *The Emperor's New Clothes*, now that the foundation of *custos morum* has been laid bare, the stage is set for a better-informed discussion of potential new political and jurisprudential models. For the muted body to play a role, it must be allowed to speak. Constitutional concepts of free exercise and free speech are often aligned and synergistic, as was the case in *Commonwealth v. Kneeland* (1838),[763] discussed earlier. There, in a blasphemy case, the Court addressed both Establishment Clause and free-speech claims advanced by a newspaper that had questioned the existence of God. The court affirmed the conviction, concluding that the state and federal constitutional guarantees of freedom of the press provided a general right of publication but did not excuse any crimes committed by use of language therein and that the Religious Freedom Clauses were not intended to prevent punishing acts that disturb the peace. There was no evidence of any actual disturbance of the peace.[764] Although blasphemy laws were declared unconstitutional in *Joseph Burstyn v. Wilson* (1952),[765] several states still have such laws on the books. Pennsylvania's General Assembly enacted a blasphemy law in 1977. The district court declared it unconstitutional in *Kalman v. Cortes* (2010) as a violation of both the Establishment and Free Exercise Clauses of the First Amendment, citing *Lemon* (1971).[766]

Penkoski v. Bowser (2021)[767] in many ways represents the culmination of the trials and tribulations of *custos morum*'s efforts to define religion and its legal privileges. Penkoski tried to reignite the Christian-nation controversy in a petition for oral argument[768] while seeking an injunction against a Black Lives Matter mural in Washington, D.C. Their plea for an injunction was denied based on free-speech protection of the artwork and lack of standing to advance an Establishment Clause claim.

The plaintiff's alleged injuries of feeling excluded and like a second-class citizen based on the mural's message were deemed insufficient to confer standing. The court declined to follow the "offended observer" theory adopted by some circuits.[769] The lack of standing foreclosed consideration of the Establishment Clause and equal-protection claims.

The "offended observer" doctrine has been employed by many courts over many years to determine standing in Establishment Clause cases.[770] The Supreme Court's most recent commentary was in the concurrence and dissents to a denial of certiorari in *City of Ocala v. Rojas* (2023), where atheists had challenged a city-sponsored prayer vigil after a mass shooting.[771]

According to Justice Gorsuch, the doctrine arose in *Lemon v. Kurtzman* (1971). The *Lemon* test that forbade anything that a reasonable observer would perceive as government endorsement of religion implied that observers must have the right to sue. Courts began to recognize Article III standing for people who were offended by such activities. Gorsuch noted that *Lemon* had been discredited and establishment claims should be measured against the Constitution's original and historical meaning, not the hypothetical reasonable observer. He suggested that offended viewers should avert their eyes or pursue political solutions.

Although the offended-observer doctrine addresses standing in Establishment Clause cases, its rhetoric is difficult to square with modern indecent exposure laws. Whereas such laws have long been defended by theories of prevention of evil example and constructive breach of peace, many modern statutes define the offense by a finding that the exposure would or did offend, annoy, or alarm an unwilling person. This critical determinant of criminal behavior is inadequate to establish standing to sue. To establish standing, Article III requires a plaintiff to show three things: (1) an injury in fact (2) that is fairly traceable to the challenged conduct of the defendant and (3) that is likely to be redressed by the requested relief.[772]

Generalized grievances are not adequate to confer standing. The murals offended and annoyed Penkoski, making him feel like a second-class citizen. It was not relevant how serious or justified these feelings of alienation and indignation toward the perceived government misconduct might be. If these feelings do not amount to a case or controversy, how can they define a crime? True, there are different objectives for the rules. Standing promotes judicial efficiency and protects separation of powers. Nevertheless, if being annoyed is insufficient to gain access to court, should it be adequate to send someone to jail? In one case, direct governmental action implicating religion is involved. In the other case, the victim's right is premised on a governmental determination that exposure of private parts is criminal. Both enforce established religion.

The argument in the motion for oral argument in *Penkoski* did not see the light of day because of dismissal for failure to establish standing to make the case. The plaintiffs' argument is illuminating and provocative. Also known as Warriors for Christ, they argued that Black Lives Matter is "inseparably linked to the religion of secular humanism".[773] and characterized the LGBTQ community as a sister denomination. They described the core belief of secular humanism as "what is right for me is right for me and what is right for you is right for you and that is ok as long as it does not hurt anybody."[774] Plaintiffs further argued that "[c]ountless religious experts have acknowledged that "irreligion" is "religion" and that a "critic of religion" is "a new religion."[775] The plaintiffs sought to counter the new religions' threats to their core value, the nuclear family. They asked that the government remain neutral on matters of religion, including those movements they defined as religions. The plaintiffs cited *Lemon v. Kurtzman* (1971), arguing that the mayor's policy decision to erect the mural failed all three prongs of the *Lemon* test. The action violated the Establishment Clause because it had no valid secular purpose; it advanced, endorsed, or inhibited religion; and it fostered excessive entanglement with religion. As we know, the *Lemon* test has been discredited but not overruled, and the preferred measure going forward is the Constitution's original and historical meaning, which we have discussed extensively.

The Warriors' argument, tests for standing, and merits of the case are recursive, taking us back to John Locke, his influence on the Bill of Rights, and his ambivalence. Locke is often credited with developing the concept of secularism and the separation of church and state. Recall that his writings evidenced some apparent contradictions about government involvement in sexual morality and indolence of the body. He believed in God and so likely would not have fully embraced secular humanism. He wrote that "the taking away of God, though but even in thought, dissolves all."[776] This, and his support for punishment of immorality, reflected his viewpoint that belief in God is fundamental to morality and societal order.

Secular humanism, Enlightenment philosophy, and classical liberalism are closely related. They share a common ground of preference for reason and empiricism over faith in divine wisdom. Enlightenment thinking and Locke, in particular, influenced the framing of the Constitution and Bill of Rights. These philosophies are part of a gestalt in American politics and law motivating increased individual liberty and reduced accountability to divine authority. Following the path of history, from humanism in fourteenth- to seventeenth-century Europe to the Enlightenment in eighteenth-century Europe to classical liberalism in nineteenth- and twentieth-century Europe and the United States, America's liberal democracy is now faced with the challenge of creating a new consensus source of moral truth or more effective means of reconciliation and accommodation.

This case illustrates the difficulty of defining a legitimate state interest in prosecuting indecent exposure without attribution to, and support for, religious doctrine. If left only to the core principle of modern laws focusing on offending, annoying, or alarming an audience, what is the principled basis upon which a court as *custos morum* can choose a side in this case? The court in *Penkoski* chose none.[777] This case exemplifies the tremendous complexity facing doctrinal efforts to resolve America's moral dilemma regarding public display of bodies. These matters beg for more and better debate, yet the body remains legally muted and expressionless, leading to constitutional questions of freedom of speech.

7. Order, Unity, Peace, and Liberty: Freedom of Expression and the Court as *Custos Morum*

The traditional justifications for indecent exposure laws are prevention of evil example and public nuisance. Prevention of evil example runs directly counter to basic principles of freedom of speech. As for public nuisance, the general legal definition is an activity, condition, or thing that interferes with the general rights and safety of the public. It affects a community, neighborhood, or substantial number of people. Typical examples of public nuisances include excessive noise, pollution, obstructed public roads, and hazardous conditions that endanger public health or safety. The scope of public nuisance as mere annoyance or bad manners has narrowed due to changes in society, growth of social media, and progressive expansion of constitutional protection of personal rights, particularly freedom of speech. This constitutional protection has served as the basis for most challenges to laws suppressing and shaping public displays of naked bodies. Most First Amendment claims have involved the role of women's bodies in commerce, politics, and motherhood. Harnessing the penis remains a rigid rule of forbidden expression.

The First Amendment guarantees freedom of speech. Scholars have characterized free-speech doctrine as "maddeningly complex,".[778] employing "marginally (at best) useful three-and-four-part tests, and slippery and hard to apply categories,".[779] and constituting "one of the most complicated and confusing areas in constitutional law.".[780] Speech has been broadly construed to mean the communication of ideas through words or expressive conduct. The only recognized exceptions are incitement to immediate lawlessness, defamation, obscenity, and live naked bodies.

First Amendment protection of nude images not intended for sexual arousal was considered by the Court of Appeals for the District of Columbia in 1940 in *Parmelee v. United States*..[781] An importer of books challenged a seizure and destruction by customs, based on a finding of obscenity, of a book entitled *Nudism in Modern Life*. The court reversed the lower court's finding of obscenity. The court noted that the *Hicklin*

(1868) test addressing the tendency of obscene materials to deprave and corrupt had been repudiated and replaced by consideration of the work as whole and its effect on all those whom it is likely to reach. The court was cognizant of the varying meaning of moral concepts over time. It cited Judge Learned Hand in *United States v. Kennerly* (1913).[782] for the definition of obscenity as "the present critical point in the compromise between candor and shame at which the community may have arrived here and now."[783]

The wellspring of obscenity judicial doctrine is *Roth v. United States* (1957), in which the Supreme Court concluded that obscenity is not constitutionally protected speech or press.[784] The case involved a statute regulating distribution of books, photographs, and magazines. The Court noted that this was the first time the constitutionality of obscenity prohibitions under the First or Fourteenth Amendment had been "squarely presented" to the Court. The Court started by asserting that there was universal agreement around the world that obscenity should be restrained and concluded that, by definition, obscenity is "utterly without redeeming social importance." Thus, obscenity should not be entitled to any constitutional protection.[785]

The Court introduced a successor to the *Hicklin* (1868) test.[786] Recall that *Hicklin* defined material as obscene if it tended "to deprave or corrupt those whose minds are open to such immoral influences, and into whose hands a publication of this sort may fall." The Court in *Roth* (1957) focused its definition on sex, distinguishing obscenity from sex: obscenity deals with sex in a "prurient" manner. Despite sex being "one of the vital problems of human interest and public concern,"[787] prurient expressions of sex have no redeeming social importance, even though the "constitution embraces at the least the liberty to discuss publicly and truthfully all matters of public concern without previous restraint or fear of subsequent punishment."[788] The Court held that the state has a legitimate interest in protecting the sanctity of traditional ideas of sex from criticism embodied in prurient expressions. It did not identify whether the prurience was an attribute of the actor or the audience. As the court in *People v. Muller* (1884) noted, "[t]he presence of a woman of the purest character and of the most modest behavior and bearing may suggest to a prurient imagination images of lust, and excite impure desires, and so may a picture or statute not in fact indecent or obscene."[789]

The Court did not explain why "prurient expressions" have no social importance or are not a legitimate means of criticism, nor did it assert that such expressions present a serious danger to civil society. The footnote defining "prurient" contained several references.[790] It opened with a dictionary definition: "Itching; longing; uneasy with desire or longing; of persons, having itching, morbid, or lascivious longings; of desire, curiosity, or propensity, lewd . . . ." The Court went on to characterize "prurient interest" as "a shameful or morbid interest in nudity, sex, or excretion, and if it goes substantially beyond customary limits of candor in description or representation of such matters."

The *Roth* (1957) test to determine whether material is obscene is "whether, to the average person, applying contemporary community standards, the dominant theme of the material taken as a whole appeals to prurient interest."[791] "Lewd," "lascivious," and "prurient"[792] are roughly synonymous. Although indecent exposure laws do not always require a showing of such intent, when present, would there be no First Amendment protection because the prurient intent made the indecent exposure obscene? The statute challenged in the case forbade the mailing of "obscene, lewd, lascivious, indecent, filthy or vile" materials.[793] The Court rejected an argument that the terms "obscene" and "indecent" are vague, stating that "applied according to the proper standard, for judging obscenity, already discussed, [they] give adequate warning of the conduct proscribed and mark boundaries sufficient to judge the law."[794] If indecent exposure is only indecent, not obscene, would its expression be protected by the First Amendment? It is unlikely that the *Roth* Court would have agreed. Although the "protection given speech and press was fashioned to assure unfettered interchange of ideas for the bringing about of political and social changes desired by the people," lewd and obscene "utterances are no essential part of any exposition of ideas, and are of such slight social value as a step to truth that any benefit that may be derived from them is clearly outweighed by the social interest in order and morality."[795]

The test of obscenity would be "whether to the average person, applying contemporary community standards, the dominant theme of the material taken as a whole appeals to prurient interest.[796]

In establishing this test, the Court secularized what was obvious in a more decent society by delegation to Everyman.[797] Would the average man find all naked bodies obscene? Or indecent? How is this impression formed if the body has no inherent expression? Normally, impressions are formed from observation of expressions or indirect evidence of the nature of the person. If nakedness informs the impression, isn't that necessarily an expression? The criticism that it would express would not have even slight social value. This Catch-22 is an example of the tangled web of self-deception and unconscious bias endemic in judicial doctrine relating to indecent exposure.

Roth (1957) and subsequent cases often assessed freedom-of-speech claims for rituals employing naked bodies as a medium of expression, primarily topless dancing in strip clubs. The courts held steadfastly to the notion that the body itself is expressionless, focusing instead on the use of the body as a vehicle of expression and the nature of such uses. This definitional artifice means that the Supreme Court has not yet confronted the question of whether simple public nakedness is protected by the First Amendment. According to *Roth*, indecent exposure pursuant to statutes that require lascivious intent might better be characterized as obscene exposures.

In *Ginsberg v. New York* (1968),[798] the Court sought to protect minors from images with presumably at least slight social value that might not be considered obscene for adults. It involved a difficult balancing "to protect the welfare of children and to see that they are safeguarded from abuses which might prevent their growth into free and independent well-developed . . . citizens"[799] while protecting access to sexual materials for adults.

The Court gave a nod to the importance of empirical evidence supporting alleged state interests in *Stanley v. Georgia* (1969).[800] Up to this point, decisions were based on presumptions, prejudice, and religious sentiment. The appellant was charged with possession of allegedly obscene material found in his home during a search for bookmaking evidence. In reversing the conviction on the basis of the First and Fourteenth Amendments, the Court found a violation of the right of privacy. It rejected the state's argument that exposure to obscene materials could lead to deviant sexual behavior or sexual violence because there was little empirical evidence to support that assertion. Another notable aspect of the case is the implicit finding that obscene materials may enjoy a presumption of intrinsic value worth protecting.

Recall that the history of indecent exposure included a case involving showing a deformed fetus for a fee. Indecency and obscenity in modern jurisprudence focus exclusively on erotica, as indicated in *Roth* (1957) and confirmed in *Cohen v. California* (1971) (the "Fuck the Draft" case).[801] The *Cohen* Court concluded that the expression incorporated into Cohen's jacket could not be reasonably interpreted to mean that he literally wanted to have intercourse with the draft. It then dismissed an obscenity argument by the state on the basis that "[t]his is not, for example, an obscenity case. Whatever else may be necessary to give rise to the states' broader power to prohibit obscene expression, such expression must be, in some significant way, erotic," citing *Roth*.[802] This is consistent with the requirement in most indecent exposure statutes of a showing of private parts with lewd and lascivious intent.

Miller v. California (1973) refined the *Roth* (1957) guidelines in alignment with this view, confining the meaning of obscenity to sexual content and proposing a three-part test:

> whether the average person, applying contemporary community standards would find that the work, taken as a whole, appeals to the prurient interest;
>
> whether the work depicts or describes, in a patently offensive way, sexual conduct specifically defined by the applicable state law; and
>
> whether the work, taken as a whole, lacks serious literary, artistic, political, or scientific value.[803]

Words like "average person," "community," "patently offensive," "prurient," and "lacks serious . . . value" left considerable discretion with courts to base decisions on personal prejudice. "Average person" sounds like a jury. While recognizing that communities differ substantially on moral matters, it left open the question of how to define the "average man" and "community" when materials are distributed nationally. The average American, according to the most recent census data, is a white woman in her early forties who has a high school education and access to a computer.[804] Seems like an odd choice as moral authority for the nation. The average American most likely has no idea what "prurient" means. The Court's delegation to a hypothetical average person to define these terms explicitly recognized differences of opinion about these characteristics, acknowledging a lack of moral consensus. Adding to the complexity, the average person may vary depending on the location, time, and context of the publication. More semantic wrestling ensued in succeeding cases.

The second prong of the test incentivized states to provide more specifics regarding all elements of the crime, especially what body parts are shown. The states have made efforts to statutorily refine the first two prongs of the test.[805] The third prong of the test could obviate the first two.[806] It defines "value" as limited to the specific disciplines of literature, art, politics, and science. It did not provide any constitutional reference for these selections. The prong-three exemptions have been a tentpole of protection of the "art" of adult entertainment and a less-reliable tool for protection of political protests. Despite its obvious infirmities, it remains the judicial gold standard for determining obscenity.

Paris Adult Theatre I v. Slaton (1973), decided in the same year, addressed an element of the crime not covered by the *Miller* test: the audience.[807] The Court found that pornographic films do not acquire constitutional immunity simply because they are exhibited to consenting adults only. This is a rare example in modern jurisprudence of support for the prevention-of-evil-example rationale.[808] The Court expressed the view that there is a legitimate state interest in "stemming the tide of commercialized obscenity."[809] The Court expressly balanced First Amendment rights and "free will"[810] claims against "legitimate state interests" to "maintain a decent society"[811] by "regulating commerce in obscene material."[812] The Court cited *Miller* (1973), finding that because obscene material lacks any serious literary, political, or scientific value, the state was not trying to control the minds and thoughts of adult theater patrons.[813] Commercial speech involving advertising contraceptives was addressed in *Carey v. Population Services International* (1977), in which a ban on advertising contraceptives was deemed unconstitutional, even though such ads might be offensive, as long as they were not obscene.[814]

During the same era, there was a case of indecent exposure as a protest against commercialization of nudity. In *State v. Nelson* (1970), the Supreme Court of Iowa addressed a First Amendment claim arising from a meeting in a dormitory at Grinnell College featuring a guest speaker from *Playboy* magazine.[815] Ten students, protesting *Playboy*'s comercialization of the nude female body, disrobed and remained undressed for approximately ten minutes. The meeting continued unabated. The students were charged with indecent exposure under a state statute making it a crime for unmarried people to "lewdly and viciously associate and cohabit together, or if any man or woman, married or unmarried, is guilty of open and gross lewdness, and designedly makes an open and indecent or obscene exposure of his or her person."[816]

The court affirmed the conviction, finding that "public order and decency by proscribing public behavior that violates well-founded and recognized norms of behavior" was a compelling state interest.[817] The statute outlawed "open and indecent or obscene" exposure. There was no requirement of a showing of lewd intent. The court addressed the question of simple public nudity, noting circumstances where no crime would be found, such as in artistic or medical settings. It found "more than mere public nudity" in this case:

> [P]ublic nudity or exposure that is intentionally undertaken to violate the accepted rules of behavior as those rules relate to the particular factual situation in which the exposure occurs. Thus, it is not the nudity alone, but it is the act of disrobing, plus the intent to do it in a place where social norms would be knowingly violated that provides the illegality. Such a rationale concentrates not on the person's actions before, during, or after his public exposure, but rather this interpretation centers primarily on the context or factual circumstances in which the exposure occurs. It does require an intent to do the exposure with the design of violating well-recognized rules of behavior for the specific context.[818]

The clear political message conveyed had no influence on the decision. The U.S. Supreme Court denied certiorari.

Two law-review case notes commented on the case.[819] In the first, Steffes argued that the government in *Nelson* (1970) was "trying to protect the reckless and criminal disregard of the decencies of life."[820] He opined that "[d]isrobing and other acts contrary to good morals were forbidden at common law," and obscenity had been found to be "utterly without social significance,"[821] an amusing perspective given that the students were protesting against *Playboy* magazine.

Michaud reviewed *Nelson* (1972) five years later, arguing an opposing view inspired by *Erznoznik v. Jacksonville* (1975), a Supreme Court case that had been decided after publication of the first note. In *Erznoznik* (1975), the Supreme Court held that a local ordinance restricting showing of movies that contained nudity was facially invalid because it did not distinguish between nudity that might be viewed as offensive and nudity that would be acceptable.[822] The Court opined that "the Constitution does not permit government to decide which types of otherwise protected speech are sufficiently offensive to require protection for the unwilling listener or viewer."[823] The ordinance was found to impermissibly discriminate against movies based solely on content. The Court quoted *Police Department of Chicago v. Mosley* (1972): "[A]bove all else, the First Amendment means that government has no power to restrict expression because of its message, its ideas, its subject matter, or its content."[824]

Justices Berger and Rehnquist dissented in *Erznoznik* (1975), noting that

> assuming *arguendo* that there could be a play performed in a theater by nude actors involving genuine communication of ideas, the same conduct in a public park or street could be prosecuted under an ordinance prohibiting indecent exposure. This is so because the police power has long been interpreted to authorize the regulation

> of nakedness in areas to which all members of the public have access, regardless of any incidental effect upon communication. A nudist colony, for example, cannot lawfully set up shop in Central Park or Lafayette Park, places established for the public generally. *Cf. Paris Adult Theatre I v. Slaton*, 413 U.S. 49, 413 U.S. 67 [*sic*] (1973); *Roth v. United States*, 354 U.S. 476, 354 U.S. 512 [*sic*] (1957) (DOUGLAS, J., dissenting).[825]

Justice White, in a separate dissent, cautioned that if the "broadside" leveled in this case is taken literally, "the State may not forbid 'expressive' nudity on the public streets, in the public parks, or any other public place since other persons in those places at that time have a 'limited privacy interest' and may merely look the other way."[826]

Should there be a constitutional right for social nudists to walk down Main Street in all their natural glory, in what they might call a "celebration of myself" and in encouragement of healthier lifestyles? Nakedness is central to the argument of nudists for an alternative lifestyle. A nudist colony in the park would be avoidable. Paradoxically, nudist motion pictures have been held not obscene.[827] It looked for a moment like there might be an abrupt change in judicial doctrine regarding indecent exposure.

Michaud noted that in *Cohen v. California* (1971), the Supreme Court protected a man's decision to place an unsightly display of the words "Fuck the Draft" on the back of his jacket. The Court in *Cohen* recognized the cognitive importance of the "emotive function" of messaging and expressed support for leaving matters of taste and style to the individual. Offensive speech deserved protection. The manner of expression was also protected.[828]

The Court in *Erznoznik* (1975) criticized the ordinance for prohibiting nudity, not just "sexually explicit nudity," saying that "to be obscene, 'such nudity must be, in some significant way, 'erotic.'"[829] The nature of presentation was such that it would be difficult for people to avert their eyes, referencing an enduring view of the Court regarding offensive public display that an unwilling audience can protect their sensibilities "simply by averting [their] eyes."[830] Michaud extrapolated from *Erznoznik* (1975) and *Cohen* (1971) that the privacy interest (right to be left alone) of people on public streets would now be severely limited, especially where the audience can avoid the unwanted experience altogether or at least minimize its annoying or alarming impact. These cases demonstrated that protection for profanity includes the mode of expression as well as its content, leading Michaud to conclude:

> A per se approach to the question of public nudity is unacceptable. Just as words may or may not be "fighting" words, depending on the circumstances of their utterance, so nudity "thrust" upon an unwilling audience may or may not violate legitimate privacy interests, depending upon the context of the intrusion.[831]

The trump card of protection of minors was argued in *Erznoznik* (1975) but did not prevail. The Court noted that "[c]learly all nudity cannot be deemed obscene even as to minors."[832] Speech that is neither obscene nor subject to other unspecified legitimate proscription cannot be suppressed just because it involves images that "a legislative body think unsuitable." It offered examples of nudity in art and news. These are media examples. This is an important distinction to keep in mind when assessing cases. There is something different about live nudity that is not articulated. Maybe it has to do with the audience feeling unsafe in such circumstances? The mention of "alarm" in some statutes may be an explicit recognition of this aspect of live nakedness, but it is usually presented in the alternative as "offend," "alarm," or "annoy" an audience. Taken at face value, *Erznoznik* (1975) looked like a strong precedent for invalidation of indecent exposure laws or, at least, a narrowing to circumstances to where the audience has a reasonable fear of imminent sexual assault.

The protection-of-minors argument needs more study and critical discussion. Despite widespread easy access by minors to naked pictures and videos, obscenity, and pornography via television and the internet, empirical evidence is inconclusive that these exposures alone cause significant harm.[833] Numerous studies have found that exposure to nakedness in safe environments does not cause harm.[834] Research indicates that exposure to nudity can have beneficial outcomes, including increased self-esteem, sexual knowledge, and comfort with physical contact and affection. Exposure to nudity in the home has also been associated with lower rates of theft and drug use in adolescence as well as improved relations with adults outside the family.[835]

The effect of obscene materials appears to be contextually determined, not inherent in nakedness. Would seeing someone walking down the street naked be harmful to children? Harm has been shown where children are forced or induced to participate in sexual activities, particularly those involving victimization by older minors and adults. These introductions to sexual relations can result in anxiety disorders, depression, substance abuse, suicide, eating disorders, posttraumatic stress disorder, sleep disorders, and difficulty establishing trust relationships.[836] Other forms of accompanying verbal and physical abuse can create similar dysfunctions. Ironically, hate speech is protected by the First Amendment. There are no mentions of the effects of hate speech on children in Supreme Court cases, despite scientific evidence of detrimental effects.[837] The same is true regarding access to violent content. Live naked bodies are considered to be less deserving of constitutional protection.

As with violent video games, the developmental consequences are uncertain and debatable.[838] Factors that are likely to influence how children react to seeing naked people include age, gender, culture, education, religious education and orientation, family environment, and personal experiences.[839] For adults and children, there is reason to believe that less restriction on nakedness may be a means of promoting healthy body image, positive self-esteem, and overall life satisfaction. Unlike video games, public nakedness is prohibited altogether.

The argument that drag shows and other "artistic" representations of sex and sexuality discussed later in this analysis could cause minors to develop unrealistic attitudes about sex and consent, more negative attitudes about roles and identities in relationships, and unrealistic views of body image, sexual performance, and its consequences has led to contradictory outcomes in leading cases. Scientific evidence is generally not considered.

The next stop on the meandering path of constitutional interpretation regarding public nudity as protected speech was a claim arising out of nude barroom dancing in *Doran v. Salem Inn, Inc.* (1975).[840] In this case, the Supreme Court upheld a preliminary injunction against enforcement of a statute banning topless dancing. In addressing the likelihood of success on the merits of this claim, the Court noted that nude barroom dancing might involve "only the barest minimum of protected expression," citing *California v. LaRue* (1972),[841] that might be entitled to First and Fourteenth Amendment protection.[842]

All right, so topless dancing might involve protectable expression. What about pornography? Seems unlikely under *Roth* (1957)? Not necessarily. In the Seventh Circuit case *American Booksellers Ass'n v. Hudnut* (1985), the Court of Appeals considered an Indianapolis ordinance that held that people who "traffic" in pornography are liable for crimes committed by people who were influenced by the exposure.[843] The district court had declared the ordinance an unconstitutional limitation on speech. The Seventh Circuit Court of Appeals agreed, finding that the ordinance failed to refer to prurient interests, offensiveness, community standards, or judging a work as a whole, as required by the *Miller* (1973) test.

The ordinance was premised on the theory that pornography influences attitudes about women in harmful ways. This was problematic. It indicated that the ordinance discriminated based on the content of speech. Indianapolis justified the ordinance on the ground that "pornography affects thoughts":

> Men who see women depicted as subordinate are more likely to treat them so. Pornography is an aspect of dominance. It does not persuade people so much as change them. It works by socializing, by establishing the expected and the permissible. In this view pornography is not an idea; pornography is the injury.[844]

The Hudnut court's reaction is fascinating:

> There is much to this perspective. Beliefs are also facts. People often act in accordance with the images and patterns they find around them. People raised in a religion tend to accept the tenets of that religion, often without independent examination. People taught from birth that black people are fit only for slavery rarely rebelled against that creed; beliefs coupled with the self-interest of the masters established a social structure that inflicted great harm while enduring for centuries. Words and images act at the level of the subconscious before they persuade at the level of the conscious. Even the truth has little chance unless a statement fits within the framework of beliefs that may never have been subjected to rational study.[845]

From this, the court easily extrapolated that the rationale for the statute "simply demonstrates the power of pornography as speech." The court continued:

> Pornography affects how people see the world, their fellows, and social relations. If pornography is what pornography does, so is other speech. Hitler's orations affected how some Germans saw Jews. Communism is a world view, not simply a Manifesto by Marx and Engels or a set of speeches. Efforts to suppress communist speech in the United States were based on the belief that the public acceptability of such ideas would increase the likelihood of totalitarian government. Religions affect socialization in the most pervasive way.[846]

The court held that such communications should not be suppressed because

> almost all cultural stimuli provoke unconscious responses. Religious ceremonies condition their participants. Teachers convey messages by selecting what not to cover; the implicit message about what is off limits or unthinkable may be more powerful than the messages for which they present rational argument. Television

> scripts contain unarticulated assumptions. People may be conditioned in subtle ways. If the fact that speech plays a role in a process of conditioning were enough to permit governmental regulation, that would be the end of freedom of speech.[847]

The judge cited numerous examples of artistic depictions of sexual domination and violence, including James Joyce's *Ulysses* and Brian DePalma's *Body Double*. He quoted John Stuart Mill's proposition in *On Liberty* (1859) that truth will prevail when freedom of speech is protected. The court viewed the city's argument that pornography is low-value speech as inherently contradicted by the premise of the ordinance that pornography led to crime.

There's a lot to unpack here. As a whole, the opinion was a broadside against the prevention-of-evil-example rationale for indecent exposure laws. The court's conclusion that depictions of deviant sex are protected speech no doubt would not have made any sense to the framers. But does it make sense now? The case was summarily affirmed on appeal by the Supreme Court, without oral argument or written opinion.[848] *Hudnut* has been cited over fifty times.

The court's common-sense finding that speech was necessarily involved, given the premise of the ordinance, made strict scrutiny the appropriate standard of review and required that there be a compelling state interest that outweighed the free-speech right. The answer would have been easy for the founders of the United States living in a society dominated by the Christian religion. Lacking that strong sense of moral authority, the court sided with individual autonomy. This court's soliloquy is a provocative example of America's modern moral dilemma. Is pornography instructive? Does protecting this category of speech contribute to the political discourse? Moral jurisprudence was losing its moorings.

John Stuart Mill had nothing to do with drafting the Constitution. He was born in 1806.[849] The *Hudnut* court's reference to him in its discussion of subconscious effects of obscenity and comparison to other kinds of offensive influences as agents of cultural change is reminiscent of the conflicting views of Thomas Jefferson and John Locke on toleration of differing views in moral matters. Would Jefferson support the court's decision, having written that "[n]othing but free argument, raillery and even ridicule will preserve the purity of religion"?[850] Mill believed that morality is not fixed or absolute, but rather a dynamic and evolving process of discovering the best rules for human well-being. He advocated that people should be free to challenge prevailing morality so long as their actions do not harm others. Mill felt that moral improvement is best fostered by cultivation of individual character, which requires freedom from external interference and enforced conformity.[851]

The individual and cultural effects of indecent exposure laws are untested outside commercial, artistic, and socially confined (nudist enclaves) contexts. Indecent exposure laws foreclose challenges to the prevailing moral order. The naked body is provocative. Public nakedness without a showing of lewd or lascivious intent would inspire discussion of important societal ideas. Despite the *Hudnut* court's appreciation for the marketplace of ideas and the potential value of pornography, it did not challenge the assumption that "prurient interest" does not express a viewpoint worthy of constitutional protection. The court's reference to religion implicates the Establishment and Free Exercise Clauses as well as free speech. This case reminds us that a robust commitment to freedom of speech and religion require tolerance for deeply offensive expressions of different morality. Are live naked bodies less instructive than pornography? Or intolerably offensive?

One way to mitigate the effects of indecency is to build a fence around it. The *Miller* (1973) and *Paris* (1973) cases gave rise to a doctrine that secondary effects around adult entertainment venues justified regulation. This was little more than a rediscovery of the nuisance theory of indecent exposure and prosecutions for frequenting of bawdy houses. The secondary-effects doctrine justifies government regulations based on the harmful effects these businesses may have on the surrounding community, such as crime, prostitution, or public health problems. The natural consequence of the doctrine is to support zoning ordinances that restrict the location of adult entertainment businesses as legitimate exercises of police power. These ordinances are considered to be constitutional because they do not regulate content, only its secondary effects. The doctrine has been criticized as a tool for suppression of speech based on moral disapproval and prejudice and for not being well-grounded in empirical evidence and analysis.[852]

In *Young v. Arkansas* (1986), the U.S. Supreme Court denied certiorari in an appeal from the conviction of a dancer for indecent exposure.[853] The Arkansas Supreme Court had affirmed her conviction, finding that the conduct violated the statute and was not protected by the First Amendment. The statute required a showing of intent to "arouse or gratify" a sexual desire. The Arkansas state supreme court did "not take issue" with petitioner's contention that "mere nude dancing" is entitled to First Amendment protection because the dancer had run her hands over her body provocatively while dancing, creating a "fair inference" that her purpose was to arouse or gratify the sexual desires of the audience. Thus, there was no mere nude dancing to consider. Petitioner did not argue that dancing with the required statutory intent qualified for First Amendment protection.

In a dissent from the denial of certiorari, Justices White and Brennan expressed concern that the statute "criminalizes nonobscene nakedness in any public place so long as its purpose is the gratify the sexual desires of another person."[854] Recall from chapter five that this paraphrases the provision in most state statutes that showing private parts with an intent to arouse is indecent exposure. They asserted that there were "repeated indications that barroom-type nude dancing is a type of expression that is protected under the First Amendment under some circumstances . . . ."[855] The justices expressed concern that the Arkansas statute might be overbroad because it was not limited to establishments possessing liquor licenses;[856] therefore, the government must demonstrate a compelling state interest sufficient to prohibit the exercise of a protected form of expression,[857] citing *Doran* (1975) and *O'Brien* (1968). Neither of those cases suggested how to discern whether protectable expression was present.

Some years later, Justice Stevens, in his dissent in *New York State Liquor Authority v. Bellanca* (1981), a case in which the Court held that the broad powers of the Twenty-First Amendment to regulate sale of liquor outweighed any First Amendment interest in nude dancing, noted that although "the Court has written several opinions implying that nude or partially nude dancing is a form of expressive activity protected by the First Amendment; the Court has never directly confronted the question."[858]

Justice White, referring to Stevens's 1981 dissent in *Young* (1986), stated it was time to call the question.[859] He observed that state courts disagreed over the reach of the First Amendment in this area. Importantly, he pointed out that the Court in *LaRue* (1972) purported to balance evidence of social harms provided in explicit legislative findings supporting the law against the value of a "slight interest" in protected expression. There were no such findings in *Bellanca* (1981). Stevens suggested that whether a state may prohibit nude or partially nude dancing in commercial establishments might best be resolved by "elected representatives of the community."[860] However, this posture would be problematic. Legislatures do not have constitutional authority to determine whether speech is present and, if it is, they can "make no law . . . abridging the freedom of speech."[861]

These First Amendment protections for barroom dancing and

pornography have not translated into protection for public nakedness outside commercial contexts. One impediment is the viewpoint that the nude body is expressionless for First Amendment purposes. It was propounded in *South Florida Free Beaches, Inc. v. Miami* (1984), which involved a challenge to a Miami nude sunbathing ordinance.[862] The case was an appeal from a denial of an injunction that had been requested on free-speech grounds. The court embraced the notion of the nude body as tabula rasa, finding that protected speech exists only when the body is combined with a recognized mode of expression, such as dance, literature, or theater, that itself is entitled to First Amendment protection.[863] The court got cute, holding that "the first amendment does not clothe these plaintiffs with a constitutional right to sunbathe in the nude." According to the court, "[n]either do they possess a constitutional right of associating in the nude. They remain able to advocate the benefits of nude sunbathing, albeit while fully dressed."[864] By analogy, pornographers and barroom dancers could entertain audiences with essays on deviant sex and masturbation. *Cohen* (1973) had already made the point that the medium of expression can be integral to the message.

As the courts as *custos morum* puzzled over the quantum of expression in nude barroom dancing and alternative means of expression outside bars, the expressionless nature of naked bodies not energized by dancing continued to be reinforced in First Amendment jurisprudence. In *New York v. Hollman* (1986), the New York Supreme Court upheld a conviction for indecent exposure in another First Amendment case concerning nude sunbathing.[865] The court found that

> [w]hile there may be contexts in which a public display of nudity would reasonably be understood as a means of communicating an idea, it cannot be said that nude sunbathing on a beach is a form of expression likely to be understood by the viewer as an attempt to convey a particular point of view.[866]

Thus,

> [e]ven if it was considered expressive conduct, such conduct was subject to regulation since prohibiting public nakedness was plainly within state's police powers. The statute was not aimed at suppressing expression of opinion concerning nakedness, but neutrally prohibited all public displays of nakedness regardless of actor's purpose, and the statute furthered an important government objective of providing recreational space for citizens and preserving character of park for its intended use.[867]

It should be abundantly clear that the message was that nude sunbathing is more enjoyable and does not lead to any detrimental secondary effects. The court chose not to recognize this message or find it worthy of constitutional protection. There was no subsequent appellate history.

Twenty years later, the U.S. District Court for the Eastern District of Pennsylvania, in *Egolf v. Witmer* (2006), cited *Hollman* (1986) for the proposition that a claim to rights to public nudity "has long been flatly rejected."[868] *Egolf* offered a glimmer of hope that the First Amendment would apply when the court stated that

> Expressive conduct exists where "an intent to convey a particularized message was present, and the likelihood was great that the message would be understood by those who viewed it," or if the nature, context and environment of the conduct "was sufficiently imbued with elements of communication to fall within the scope of the First and Fourteenth Amendments."[869]

Despite this view and acceptance that the plaintiffs' activities would be understood as a political protest, the court found that the Pennsylvania indecent exposure statute was content neutral: it did not target expressive conduct because it applied to all "publicly lewd and indecent conduct." The problem for the plaintiffs was that the nudity was merely "accompanied by expressive activity."

These cases did not capture the attention of the Supreme Court, which continued to find striptease more intriguing than sunbathing and protests against exploitation of women. The Court continued its ruminations about commercial nudity in *Barnes v. Glen Theatre, Inc.* (1991), in which, in a 5-to-4 opinion, it upheld an Indiana law requiring nude dancers to wear pasties and G-strings.[870] The plurality found the expression in commercial nude dance to be "only marginally so."[871] Applying the symbolic-speech standard from *United States v. O'Brien* (1968) (burning a draft card),[872] they concluded that the law imposed only "incidental limitations on some expressive activity,"[873] which was justified to "protect[] order and morality."[874]

The Court then turned to the common law, citing *Winters v. New York* (1948)[875] for the proposition that nudity was considered a crime of "gross and open indecency."[876] It cited *Sedley's Case* (1663) and the proliferation of public indecency statutes as evidencing "moral disapproval of people appearing in the nude among strangers in public places."[877] Continuing down the ecclesiastical path mapped here, the Court reinforced its reasoning with *Ardery v. State* (1877), noting with approval the *Ardery* court's tracing of the offense to the biblical story of Adam and Eve.[878] Despite this evidence of doctrinal origins, the Court attributed authority for such prohibitions to the police power. The legitimate state interest was in protecting order and morality.[879]

The perceived evil to be suppressed was not the erotic messages of barroom dancers. It was public nudity, whether or not it combined with expressive activity. Justice Scalia, concurring, reinforced the plurality view with an attempt to revive prevention of evil example. Public nudity is a crime, he stated, not just because it is annoying; it is "*contra bonos mores*"—immoral.[880] This, alone, was all that was needed in this case, given the rights involved. He cautioned would-be naked protestors that those who choose public nudity as a means of communication should "make sure that the conduct they select is not generally forbidden."[881] Justice Souter, concurring, opined that performance dancing is inherently expressive; "nudity *per se* is not."[882]

The Court's most provocative remark on the topic was that "[w]here the government prohibits conduct precisely because of its communicative attributes, we hold the regulation unconstitutional."[883] The plurality cited cases involving flag burning, wearing arm bands, and engaging in sit-ins.[884] A critical element of most indecent exposure statutes is a communication attribute, an intent to arouse or lewdness or lasciviousness that annoys or alarms people in public places. Such conduct is prohibited solely due to its "communicative attributes."

Concurring, Justice Scalia opined that there was no need to apply the *O'Brien* test because "[a]lmost the entire domain of Indiana's statute is unrelated to expression, unless we view nude beaches and topless hot dog vendors as speech."[885] Although the topless hot dog vendor has not had her day in court, topless baristas and nude beachgoers will plead their cases later in this chapter. Justice Souter concurred based on a nuisance theory of potential secondary effects on adjacent property values and crime rates. Four justices dissented. They focused on nuisance theory and the presumption that a willing audience would not be annoyed or alarmed by the dancing in a relatively private place.

The Supreme Court demonstrated its continuing fascination with nude dancing a decade later in *City of Erie v. Pap's A.M.* (2000), in which a 6-to-3 majority upheld a statute like the Indiana statute at issue in *Barnes* (1991).[886] The Court relied on a secondary-effects rationale, quoting the preamble to the ordinance for the proposition that such activities create "an atmosphere conducive to violence, sexual harassment, public intoxication, prostitution, [and] the spread of sexually transmitted diseases."[887]

The secondary-effects doctrine has helped localities and lower courts manage adult entertainment. The Supreme Court encouraged the use of empirical evidence to support such theories in *City of Los Angeles v. Alameda Books* (2002).[888] It has not suggested that the same scientific rigor should be applied to determining whether naked bodies are expressive, whether there are ways in which such protectable expression might be identified and measured, or whether there is any actual harm from such exposures other than annoyance.

Sable Communications of California v. FCC (1989) addressed an open issue in the *Miller* (1973) "contemporary community standards" requirement.[889] In this case, the Court affirmed a district court ruling that enjoined enforcement of the Communications Act of 1934 against a "dial-a-porn" phone sex service. Given the nationwide reach of the service, the Court pondered what community standard should apply, noting that nuisance theory was not relevant due to the dial-up nature of the service. Although the Court did not show any awareness of the prevention-of-evil-example rationale, it found such activity to be constitutionally protected, merely indecent speech.[890]

The Court gave no guidance as to what is "merely indecent" yet not obscene. There was also no helpful guidance regarding why the expression of lewd or lascivious intent in indecent exposure statutes and common-law cases would not qualify the exposure for First Amendment protection, given that such expressions in barroom dancing are protected. The consenting audience could be a differentiator, assuming nuisance theory, but it would not obviate the state interest in preventing evil example.

The *Roth* (1957) Court did not try to define indecency. In *Reno v. ACLU* (1997), a case assessing the constitutionality of the Communications Decency Act of 1996 as a means of protecting minors from internet distribution of pornography, the Court finally addressed the obscenity/indecency distinction: "In evaluating the free speech rights of adults, we have made it perfectly clear that '[s]exual expression which is indecent but not obscene is protected by the First Amendment.'"[891] "Perfectly clear"—really? In this case, the Court was trying to justify allowing adults access to sexually explicit materials while keeping them from children. The Court's rhetoric could be taken to mean that public nakedness, even when accompanied by lewd or lascivious intent, should enjoy First Amendment protection because it is indecent but not obscene. In cases where intent is shown, First Amendment protection would apply to the "sexual expression" akin to the expression forming the entertainment in barroom dancing.

Simple public nakedness would still be caught in the Catch-22 of the expressionless body. As with indecency, there is no secular rationale for the legal characterization of expressionless bodies. The courts have indicated ways in which the body can be used for expression but continue to deny its inherent communicativeness. *Reno* (1997) might be distinguishable as reiterating precedent to the effect that an unwilling audience can protect their sensibilities "simply by averting [their] eyes"[892] because it was a dial-up service.

Cohen (1973) established that "Fuck the Draft" on clothing was not obscene. But surely it was indecent? This historical study has provided numerous examples of public indecency prohibited by law that did not involve nakedness. Recall, for example, that the first case of indecent exposure in America involved public display of an aborted fetus.

In *United States v. Stevens* (2010), when assessing the constitutionality of a statute banning depictions of animal cruelty,[893] the Court observed that "[d]epictions of animal cruelty are not, as a class, categorically unprotected by the First Amendment. Because § 48 explicitly regulates expression based on content, it is "'presumptively invalid,' . . . and the Government bears the burden to rebut that presumption."[894] So, because depictions of animal cruelty are not "categorically unprotected" by the First Amendment and the statute regulates these expressions based on content, the statute was presumed invalid, yet indecent exposure statutes that regulate expressions of the body based on indecent (lewd, lascivious, etc.) content are presumed valid? Is animal cruelty a worthier category of speech? Is "intent to arouse" content more worthy of protection in commercial contexts? These inconsistencies are puzzling.

The Court in *Stevens* opined that while the prohibition of animal cruelty has a long history in American law,[895] there is no evidence of a similar tradition prohibiting *depictions* of such cruelty.[896] The government's proposed test would broadly balance the value of the speech against its societal costs to determine whether the First Amendment should be applied. The Court rejected this test, noting that the First Amendment's free-speech guarantee does not extend only to categories of speech that survive an ad hoc balancing of relative social costs and benefits.[897] This sure seems like a case of ad hoc balancing and viewpoint restriction. Viewpoint restrictions will be addressed later in the chapter.

Explicit use of live naked bodies as vehicles of political protest against legal repression of the body does not enjoy the same protection as canine blood sports. In the most recent federal appellate court ruling on public nakedness, *Taub v. City of San Francisco* (2017), the Ninth Circuit upheld a San Francisco ban on public nakedness in a case involving naked political protesters.[898] The ordinance provided exceptions for permitted parades, fairs, or festivals. Such a permitting process might raise the specter of prior restraints, a topic also covered later.

The plaintiffs did not obtain a permit for their protest. They referred to themselves as "body freedom advocates." Unfortunately, the appellants admitted in their briefs that "mere nakedness is not speech,"[899] so the question of whether simple public nakedness deserved protection was obviated. Nevertheless, the court opined that "[p]ublic nakedness is not inherently expressive" in finding that the city ordinance was "a valid, content neutral regulation" of their expressive conduct, based on the four factors set forth in *O'Brien* (1968):

- The ordinance falls within traditional police powers.[900]
- It furthers important and substantial interests in protecting individuals "who are unwillingly or unexpectedly exposed" to the nakedness and avoids secondary effects of distractions, obstructions, and crowds that might interfere with safety and free flow of pedestrian and vehicular traffic.[901]
- The prohibition "is unrelated to the suppression of free expression, because the ordinance regulates public nakedness whether or not it is expressive."[902]
- "[T]he incidental restriction on alleged First Amendment freedoms is no greater than is essential to the furtherance of that interest."[903]

The third point is curious and contrary to several important precedents involving barroom dancing. It also would seem to ban artistic and political activities involving nudity or indecent expression, as in *Cohen*, the "Fuck the Draft" case. In fact, one could make similar arguments regarding the *O'Brien* test for Cohen's provocative jacket. The First Amendment has been interpreted to permit restrictions on several categories of speech—including obscenity, defamation, fraud, incitement, and speech integral to criminal conduct—that "have never been thought to raise any constitutional problem."[904] Here, there was no assertion that the activities were anything more than indecent. The actors' intent was political. There was no doubt about the message being conveyed.

The city allowed nakedness in permitted activities such as gay pride celebrations where the focus is on entertainment rather than political protest. No one was prosecuted for a topless Iraq war protest by a group known as "Breasts not Bombs" in the same city twelve years before *Taub*

(2017) and eight years before enactment of the nudity ban.[905] The protesters in the Iraq war protest used their bodies to complain about an unrelated problem, war, asserting that the war in Iraq, not their nakedness, was indecent. A thousand years ago, Lady Godiva rode naked to protest burdensome taxation of the people of Coventry.[906] There was no appellate history in *Taub* (2017) despite the obviously political nature of the expression that was banned, the presence of prior restraints due to the permitting requirement, and content and viewpoint restrictions regarding the subject matter of the protest.

This is one of many naked political protests against topless prohibitions and regulations, in and out of commercial contexts. These cases typically involve claims of invalidity based on equal protection and free speech. The equal-protection claims will be addressed in a subsequent chapter. A short time after Taub's failed initiative, a protest was staged in Fort Collins, Colorado, resulting in *Free the Nipple-Fort Collins v. City of Fort Collins* (2019).[907] It is a provocative case. The appellants did not allege a free-speech violation, nor did the court address it directly, but the dictum in the court's opinion had many interesting implications worth addressing here. The plaintiff was a political organization. The target was simple public nudity, a notionally expressionless phenomenon. Unlike in *Taub* (2017), the nakedness was limited to women's breasts. The plaintiff sought an injunction based on violation of equal protection due to a ban on naked breasts in public. No showing of lewd intent was required under the statute.

The Tenth Circuit Court of Appeals considered an appeal from an injunction forbidding the city from implementing the ordinance.[908] The court noted that the gender-based classification at issue should invoke intermediate scrutiny, meaning that the classification needed "an exceedingly persuasive justification."[909] In affirming the injunction, the Court of Appeals made a number of bold statements: "Any law premised on 'generalizations about "the way women are"'."—or the way men are—will fail constitutional scrutiny because it serves no important governmental objective."[910] "Laws grounded in stereotypes about the way women are serve no important governmental interest. . . . To the contrary, legislatively reinforced stereotypes tend to 'create a self-fulfilling cycle of discrimination.'"[911] The court cited *People v. Santorelli* (1992) for the proposition that "[o]ne of the most important purposes to be served by the Equal Protection Clause is to ensure that 'public sensibilities' grounded in prejudice and unexamined stereotypes do not become enshrined as part of the official policy of government."[912]

The city justified the ordinance as a means to protect children, maintain public order, and promote traffic safety. Evidence was lacking or contradictory. An exemption for breastfeeding in state law had already created risks that children might see a naked breast in public. There was no evidence of harm to children or anyone else in neighboring cities that allowed toplessness. As to public order, the court doubted that topless women would regularly walk through downtown Fort Collins past elementary schools or swim in public pools. It did not hint at what it would do if they did. Obviously, they would be legally entitled to do so. The court rejected the city's traffic safety justification as overbroad.[913]

The district court had heard expert testimony that "the naked female breast is *seen* as disorderly or dangerous because society, from Renaissance paintings to Victoria's Secret commercials, has conflated female breasts with genitalia and stereotyped them as such."[914] The court preferred local understanding to this "scientific evidence." The expert testimony obviously oversimplified and distorted the naturally erotic meaning of women's breasts to men.[915] Rather than being dangerous or disorderly, they have generally been an enticement, whether intended or not, to sexual fantasy. Striptease comes to mind. So does courtship. And fashion.

The court was convinced that the true motive for the ordinance was to protect the moral sensibilities of the public. It noted the city's citation to *Biocic* (1991) as upholding "nebulous concepts of public morality."[916] The court in *Biocic* also had concluded that scientific evidence and theory were outweighed by obvious local public sentiment. This precedent emboldened the court in *Free the Nipple-Fort Collins* to apply personal moral theory in its interpretation of the Constitution. This approach is known as Lochnerizing, a discredited practice where courts dismiss the judgment of elected officials and substitute their own theories of economic or social justice.[917] *Free the Nipple-Fort Collins* has remained an outlier.[918] The ruling effectively allows women in six states to go shirtless in public. Few have done so. Federal courts in other jurisdictions generally continue to uphold laws banning toplessness in public.[919]

The Tenth Circuit's rationale that any law premised on generalizations about "the way women are"—or the way men are—should fail constitutional scrutiny because it serves no important governmental objective would seem equally applicable to indecent exposure more generally. The court dug deeper into its rationale, stating that legislatively reinforced stereotypes tend to create a self-fulfilling cycle of discrimination and that public sensibilities grounded in prejudice and unexamined stereotypes should not become enshrined as part of the official policy of government.[920] If a woman exposing her breast in public expresses such important legal and political principles, it seems that adding the rest of the exposure ought to make the point more emphatically. The same motives articulated by the state for the topless ban would defend a ban on complete nakedness.

There is little research and even less discussion in First Amendment cases involving general public nudity about the influences that create the negative audience reaction. It is likely that most people who find the exposure offensive would attribute it to religious beliefs or a sense of modesty, which are based on unexamined stereotypes and influence opinions of both men and women.

There was a contemporaneous challenge to a topless ban in the Supreme Court of New Hampshire. The leader of the appellants in *State v. Lilley* (2019) claimed to be a pioneer in bringing the Free the Nipple movement to New Hampshire.[921] She argued that breasts have been hypersexualized and considered pornographic and taboo, creating stigma that contributes to less breastfeeding in the United States. The appellants claimed that the ordinance violated free speech and equal protection rights. Her free-speech claim was not persuasive. The court was steadfast—bodies are not inherently expressive. Even if there was expression present, the limitation imposed by the ban was not a total denial. The court applied a rational review standard and found that the "defendants have not carried the heavy burden of mounting a successful facial attack to an ordinance analyzed only for rationality."[922]

The *Lilley* (2019) court asserted that the prohibition at issue was not a content-based restriction because it banned all nudity. It did not target women's breasts. There was no viewpoint restriction (except for the view that the body is expressionless) because the ordinance "merely regulates the manner in which activities may be carried out in that they cannot be carried out in the nude."[923]

Highly offensive speech continues to warrant protection. Findings in the *Cohen* (1971) "Fuck the Draft" case were revisited in a school context in *Mahanoy Area School District v. B.L.* (2021),[924] which featured a high school student using a social network (Snapchat) to criticize her school and cheerleading team by showing images with "a friend with middle fingers raised; it bore the caption: "Fuck school fuck softball fuck cheer fuck everything."[925] The Court first noted that "putting aside the vulgar language, the listener would hear criticism" and then went on to say that her speech "was not obscene as this court has understood that term."[926] It buttressed this view by reference to *Snyder v. Phelps* (2011) and *Rankin v. McPherson* (1987):

> To the contrary, B. L. uttered the kind of pure speech to which, were she an adult, the First Amendment would provide strong protection. See *id.*, at 24 ; cf. *Snyder* v. *Phelps*, 562 U. S. 443, 461 (2011) (First Amendment protects "even hurtful speech on public issues to ensure that we do not stifle public debate"); *Rankin* v. *McPherson*, 483 U.S. 378, 387 (1987) ("The inappropriate . . . character of a statement is irrelevant to the question whether it deals with a matter of public concern").[927]

Again, in the opinion of the Court in *Mahanoy* (2021), referencing *Tinker* (1969): "As we have previously said, simple 'undifferentiated fear or apprehension . . . is not enough to overcome the right to freedom of expression.'"[928] The Court rejected the notion that her comments were unworthy of protection because of

> the robust First Amendment protections discussed herein. But sometimes it is necessary to protect the superfluous in order to preserve the necessary. See *Tyson & Brother v. Banton, 273* U.S. 418, 447, 47 S. Ct. 426, 71 L. Ed. 718 (1927) (Holmes, J., dissenting). "We cannot lose sight of the fact that, in what otherwise might seem a trifling and annoying instance of individual distasteful abuse of a privilege, these fundamental societal values are truly implicated." *Cohen*, 403 U.S., at 25, 91 S. Ct. 1780.[929]

Justice Thomas, dissenting in Mahanoy (2021), criticized the majority for ignoring history:

> The majority declines to consider any of this history, instead favoring a few pragmatic guideposts. This is not the first time the Court has chosen intuition over history when it comes to student speech. The larger problem facing us today is that our student-speech cases are untethered from any textual or historical foundation. That failure leads the majority to miss much of the analysis relevant to these kinds of cases.[930]

The statute at issue in *Mahanoy* (2021) paraphrased the *Miller* (1973) test, defining "harmful to minors" as any description or representation of nudity that

> (i) taken as a whole, appeals to the prurient interest in sex of minors;
>
> (ii) is patently offensive to prevailing standards in the adult community as a whole with respect to what is suitable material for minors; and

(iii) taken as a whole, does not have serious value for minors.[931]

This case is reminiscent of *Baker v. Glover* (1991), in which a federal court in Alabama held that applying Alabama's obscenity statute to criminalize the phrase "Eat Shit" on a bumper sticker violated the plaintiff driver's First Amendment rights.[932] In *Baker*, the government urged the court to interpret the phrase "Eat Shit" as a prurient reference to sexual pleasure related to "coprophilia" (the fixation upon the products of bodily excretion), "coprophagy" (erotic interest in consuming fecal excrement), and "coprolalia" (the uttering of obscenities to achieve sexual gratification), a position the court swiftly rejected.[933] It found that the sticker had serious literary and political value. The sticker protested other stickers that urged people to report the indiscretions of truck drivers, and the court compared it to a riddle or pun. The sticker also provided an outlet to convey a political message inexpensively.[934] The court found that there was no evidence that the sticker appealed to the prurient interests of minors. Even under a standard modified for children, the bumper sticker still had serious literary and political value. The sticker did not contain fighting words, and the law was not aimed at traffic regulation.[935]

Each of the defendants in these cases was angry. The prurient expressions added no substantive communication. Many implied messages might be inferred, such as bad morals or upbringing, lack of respect for others, inability to better articulate the depths of their feelings, etc. None of them contribute meaningfully to political or social discourse or advancement of the arts.

Whereas in *Lilley* (2019) the free-speech claim was easily dismissed because bodies are expressionless, the court in *Free the Nipple-Fort Collins* (2019) ascribed great meaning to the naked breast as a powerful statement against public sensibilities grounded in prejudice and unexamined stereotypes that foster discrimination against women. In *Cohen* (1971), an alternative to "Fuck the Draft" on Cohen's jacket, such as a petition opposing the system, would not be an adequate alternative channel of communication. The Court concluded that it's just not the same message. The court in *Lilley* did not suggest what it felt might be adequate alternatives, but it did view the ordinance as not imposing content or viewpoint restrictions.[936] Like the particular instantiation in *Cohen* (1971) and the choice words in *Mahanoy* (2021), there is something special about a live naked breast that is difficult to communicate in other ways that does not apply to other erogenous zones of the body.

It appears to be settled that simple public nakedness is only indecent, not obscene..[937] It is well settled that the naked body is viewed as expressionless, a tabula rasa, for First Amendment purposes, so no protection is afforded. This view of naked bodies was first articulated as a principle of constitutional analysis in 1984 in *South Florida Free Beaches, Inc. v. Miami*..[938] Naked bodies may be used in protected expression such as dance or theater. These exposures in art and commerce are not considered obscene and may be protected by the First Amendment even if the performances are lewd, lascivious, or intended to sexually arouse the audience. These exposures are sometimes regulated as to time, place, and manner when regulating them is justified by legitimate state interests concerning local morality or effects on quality of life and commerce in neighboring areas. Such exposures outside these contexts are not protected.

No cases have squarely addressed scientific justifications for prohibitions against live nakedness. Use of naked bodies in political expression has not garnered protection. Exposure of women's breasts has produced mixed results. Whether nakedness coupled with lewd or lascivious intent or intent to sexually arouse oneself or an unwilling audience is indecent or obscene is an open question. Expression of such intent is a crime in most circumstances except where there is a paying audience.

Without augmentation, acceptable motion, or context, public nudity is just conduct; that is, action that does not communicate protectable ideas unless it is in a play, art exhibit, strip club, or political protest. There is some innuendo in Supreme Court cases suggesting that whatever the body expresses, it is not worthy of First Amendment protection or that protection of its nominal value is outweighed by legitimate state interests. For some or all of these reasons, simple public nudity has not yet proven worthy of First Amendment protection.

As indicated in this review of First Amendment case, courts generally dismiss communicative attributes of the body with a figurative wave of the hand. It is not possible to discern from case-law precedent whether they believe that the body is truly expressionless or that its expression is not worthy of constitutional protection. The assertion that the body is expressionless is not true. The surface of the body inherently communicates a wealth of information. Here are a few examples:

- *Health status*: Changes in skin color, texture, or appearance can indicate underlying health conditions. For example, yellowing of the skin can indicate liver disease, while a blue tint can suggest oxygen deprivation.

- *Emotional state*: The skin can indicate a person's emotional state. For instance, blushing can indicate embarrassment or excitement, while paleness might suggest fear or shock. Body position can indicate fear or welcoming, indifference or engagement.
- *Age*: The skin can provide clues about a person's age. Wrinkles, age spots, and the loss of skin elasticity are all associated with aging.
- *Hygiene*: The condition of a person's skin can also reflect their personal hygiene. Clean, well-cared-for skin might suggest that a person places a high value on cleanliness and personal care.
- *Physical condition*: Athletes often have more defined muscles that can be seen under the skin, indicating their physical fitness.
- *Temperature and circulation*: The skin can feel warm or cool to the touch, which can indicate body temperature and blood circulation.
- *Pain or discomfort*: If a person is in pain or discomfort, one might see bruising, swelling, or other signs of injury.
- *Sexual appeal*: Erogenous zones provide clues to courtship and sexual fantasies.
- *Tattoos and piercings*: Tattoos and piercings provide insights into experiences, affiliations, memories, and strongly held beliefs.
- *Contextual meaning*: For nudists, nakedness is an easily understood expression of self-identity.[939] When women engage in political protests with breasts exposed, the message intended to be conveyed should be easily understood.[940] Expressions of lascivious intent in topless dancing are well understood. Sunbathing on clothes-optional beaches, likewise easily understood. Topless women selling coffee. Etc.

The list goes on and on, yet the judiciary continues to assert that the naked body does not communicate expression worthy of First Amendment protection. No explanation is required. This confounds a search for the boundaries of protectable expression.

The *Miller* test requires literary, artistic, political, or scientific value. The science of body language is well-established. It operates under the umbrella of semiotics, the science of signs. The body is a rich and complex source of semiotic value and potential. Semiotics of the body refers to the study of how our bodies communicate meaning, both to ourselves and to others. This can include a wide range of signals and signs, from facial expressions and other body movements and positioning to clothing and adornments.

Body language is a nonverbal communication system that uses facial expressions, gestures, posture, and other body movements to convey meaning and emotions; for example, smiles, frowns, crossed arms, erect penises, hard nipples, and eye contact. Gestural and mimogestural semiotics focus on the meaning conveyed through such gestures and mimed gestures. In an integrated semiotic approach, communicative gesture involves the construction of a syncretic expression plane, combined with verbal discourse.[941] Semiosis is any activity, conduct, or process that involves signs, where a sign is defined as anything that communicates meaning to the sign's interpreter.[942]

Indecent exposure laws deny these obvious communicative characteristics unless the resulting communication is shaped in acceptable ways. Cultures and societies consciously and unconsciously shape the rhetoric of body language. Individuals exercise choice within permissible frameworks for clothing, hair style, adornment, and other symbols of acceptance and rebellion regarding those norms. These choices non-verbally convey information about our identities, attitudes, and affiliations. Semiotics of the body is a complex field that intersects with other disciplines, including sociology, anthropology, political science, psychology, and communication studies.

Indecent exposure laws suppress, shape, and channel aspects of body language. The source of authority for these laws has been made obvious in this historical study: the teachings of Christian theology and the vicissitudes of government policy in relation to religious moral authority. The design of the First Amendment was to tolerate criticism as a path to enlightenment and social progress. The effect of broad-based tolerance of the language of naked bodies is uncertain due to unquestioned maintenance of laws of suppression and repression. However, these laws are losing the moral authority that has sustained them since inception of the nation, as of yet allowing only nuanced communication.

Fuck the draft. Fuck cheer. Eat shit. All are important expressions worthy of First Amendment protection, according to federal courts. One of the Supreme Court's important responsibilities is to ensure a marketplace of ideas. The First Amendment is the primary means of protecting this necessary element of a workable democracy. When interpreting this amendment, the Court should be mindful of basic constitutional purposes to establish a workable democracy, protect basic human rights, and hold together a highly diverse society. In each of the cases reviewed above where the defendants used indecent expressions, the court concluded that alternative, more decent, means of expressing the underlying messages would not convey the same meaning, yet courts have refused to apply the same reasoning to naked bodies outside commercial and artistic contexts. The verbal indecent expressions were protected despite unrestricted public access. No audiences consented. It is likely that some observers were offended, annoyed, or alarmed by what they witnessed.

This review of free-speech cases has demonstrated the natural tension of interpretation of principles of freedom of expression when the courts are acting as *custos morum*. Indecent exposure and public indecency laws are powerful government tools for control of bodies. The laws embody the well-known maxim "out of sight, out of mind." The opinions in these cases evidence a desire to confine naked bodies to defined activities in spaces populated with consenting adult audiences who pay for the privilege of witnessing the exposures.

These rules displace real bodies from promiscuous social intercourse. There is no doubt that naked bodies are inherently rich in expressiveness, with unclothed surfaces exposing indicia of attitudes, health, experiences, and genetics. They can express many things, including beauty, pain, joy, abilities, fitness, obesity, disabilities, and arousal in ways not adequately addressed by alternative channels of communication. Naked bodies are a cornucopia of expression. None of these communications has proven worthy of First Amendment protection. Rather, protection has been a tool of adult entertainment and a backstop for crude, inarticulate criticism. Fuck the draft. Eat shit. Fuck cheer. All much more important political and social commentary worthy of First Amendment protection.

The marketplace of ideas, a central concept in America's constitutional system, obviously is not a marketplace of expressions. Certain ideas may be communicated only in certain expressions. Some expressions are wholly forbidden regardless of their associated ideas. Other forbidden expressions are said to have no associated ideas. The forbidden expressions that are "indecent" or "obscene" are "utterly without redeeming social value" unless reconstituted in certain contexts (e.g., strip clubs and movies) and modes of expression (such as dance and acting).

The purported justification for laws suppressing indecency and obscenity is furtherance of the "important or substantial governmental interest" in protecting morals.[943] by "preventing acts which shock the sense of decency of the community, or which tend to lower the moral standards."[944] It has been said, and repeated through the years, that the right of individuals to express themselves in these ways is overborne by the "right of the Nation and of the States to maintain a decent society."[945] What exactly is the indecency that the nation and states have such a substantial interest in suppressing that is not undermined by the unnecessarily filthy language in *Cohen* (1973), *Baker* (1991), and *Mahanoy* (2021) and by Ku Klux Klan speeches advocating overthrow of the government, Nazi party parades in Jewish neighborhoods, burning a cross on the lawn of an African-American family, and picketing at funerals of a gay man and an Iraq war veteran?[946]

Recall that in *Hicklin* (1868), the English common-law case in which the first judicial definition of obscenity was established, the "obscene" publication was a pamphlet promoting the Romish Church. It was obscene because it was "calculated to produce a pernicious effect in depraving and debauching the minds of the persons into whose hands it might come." Indecency was well understood in the seventeenth century. Courts, acting as *custos morum,* have not been able to provide a clear modern version of public decency, even though "indecent" exposure has been defined by statute at the microscopic level in many jurisdictions.

According to courts that have commented on it, "'[i]ndecent' may include anything from vulgarity or impropriety to real obscenity."[947] It also means "offensive to public prosperity, offending against delicacy, unfit to be seen, and gross or immodest."[948] "Obscene" and "indecent" are said not to be technical terms but rather common words that are to be understood according to their common meaning.[949] Their legal meaning is understood to encompass less than their conventional meaning:

> An act may be unconventional, may be such as to give offense to the finer sensibilities, may relate to acts which would bring a blush (real or feigned) to the cheeks of the prudish, and yet not be indecent. To determine whether an act is indecent within the purview of the statute, the time, the place, the circumstances, and the motives of the actors must be considered.[950]

For example:

> Doubtless an artist, when looking in his studio upon the model before him, in the figure of a perfectly formed young woman standing completely nude, may be so much under the influence of the aesthetic principles of his profession, and so intent in his wish to copy with perfect exactness the living picture, as not to have one obscene, indecent or impure thought or the slightest sexual desire, but on the contrary he may be perfectly absorbed in the purest

> feeling of admiration and wonder at the artistic beauty of the creation before him. But it by no means follows that if he should open wide the doors of his studio and fill it with people from the crowded streets, they would be moved by the same lofty and pure feelings. And in passing upon the question whether such an exhibition was obscene or tended to corrupt the morals of youth, a jury would not be justified in considering only the feeling of the artist. They should consider that not every person is so much absorbed in the artistic features, and that the exhibition of such a model may rather arouse in many spectators' passions of a merely animal nature.[951]

A widely promulgated and well-accepted early definition of indecency was enunciated in *Ardery v. State* (1877), a nineteenth-century Indiana case in which Chief Justice Perkins artfully described the genealogy of the concept:

> Immediately after the fall of Adam, there seems to have sprung up in his mind an idea that there was such a thing as decency and such a thing as indecency; that there was a distinction between them; and since that time the ideas of decency and indecency have been instinctive in, and, indeed parts of, humanity.[952]

Compare *Ardrey* with another nineteenth-century view, that of the poet Walt Whitman, who wrote:

> Sweet, sane, still nakedness in Nature:—ah if poor, sick, prurient humanity in cities might really know you once more: Is not nakedness then indecent? No, not inherently. It is your thought, your sophistication, your respectability, that is indecent. There come moods when these clothes of ours are not only too irksome to wear, but are themselves indecent. Perhaps indeed he or she to whom the free exhilarating ecstasy of nakedness in Nature has never been eligible (and how many thousands there are!) has not really known what purity is nor what faith or art or health really is.[953]

In America there is no choice between these decencies. There is no experimental, expressive, unbridled communication. People who want to be naked in public can just eat shit. Fuck them. Or, I guess, tell them "Tough luck." How does the underlying message differ? Does this distinction implicate a compelling state interest? "In the vast fields of inheritance, environment, and mores we find great differences in individual concepts and judgments of what constitutes vulgarity, obscenity, and indecency. The decency which is protected . . . is that which the predominant majority of minds agree upon."[954] Laws passed by legislatures, enforced by the police, prosecuted through the courts, and punished in prisons, enforce a majoritarian Christian view of degenerate flesh upon excessively expressive iconoclasts.

All this may be changing. Fifty years after *Miller* (1973) and *Paris* (1973), witness *Woodlands Pride, Inc. v. Paxton* (2023), a district court case concerning prohibition of drag-queen performances.[955] It provides a powerful demonstration of the political nature of judicial discharge of *custos morum* responsibilities and continuing changes in American society and politics. The plaintiffs sought an injunction against enforcement of a Texas drag ban law prohibiting "sexually-oriented performances" on constitutional grounds.[956]

The statute established five categories of "sexual conduct":

- "the exhibition or representation, actual or simulated, of sexual acts, including vaginal sex, anal sex, and masturbation;"
- the "exhibition or representation, actual or simulated, of male or female genitals in a lewd state, including a state of sexual stimulation or arousal;"
- "the exhibition of a device designed and marketed as useful primarily for the sexual stimulation of male or female genitals;"
- "actual contact or simulated contact occurring between one person and the buttocks, breast, or any part of the genitals of another person;" and
- "the exhibition of sexual gesticulations using accessories or prosthetics that exaggerate male or female sexual characteristics.[957]

A person who is "nude" or "engages in sexual conduct" during a performance is deemed to engage in an illegal "sexually oriented performance" if the conduct "appeals to the prurient interest in sex." The statutory definition of "nude" includes "entirely unclothed" or "clothed in a manner that leaves uncovered or visible through less than fully opaque clothing any portion of the breasts below the top of the areola of the breasts, if the person is female, or any portion of the genitals or buttocks." "Prurient interest" was not specifically defined.[958]

The court began its constitutional analysis by examining the legislative history. The statute was inspired by a recent cultural trend of drag-queen shows in Texas. The legislature proposed broader purposes of protecting children and avoiding other unspecified types of future performances. Attorneys for the state expressed concern that such performances were happening at Woodlands Pride gay pride festivals and children could sneak in or inadvertently witness the performances while passing by.[959]

Woodlands Pride enlisted additional plaintiffs to launch a broad-based constitutional attack alleging that the statute was a content-based restriction, a viewpoint restriction, overbroad, vague, and a prior restraint on speech. Plaintiff Abilene Pride argued that its shows were meant to promote "belongingness" and challenge gender stereotypes. Plaintiff Extra-grams delivered drag shows to private venues, with no age restriction. Plaintiff Queen Entertainment produced dinner shows at a restaurant where children could casually observe the entertainment or join the audience with parental permission. Plaintiff Brigitte Bandit, an individual performer, argued that the court should consider her "drag to be an artistic endeavor that allows her to express herself, explore her identity outside of traditional gender norms, share messages of kindness and acceptance, and convey political messages."[960]

The district court granted the injunction. The plaintiffs, collectively, argued that their performances conveyed messages of celebration, equality, acceptance, and political and social justice. The court opined that the shows constituted expressive content and that First Amendment protection extends to "all types of activities, even some that are untasteful to society." Regardless of the messaging, the performances were intended as art. The court also concluded that there was content-based restriction. It then applied strict scrutiny to determine whether the restrictions could be justified by a narrowly drawn prohibition justified by a compelling state interest. Again, the statute failed to pass constitutional muster.[961]

The court also found targeting of drag shows to be an unconstitutional viewpoint restriction, citing *Rosenberger v. Rector*'s[962] conclusion that "regulating speech when the specific motivating ideology or the opinion or perspective of the speaker is the rationale for the restriction" is "an egregious form of content discrimination."[963]

The Texas Penal Code defined obscenity in a manner consistent with *Miller v. California*.[964] The *Woodlands Pride* court cited *Sable Communications of California v. FCC* (1989)[965] for the proposition that the First Amendment can protect sexual expression if it is indecent but not obscene. The Supreme Court in *Sable* (1989) was concerned that adult entertainment in general should not be criminalized and suggested that the distinction was an important recognition of the compelling state interest in protecting the physical and psychological well-being of minors from obscenity but not indecency. The legislative history of the Texas ban indicated to the court that the protection-of-minors argument was a red herring.[966]

The drag ban statute was found to have another fatal flaw: not specifying a child's age for determining whether the acts would appeal to a prurient interest. The court also concluded that the law was overbroad and vague, without clearer definitions of "prurient sexual interest," "lewd," and "performer."[967] The term "prurient" was first used to judge obscenity in *Roth* (1957) and was carried over to the *Miller* (1973) test that has been employed as precedent for the past fifty years. The court found that failure to include all prongs of the Miller test in the statute caused the term to be unconstitutionally vague and that the understanding of "lewd" was made "problematic" by the vagueness. The court noted "great divergence amongst the population" about what is considered lewd, evidencing decay in moral consensus that has ruled for more than two centuries. Thus, the statute was both too narrow and specific in that it focused on drag shows and too broad and vague with respect to specifications of age, intent, and actor.[968]

Woodlands Pride (2023) represents the state of the art in First Amendment jurisprudence. The court found that the drag ban law violated the First Amendment as an unconstitutional restriction on these expressive performances. The law was a content-based restriction subject to strict scrutiny, which failed; was viewpoint discrimination, which also failed strict scrutiny; and was substantially overbroad, unconstitutionally vague, and an impermissible prior restraint on speech. The plaintiffs pitched a shutout.

So, what does it teach us about indecent exposure? Drag shows can convey noble messages, as plaintiff Bandit alleged. They also can express lewd and derisive intent, although generally in comedic fashion, as alleged in *Spectrum WT v. Wendler* (2023), which featured a college president who decried such shows because they "stereotype women in cartoon-like extremes for the amusement of others and discriminate against womanhood . . . . Drag shows are derisive, divisive and demoralizing misogyny, no matter the stated intent."[969] How would the tests regarding breadth, vagueness, viewpoint, and content employed in *Woodlands Pride* (2023) map to indecent exposure?

Overbroad and Vague

A law is overbroad if it substantially prohibits conduct protected by the Constitution, such as forms of protected speech. For example, in *United States v. Stevens* (2010), discussed earlier, the Supreme Court found that a law banning the commercial creation, sale, or possession of depictions of an animal being intentionally and illegally mutilated, tortured, wounded, or killed was unconstitutional because it was overbroad.[970] Although it would prohibit pornographic images, it could also apply to protected speech. The law could, in some cases, criminalize photographs of hunting and livestock, art, and news footage. So, would a law that criminalizes any live appearance in public of an unclothed person also be overbroad? Although the law might constitutionally prohibit pornographic expressions, it would also criminalize indecent exposure and some artistic and political expressions and news footage.

Vagueness is a different attribute but is often present in a statute that is overbroad. A statute is too vague if people of common intelligence would have to guess at the statute's meaning. For example, in *Coates v. Cincinnati* (1971), the Supreme Court held that a statute that criminalized three or more people congregating on a sidewalk and "annoying" other people was too vague.[971] People would have to guess as to what conduct law enforcement would consider "annoying." By forcing people to guess what the statute meant, the law violated the constitutional right to the due process of law. The law was also overbroad because although it applied to behavior that a state can constitutionally prohibit, such as obstructing a sidewalk, the language of the law would also criminalize constitutionally protected conduct.

The *Woodlands Pride* (2023) court found the Texas drag show ban to be both overbroad and vague, as it lacked adequate definitions of "prurient sexual interest," "lewd," and "performer." The statute was both too narrow and specific—focusing on drag shows—and too broad and vague—regarding specifics of age, intent, and actors. These findings are directly on point concerning indecent exposure statutes, wherein "lewd and lascivious" intent and offending, annoying, or alarming audiences are critical elements. Per *Coates* (1971), "annoying" is impermissibly vague as well. Many state statutes contain vague terms such as "private parts," and "person,"[972] none of which would pass muster under *Woodlands* (2023) and *Coates* (1971).

Viewpoint Restriction

The First Amendment prohibits the government from restricting speech based on its content or viewpoint, with few exceptions.[973] Viewpoint restrictions must survive strict scrutiny of a showing of a compelling state interest. The historical analysis of indecent exposure laws shows that the prohibition of public nakedness is rooted in Christian theology. These laws suppress any alternative viewpoints expressed in the form of public nakedness. The suppression is reinforced by another viewpoint that bodies are expressionless. This judicial view contradicts fundamental principles of semiotics and communication theory.[974] It is also difficult to reconcile with the notion of use of the body as a vehicle for expression and the kinds of such uses that are judicially favored and disfavored.

In 1952, the Court identified a narrow class of speech that could be curtailed, including "lewd and obscene, the profane, the libelous and the insulting or 'fighting' words—those which by their very utterances inflict injury or tend to incite an immediate breach of the peace"—"the prevention and punishment of which have never been thought to raise any Constitutional problem . . . because their very utterance inflict injury or tend to incite an immediate breach of the peace."[975] The Court opined that such utterances have, at best, slight social value that is outweighed by the "social interest in order and morality." Nevertheless, subsequent cases confirmed First Amendment protection for Ku Klux Klan speech advocating overthrow of the government, Nazi party parades in Jewish neighborhoods, burning a cross on the lawn of an African American family, and picketing at funerals of a gay man and an Iraq war veteran.[976] Are these not indecent activities? Even pornography is protected by the First Amendment. Whose concept of decency justifies legal protection?[977]

None of this litany of annoying and alarming expression has led to reconsideration of the Court's views on the presumed lewdness and profanity of indecent exposure. If an audience cannot be legally protected from pornography, bigotry, intimidation, and hatred by nuisance theory, why can audience sensibilities be protected by nuisance from the sight of naked bodies? No source for this distinction has been expressed anywhere except for the Pauline conception of depraved flesh.

Articulating the rationale for distinguishing sex speech from obscenity in *Roth* (1957), Justice Brennan unconsciously engaged in viewpoint restriction by stating that appeal to prurient interest is not protected without identifying the compelling state interest served by its suppression. Virtually all the moral crimes of the colonial era have been decriminalized. Many have been deemed to be protected constitutional rights. Nudity exhibited with prurient intent is protected, but only in commercial contexts. Nudity without expression of prurient intent or other independent protectable expression using the body is viewed as not speech and, therefore, not protected. One form of bodily expression is defined as not worthy and the other as nonexistent. This is an arguable point of view.

Most indecent exposure statutes identify avoiding offense, annoyance, or alarm as the state interest being protected. The Supreme Court, in *Matal v. Tam* (2017), found that a refusal to register a trademark containing a derogatory term for Asian persons violated the First Amendment.[978] In so doing, a divided Court agreed that the disparagement bar to registration was an unconstitutional viewpoint restriction. The bar violated a "bedrock principle" established in *Hudnut* (1985) that "the government may not prohibit the expression of an idea simply because society finds the idea itself offensive or disagreeable." Indecent exposures provoke many points of view, meaning that the exposures are communicating something that inspires a response, often indicating that the audience finds the expression offensive or disagreeable.

The Supreme Court subsequently held that regardless of the government's interest in regulating indecent expression, it cannot engage in such regulation just because the "messages defy society's sense of decency or propriety." In *Iancu v. Brunetti* (2019), another trademark case, the Court invalidated a prohibition against registration of "immoral" trademarks.[979] The Court found that the "immoral or scandalous" criterion was viewpoint based. The federal statute involved "on its face, distinguish[ed] between two opposed sets of ideas: those aligned with conventional moral standards and those hostile to them; those inducing societal nods of approval and those provoking offense and condemnation. This facial viewpoint bias in the law results in viewpoint-discriminatory application." The Court called the prohibition against viewpoint discrimination "a core postulate of free speech law" and cautioned that the "government may not discriminate against speech based on the ideas or opinions it conveys."[980]

Naked bodies are targeted based on the viewpoint that they express nothing worthy of protection, a view that is disputed by many sources referenced herein. Display of naked bodies with lewd or lascivious intent outside of commercial contexts also expresses views of the actor that some audience may find offensive, alarming, or annoying. The Court has protected speech criticizing a cheerleading squad couched in "vulgar and offensive" terms, citing *Iancu*.[981] How is this student's indecency more worthy of protection or otherwise distinguishable?

Content-based Restriction

Justice Douglas, referring to the history of obscenity prosecution in his concurrence in *A Book Named "John Cleland's Memoirs of a Woman of Pleasure" v. Attorney General of Massachusetts* (1966), said, "Neither reason nor history warrants exclusion of any particular class of expression from the protection of the First Amendment on nothing more than a judgment that it is utterly without merit."[982] This is precisely the case with indecent exposure.

Roth (1957) ruled that if material, taken as a whole, appeals to prurient interest in sex, is patently offensive to contemporary community standards, and is "utterly without redeeming social value," it is obscene. The content of the expression of naked bodies is a priori judged to be utterly without merit and offensive or annoying. Content-based restrictions must survive strict scrutiny.[983] This class of restrictions in First Amendment cases comprise regulations that apply to specific speech due to the topic discussed or the idea or message expressed.[984] Such restrictions are inherently suspect and considered presumptively unconstitutional.[985] The government bears the burden of proving that these restrictions are narrowly tailored to serve compelling state interests.[986] This means that the restriction must serve a compelling governmental interest, be narrowly tailored to achieve that interest, and be the least restrictive means of advancing that interest.[987] A regulation that serves purposes unrelated to the content of expression may be deemed neutral, even if it has an incidental effect on some speakers or messages but not others.[988]

Content-based restrictions have been permitted only for a few categories of expression: advocacy of imminent lawless action, defamation, speech integral to criminal conduct, fighting words, child pornography, fraud, true threats, speech presenting some grave and imminent threat the government has the power to prevent, and obscenity.[989]

Indecent exposure laws impose content-based restrictions when they outlaw exposures that are sexually explicit or indecent without applying the *Miller* test.[990] For example, incidental nudity is not criminal, but intentionally exposing genitals in a sexual manner is. This is a statement. It has content. People may find it offensive. That is their view.

There is a well-documented moral philosophy known as "libertinism." The expression was coined by John Calvin in the sixteenth century when he was describing opposition to insistence that church discipline should be enforced uniformly against all members of Genevan society.[991] Libertines placed great value on physical pleasures and exploring the senses, including sexuality. Their philosophy grew over time into broad-based opposition to restraints in sexual morality. They are, in many ways, a counterpoint to the depravity of the flesh advocated by Apostle Paul.

Calvin's works were a major source of authority for Puritans. The majority of delegates to the Constitutional Convention in 1787 were Calvinists. The law has defended this philosophy against critical expression by libertines for more than three hundred years. Literary works have been allowed from major literary figures like John Wilmot, Second Earl of Rochester, and the Marquis de Sade, whose works are readily available to all audiences. Expressions of the philosophy in pornographic poetry, art, and fiction faced resistance, most of which has been overcome.

The most severe and enduring suppression of libertinism has been in indecent exposure laws that require evidence of lewd or lascivious intent or intent to sexually arouse the actor or an unwilling audience. These laws are content-based rejections of libertine philosophy, as evidenced in the obscenity tests of *Roth* (1957) and *Miller* (1973). More detailed discussion of the political, social, and moral effects of libertinism is beyond the scope of this initial work. Many would argue that the marketplace of ideas has benefited from its views. Those views are muted by American indecent exposure laws.

What, then, should be done where there is no such evidence of intent? Why are messages of naked human bodies that are not intended to be sexually provocative denied a right of expression? Naked bodies displayed in public can convey messages of celebration, equality, acceptance, and political and social justice, as Brigitte Bandit alleged in *Woodlands Pride*. The naked body is a tableau of experience where messages of hardship, pain, poor health, and disability may be inscribed on its surface. The suppression and sculpting of eroticism in drag shows creates expression more worthy of strict scrutiny than the communications of the natural naked body. Is there something in the messages of drag-queen shows that is more important to America's liberal democracy than the messages of the naked body? Judicial precedents seldom cite any evidence to support the state interest in legal repression of the body, relying instead on a simple presumption that it is expressionless and may be used for expressive purposes only in regulated places.

Native expression of the body in a commercial context was denied protection in *Edge v. City of Everett* (2022), a case that arose when a group of "bikini baristas" petitioned the District Court for the Western District of Washington to challenge the constitutionality of two city ordinances criminalizing lewd conduct and improper dress.[992] Similar to plaintiffs in *Woodlands Pride* (2023), the baristas argued that clothing (or lack of it) conveys important messages, including "female empowerment, positive body image, freedom of choice, and personal and political viewpoints."[993] The city alleged that there had been a proliferation of sex crimes at the barista stands. Police investigations allegedly found that "baristas routinely appeared in the windows of coffee stands nude or partially nude, posed in various states of nudity, allowed customers to photograph and/or touch them for a fee, performed sexual 'shows,' openly advertised prostitution activities, and allowed customers to masturbate while watching them perform, all within public view."[994]

The initial findings of the district court were appealed to the Ninth Circuit. On remand, the court considered the Ninth Circuit's view that the plaintiffs' First Amendment claims failed to "show a likelihood that their intended message will be understood by those who receive it."[995] The baristas had denied engaging in nude dancing or erotic performances, so they were not eligible for protection under *Barnes* (1991). Wearing pasties and G-strings alone would not transform their nakedness into "expressive conduct" within the meaning of the First Amendment, so that claim failed. The rational-basis standard of review was applied because the court concluded that no fundamental rights were involved. The Lewd Conduct Ordinance was upheld. The Dress Code Ordinance was held to violate the Equal Protection Clause because its restrictions were excessive and not substantially related to the city's objectives. The equal-protection claims will be examined in chapter nine.

Edge (2022) and *Woodlands Pride* (2023) expose a lack of intellectual discipline about the nature of protected speech. Two different commercial applications of sexual innuendo produced contradictory results. Both were sexual entertainment for profit. The state interest in protecting community standards was deemed an important government interest in *Edge*. The ban on drag shows in *Woodlands Pride* was found to be a content-based restriction, a viewpoint restriction, overbroad, vague, and a prior restraint on speech. The expressive content of the conduct is employed to support the differential treatment. Entertainment is the focus in both cases. Parties in both cases alleged similar messages. The plaintiffs did not contest dismissal of their First Amendment challenge to the Lewd Conduct Ordinance on remand. The court found that the government interest in reducing crime associated with the barista stands in *Edge* was sufficient to justify the Dress Code Ordinance against First Amendment claims. There was no crime study done in *Woodlands Pride*.

There are various theories about the basis for the guarantee of free speech. The search for truth is the most obvious. The truth of the naked body in American society is murky at best. There are many restrictions on it as a medium of expression that identify restricted erogenous zones and define permissible expressive content, acceptable audiences, and channels of communication. These restrictions confine and distort messages of the body, contradicting the fundamental value of search for truth. All of this is lost on the courts.

Constitutional values other than freedom of speech are implicated in this denial of expression of the body, such as deference to individual conceptions of dignity and autonomy, the concept that government has limited powers surrendered with the consent of citizens, and that freedom of expression is a residual natural right. Many political and human virtues have been ascribed to these values.[996]

The social and political values of various forms of artistic and commercial display of naked bodies that are protected speech range from sacred to profane, enriching and inspirational to sexually gratifying. These channelizations of nakedness confirm the extension of protection beyond linguistics to bodily movements, facial expressions, and selective exposure of body parts. The courts can regulate behavior that is not primarily communicative, but this does not explain the anomaly of the simple naked body. Nevertheless, this paradigm supports the artifice that justifies differential treatment for simple public indecency. The body is expressionless because it is deemed to be so. This tautology is fundamental to judicial refusal to recognize whatever such bodies might express.

Where an indecent exposure with lewd and lascivious intent creates alarm in the unwilling audience, there are other legal theories to support prosecution, such as assault. Just as physical attacks can injure the victim, the unwanted sexual overture of lewd and lascivious conduct could cause psychic injury. This is a difficult argument to sustain, given that there is little evidence to support the proposition that indecent exposure causes deep and lasting harm to its victims.[997]

There is considerable evidence that certain exposures of naked bodies to willing audiences can be beneficial, some of which has been summarized previously. It is difficult to defend the status quo legal judgment that the naked body is expressionless or that a finding of lewd and lascivious intent does not imply the presence of speech.

Although obscenity generally has not been protected speech, its definition and consequent scope of exclusion from protection have diminished radically since the middle of the twentieth century. Enforcement has effectively devolved to prohibition of child pornography. The rationale for not protecting it had been a presumption that it is intended merely to satisfy sexual desires, not to communicate ideas. Despite not warranting First Amendment protection, the flow of erotic material is largely unregulated. As we have discussed, it is no longer clear that pornography may not be considered protected speech in some circumstances.[998] The internet has made access to such material easy and universal.

The pornography wars of the 1970s and 1980s led to clashes between anti-pornography activists, who claimed that it harmed women, and an unprecedented alignment of activists focused on civil rights, censorship, gay rights, and adult entertainment. What the opposition had in common was that pornography is a marketplace of ideas that expresses views about sex, morality, and the role of women in society.

The history of indecent exposure laws points to Pauline concepts of the depravity of the flesh as the source of the prohibition. Secular justifications may hypothesize harmful effects on family concepts, denigration of women, or incipient sexual crimes, yet there is a dearth of evidence supporting these theses. Only violently pornographic presentations have shown such effects. Simple public nudity has not. The bottom line is an intuitive presumption that there is little or no speech value that is outweighed by a presumption of serious harm unsupported by scientific evidence. The classic state interests in prevention of evil example and avoidance of public nuisances have eroded in modern constitutional jurisprudence without a corollary effect on indecent exposure laws.

A central tenet of First Amendment law is aversion to content distinctions. The legal system is committed to content-neutral restrictions except where expressions of the body are involved. The viewpoint restriction is particularly interesting in this regard. According to this principle, the government cannot allow speech offering one viewpoint and forbid competing assertions—that is, once again, except for expressions of the naked body. Subject matter distinctions are similarly disfavored. Such restrictions warrant strict scrutiny, except for those related to the naked body, leaving body-freedom advocates stymied, frustrated, and without a voice. "Fuck the Draft," "Fuck Cheer," "Eat Shit"—all constitutionally protected speech delivering adequate value to society to warrant strict scrutiny of the state interest competing with the right of free speech.

Fucking and eating shit are often associated with prurient interest in sex. "Fuck" is being used metaphorically, but should the crude poetry of this use elevate its offensiveness to protected speech? These expressions are obviously intended to be patently offensive and are generally perceived by audiences as such. So, it all comes down to whether they have serious literary, artistic, political, or scientific value, according to the *Miller* (1973) test. This criterion has not been measured against the weight of evidence presented, and alluded to, in this study of indecent exposure laws.

The withering of the Christian-nation authority creates needs and opportunities for experimentation with alternative moral models, such as social nudism. The science of semiotics offers unexplored opportunities for potential social scientific progress if individuals have the right to choose not only the clothes they wear but whether to wear them. There are people whose bodies are beautiful art. Recognizing a right to display this beauty in public without charging the audience might lessen the burden of adult entertainment venues on communities, the women who work there, and the men who go there to see naked women. Regardless of the level of judicial scrutiny, there is nothing more than tradition to support the laws nowadays. In many instances in modern American society, community members are expected to tolerate activities creating offense, annoyance, or alarm, so the state interest in this particular activity is suspect.

Prior Restraint

Woodlands Pride (2023) found that the drag ban statute imposed an impermissible prior restraint on speech by providing local governments with authority to regulate sexually oriented performances on public property or in the presence of children.[999] The City of San Francisco prohibits exposure of private parts in public. The ordinance prohibiting public nudity provides an exception for permitted parades, fairs, or festivals.[1000] It references another provision of the Police Code to prohibit public nudity while serving customers in restaurants and when on public seating without a barrier.[1001] Many constitutional issues arise from these ordinances. They express viewpoint and content restrictions preferring nudity done in enumerated contexts and do so using a permitting process. This licensing regime authorizing certain transgressions of the public nudity ban is an insidious tool for shaping public discourse about the body that is obviously inspired by a powerful LGBTQ political influence in the city. Such practices affirm the limits of the dress regulations that they superficially appear to challenge.[1002] The permitting process reaffirms the general prohibition and forecloses alternative and competing public expressions of public nudity that do not satisfy the discretion of local authorities.

This chapter explored the impact of the evolution of free speech doctrine on the crime of being naked in public. Difficult questions were addressed: What if the actor intends the exhibition to be an expression? What if that intention has religious, political, or commercial motives? Why aren't lewd and/or lascivious communications worthy of First Amendment protection when profanity and pornography are protected? They are a constitutionally protected value in commercial contexts. Would it be more reasonable to view indecent exposure laws as regulating the manner of expression? Is decency a restriction on both the substance and manner of expressions involving public display of the body? What is the role of the audience in determining constitutional protection? What is the effect of place on freedom-of-speech claims for this crime? Freedom of speech is a complex and treacherous area of constitutional interpretation often influenced by unconscious forces.

Whether the naked body is viewed as expressionless or a canvas on which expression can be painted, if the free-speech argument fails, there may be a credible argument that such uses of the body are the business of its owner as a matter of due process and natural rights.

8. To Maintain a Decent Society: The Government's Power to Regulate Morals in Relation to the Individual's Rights to Bodily Autonomy

It has been said that liberty and privacy come down in the end "to a control over the most basic vehicle of selfhood: the body. For control over the body is the first form of autonomy and the necessary condition, for those who are not saints or stoics, of all later forms."[1003] Leaving aside the religious genesis of indecent exposure laws and arguments that naked bodies are natively expressive or their use as a vehicle of expression is worthy of First Amendment protection, questions remain whether offense to the opinions of others should be sufficient to justify state regulation of personal appearance.

Dress, makeup, and adornment, including expressions of affiliations with social, political, and religious organizations and subcultures, are common ways to express individuality. Personal choices in attire, hairstyle, and other aspects of appearance may collide with school and workplace rules, creating legal conflicts. U.S. law prohibits employers from discriminating in dress codes against protected classes.[1004] State and local laws on these subjects exist as well. This chapter will focus on judicial doctrines that inform an assessment of rights of undress as a matter of due process and natural rights.

The Supreme Court has found fertile ground for implicit rights to liberty and privacy in the First, Fifth, Ninth, Tenth, and Fourteenth Amendments. The Fifth and Fourteenth Amendments provide, among other things: "No person shall be . . . deprived of life, liberty, or property, without due process of law."[1005]The Fifth Amendment constrains the federal government from violating due process of law, and the Fourteenth does likewise vis-à-vis state governments.

The Supreme Court has developed a doctrine of substantive due process based on these amendments to protect from government interference certain individual rights deemed by the Court to be fundamental, even if such rights are not enumerated in the Constitution. It has been said that the amendments give the courts the power to guarantee "freedom from all substantial arbitrary impositions and purposeless restraints."[1006] This doctrine has been a bulwark of *custos morum*. Substantive due process is distinguished from procedural due process. The latter protects individuals from the coercive power of government by ensuring that adjudication processes, under valid laws, are fairly and impartially enforced.

Substantive due process is often criticized, including by Justice Thomas in his concurring opinion in *Dobbs* (2022); he sees the amendment as only a guarantee of good process, not a protection of unenumerated liberty interests.[1007] He argues that the doctrine lacks any basis in the Constitution. What he doesn't say is that the drafters of the Bill of Rights expressly disclaimed that the Bill of Rights was an exclusive list of individual rights, inferring that there are other individual rights. Natural rights theories, arguing that individual rights are residual, not granted, represent a counterforce consistent with the Bill of Rights and constitutional democracy more generally. The Ninth and Tenth Amendments provide an alternative theory of unenumerated rights: protecting the natural rights of people not surrendered to the government. This idea has been disfavored by courts as they have expended more intellectual energy defining the contours of rights than limitations on the power of government despite there being no constitutional basis for the bias. Only the compelling-interest approach evidences serious interest, and it is limited to court-defined "fundamental" individual interests.

We will begin by exploring potential application of substantive due process to indecent exposure laws. The focus is on the Fourteenth Amendment, given its nature as a limitation on state government powers. Decisions regarding contraception, procreation, marriage, family relations, child-rearing, and education have been included within a "right to privacy."[1008] All these matters were at one time the concern of religion. Now state control of these aspects of life is limited by privacy doctrine as an aspect of individual liberty. Indecent exposure laws have withstood the judicial expansion of rights as affected state interests have diminished in credibility. Are they still sufficient to overcome the individual's right to be left alone to enjoy life, liberty, and the pursuit of happiness? Does that right include one's appearance in public?

The constitutional source of the right of privacy is not settled. One possible source is the Fourteenth Amendment's concept of personal liberty.[1009] Another is implicit in the penumbra of the Bill of Rights presumed to be incorporated into the Fourteenth Amendment.[1010] A third possibility is the Ninth Amendment's reservation of rights to the people.[1011] The boundaries of the constitutionally protected right of privacy have not been settled. The choice of rationale is important because it affects the scope of rights and the tests for measuring affected state rights and powers. This chapter discusses the kinds of rights that have been protected by these principles, those that have not been protected, the state interests implicated in each class of situations, and analytic approaches adopted by the Supreme Court in making such determinations that may be relevant to possible indecent exposure claims.

At least two distinct kinds of interests have been protected under the right of privacy. "One is the individual interest in avoiding disclosure of personal matters, and another is the interest in independence in making certain kinds of important decisions."[1012] It is this latter interest, which might more fairly be characterized as a liberty interest or the protection of autonomy,[1013] that is impaired by indecent exposure laws. The right of personal autonomy subsumed under the right of privacy is not limited to acts that are not observable to the public.[1014] This right is distinguishable from an individual's general right to liberty in the degree of personal intimacy involved, so that claims of autonomy for decisions regarding such matters as contraception, procreation, and marriage are treated under the rubric of privacy rather than liberty.[1015]

The distinction has legal significance. When a court finds a right of privacy at risk with respect to autonomy in decision-making, the right to make that decision is considered to be fundamental.[1016] Government interference with a fundamental right is subjected to strict scrutiny when challenged in the courts and must be justified by compelling state interests.[1017] Not all liberty interests are considered fundamental. Where non-fundamental rights are involved, government interference can be justified by a reasonable relationship to a legitimate legislative aim.[1018] The probability that a law will be invalidated is much greater when strict scrutiny is applied.

Boundaries of the privacy right in decision-making are not neatly drawn. The Court has proceeded on a more or less ad hoc basis in defining the right. Early definitions were grand and broad. In 1879, Judge Cooley termed it simply the "right to complete immunity: to be let alone."[1019] Fifty years later, Justice Brandeis endorsed Cooley's "right to be let alone," calling it "[t]he most comprehensive of rights and the right most valued by civilized men."[1020] The decisions of the Supreme Court since

Brandeis's pronouncement demonstrate a more restrictive view of the right to be let alone.

Commentators have outlined principles that distinguish privacy-autonomy rights from less fundamental liberty interests. Tyler Baker's note in the *Stanford Law Review* identified "impact on the individual" as the primary determinant.[1021] The author highlighted reference by the court in *Eisenstadt v. Baird* (1972) to "matters so fundamentally affecting a person" as an indication of a theme "which seems to run through the more recent cases."[1022] The decision in *Roe v. Wade* (1973) that a pregnant woman's decision to abort is protected by a right of privacy appeared to be based on recognition of the extreme hardship presented by alternatives to abortion in a matter fundamentally affecting her person.[1023] The refusal to extend the privacy right to obscenity in *Paris Adult Theatre I v. Slaton* (1975)[1024] could be distinguished because of a presumption that the desire for obscenity does not so fundamentally affect a person as does an undesirable pregnancy and the denial of access to obscenity imposes less hardship than a ban on abortion.[1025]

Impact on matters fundamentally affecting persons appears to be the common denominator in cases declaring autonomy in decision-making a fundamental right of privacy. Personal relationships seem to be a particularly important category of fundamental matters,[1026] yet only the most intimate aspects of those relations, those regarding sexuality, such as contraception, procreation, abortion, and the usual accoutrements of normal sexual relations—marriage, the family, and child-rearing—have been brought within the protective ambit of the right to privacy.[1027]

Thus far the Supreme Court has not characterized its decisions in terms of deregulating sexuality. It has continued to cite with approval statutes outlawing adultery, fornication, bigamy, and prostitution as well as court decisions upholding such laws.[1028] This distinction between the classes of sexual activity is difficult to explain other than by reference to contemporary morality. If these various sexual activities were ordered on a continuum from most acceptable to least acceptable, a positive correlation is observable between the degree of popular acceptance or tolerance of the activity and whether it has been included within the right of privacy. The correlation is quite high except for abortion, and this may have been due to concern over the extreme hardships that would result if the decision were not protected. This may distinguish it from unprotected sexually related activities. The finding of a constitutional right to abortion was overturned in 2022.[1029]

Using contemporary morality to define the limits of the right comports with an early directive by Justice Cardozo that the Court should turn to the "traditions and conscience of our people" to determine which rights are to be considered fundamental.[1030] Under this approach, the Court determines when the moral consensus reaches a point where a particular kind of activity no longer may be subjected to legal regulation absent a compelling state interest. In so doing, the Court overrides the judgment of the legislature and forbids as a matter of constitutional principle any further intrusions into the area.

The oddity of this scheme is that the judgment of nine appointed officials with life tenure regarding the state of contemporary morality is preferred to the decision of elected representatives whose traditional function is to reflect popular sentiments and who are subject to removal every few years if they do not do so. In effect, in most cases, the decision to overturn a legislative determination on a moral issue serves more to insulate certain activities from the community's prevailing moral views than to articulate contemporary morality. This practice will hardly lead to the ideal of developing neutral principles defining privacy.[1031] Furthermore, it presumes the legitimacy of majoritarian morality, a premise discussed elsewhere. Privacy is not a concept that can be simply determined by the vicissitudes of public opinion, and the Court should not define it in such terms. It is more useful and more reasonable to consider public opinion, as embodied in the laws passed by the several legislatures, to be a limitation on the right. The impact of these laws on the exercise of that right can then be measured by the appropriate constitutional standard.

According to Professor Tribe of Harvard Law School, regardless of whether one terms it a right of privacy, autonomy, or intimate decision, "any plausible definition of privacy, then, whatever the sources of its normative commitments, must take the body as its first and most basic reference for control over personal identity."[1032]

Professor Tribe embraced this as the correct starting point, but he believed that it was only a starting point. Principles still need to be developed to determine the nature and extent of emanations from the hub of personality that ought to be considered fundamental. Professor Tribe's discussion of this point confuses effect and justification. He wrote that "[n]ot all forms of bodily compulsion, and not even all actions that entail an unwanted touching or intrusion into the body, can plausibly be regarded as violations of the self or usurpations of personality."[1033]

He offered as an example of bodily compulsion that does not violate the self or usurp personality a situation where "the intrusion [is] caused by the police officer who gently shoves a person back to clear the way for an ambulance." However, the effect of being shoved is certainly an intrusion upon the self or personality of the individual. In Professor Tribe's hypothetical, the police officer's legitimate concern for health and safety justifies the intrusion.[1034] The justification does not mollify the effect. It provides a defense to the shoved individual's claim of a right to a remedy.

Despite this conceptual confusion,[1035] Professor Tribe went on to assert that civil rights can be adequately protected from unwarranted intrusion "only if the interest intruded upon is scrupulously defined at a level of generality sufficient to protect persons who deviate from the norm." In his opinion, a right to bodily autonomy[1036]—the right to do with one's body as one pleases—is such a sufficiently general principle.

Professor Stanley Benn proposed as a foundation for the right "respect for persons,"[1037] which should encompass three ideals:

- the ideal of personal relations;
- the Lockian ideal of the politically free man in a minimally regulated society, and
- the Kantian ideal of the morally autonomous man, acting on principles that he accepts as rational.[1038]

Political choice, moral choice, and the choice of friends are all decisions at the heart of personality. Only moral choice does not enjoy undisputed freedom from government compulsion. Is this exception defensible? Do individuals have less right to moral autonomy? Or, alternatively, does the government have more power to regulate morals than politics or personal relations? If so, why?

There are other unquestioned limitations on the right to bodily autonomy. According to Justice Blackman, writing for a nearly unanimous court in *Roe v. Wade* (1973),

> [t]he privacy right involved [in the abortion decision], therefore, cannot be said to be absolute. In fact, it is not clear to us that the claim asserted by some amicae that one has an unlimited right to do with one's body as one pleases bears a close relationship to the right of privacy previously articulated in the Court's decisions. The Court has refused to recognize an unlimited right of this kind in the past.[1039]

These limitations are imposed on interrelated dimensions of location and action.[1040] For instance, the decision in *Stanley v. Georgia* (1969) to protect private possession of obscenity in the home from prohibitive legislation demonstrated a special constitutional concern for the sanctity of the home.[1041] Although possession of obscenity in the home is protected, the relationship between the right of privacy and the degree of publicity involved is not linear. The Supreme Court in *Paris* (1973) refused to extend the home privilege to a limited-access commercial theater.[1042] Baker's law review note suggests two bases for the special privilege of privacy in the home:

- "activities in the home harm others only to the extent that they cause offense resulting from the mere thought that individuals might be engaging in such activities and that such 'harm' is not protectable by the state;" and
- "individuals need a sanctuary where they can be freer from social control."[1043]

The Court's reference to the adage "a man's home is his castle"[1044] signals an implicit preference for the latter rationale. Furthermore, the Court has refused to recognize a right to access obscenity for private use in the home,[1045] so outside the haven of the home the refusal to afford constitutional protection to obscenity is unaffected. Greater freedom in the home cannot be unlimited. Presumably, the sanctity of the home would not insulate all kinds of criminal activity from governmental intervention.[1046] Yet, except for activities that threaten the person or property of others, in the castle, "we can drop the mask, desist for a while from projecting on the world the image that may reflect the values of our peers rather than the realities of our natures."[1047] What about the prevention of evil example? Recall common-law cases where public knowledge of private indecencies supported convictions.

Despite lessened concern for the insidious effect on public morals that such actions might foster, this idea of a sanctuary leaves intact government power to force its citizens outside the home to wear a mask of alternative morality, but what legitimate governmental interest justifies such compulsion? Prevention of evil of example is no longer a credible state interest. The public/private distinction aligns with the remaining justification of avoiding public nuisance. This interest has been undermined by precedent discussed in chapter seven. Immoral activities protected in the home are criminal when done in public because they are offensive, annoying, or alarming to offended observers. People must "wear the mask" or be punished.

Some privacy rights extend beyond the home. For instance, "the constitutionally protected privacy of family, marriage, motherhood, procreation, and child-rearing . . . extends to the doctor's office, the hospital, the hotel room, or as otherwise required to safeguard the right to intimacy involved."[1048] Privacy rights can exist independent of place, as with access to contraceptives. Nakedness enjoys limited place-based relief in strip clubs, other entertainment venues, art displays, nudist colonies, and virtual renditions via media technologies.

Justice Blackman in *Roe v. Wade* (1973) cited two cases as examples of limitations on an individual's right to bodily autonomy: *Jacobson v. Massachusetts* (1905)[1049] and *Buck v. Bell* (1927).[1050] A claimed constitutional right to refuse to submit to compulsory vaccination was rejected in *Jacobson.* The right of "mental defectives" to avoid sterilization was denied in *Buck v. Bell.* The decision in the former rested on concern for public health.[1051] The decision in the latter, sanctioning sterilization of Carrie Buck, was made after weighing the detriment to her against the privations expected to be endured by a fourth "generations of imbeciles."[1052] In each case, compelling state interests justified the bodily intrusions. Protection of health and safety are legitimate state aims from which no individual may find a sanctuary. No person can kill, steal, or conspire to do the same with immunity from prosecution simply because they did so in the home.

The only traditional state interest affected by the location of a person's action is the protection of morals by preventing evil example and avoiding public nuisances. With every accretion to the class of activities in the personal-autonomy aspect of the right of privacy, a suggestion that the Court is unconsciously and indirectly, but steadily, undermining this tradition grows more plausible. Rather than face the issue of the constitutionality and efficacy of legal enforcement of public morals foursquare or straightforwardly consider the "Kantian ideal of the morally autonomous man," the Court persists in weaving a treacherous intermingling of the countervailing forces of majority rule and individual liberty. As in the choice among various sexual activities described above, the Court is imposing implicit moral judgments during the definitional process. Like Professor Tribe, the Court is merging analytically separable concepts of individual liberty and state interest.

Thus, a fundamental right to bodily autonomy as to states of dress and undress can be grounded in the liberty guaranteed in the Fourteenth Amendment under the penumbra theory or as suggested by Justice Goldberg, in the Ninth Amendment, by recognizing the body as the source from which all liberty, autonomy, personality, and the very concept of the self emanates.

The Supreme Court has favored the penumbra theory as the basis for the autonomy aspect of fundamental rights of privacy. Justice Douglas first articulated the theory in *Griswald v. Connecticut* (1965).[1053] There, he wrote that

> [v]arious guarantees [in the Bill of Rights] create zones of privacy. The right of association contained in the penumbra of the First Amendment is one, . . . the Third Amendment in its prohibition against the quartering of soldiers "in any house" in time or peace without the consent of the owner is another. . . . The Fourth Amendment explicitly affirms the "right of the people to be secure in their persons, houses, papers, and effects, against unreasonable searches and seizures." The Fifth Amendment in its Self-Incrimination Clause enables the citizen to create a zone of privacy which government may not force him to surrender to his detriment. The Ninth Amendment provides: "The enumeration in the Constitution, of certain rights, shall not be construed to deny or disparage others retained by the people."[1054]

In the opinion of the Court in *Griswold* (1965), use of contraceptives fell within a zone of privacy created by several of these fundamental guarantees. The Court's failure to explain which of the fundamental guarantees were involved or offer conceptual discussion regarding the central value of this new general right to privacy raised the ire of commentators, who for years since the decision have searched for the touchstone of this brand of privacy.[1055]

The Supreme Court's most recent guidance on substantive due process is *Dobbs* (2022), where the Court overruled *Roe v. Wade* (1973), finding that abortion is not implicitly protected by the Constitution, deeply rooted in America's history and tradition, implicit in ordered liberty, or justified as a component of a broader right. The ruling marks a significant retreat from assertion of *custos morum* authority. Its application to indecent exposure is complex due to fundamental differences in the rights involved, their histories and traditions, relationships to constitutional principles embodied in the original meaning of the Constitution, effect on ordered liberty, and implications for broader recognized rights:

- *Fundamental differences in the rights involved.* Both cases involve control of the body and morality. Rightly or wrongly, the focus in *Dobbs* was on health and safety. The case involved countervailing arguments about individual interests in balancing concepts of the beginning of life versus women's control of their bodies. Indecent exposure laws affect control over personal identity and voice, the nature and quality of interpersonal relations, and concepts of public decency. The balancing of rights of individuals weighs these values against much less consequential state interests in avoiding offense, annoyance, and alarm of unwilling viewers.

- *Histories and traditions.* This deeply rooted history test for the Due Process Clause is ironic, given that the amendment was enacted to outlaw slavery, which, at the time, was such a tradition. Nevertheless, a right to be naked in public has support in the long histories and traditions of social nudism, nude sunbathing, and libertinism.
- *Relationships to constitutional principles embodied in the original meaning of the Constitution.* There are no references to abortion in the Constitution, nor are there reasonable implications of protection by any constitutional provision. Although there are no references to indecent exposure in the Constitution, there is considerable relevant precedent and documentary evidence regarding the original meaning of the Constitution implicating numerous constitutional clauses and principles, as discussed elsewhere in this study.
- *Effect on ordered liberty. Dobbs* presented an unavoidable conflict between the health and well-being of pregnant women and the termination of fetuses. With no clear guide to resolution, the Court abnegated responsibility in favor of the legislative process and noted the important roles played by scientific evidence and the political process. Constitutional democracy rests on a foundation of the marketplace of ideas. Indecent exposure laws mute and distort messages and images of the body, inhibiting better understanding of the role of the body in the definition of self and good order of society. No scientific evidence has been offered to support the laws. The laws, as written, have many possible constitutional infirmities. Properly drawn laws narrowly tailored to protect legitimate state interests supported by sufficient credible evidence might survive constitutional scrutiny.
- *Implications for broader recognized rights.* Freedom of speech, association, and the exercise of religion in the First Amendment, freedom from unreasonable searches and seizures of the person in the Fourth Amendment, and freedom from self-incrimination in the Fifth Amendment are all specific descriptions of liberty of the body.

Communication, movement, religiosity, and physical integrity of the body as integral rights of the individual are central values of the Bill of Rights. Except for religion, which is also governed by an anti-establishment constitutional mandate, one would suppose the government is free to promote these individual interests in furtherance of the general welfare of the nation. However, when a government action opposes these individual interests, shouldn't that action necessarily be the result of a compelling state interest? Professor Tribe's premise is flawed: all compulsory governmental touching or intrusion into the body is a violation of the self and usurpation of personality. Because the body is the foundation of all other rights, all nontrivial actions of this sort ought to be justified by compelling state interests. No such interests have been advanced to justify indecent exposure laws.

Substantive due process may be the weakest constitutional claim after *Dobbs*. The effect of *Dobbs* on Ninth and Tenth Amendment claims in unclear but probably negative. At a minimum, *Dobbs* should invalidate statutes that ban all public nudity regardless of intent as overbroad as a matter of procedural due process, given the long, well-ordered tradition and history of social nudism. The Court's notion that profound moral and social questions should be left to the people does not absolve the Court from its duty to assess the constitutionality of the process employed to effectuate the outcomes.

The reservation of rights to the people in the Ninth and Tenth Amendments when read in conjunction with the Fifth and Fourteenth Amendments support a different due process argument questioning the validity of indecent exposure laws. The Ninth Amendment reads:

> The enumeration in the Constitution, of certain rights, shall not be construed to deny or disparage others retained by the people.[1056]

And the Tenth Amendment adds:

> The powers not delegated to the United States by the Constitution, nor prohibited by it to the States, are reserved to the States respectively, or to the people.[1057]

As discussed above, due process under the Fifth and Fourteenth Amendments has been interpreted to not only guarantee procedural fairness but also limit the substance of governmental actions to furtherance of aims not in conflict with constitutional principles regarding the powers of government and rights of individuals.[1058] The nebulous concept of substantive due process is not necessary to protect unenumerated rights. The Ninth and Tenth Amendments reinforce the constitutional concept of limited government. They represent further evidence of the concern of drafters of the Bill of Rights that its list of protected rights might be construed as exclusive.

Perhaps guided by unconscious fears about individual liberty, the Court has virtually written "the people" out of the Ninth and Tenth Amendments, undermining the framers' concept of limited government. The Ninth Amendment has been called "the forgotten amendment."[1059] Judicial views of the Tenth Amendment have largely limited its application to issues of federal/state relations.[1060] The Supreme Court has given virtually no credence to the Ninth Amendment's explicit recognition of retention by the people of an undifferentiated residuum of rights not expressed in the first eight amendments to the Bill of Rights. The Tenth Amendment reserved powers not delegated by the Constitution not only to the states, but to the people.

In his book *The Forgotten Ninth Amendment*, Bennett Patterson called the amendment a "declaration and recognition of individualism, which is the cardinal virtue of democracy; a succinct expression of the dignity and liberty of the individual and a recognition of the soul of mankind."[1061] Justice Goldberg, in his concurring opinion in *Griswold*,[1062] directed the Court's attention to these values in the Ninth Amendment, yet he managed to convince only Chief Justice Warren and Justice Brennan that the amendment was a proper basis for invalidating a state ban on the sale of contraceptives. According to Goldberg's approach, the right to marital privacy, including access to contraceptives, flows from the "entire fabric of the Constitution and the purposes that clearly underlie its specific guarantees."[1063]

In structuring the Constitution, the framers proposed that the people retain not only rights but also powers. Under the Tenth Amendment, all powers that are not conferred on the federal and state governments by their respective constitutions, and those forbidden to the states, are reserved to the people. As Story remarked in his *Commentaries on the Constitution*:

> Being an instrument of limited and environmental powers, it follows irresistibly, that what is not conferred is withheld, and belongs to the State authorities if invested by their constitutions of government respectively in them; and if not so invested, it is retained BY THE PEOPLE, as part of their residual sovereignty.[1064]

The Tenth Amendment is not, as suggested by Justice Stone in *United States v. Darby* (1941), simply "a truism that all is retained which has not been surrendered."[1065] His reasoning was rejected in *New York v. United States* (1992).[1066] The amendment is an emphatic statement on the nature of government. In a democracy, the people are the original sovereigns who delegate to the government certain limited powers. It is not the government that grants the people limited rights, but vice versa. This natural order reflected in both the Ninth and Tenth Amendments implies a broad concept of individual liberty. The people retain all powers and rights not surrendered to the government. Detailed study of evidence of the original intent of the framers of the Constitution and the understanding of the ratifiers indicates that the Bill of Rights should be read more as placing limits on government than as granting rights.[1067] It did not give rights to the people, because such rights already belonged to them.[1068] The Supreme Court has never embraced this notion, preferring instead to exercise its *custos morum* authority to parse out discrete rights based on application of precedent to the Court's assessment of social conditions.

When determining the balance of powers and rights between individuals and their government, the Court begins by defining the extent of the individual right. This practice invariably leads to conceptions of a limited right; for instance, the right to liberty, which is then "balanced" against the means and aims of the infringing governmental action. The right is *doubly* balanced: first in the definitional process and then in the relationship. A proper understanding of the relationship of the individual to the government can be more justly determined according to the intent of the framers by recognizing that the liberty of the individual is in the first place unlimited, as broad as imagination can carry it.[1069] The only limitations are those imposed by conscience, society, and laws based on delegated powers. This reconciles and synthesizes the intent of the Fifth, Ninth, Tenth, and Fourteenth Amendments.[1070]

The "concept at the root of any decent system of ordered liberty" is recognition of the "dignity and worth of every human being."[1071] Government may "order" liberty only to promote these values by imposing limitations on actions that threaten the lives, property, or personality of its citizens. Every encroachment on liberty must be carefully measured to promote these aims to avoid unjustified waste of precious liberty, for no theorist of American democracy would presume the people to have given the government power to introduce arbitrary tyranny or that the citizens lightly abnegated their autonomy to the state.

The Supreme Court announced its rule for balancing the liberty of the individual and the interests of government in *McLaughlin v. Florida* (1964). It stated that "where there is a significant encroachment upon personal liberty, the State may prevail only upon showing a subordinating interest which is compelling."[1072] The means chosen to effectuate that aim must be "necessary, and not merely rationally related," to it.[1073] This "compelling interest" test is a judicial concept also known as strict scrutiny. It has developed on a case-by-case basis. The three types of interests that have been determined to be compelling are the following:

- *Protection of life and property*. The prevention of local crime[1074] and maintenance of domestic peace[1075] have long been considered compelling state interests. Measures to control fraud, undue influence, intimidation, overreaching, and other forms of vexatious conduct in commercial dealing[1076] are usually included. Concerns for the safety and health of citizens, such as in actions promoting highway safety[1077] regulating the medical profession,[1078] providing for the removal of victims of child abuse from their parents,[1079] and suppressing intimidation and threats of violence1080 are also compelling.
- Ensuring the integrity of the political system. The government has a compelling interest in "self-preservation" that allows it to use reasonable means to suppress subversive activity[1081] and preserve important state documents.[1082] Maintenance of the integrity of the electoral process is a compelling concern,[1083] as is the fostering of public education, which is vital to the perpetuation of the democratic ideal.[1084] Ensuring high standards in the legal profession to safeguard the political rights of citizens is, likewise, a compelling state interest.[1085]
- Protecting individual liberty. Eliminating racial discrimination, integrating the medical profession, and increasing the number of doctors willing to serve minority patients are compelling state interests.[1086] The right to marry, which is not expressly provided for in the Constitution, was deemed a compelling interest.[1087]

This curious third category of individual liberties that have been deemed to be "compelling interests" of government implies a secondary balancing of constitutional rights. Those rights that are not fundamental and that the government has a compelling interest in may be preferred to other less fundamental rights.[1088] It is noteworthy that support of marriage is one of only two individual rights considered to be a compelling interest of government. The interest of government in promoting racial integration in the 1970s is easy to understand. The interest in marriage may not be so obvious. When viewed in the context of moral jurisprudence, it is understandable why governmental support is so strong. Dating to the colonial era, the family was the backbone of civil order and the wellspring of productivity and decency.

The principles regarding compelling state interests that emerged in this distillation of cases conform remarkably well to those described in the Preamble to the Constitution:

> We, the people of the United States, in order to form a more perfect union, establish justice, insure domestic tranquility, provide for the common defense, promote the general welfare, and secure the blessings of liberty to ourselves and our posterity, do ordain and establish this Constitution for the United States of America.

According to Justice Story, the Preamble's "true office is to expound the nature and extent and application of the powers actually conferred by the Constitution . . . ."[1089] The Fifth, Ninth, Tenth, and Fourteenth Amendments reserve all other powers and concomitant rights to the people. Government interests are subordinated in the Constitution to the ideals of protection of life, property, and individual liberty.

State interests that have been found to be subordinate and not compelling include concern about incipient threats of welfare fraud,[1090] racial conflicts,[1091] excessive lawsuits,[1092] and damage to public confidence in the integrity of the political process.[1093] Thus, mere apprehension of damage to otherwise compelling interests is not sufficient to justify infringement of fundamental individual rights. Also, mere historical accident[1094] cannot give rise to a compelling state interest. The preceding analysis reveals the proper principles describing individual liberty indicated by the text of the Constitution, evidence of the likely intent of the framers, understanding of the ratifiers, and common public meaning at the time:

- The Constitution created a government of limited powers.
- All powers not delegated to the government were retained by the people.
- The rights given up are those necessarily forfeited because of the delegation of powers. A gratuitous abrogation of rights should not be presumed.
- The government has compelling interests in national defense, commerce, and protection of life, liberty, and property and may exercise the powers necessary to effectuate these aims.
- Individual liberty should not be sacrificed to any other ends. Residual sovereignty reposes in the people, not the government.

- The government is the servant of the people, not their master, when considering interests that are less than compelling.[1095]

The government has no delegated power to define liberty in terms that allow it to expropriate individual choice to further interests that are not compelling. The Constitutional guarantee of liberty is "an incomplete protection if it encompasses only the right to do momentous acts, leaving the state free to interfere with these personal aspects of our lives which have no direct bearing on the ability of others to enjoy their liberty."[1096]

The right to bodily autonomy is an essential aspect of individual liberty. Control over one's body is a central value of a healthy personality. The choice of whether, with what, and to what extent to cover the body is an integral expression of the self.[1097] Judge Wisdom, in a case involving the right of a young man to wear his hair longer than convention condoned, explained that a man deprived of freedom to dress as he pleases

> is forced against his will to hold himself out symbolically as a person holding ideas contrary, perhaps, to ideas he holds most dear. Forced dress . . . humiliates the unwilling complier, forces him to submerge his individuality in the "undistracting" mass, and in general, smacks of the exaltation of organization over member, unit over component, and state over individual.[1098]

The inversion of values described in the Constitution that Judge Wisdom warned against seems eerily consistent with the Supreme Court's modern jurisprudence before *Dobbs* (2022). The Ninth Amendment was drafted to avoid this very problem, as noted by James Madison, principal author of the Bill of Rights:

[B]y enumerating particular exceptions of the grant of power, it would disparage those rights which were not placed in that enumeration, and it might follow by implication, that those rights which were not singled out, were intended to be assigned into the hands of the general government, and were consequently insecure.[1099]

A long-hair controversy reached the Supreme Court in 1976 in *Kelley v. Johnson*, in which a policeman unsuccessfully sought to invalidate a local regulation of the length and style of policemen's hair.[1100] Justice Marshall, dissenting, joined by Justice Brennan, shared the understanding of Judge Wisdom regarding the importance of individual control over personal appearance. He thought it "clear that the Fourteenth Amendment does indeed protect against comprehensive regulation of what citizens may or may not wear." Further, he wrote, it seemed to him

> manifest that the "full range of conduct" [free from governmental control] must encompass one's interest in dressing according to his

> own taste. An individual's personal appearance may reflect, sustain, and nourish his personality, and may well be used as a means of expressing his attitude and lifestyle. In taking control over a citizen's personal appearance, the government forces him to sacrifice substantial elements of his integrity and identity as well. To say the liberty guarantee of the Fourteenth Amendment does not encompass matters of personal appearance would be fundamentally inconsistent with the values of privacy, self-identity, autonomy, and personal integrity that I have always assumed the Constitution was designed to protect.[1101]

The majority, led by Justice Rehnquist, had a different view of the liberty interest involved. It was distinguishable from other "fundamental" liberties involving matters of procreation, marriage, and family life. Prior Supreme Court decisions offered little guidance for determining "whether the citizenry at large has some sort of 'liberty' interest within the Fourteenth Amendment in matters of personal appearance"; nevertheless, the majority was willing to "assume an affirmative answer for purposes of deciding this case"![1102] Wide latitude traditionally accorded government in handling its "internal affairs" implied that the regulation should be upheld if rationally related to legitimate state interests; no necessary connection to a compelling interest needed to be shown.[1103]

Although the state interest involved in regulating the conduct of police officers is a compelling one of protection of life and property, maintenance of esprit de corps and discipline is akin to the sort of incipient threats to compelling interests that have traditionally given way in confrontations with individual liberty. In choosing the standard of review by reference to the nature of the governmental interest, the majority departed from a long, unbroken history of basing that decision on the nature of the individual rights involved.[1104] Undoubtedly, the choice of the standard of review was also based to a considerable degree on the implicit judgment of the justices in the majority of the relative unimportance of the right to personal appearance. But what was the source of the Court's authority to make such judgments? What delegated power authorizes the government to determine the relative significance of decisions regarding individuals' personal appearance? The infirmity of the majority's approach lies in its insidious double balancing.

The proper analytic approach was suggested earlier: the people are the original sovereigns. As such, their liberty is unlimited. When the framers created our form of constitutional government, they delegated certain powers to it. In so doing, they necessarily sacrificed the implicated individual rights. All powers not delegated and all rights not appurtenant to the delegated powers were retained by the people. Therefore, to be constitutional, any governmental action that infringes on liberty must be an exercise of the delegated powers. The government owes a duty of efficiency given the nature of its relationship to the individual: it should choose means that minimally impact on powers and rights retained by the people.

Liberty is not a right granted to various degrees to the people by the government. As the majority in *Kelley* (1976) suggested, it is inherent in their natural sovereignty. The Court does not have the power or right to judge the personal significance of aspects of liberty. Its duty is limited to assuring that the actions of the coordinate branches and of the states are motivated by proper aims and conducted through efficient means. In the Court's terminology, encroachment on individual liberty must be "necessarily related" to a "compelling state interest." A presumption favoring liberty is implicit in the concept of a limited government of delegated powers expressed in the Constitution. The approach suggested in Marshall's dissent in *Kelley* (1976) fairly approximates this model.

The great vice of the double-balancing approach is the unfettered and unprincipled discretion in the first step. The people are the only competent judges of whether any activity is or is not fundamental. The personal preferences of nine justices are not indicative of the values of every citizen. Neither is history a certain guide to the balance of values in any individual's personality. The Constitution nowhere establishes a class of non-fundamental liberties. The express purpose of the Ninth Amendment was to erase any implication of limiting liberty to the rights specified in the first eight amendments. The Fifth and Fourteenth Amendments guarantee liberty, not just "fundamental" liberties. As former Justice Harlan emphasized in *Cohen v. California* (1971), "the Constitution leaves matters of taste and style . . . largely to the individual . . . because government cannot make principled distinctions in this area."[1105]

The first step is truly unfettered: individual liberty can be entirely wiped out by it, as in the case of *Ball v. Board of Trustees of Kerrville* (1978), where the Fifth Circuit dismissed a claim by a schoolteacher that being discharged from employment for refusal to shave his beard was an infringement of liberty.[1106] His liberty claim was deemed "wholly insubstantial and frivolous." The court reinforced this conclusion by saying, "Federal Courts do not sit to entertain such claims."[1107] Would these same judges object if tomorrow they were told they must grow beards or lose their jobs? Wear their hair shoulder length or longer or lose their jobs? Wear pink leotards while the court is in session or lose their jobs? Or would they good-naturedly acquiesce, realizing that objections to these impositions of taste and style in personal appearance would be "wholly insubstantial and frivolous?"

Compare the reasoning in *East Hartford Education Ass'n v. Board of Education* (1977).[1108] A local regulation requiring that a teacher wear a necktie in the classroom was struck down as a violation of the rights of free expression, privacy, and individual liberty. The alleged state interests were inadequate to overcome these individual rights: a desire to establish a professional image for teachers was outside the delegated powers of the local authority. Promoting good grooming among students was likewise, ultra vires and tenuous. Maintenance of respect and decorum in the classroom was found to be not necessarily furthered by the tie ordinance.[1109] Judge Oakes reinforced the liberty claim by explaining the personal and political significance of control over appearance:

> The right to control one's own body . . . extends in the minds and hearts of many individuals to the body's teguments, be they clothing or hair.
>
> . . .
>
> Substantial creative efforts of mankind have been devoted to matters of dress . . . [throughout history], and dress has often conveyed a message[,] . . . [sometimes as] a symbol of wisdom, authority, . . . [or] affluence.
>
> Conversely, recognizing the role clothing plays in giving individuals a sense of freedom and identity, the military, prisons, and other authoritarian institutions have long used strict uniformity of dress and hair style to effectuate conformity. Their purpose has been to deprive a person of his individuality in the interests of better discipline and related aims.
>
> . . .
>
> History is replete with instances of oppression accomplished by body-tegument conformity . . . . [D]ictatorships of both the left and the right use hair and dress regulation as part of their program of behavior regulation.[1110]

Even within the traditional system of defining degrees of liberty interest, surely the personal significance and potential for political manipulation described in this passage imply that the control of personal appearance is an issue of fundamental importance to our system of ordered liberty.[1111] But, in the end, the most important question is, What are the state aims that may constitutionally infringe on individual liberty? The answer should be protection of life, property, and liberty, the compelling interests of the government and the sole aims that may be pursued without voluntary individual participation.

However, Justice Stevens, while a judge on the Court of Appeals, gave a different answer:

> From the earliest days of organized society, no absolute right to an unfettered choice of appearance has ever been recognized; matters of appearance and dress have always been subjected to control and regulation, sometimes by custom and social pressure, sometimes by legal rules. A variety of reasons justifies limitations on this interest. They include a concern for public health or safety, a desire to avoid specific forms of antisocial conduct, and an interest in protection of the beholder from unsightly displays. Nothing more than a desire to encourage respect for tradition, or for those who are moved by traditional ceremonies, may be sufficient in some situations. Indeed, even an interest in teaching respect for (though not necessarily agreement with) traditional manners, may lend support to some public grooming requirements. Therefore, just as the individual has an interest in a choice among different styles of appearance and behavior, and a democratic society has an interest in fostering diverse choices, so also does society have a legitimate interest in placing limits on the exercise of that choice.[1112]

The paramount state interest in health and safety are indisputable, but what of Stevens's suggestion of purposes to avoid "antisocial conduct" and "unsightly displays" or further the "desire to encourage respect for tradition?" The latter two are squarely contradicted by prominent Supreme Court precedent, beginning with *West Virginia State Board of Education v. Barnette* (1943), in which Jehovah's Witnesses challenged a school requirement that pupils salute the flag.[1113] Their refusal to salute was no doubt offensive. Thirty years later, in *Cohen v. California* (1971), the Court protected a man's decision to place an unsightly display of the words "Fuck the Draft" on the back of his jacket.[1114] Use of language commonly considered obscene in criticism was revisited forty years after *Cohen* in *Mahanoy Area School District v. B.L.* (2021).[1115] In this case, analyzed in chapter six, a high school student used a social network (Snapchat) to criticize her school and cheer team by showing images with "a middle finger raised; it bore the caption: Fuck school fuck softball fuck cheer fuck everything."[1116] The Court first noted that "putting aside the vulgar language, the listener would hear criticism," and then went on to say that her speech "was not obscene as this Court has understood that term."[1117]

What of the remaining objective of avoidance of "antisocial conduct" raised in *Miller* (1974)? Justice Stevens offered as an example of such conduct indecent exposure, the prohibition of which, he said, "is intended to arrest other antisocial behavior . . . at its incipiency."[1118] If this is the purpose of indecent exposure laws, then the line of cases supporting the right to express dissatisfaction with the patently offensive language described above demonstrates that the fear of incipient threats to legitimate state interests is not compelling and cannot justify significant infringement of important individual rights.

Avoidance of the treacherous double-balancing mode of analysis devolves to a question of the proper purposes of government. The blinding force of tradition was overcome in 1975 in *O'Connor v. Donaldson*.[1119] The action was a suit for damages by a mental patient alleging wrongful confinement. A unanimous Court held that confinement of a person who is not dangerous to self or others works an unconstitutional deprivation of liberty. Protection of citizens "from exposure to those whose ways are different, . . . [or] who are physically unattractive or socially eccentric," does not justify depriving a person of his or her liberty.[1120] "Mere public intolerance or animosity cannot constitutionally justify the deprivation of a person's physical liberty."[1121]

Professor Tribe recognized the implications of this holding:

> What seems most significant about Donaldson as its extension of those [First Amendment] precedents to a setting not involving first amendment freedoms. Even without establishing that apparel, appearance, or lifestyle touch upon these freedoms, therefore, one can argue strongly that "the Constitution leaves matters of taste and style . . . largely to the individual," so that, outside such special contexts as that of intrusion into privacy or imposition upon a captive audience, government may not dictate how a person or group chooses to appear or to interact solely on the ground that others may find the display distasteful. This is as it must be if rights of personhood are to retain significance.[1122]

At least two purposes not mentioned by Justice Stevens mirror the traditional justifications of indecent exposure laws. As discussed earlier, the legitimacy of prevention of evil example would seem to have been seriously undermined or wholly discredited by *Donaldson* (1975) and *Cohen* (1971). The rejection of compulsory participation to promote a good example in *Barnette* (1973) should raise serious doubts about the constitutionality of legal actions aimed at preventing evil examples that extract significant costs in terms of individual liberty. The Supreme

Court's characterization of incipient threats as non-compelling interests reinforces these doubts. Effectively unlimited access to such examples via the internet guts whatever is left over.

The government interest in suppressing public nakedness can be assessed from still another perspective by analyzing the more general interest in "maintaining a decent society" suggested by Chief Justice Warren, dissenting, in *Jacobelli's v. Ohio* (1964).[1123] His premise harkened back to the roots of moral jurisprudence but lacked a constitutional basis. Perhaps it could find a home in the police power? The fundamental weakness in such an approach has been chronicled here—America's moral authority has been Christianity. Although decency is treated as a unitary concept, it may be that only certain elements should be legitimate concerns of government, such as those that affect protection of life and property—for instance, fairness, truthfulness, charity, and other values that warrant promotion and regulation. Other aspects of decency that have no material consequences could be left to individuals, families, social organizations, schools, churches, and other religious institutions.

The sodomy cases can be rationalized in this way. In *Bowers v. Hardwick* (1986), the Supreme Court upheld a Georgia law against homosexual sodomy, finding no fundamental rights were involved.[1124] Seventeen years later, the Court in *Lawrence v. Texas* (2003) overruled *Bowers* (1986), striking down a Texas law that prohibited sodomy regardless of the gender or marital status of the participants.[1125] In a wide-ranging opinion, Justice Kennedy concluded that the *Lawrence* case involved individual liberty "both in its spatial and more transcendent dimensions,"[1126] writing, "Freedom extends beyond spatial bounds; and Liberty presumes an autonomy of the self that includes freedom of thought, belief, expression, and certain intimate conduct."[1127]

The Court concluded that the sodomy prohibition violated the Fourteenth Amendment. It began its analysis with a brief history of enforcement of sodomy laws consistent with the findings reported here, noting a lack of material enforcement when the activity was private and consensual between adults. The Court then recounted its statement in *Planned Parenthood of Southeastern Pennsylvania v. Casey* (1992): "At the heart of liberty is the right to define one's own concept of existence, of meaning, of the universe, and of the mystery of human life."[1128]

The Court then cited with approval a remarkable statement of moral jurisprudence in Justice Stevens's dissent in *Bowers* (1986): "the fact that the governing majority in a State has traditionally viewed a particular practice as immoral is not a sufficient reason for upholding a law prohibiting the practice; neither history nor tradition could save a law prohibiting miscegenation from constitutional attack."[1129] The findings in *Lawrence* (2003) have caused commentators to question whether any obscenity laws could survive future constitutional challenges.[1130] After *Lawrence* (2003), what would justify a finding that a particular immoral practice should be illegal? The court did not provide an answer. It provided hints with references to minors, potential for injury, and coercion. The Court further noted that the present case did not involve public conduct or prostitution. Themes of privacy and adult, consensual, safe behavior are evident. No legitimate state interest that could justify the intrusion was found.

The public/private distinction has been a cardinal principle of indecent exposure precedent. The Court's reasoning in *Bowers* is murky. Privacy alone may have sufficed to justify its finding regarding limitations on the police power of the state. In any case, it is reasonable to infer that the prevention-of-evil-example rationale for indecent exposure suffered a potentially fatal blow in this case, leaving only public nuisance, with its First Amendment vulnerabilities, as the sole defense for the laws.

The history of indecent exposure laws began with the Charles II proclamation against vicious and debauched persons, where he entreated such persons to "become examples of sobriety and virtue," and colonial acts that sought to punish wantonness, lasciviousness, and filthy acts of uncleanness, scandalous living, and numerous biblical crimes of sexual indulgence. There was no express concern about nuisance. Prevention of evil example was seen as fundamental to the maintenance of good order in society. This orientation naturally exempted private activities. As the balance of state interest reliance shifted over time from evil example to nuisance, the boundary of privacy became more resolute. Thus, the concept of privacy in indecent exposure jurisprudence has a long history and tradition with a practical foundation. Before this shift, nuisance was more a byproduct and premise for prevention of evil example. The concern was not with offending, annoying, or alarming audiences as much as it was with informing and inspiring them. Precedents in chapter four show how nuisance gained ground over time in managing unwanted courtship and protecting the sensibilities of women while they travel roads and highways. Now, with the presence of so much offensive behavior everywhere one turns, reliance on nuisance appears antiquated and feckless, a remnant of nineteenth-century society.

Justice O'Connor concurred in *Lawrence*, arguing that the statute violated the Equal Protection Clause by discriminating against gay people.[1131] The government was focused on homosexual sodomy and not "deviate sexual intercourse," thus targeting a recognizable subculture.[1132] She then embraced the view that moral disapproval of a group cannot be a legitimate governmental interest under the Equal Protection Clause because legal classifications must not be "drawn for the purpose of disadvantaging the group burdened by the law."[1133] O'Conner continued: "A State can of course assign certain consequences to a violation of its criminal law. But the State cannot single out one identifiable class of citizens for punishment that does not apply to everyone else, with moral disapproval as the only asserted state interest for the law."[1134] The Justice closed her soliloquy with acknowledgement of the public/private distinction and of moral disapproval of a class not being an adequate state interest under any standard of review. These remarks provide a provocative segue to the ensuing consideration of equal-protection implications of indecent exposure laws.

9. Equal Protection and the Legal Topology of Bodies

The Fourteenth Amendment includes a guarantee of equal protection of the laws. Free-speech claims are often advanced alongside equal-protection claims; therefore, many of the relevant precedents discussed in this chapter were also covered in chapter seven. No equal-protection cases challenging indecent exposure laws have reached the Supreme Court. Lower court equal-protection claims have focused mainly on gender differentials. Most have failed.

Distinctions that are relevant in enforcement of indecent exposure laws may be vulnerable to equal-protection arguments. Not all parts of bodies are proscribed from public view. The common ground of proscribed areas of the body is their linkage to birth and death via sexuality: penis, vulva, anus, and breasts. Not all contexts of exposure are treated alike. Not all intentions support arrest and conviction. Not all audiences feel the same way about the exposures. No subcultures that embrace naked lifestyles, such as social nudism, are protected by law from discrimination. Statutes describe the prohibited areas of the body with varying degrees of specificity.

The equal-protection analysis begins with body-part differentiation. Women's breasts have accounted for a disproportionate share of judicial scrutiny and legislative action regarding this aspect of indecent exposure laws. State and local laws governing such exposures vary considerably.[1135] All states have made allowances for breastfeeding. Toplessness is explicitly illegal in only three states. Laws are ambiguous in fourteen more states, with public display of breasts generally allowed in the remaining states. In those states that prohibit toplessness, women have objected to being treated differently than men with respect to breasts. Litigants claim that this distinction is evidence that indecent exposure laws unfairly exercise control over women's body image and sexuality.[1136]

The differential treatment has inspired organized protests, leading to significant legislative accommodations but little sympathy from most courts. Discrete breastfeeding in public is okay everywhere. It is a convenience and presumably not terribly erotic. Breasts presented in other contexts are assumed to have a measure of eroticism and usually constitute indecent exposure unless the exposure is done in a secluded or designated space, usually a beach, or there is a paying audience—the latter circumstance being a modern limitation of the prevention of evil example. Topless dancing in adult entertainment enjoys First Amendment protection and may be subjected to time, place, and manner restrictions.

Women's breasts are the usual focus of entertainment in strip clubs. Paradoxically, the expression that garners First Amendment protection in such environments is distinctly erotic, intended to satisfy the prurient interests of male patrons. Such expressions are a key element of the definition of indecent exposure in many state statutes. The willing audience obviates nuisance theory, leaving prevention of evil example as the implicated state interest, along with the secondary-effects doctrine discussed previously. The prevention-of-evil-example rationale, caught in a crossfire of diminishing influence of Christian moral principles and expansion of constitutionally protected individual rights, has steadily weakened since the end of the nineteenth century.

Although a substantial and enduring industry has developed around such entertainment, the crux of most equal-protection claims outside the industry allege that women's and men's breasts should not be treated differently in indecent exposure laws. The keys to differential treatment are the manner of the display and its context. Recall from the description of modern laws the importance of the interplay of act, actor, place, and audience. Understanding these factors helps to explain and justify distinctions in treatment of breasts and the quality and legitimacy of those judgments.

The Supreme Court addressed the importance of context for exposure of breasts in freedom-of-expression cases, as discussed in chapter seven. For example, in *Barnes v. Glen Theatre, Inc.* (1991), the Court upheld a requirement that nude dancers wear pasties and G-strings as incidental limitations on the "marginal" expression involved, so even in this context cover was legally justified.[1137] In the context of adult entertainment with voluntary audiences, the market appeal of the breast is that it is erotic and enhancing the eroticism through associated expression is a virtue. The relevant expression is lewd intent, so modulation of this expression was seen by the Court as a reasonable measure to "protect societal order and morality" by mitigating sexual stimulation and fantasy or distorting its effects.

Another common characteristic of such venues is the sale and consumption of alcoholic beverages. This brings the Twenty-first Amendment and other sources of governmental authority to regulate alcohol consumption into play, justifying regulation of conduct where the sale of alcoholic beverages is offered[1138] and creating contention in the interplay of these amendments.[1139] The relevance of the physical location is evident in application of the secondary-effects rationale.

The Court has not addressed barroom dancing or striptease since *City of Erie* (2000). The secondary-effects doctrine employed there has evolved as the primary means of regulation. It posits that such entertainment produces collateral effects in the neighboring areas, such as increased crime and decreased property values. Concern about these effects is considered a legitimate state interest justifying time and manner restrictions on the entertainment but not outright bans. Local ordinances often govern whether alcohol can be served and the degree and nature of displays of nudity.[1140] The display of breasts in this context is a First Amendment right that must be carefully managed. Acceptance of this form of entertainment violates traditional principles of prevention of evil example, consistent with the general decline of this rationale as a force of law.

Commercial exploitation of the appeal of topless women outside of barroom dancing was considered in another topless case discussed earlier, *Edge v. City of Everett* (2022).[1141] There, a group of "bikini baristas" petitioned the District Court for the Western District of Washington to challenge the constitutionality of two city ordinances criminalizing lewd conduct and improper dress. The plaintiffs' First Amendment challenges failed. Their equal-protection claims were upheld. The court had employed a rational-basis standard of review for the First Amendment claims. It applied intermediate scrutiny when assessing equal protection claims targeting the Lewd Conduct Ordinance and Dress Code Ordinance. The court found that the city had provided an adequate justification for the Lewd Conduct Ordinance treating male and female breasts differently.

With respect to the Dress Code Ordinance, the court found an equal-protection violation because the ordinance included gender-based classifications banning a wide variety of women's clothing, the justifications for these distinctions were unpersuasive, enforcement might prove awkward, and the law effectively prescribed how women, but not men, in such establishments ought to dress. The constitutional problem was in detailed prescription of dress, not the exposure of breasts. The disparate treatment of women was unwarranted. A pyrrhic victory.

These cases illustrate contradictory views on constitutional protection of commercial uses of naked breasts. Meanwhile, exposure of breasts in open public spaces remains a crime in most jurisdictions. Naked breasts are a cornerstone of strip clubs, where they are considered distinctly erotic, stimulating, and entertaining by dominantly male audiences. There are many such clubs catering to primarily male audiences and very few with male dancers and female audiences. The women baristas in *Edge* sought to brighten the day for gentlemen enjoying a jolt of latte but were shut down. At first blush, the commercial success of exposure of women's breasts appears to contradict the argument in most noncommercial topless cases that female and male breasts are, or should be considered, fungible.

Most efforts to free the breast outside of commercial contexts have failed. *Free the Nipple-Fort Collins v. City of Fort Collins* (2019),[1142] a case discussed in chapter seven,[1143] which occurred a short time after *Taub*'s failed full nakedness free-speech initiative, is an exception. As in *Taub*, the plaintiff was a political organization. Whereas *Taub* involved total nudity, *Free the Nipple-Fort Collins* targeted public display of women's breasts. The plaintiff sought an injunction based on violation of equal protection by a ban on naked breasts in public. No showing of lewd intent was required under the statute.

The Tenth Circuit Court of Appeals in *Free the Nipple-Fort Collins* affirmed a preliminary injunction, citing *People v. Santorelli* (1992): "One of the most important purposes to be served by the Equal Protection Clause is to ensure that 'public sensibilities' grounded in prejudice and unexamined stereotypes do not become enshrined as part of the official policy of government."[1144] The court did not offer any evidence or arguments to support its conclusion that the city's fears arose from a "sex object stereotype of women's breasts."[1145] It most likely resulted from their own different unexamined stereotype.

The court was convinced that the true motive for the ordinance was protecting the moral sensibilities of the public that were based on prevailing morality and that that it is not a legitimate basis for identifying areas of the body that should be covered in public. The court did not suggest how to make such determinations or what other exposures might be legitimate under this theory, leaving open the question of exposure of other body parts and full body nakedness. The history of indecent exposure laws identifies an ecclesiastical foundation for the presumed prevailing morality—a foundation that has weakened considerably. The court deemed there to be no justiciable nuisance by finding that the audience sensibilities did not warrant protection. No state statute requires that the audience offense, annoyance, or alarm be reasonable. No court has suggested a test for indecency in indecent exposure cases. The *Miller* (1973) test still reigns as the standard for determining obscenity, but it does not purport to measure the reasonableness of the average person used in that test.

The Tenth Circuit's rationale that any law premised on generalizations about "the way women are" could be applied to notions of the way that men are or notions of other areas of the body that are considered indecent. The court was adamant that public sensibilities grounded in prejudice and unexamined stereotypes should not become enshrined as part of the official policy of government. If a woman exposing her breast in public expresses such important legal and political principles, it seems that adding the rest of the exposure ought to make the point more emphatically. *Free the Nipple-Fort Collins* has remained an outlier.[1146] The ruling effectively allows women in six states to go shirtless in public. Federal courts in other jurisdictions have generally continued to uphold laws banning toplessness in public.[1147]

The Court of Appeals for the Eighth Circuit reached the opposite conclusion in an analogous case three months later. In *Free the Nipple v. City of Springfield* (2019), the circuit court affirmed a summary judgment for the city against a claim that its ordinance prohibiting women from exposing their areolas and nipples in public violated the Equal Protection Clause.[1148] The appellants unsuccessfully cited *Lawrence v. Texas* (2003) and *Bowers v. Hardwick* (1986), arguing that the city's interest in prohibiting immoral acts was not a sufficient justification, and *Sessions v. Morales* (2017)[1149] for the proposition that the ordinance was based on outdated stereotypes. The court countered that the city's police power protected a sufficient legitimate state interest in "preventing the secondary adverse effects of public nudity and protecting the order, morality, health, safety, and well-being of the populace. . . ."[1150] It provided no additional details or evidence to support this assertion. The ordinance provided an exemption for adult entertainment.

In a third 2019 case driven by the Free the Nipple movement, also discussed earlier in chapter seven, the Supreme Court of New Hampshire considered equal-protection and free-speech challenges. In *State v. Lilley* (2019),[1151] the court applied a rational-review standard and found that the "defendants have not carried the heavy burden of mounting a successful facial attack to an ordinance analyzed only for rationality."[1152] The plaintiff's free-speech claim was not persuasive. The court concluded that there was no equal-protection violation because the statute did not target women's breasts. It banned all nudity and "merely regulates the manner in which activities may be carried out in that they cannot be carried out in the nude."[1153] It banned nudity for both men and women, including women's breasts in the definition due to the common understanding of the term. It "merely reflects the fact that men and women are not fungible with respect to the traditional understanding of what constitutes nudity."[1154]

A dissent that took the position that there was "no principled reason why" the majority's approach "would not apply with equal force to other laws" that afford differing treatment to people of different races, religions, colors, or national origins.[1155] *Lawrence v. Texas* (2003) was cited to no avail. The majority did not respond directly to the criticism, replying instead that gender differences in defining nudity are due to a unique "traditional understanding."[1156] It closed the opinion with an homage to the role of legislatures in assessing changes in morality: it's up to the people of Laconia to make such decisions. The U.S. Supreme Court denied certiorari.

In a more recent case, *Eline v. Town of Ocean City* (2021),[1157] the Fourth Circuit employed nuisance theory to uphold a city ordinance in Maryland that prohibited women from going topless on city beaches, finding that protecting the public sensibilities from the public display of areas of the body traditionally viewed as erogenous zones—including female, but not male, breasts—is an important government objective that satisfies the Equal Protection Clause's heightened scrutiny requirement. The court once again noted that "the two sexes are not fungible."[1158] The relevant ordinance did not require any showing of willfulness or lewd intent:

> Nude, or a State of Nudity means the showing of the human male or female genitals, pubic area, vulva, anus, or anal cleft with less than a full opaque covering, the showing of the female breast with less than a fully opaque covering of any part of the nipple, or the showing of the covered male genitals in a discernibly turgid state.[1159]

The court acknowledged that topless women on the beach might not offend everyone, but it "is still seen by society as unpalatable."[1160] The plaintiff offered scientific research contradicting this presumption and further research that not treating males and females alike would have harmful secondary effects, such as discouraging breastfeeding and promoting a cultural over-sexualization of women and girls. The court rejected the research as being proscriptive rather than descriptive regarding local moral values, deferring to evidence provided by city that the topless women offended residents and vacationers. The court relied on *United States v. Biocic* (1991),[1161] a Fourth Circuit case involving topless sunbathing in a national wildlife refuge, in which the court confessed that "[i]n common understanding and practice the only reason for prohibiting public nudity by law is because of the perception (right or wrong) that it is 'indecent.' No other reason is apparent in common understanding and practice in this society."[1162] The circuit court in *Biocic* (1991) had applied an intermediate level of scrutiny in summarily dismissing an equal-protection argument, noting that an important government interest in protecting the moral sensibilities of a substantial segment of society was sufficient to overcome the individual rights involved. The court went on to note that female breasts have traditionally been viewed as erogenous zones and male breasts have not.[1163]

These cases differ on standards of review, outcomes, and theories of constitutional interpretation. Despite these disparities, the Supreme Court has not accepted the challenge. The *Free the Nipple-Fort Collins* court's view of the Fourteenth Amendment starkly contrasts with the Supreme Court's notion in *Dobbs* (2022), decided three years later, that "the claimed right is deeply rooted in the Nation's history and tradition and implicit in the concept of ordered liberty." There was no discussion of such criteria. The city justified the ordinance as a means to protect children, maintain public order, and promote traffic safety, and it proffered expert testimony. Even if a right were established, this rationale probably would have sufficed under a rational-basis standard of review.

Examination of the topology of the body viewed through the lens of equal protection exposes context sensitivities that may reconcile apparent paradoxes and contradictions in legal reasoning on the subject. The lack of historical knowledge about the laws leaves courts looking like they are adrift in a sea of moral ambiguity. Freeing women with naked breasts from prosecution for indecent exposure is a slippery slope. The accommodation for commercial exploitation of naked breasts is consistent with the more general toleration of obscenity in American society and generally limited access for audiences. These commercial activities foster images of sexualization of the breast, disadvantaging those that argue for a more general lessening of the prohibition of naked breasts in public. Statutory reform has created exceptions for breastfeeding, which involves a presumed diminishment of erotic appeal and enhanced convenience, in all states. None of these tolerances have fomented a radical change in public exposure of breasts in affected areas.

The key differentiator in jurisdictions where the topless prohibition exists is contextual. Breasts are provocative. It is a marketable characteristic. Commercial exploitation of this quality is permitted in commercial venues in most states. These activities benefit from the patina of constitutionally protected expression yet are often subject to reasonable time, place, and manner restrictions. The audience is entertained rather than annoyed. In other public places where unwilling audiences may be present, the prohibitions are maintained to avoid annoyance and alarm of the audience. Mere exposure is legally deemed to have no expression, even though it is simultaneously declared offensive and, in fact, usually is so for some audience members. Prevention of evil example has faded away under the weight of commerce and political pressure, leaving nuisance theory standing alone as justification for the prohibition.

These observations rationalize differential treatment of women's breasts in different contexts. They do not, however, explain prohibitions of other areas of the body associated with birth, death, and sex. Consider for a moment an argument extrapolating the accommodations made to women for breastfeeding in public to allow men to urinate in street storm drains. Although not always specified, urinating in public is illegal in every state, generally as a public nuisance or indecent exposure.[1164] Breastfeeding exemptions appear to be a convenience for mothers enacted because of political pressure and good sense, given the generally non-erotic perception of such displays in customary characterizations of them. However, couldn't the same be said about a man urinating in a street storm drain? Lewd intent is unlikely. His penis is likely to be flaccid. There is no incipient threat of an unwanted sexual advance. Women could share the privilege by just squatting over a convenient drain. This feels different. Why? What is the state interest that justifies the differential treatment? This is where the waning influence of prevention of evil example and a consensus moral authority to rely upon fosters ambiguity about managing such exposures and exceptions for women's breasts. It just feels more annoying or offensive.

Understanding history and appreciating the importance of context unearths at least two novel equal-protection arguments: (1) discrimination against social nudists and libertines as discrete and insular disfavored classes and (2) favoring nudity as adult entertainment over what is communicated by naked bodies in other contexts. Social nudism poses the more obvious equal-protection challenge. Social nudists suffer as a class from the discriminatory effects of indecent exposure laws.[1165] Libertines are less organized and less easily described as a class. Nudists do not enjoy the same privileges and immunities as other subcultures in America. The laws are not justified by compelling state interests. With the withering of prevention of evil example as a legitimate state interest, avoidance of nuisance is not sufficient to overcome constitutional claims for equal protection, religious freedom, freedom of speech, and other aspects of due process due to the magnitude of the impact on their pursuit of life, liberty, and happiness.

Progress in gay rights provides a roadmap for social nudism. The nudism subculture has a long and well-documented history in America.[1166] Its adherents sometimes refer to clothed people as "textiles."[1167] Nudists have long suffered discrimination by textiles. *Woodlands Pride* (2023) and *Hudnut* (1986) precedent support claims of social nudists. They also provide arguments for libertines to challenge pornography bans, given that such expression is the lingua franca of libertine philosophy. The historical analysis directive for considering substantive-due-process claims in *Dobbs* (2022) would yield interesting findings for both challenges. These classes have long histories. Could the secondary-effects doctrine be invoked to impose restrictions? Yes, for libertinism. Seems unlikely for social nudism given lack of evidence of collateral damage to areas neighboring nudist colonies and clothes-optional beaches.

Adult entertainment poses a legal paradox: a critical element of indecent exposure in most statutes is a showing of lewd intent. Expressions of such intent by topless women makes for appealing adult entertainment that enjoys First Amendment protection. Exposure of breasts without evidence of such intent in other public places leads to arrest and prosecution—despite the judicial view that nude bodies are expressionless. History provides a credible explanation for the differential treatment. The plaintiff in *State v. Lilley* (2019) argued that breasts have been hypersexualized and considered pornographic and taboo, creating stigma and contributing to less breastfeeding in America.[1168] She made this argument while seeking freedom to exhibit her breasts in public places. Suppose, instead, that she argued that the exception for commercial exploitation of the often lewd and lascivious exhibitions of breasts in barroom dancing while prohibiting general display of women's breasts fosters an environment where negative visions, fantasies, and stereotypes are magnified, creating harm for women who do not participate in the industry? These women are denied an equal opportunity to portray more wholesome images of women's breasts. Channelization of images of naked women into the commercialization of sex supports what Bateman calls the "cult of female modesty," where a woman's worth, value and respect depend on her bodily modesty.[1169]

The prohibition of public nakedness presents only one view, reinforcing negative stereotypes and intimidating women seeking respect for public exposure of their bodies. Existing constitutional interpretation of indecent exposure laws represents an "entrenchment of values, or of conceptions of the right and the good, [that] necessarily favors certain conceptions over others by essentially shielding some favored moral-political conceptions from the democratic decision-making process."[1170]

Directing constitutional claims in this manner would set up a confrontation between First Amendment protection of marginal expression with Fourteenth Amendment equal protection and due process.[1171] Simple public exposure of breasts is banned and defined as expressionless or having expression not worthy of constitutional protection. Simultaneously, the sale of erotic images of the breast is permitted and protected. This creates a semiotic imbalance, distorting the meaning of the breast in society. The noncommercial exhibition is denied equal protection of the law.

Perhaps a stronger case could be made by adding a strip club patron to the class—his harm is twofold: having to pay to see live women's breasts rather than satiate his appetite by viewing them for free in other public places and suffering from negative stereotypes associated with men who frequent strip clubs. Another source of support for this claim can be found in viewpoint-restriction cases described in chapter seven. In particular, in *Iancu v. Brunetti* (2019), one of the trademark registration cases, the Court decried inequality in opportunities for expression of viewpoints on conventional moral standards, "those inducing societal nods of approval and those provoking offense and condemnation."

Courts often reach paradoxical and contradictory conclusions when assessing equal-protection arguments concerning indecent exposure due to inadequate understanding of the history of the laws. The opinions often purport to represent community sentiment. It seems in many cases that the decisions reflect the personal moral views of the judges. Neither of these approaches delivers the predictability and credibility of the previous Christian moral regime.

In choosing between moral hegemony of judges or the community, the findings in this study suggest that morality of the relevant community, as expressed in local regulations, and not contradicted by empirical evidence, may be a better model for management of morals than *custos morum*. Improved understanding of the value, costs, and contours of indecent exposure laws in the maintenance of civil society would encourage more robust legislative debates, more defensible statutes, and a more just and predictable judicial process. Even such changes, however, may not effectively address the issue of erosion of America's Christian moral authority.

10. Legal Management of Naked Bodies in a Religiously Unaffiliated or Polytheistic Society

> We Are Founded on Judeo-Christian Principles – Trump Vows to End Religious Freedom for Non-Christians in the United States.[1172]
>
> Christianity Will Be the Law: High-Profile Advocate for Ending the Separation of Church and State Is Well Acquainted with Speaker Mike Johnson".[1173]
>
> The sum of all is, if we would most truly enjoy the gift of Heaven, let us become a virtuous people; then shall we both deserve and enjoy it. While on the other hand, if we are universally vicious and debauched in our manners, though the form of our Constitution carries the face of the most exalted freedom, we shall in reality be the most abject slaves (Samual Adams (1776)..[1174]

Returning to the questions that we opened with: Caesar or God? Poet or fascist? How should indecent exposure be managed? In the larger context, should America be a Christian nation, a secular state, or a federation of moral diversity? The Supreme Court's performance as *custos morum* has led it to a conundrum. As Justice Kenney wrote in *Obergefell v. Hodges* (2015), "the Court has recognized that new insights and societal understandings can reveal unjustified inequality within our most fundamental institutions that once passed unnoticed and unchallenged.".[1175]

The traditional rationale of prevention of evil example began to decay long ago. The scope of moral crimes emblematic of evil example has narrowed considerably. Access to such forbidden knowledge has expanded exponentially in an internet-charged modern American society as information flows freely with unprecedented breadth and depth. The internet has effectively abolished limited access to evil examples. Television is rife with movies and shows illustrating the forbidden knowledge formerly protected by public indecency laws.

Nuisance as the remaining tentpole of indecent exposure has lost credibility because increased toleration of offensive public displays and lack of law enforcement against such actions are commonplace. As these changes have been happening, First Amendment doctrine has been expanding to protect just about all offensive expression except for advocacy of immediate lawlessness and public nakedness. Nuisance may have suffered death blows in *Hudnut* (1985) and *Lawrence* (2003).

The last bastion of moral defense against indecent exposure is protection of children. The long history of social nudism presents a counterpoint to this concern.[1176] Credible scientific evidence contradicts the thesis that seeing adults naked harms children. Research indicates that content and context are important.[1177] This may imply that the intent of the actor and the nature of the expression of the body are relevant.[1178] Whether perpetrators are naked or not, sexual violence against children is harmful. Is it the nakedness or the violence that creates the harm? Violence without nakedness is harmful. Is nakedness without violence harmful? This is where popular perceptions and scientific evidence diverge, as evidenced in numerous court opinions discussed previously.

More research and sophisticated, unbiased methodologies are needed to thoroughly vet this important issue. At this point, it looks like use of the protection argument is overbroad and difficult to reconcile with the lack of protection by the Supreme Court, as *custos morum*, of children being exposed to nakedness and sexual content on the internet and television, live caricatures of sexuality, hate speech, and depictions of violence.

The following series of cases illustrates the rambling evolution of moral jurisprudence in the second half of the twentieth century. Simple public nudity is still in search of a constitutional "right." Without such a right, courts continue to uphold regulations and affirm convictions. For instance, in *Eckl v. Davis* (1975), a group of nudists brought a class action in a California court seeking a preliminary injunction against enforcement of a Los Angeles city ordinance banning simple public nudity.[1179] They alleged a host of constitutional infirmities, including violations of freedom of religion, free speech, equal protection, and due process. The appellants wanted to use local beaches for sunbathing and swimming nude. The ordinance banned public display by anyone above the age of ten of "the genitals, vulva, pubis, pubic, symphysis, pubic hair, buttocks, natal cleft, perineum, anus, anal region, or pubic hair region of any person, or any portion of the breast at or below the upper edge of the areola thereof of any female person." There was an exception for theatrical performances.

Without stating it, the court appeared to apply the rational-basis standard of review; it found that the purpose of the ordinance was to "to insure the peaceful and undistracted enjoyment of the parks and public beaches of the city by all persons who choose to come there" was adequate justification, presumably based on nuisance theory. The court concluded that there were no violations of constitutional rights for the following reasons:

- The ordinance was directed at conduct, not words or speech.
- Even assuming there was a communicative element in the proscribed conduct, the First Amendment right was outweighed by the substantial public interest of ensuring the peaceful and undistracted enjoyment of the parks and public beaches of the city by all persons choosing to go there.
- The fact that the ordinance was consonant with moral principles espoused by religious bodies did not implicate the constitutional concept of separation of church and state.
- Nudity for women is commonly understood to include uncovering of breasts. The classification was therefore reasonable, not arbitrary, and rested on a difference having a fair and substantial relation to the objectives of the legislation, so all persons similarly circumstanced were treated alike.
- The ordinance was not unconstitutionally vague. The language was sufficiently definite to provide adequate warning of the proscribed conduct when measured by common understanding and practices.

The appellants argued that the "expressive conduct" involved was taking off their clothes, so the ordinance presented a direct conflict, and that the ordinance was "an attempt to prohibit 'sin' by use of its criminal laws," violating the Establishment Clause.

The court's reasoning regarding the constitutional issues relied on the analysis in the California Supreme Court case *Crownover v. Musick* (1973).[1180] *Crownover* considered free-speech, equal-protection, and due-process challenges to city and county ordinances that forbade topless-woman or bottomless-person entertainment in commercial establishments. The purpose of the ordinances was "preservation of the public peace, health and safety."[1181] In upholding the regulations, the *Crownover* court asserted that the ordinances regulated conduct, not words or speech, and did not "restrict a particular form of speech considered outside the scope of constitutional protection," citing *Roth* (1957) (adult entertainment books and photos) and *Chaplinsky* (1942) (hate speech).[1182]

The plaintiffs in *Crownover* (1973) had made the following arguments:

- Since entertainment is communicative, it is a form of speech, so the ordinances prohibit speech.

- "Topless" waitresses, as well as "topless" or "bottomless" dancers, are entertainment that cannot be prohibited unless obscene.
- The ordinances are unconstitutionally overbroad because they prohibit non-obscene speech.
- Even assuming prohibition of non-obscene nude entertainment is merely incidental to the purposes of the ordinances, they are unconstitutional for lack of a compelling public purpose.

The defendants argued that the ordinance was a valid exercise of the police power regulating conduct. The court engaged in a comprehensive review of U.S. Supreme Court precedent and concluded that nothing more than conduct was involved and that if there was protectable speech, the value of such symbolic speech must be weighed against the implicated state interests to determine the level of appropriate protection, if any.

The *Crownover* (1973) court chose *O'Brien* (1968) (burning a draft card) as its guide to evaluating potentially expressive conduct. The court characterized the value of commercial expressive conduct involved as unimportant to bringing about political or social change. It was just marketing. The court cited *Miller* (1952) for the proposition that substantial deference should be shown to legislative judgments about public health, safety, and morals. It then hypothesized, without any supporting evidence, that topless waitresses might inspire brawls and their tawdry practices could have secondary effects in the neighborhood. The court further noted that these ordinances regulated only the manner of food service, so a rational-basis review was appropriate.

The reign of *Crownover* (1973) as precedent did not last long. The case was overruled in *Morris v. Municipal Court* in 1982.[1183] *Morris* involved a challenge to an ordinance restricting venues for nude-dancing entertainment. The court held that the ordinance was overbroad and that the holdings in the *Crownover* (1973) case had "crumble[d] under the force of later decisions."[1184] However, none of these later decisions addressed a core issue in *Eckl* (1975): does simple public nudity exhibit any constitutionally protected expression?

Crownover (1973) did appear to have been dispositive California precedent for *Eckl* (1975) at the time. The overruling of *Crownover* did not address the implicit finding in *Eckl* (1975) that naked bodies alone had no protectible expression even when used for marketing in a commercial context. The ordinance in *Eckl* (1975) was directed at "conduct, not words or speech." Even if there were protectable expression involved, the *Eckl* court concluded that all four prongs of the *O'Brien* (1968) test had been met.[1185] It gave short shrift to the plaintiffs' claim that the ordinances infringed their rights to the pursuit of happiness and privacy (presumably meaning autonomy). As for the equal-protection claim, nature created the classification. It's "reasonable, not arbitrary, and rests upon a ground of difference having a fair and substantial relation to the object of the legislation, so that all persons similarly circumstanced are treated alike."[1186] The plaintiffs' complaint that the under-ten-years age exemption was unjustified was also rejected. As in *Crownover* (1973), the views expressed in *Eckl* (1975) were dismissed as antiquated by the Colorado District Court in *Free the Nipple-Fort Collins* (2016). So, what's the modern view that makes these cases seem antiquated?

Fifty years after *Eckl* (1975) and thirty years after *South Florida Free Beaches, Inc. v. Miami* (1984), a naturist tested the waters for nude sunbathing with a free-exercise claim in the federal district court in Miami-Dade County. By this time, nude sunbathing was being tolerated in designated areas. The plaintiff challenged an ordinance that prohibited nude sunbathing outside a posted area. The court denied his claim in *Wittbold v. Miami-Dade County* (2013), citing *South Florida Free Beaches* (1984) for the proposition that there is no constitutional right to sunbathe nude.[1187] The plaintiff had also brought a due-process claim. It was denied, with the court finding that he did not have a liberty interest in public nudity. At this point, the state of the law appeared to be that the body must be characterized or embellished to gain a protected voice. The latest federal court ruling on the subject, in *Woodlands Pride, Inc. v. Paxton* (2023),[1188] appears to have validated this viewpoint.

The plaintiffs' strategy in *Woodlands Pride*, discussed in chapter seven, may have shown the way to giving the body such a voice, as attorneys for the plaintiffs executed a brilliant battle plan attacking a Texas ban on drag-queen shows, achieving a radically different result than in *Eckl (1975), Crownover* (1973), and *Florida Beach* (1984). In this 2023 federal district court case, the attorneys organized a team of plaintiffs that included two nonprofit festival organizers, a drag entertainment and delivery service for private events, a production company, and an individual performer. The plaintiffs made a multipronged attack on the statute's constitutionality, attacking perceived vulnerabilities in the act, place, audience, and state-interest elements of the crime.

Woodlands Pride (2023) provides inspiration and a battle plan for a full-frontal, multipronged assault on the constitutionality of indecent exposure laws. As we have explained in detail, the constitutional landscape regarding naked bodies has become a minefield of potential constitutional infirmities. Different times, different states, and different courts (state and federal) have yielded different results, although in all cases the expressionless body remains closeted. The legal history presented here shows the effects of fragmentation and diminishment of traditional moral authority based on Christian doctrine. These changes interact with maturation of America's constitutional democracy. The history and analytical constructs that we have discussed expose the messy outcomes of these interactions, providing fuel for new political, social, and constitutional perspectives about indecent exposure laws. The following scenario illustrates the resulting complexity and risks to the validity of indecent exposure laws. It is also intended to bring together many threads from this historical study into a provocative, more-expansive description of the crime that has long been lurking in the shadows of academia as the province of perverts.

Taking cues from the *Woodlands Pride* plaintiffs' legal team, consider the following scenario describing what a better-informed constitutional challenge to indecent exposure laws might look like in one of the most restrictive jurisdictions in the country: Berkeley, California.[1189] Both simple public nakedness and nakedness with lewd intent are illegal in this city. The state prohibits public nudity with lewd intent. The liberal university town of Berkeley, California, bans simple public nudity.

Consider this test case: a class action seeking declaratory relief in federal district court and challenging the facial validity of the state statute and city ordinance.[1190] The Berkeley Municipal Code bans nudity in any public place[1191]:

> 13.32.010 Nudity prohibited in any public place.
>
> It shall be either a misdemeanor or an infraction, in the discretion of the prosecutor, for any person to appear nude in any place open to the public or any place visible from a place open to the public. "Nude" within the meaning of this section means the absence of an opaque covering which covers the genitals, pubic hair, buttocks, perineum, anus or anal region of any person or any portion of the breast at or below the areola thereof of any female person.
>
> 13.32.020 Exceptions.
>
> The provisions of this chapter shall not apply to:
>
> A. Any person ten years old or younger.
>
> B. Any female exposing her breast to the extent such exposure is necessary to breast-feed a child.

> C. Performers who are engaged in live theatrical performances performed in a theater, concert hall or other such establishment which is primarily devoted to theatrical performances.

Local laws like these operate in the state under the umbrella of section 314 of the California Penal Code, which is entitled "Indecent Exposure, Obscene Exhibitions, and Bawdy and Other Disorderly Houses."[1192] The state statute provides as follows:

> Every person who willfully and lewdly, either:
>
> 1. Exposes his person, or the private parts thereof, in any public place, or in any place where there are present other persons to be offended or annoyed thereby; or,
>
> 2. Procures, counsels, or assists any person so to expose himself or take part in any model artist exhibition, or to make any other exhibition of himself to public view, or the view of any number of persons, such as is offensive to decency, or is adapted to excite to vicious or lewd thoughts or acts, is guilty of a misdemeanor.

The elements of the crime under state law include willful and lewd exposure of one's "person" or "private parts" in any public place where there is an audience to be offended or annoyed. The Berkeley ordinance is more specific about body topology and does not require proof of lewd intent or presence of an audience. It exempts breastfeeding, theatrical performances, and naked children under eleven years of age.

More than a dozen people have been arrested for participating in a public meeting in Berkeley and charged variously with indecent exposure under the state statute and local ordinance. The class has been certified. There are fourteen plaintiffs:

- a member of the American Association for Nude Recreation
- an adherent to the Garden of Eden Church naturist religion
- a social reformer
- a poetry professor
- a doctor
- a male "body freedom advocate"
- a female exotic dancer
- a topless female hot dog vendor
- a homeless man
- a well-endowed male adult film star
- a street performer whose signature performance is "statue of David,"
- Joe, the plumber (everyman)

- a PhD candidate in criminology
- a schizophrenic

They gathered on the first of October 2023 in Sproul Plaza on the UC campus—buck naked, of course—for an organizational meeting of a new social organization dedicated to body freedom, with plans for lunch at a restaurant on Hearst Avenue afterward. Someone in the group had a small Bluetooth speaker playing songs from Woodstock in the background. Dozens of students gathered, and some began to strip and dance in solidarity. Their meeting was cut short by a phalanx of campus security and Berkeley police arresting them and members of the audience for indecent exposure.

As in *Woodlands Pride* (2023), the plaintiffs generally allege that their naked appearances in public convey salutary messages. In addition to the drag queens' messages of celebration, equality, acceptance, and pleas for political change and social justice, these plaintiffs argue that their naked appearances raise awareness about important health issues, bodily acceptance, human vulnerability, and personal reflection. They further allege that indecent exposure laws discourage respect for the body, leading to deleterious physical and psychological consequences, including obesity and depression, and contradict deeply held religious beliefs or matters of conscience. More specifically:

- The AANR [1193] member points to a century-long tradition of peaceful and positive naked social experience.
- The Garden of Eden Church[1194] member believes nakedness is a celebration of the body ordained by God.
- The social reformer points to worrisome statements from a famous Nazi about the supposed virtues of indecent exposure laws.[1195]
- The poetry professor is holding a copy of Walt Whitman's "Song of Myself."[1196]
- A Quaker historian seeking revival of the seventeenth-century practice of "going naked as a sign"[1197] is exploring the politicized conversion of going naked as divine into a mundane representation forbidden by law.
- The doctor is advocating for better health and hygiene, pointing out the wide variations in morphology, disability, injury, and effects of diet and exercise in the group.
- The body freedom advocate sees no reason to relent to forces of repression forcing him to hide his body in shame.

- The exotic dancer is demonstrating her latest routine and has the name of her commercial venue body-painted across her buttocks.
- The hot dog vendor's business[1198] has doubled since she went topless. A long line has formed at her food cart on the border of the event. She is visible only to customers who choose to do business with her. A prominent sign cautions: "Naked woman serving your dogs!"
- Rock Hard, the porn star, views his public nakedness as advertising for his extraordinary physical gift, which he strokes from time to time for emphasis.
- The living-statue street performer has an amazingly sculpted body. He is a Berkeley graduate student studying Renaissance art, and the street performances are part of his master's thesis.
- The plumber is obese and has a scar on his hip from hip replacement surgery. He has Peroni's disease. The doctor noticed a suspicious lesion in Joe's groin area. A subsequent tissue sample confirmed melanoma.
- The PhD candidate is engaged in participant observer research[1199] on indecent exposure laws. He is holding a sign that says, "Offended observers, shout 'Fuck all this nakedness.'"
- The schizophrenic . . . who knows why he's doing what he is doing. He's been around campus before. Students have dubbed him "Naked Guy II."[1200]

The plaintiffs assert the following constitutional challenges:

- The laws are vague and overbroad.
- The Establishment and Free Exercise Clauses prohibit the government from forcing individuals to practice a religion and from interfering with free exercise of their chosen religious practices, acknowledging the Supreme Court's broad definition of religion.
- The Free Speech Clause prohibits government from silencing expressive conduct that is not obscene. The Berkeley and California laws impose prior restraints, content-based restrictions, and viewpoint restrictions.
- Due process prohibits the government from interfering with individual liberty without a showing of a compelling state interest justifying the government action.
- The state statute violates equal protection in discriminating against social nudists and libertines and banning public nakedness while allowing commercial nakedness.

- The activities of the group express serious literary, artistic, political, and scientific value.
- Given the fundamental interests involved, strict scrutiny should be applied to all claims.[1201]
- Prevention-of-evil-example and public-nuisance rationales for indecent exposure laws are no longer legitimate state interests.
- No other compelling state interest has been shown. In fact, no reasonable argument that there is a legitimate state interest has been made or shown.
- There are no less-restrictive means of furthering any legitimate state interest if one exists.

Selection of the plaintiffs and their arguments is aligned with constitutional issues discussed in prior chapters. These people are all criminals. Do you agree? If not, where would you draw the line? How do you justify your decision? The history and analyses of indecent exposure laws provide a wealth of material to support drafting the complaint and planning litigation strategy to challenge any or all of the crimes. Construction of such a brief is beyond the scope of this work. Facilitating such exercises is an important goal. This storyline is also intended to inform discussion of potential revisions to indecent exposure laws to better align them with current moral sentiments, political theory, and constitution interpretation of individual rights.

There is no doubt that these naked bodies are rich in expressiveness, with unclothed surfaces exposing indicia of health, experience, and genetics. They inherently express messages, including beauty, pain, joy, abilities, fitness, obesity, disabilities, and arousal. The motives involved and integration of messaging enhance and augment intrinsic expressions of the bodies of participants. Some of these bodies are tools of commerce. Others are symbols of rebellion. Still others, images of faith. Together they form a cornucopia of expression. All this begs the question of the nature and value of the prohibition to society balanced against individual and social interests in free expression, autonomy, and equal protection of the law. These exposures represent critiques of religious, political, and social regimes that have been suppressed and shaped by legal precedents that we have discussed..[1202]

Determining the proper balance between the government's regulation of morals and individual bodily rights, the yin and yang of the poet and the fascist, is obscure. William Bradford, founder and longtime governor of the Plymouth Colony, framed the question at the inception of America when he wrote in 1642,

> An other reason may be, that it may be in this case as it is with waters when their streames are stopped or damed up, when they get passage they flow with more violence, and make more noys and disturbance, then when they are suffered to rune quietly in their owne chanels. So wikednes being here more stopped by strict laws, and ye same more nerly looked unto, so as it cannot rune in a comone road of liberty as it would, and is inclined, it searches every wher, and at last breaks out wher it getts vente.[1203]

Two hundred years later, American poet Walt Whitman celebrated the body in his "Song of Myself," a vision of the splendor of the body exemplified in the following verse from that poem:

> Welcome is every organ and attribute of me,
> And of any man hearty and clean,
> Not an inch, nor a particle of an inch is vile
> And none shall be less familiar than the rest.[1204]

Indecent exposure laws express a preference for Bradford's Hobbesian vision[1205] over Whitman's ideal of bodily familiarity. Like John Dunne's vision, Whitman's poetry has no credibility in management of public decency. Indecent exposure laws impose upon all people a vision of vile flesh and indolent bodies, reinforcing a public life of modesty and shame. The reluctance of American courts to support the right of the individual to resist the imposition rather than the right of the state to impose it is becoming more vulnerable. Other than nudist society, long ago banished to the hinterland, resistance largely has been quashed or channeled into regulated commerce. The voice of the body has been muted, its speech distorted and its messages unheard.

These laws impede understanding of the role of religion and management of the body in civil order. Keeping people covered in public and managing nudity in media and entertainment may be important to maintenance of civil society. Although poorly understood, indecent exposure laws and customs appear to have played a central role in civilization. This hypothesis deserves more scholarly attention. In the meantime, if indecent exposure should continue to be a crime, this maintenance would benefit greatly from more research and scholarship to provide a constitutionally acceptable secular purpose and to define optimal contours of the prohibition. The traditional rationales are no longer persuasive and are entangled in constitutional risks.

It is helpful to decouple links between rights, justice, and policy. According to the original meaning of the Constitution, moral rights are natural rights of people, not delegations from the judiciary. Justice is an ideal of mutual respect. Rights and justice are not always aligned with policy, leading to political disputes often framed as legal disputes. In these situations, constitutional rights polarization aligns with political polarization.[1206] The history here demonstrates the loss of recognition of natural rights in an interplay of politics and a Christian sense of moral justice. Political controversies are the responsibility of our elected representatives in America's constitutional democracy. Good policy flows from understanding the goals and effects of government policies and associated costs and benefits. These outcomes require study, debate, and citizen involvement in selecting and influencing representatives. Indecent exposure laws have been mired in self-deception and obfuscation for an exceptionally long time, indicating a need for new approaches to foster a better understanding of the crime and more effective management.

In *Dobbs* (2022), the Supreme Court remarked that "[a]bortion is nothing new. It has been addressed by lawmakers for centuries, and the fundamental moral question that it poses is ageless."[1207] The Court found that the *Roe v. Wade* (1973) decision had "usurped the power to address a question of profound moral and social important that the Constitution unequivocally leaves for the people."[1208] The opinion in *Dobbs* (2022) does not directly address the fundamental issue of whether the United States is a Christian nation. If it had embraced this conception, the analysis would have been straightforward and the conclusion irrefutable, based on divine law. The Court, instead, insidiously infused Christian-nation morality into its analysis by purporting to incorporate history, traditions, and precedent, all of which were built on Christian theology, into its rationale. In doing so, it continues to submerge the religious basis of the nation's legal management of morality in a cloak of nominally secular history and tradition.

The Court used history to show the lack of precedent for a right to abortion. This approach left open questions regarding litigation of other moral judgments. Perhaps the rationale for overturning *Roe v. Wade* would have been better served by quoting Thomas Jefferson on the tremendous costs of regulation intended to produce religious uniformity: "Millions of innocent men, women, and children, since the introduction of Christianity, have been burnt, tortured, fined, imprisoned; yet we have not advanced one inch towards uniformity. What has been the effect of coercion? To make one half of the world fools, and the other half hypocrites."[1209]

Other aspects of the Court's opinion opened the door to designing a model of national moral governance more consistent with original constitutional principles of limited federal government powers over such matters. On the positive side, the Court expressly rejected its role as *custos morum*, abnegating the authority to local legislatures to manage such matters according to the will of the people as expressed in the legislative process conducted by duly elected representatives.

The Court noted that abortion was a matter left to local customs for the first 185 years after ratification of the Constitution. It opined that the question of whether the Constitution confers a right to abortion is determined by standards for analysis of the Fourteenth Amendment concept of "liberty," our nation's history, traditions essential to "our scheme of ordered liberty," and support from judicial precedents.[1210] The opinion notes, as indicated by the review of cases, that no historical precedent supports the decision in *Roe v. Wade* (1973).[1211] Although not directly addressing abortion, the history of indecent exposure laws presented here shows how legal enforcement of moral decisions have been guided by Christian principles since the nation's inception.

The Court instructed that its ruling would not prevent elected representatives in the states from regulating abortion. The natural effect of this deference is to foster development of communities of common interests that would be generalizable to other moral issues, reducing the scale of contention and simplifying consensus building in those communities. The Court concluded that *Roe* (1973) had "short-circuited the democratic process"[1212] as the proper means to address this "fundamental moral question."[1213] This perspective was presaged in Justice Harlan's concurring opinion in *Roth v. United States* (1957), in which he noted that "[s]ince the domain of sexual morality is pre-eminently a matter of state concern, this Court should be slow to interfere with state legislation calculated to protect that morality."[1214]

Justice Harlan recognized the role of scientific substantiation in assessing the presumed effect of the alleged acts on the "moral fabric of society"[1215] and that such matters are the proper domain of state legislatures. Justice Stevens advocated for both of these principles in his dissent in *New York State Liquor Authority v. Bellanca* (1981), discussed in chapter seven. The need for empirical evidence to support the secondary-effects doctrine was emphasized by the Supreme Court in *City of Los Angeles v. Alameda Books* (2002),[1216] but the Court has yet to suggest that the same scientific rigor should be applied to determining whether naked bodies are expressive or ways in which protectable expression might be identified and measured.

The intent of the framers, demands of the ratifiers, and common public original meaning of the Constitution were to respect differing local customs and religious protocols of the colonies. Aspects of the *Dobbs* (2022) opinion open the door to rediscovery of this principle of American constitutional democracy, providing judicial deference to a confederation of states with common economic and security interests that can, at the same time, accommodate different moral practices, social models, and religious orientations, leaving the federal government to focus on economic and defense matters that affect the strength and safety of the union. This model presumes that matters of bodily morality could vary without seriously undermining the cohesiveness of American national identity.

As for the Court's role as *custos morum*, the Court in *Dobbs* (2022) cited *Ferguson* (1963) for the proposition that courts should not "substitute their social and economic beliefs for the judgment of legislative bodies" and cited several other precedents for the proposition that courts must show "respect for a legislature's judgment . . . even when the laws at issue concern matters of great social significance and moral substance."[1217]

This is a time of great change in American society and its moral fabric. The Court in *Dobbs* (2022) characterized the rights involved as health and welfare, indicating that the laws must be sustained if there is a rational basis on which the legislature could have thought it would serve legitimate state interests.[1218] The Mississippi legislature justified its abortion law with an abundance of factual and statistical information, further illuminating a path forward for a new model of moral jurisprudence. The Court suggested a framework for analysis wherein "ordered liberty sets limits and defines the boundary between competing interests." The complexity of such fact-based determinations would tend to expand exponentially with scale, supporting the wisdom of reservation of rights and powers to individuals and states as envisioned by the framers of the Constitution.

The effects of loosening of the Christian religion's influence over American morals and increasing fragmentation of religion in the country can be accommodated by employing these fundamental principles of democracy that hearken back to the formation of the nation. The founding fathers crafted the Constitution to protect the colonies from establishment of a national religion, allowing for diversity of local beliefs and practices. This is a mitigation, not an ideal.

The *Dobbs* (2022) opinion contains a pearl of wisdom in its deference to the judgment of legislative bodies on the moral question of abortion: "It is time to heed the Constitution and return the issue of abortion to the people's elected representatives. 'The permissibility of abortion, and the limitations, upon it, are to be resolved like most important questions in our democracy: by citizens trying to persuade one another and then voting.'"[1219]

On the other hand, the Court's notion that an individual right not expressed in the Constitution can be recognized only if it is deeply rooted in the nation's history and tradition is exactly the fear expressed during the drafting of the amendments that they might be interpreted as exhaustive rather than exemplary. The second part of the *Dobbs* (2022) test is whether the claimed right is essential to the nation's scheme of ordered liberty. The Constitution contemplated a government with limited powers surrendered by the people, not one that would require that the residual rights satisfy tests.

From what we have learned in this journey, it may be time to transcend the court as *custos morum* and recognize that the secular equivalent of religion in a society committed to respect for diversity of religion and conscience and accommodating an increasing share of the religiously unaffiliated is the voice of democratically elected legislatures.[1220] Delegation of these mythmaking and maintenance responsibilities in this manner facilitates evidence-based experimentation and flexibility to accommodate changing mores, untethered from their ecclesiastical foundation.

Moral diversity is also a potentially viable path forward,[1221] based on revitalization of Jeffersonian ideals and basic constitutional principles of limited federal government. The quest for new moral authority and accommodation of conflicting doctrine could be more clearly delegated to state and local authorities, allowing some pluralism at the national level. Greater deference to local authorities is consistent with maturation of America's constitutional democracy. More effective processes to accommodate moral diversity need to be developed. This may be a better route than pursuit a new source of consensus moral truth. With so many sources of moral authority circulating in American society, it may not be possible. An explicit hybrid model may be optimal. There is no process today for educating policymakers about areas of common moral understanding, opportunities for accommodation, and challenges of conflicting views. No "U.S. Moral Code" has been developed to fill the void of the diminishing authority of Christianity. Perhaps a modern version of England's Society for the Reformation of Manners, discussed earlier, which was formed in 1692, should be established as a counterforce against the prevailing tide of immorality? The divisiveness in American society may have gone too far. A studied "civil" outcome, if possible, would need to be well articulated and promoted by recognized authorities to gain credibility and adherence. Criminal justice scholarship could play a substantial role in the reformation efforts.

When legitimate national interests are implicated, congressional action is more consistent with the Constitution than the court as *custos morum*. As in the cases of gay marriage and marijuana, federal courts can play a role in calling the question where there is confusion and contradiction at state and local levels that jeopardizes legitimate national interests in defense, commerce, or the political process. An early example of morals-based legislation grounded in a legitimate national interest in interstate commerce was the White-Slave Traffic Act enacted in 1910.[1222] It prohibited the transportation across state lines of women and girls for immoral purposes. The Act inspired later federal laws to manage transportation of obscene and indecent publications.[1223] In such cases, regulation of commerce provides constitutional authority for assertion of federal intervention. These laws engendered numerous challenges from the adult entertainment industry.[1224]

Legal management of morals not essential to national unity should be the province of local legislatures. Indecent exposure is well suited to local regulation. Similar thinking could be applied to state versus local management of morality. In one such experiment, California amended its penal code in 1969 to delegate responsibility for regulating nudity in adult establishments to local governments.[1225] Federal courts can and should provide guidance about the need for, and adequacy of, empirical evidence supporting local laws and ordinances that may implicate constitutional rights.

Such a cascading of moral legislation has been in place for some time for indecent exposure. It appears to have been reasonably effective and efficient, creating an interesting mix of moral subcultures. This approach has resulted in a wealth of protocols, as well as anomalies such as the ironic banning of simple public nakedness in the notoriously liberal cities of Berkeley and San Francisco. In quixotic fashion, San Francisco, where simple public nakedness is banned, allows overtly sexual celebrations in gay festivals while prosecuting naked political protestors. Up north in Washington state, Seattle failed to prosecute full nakedness in a Gay Pride parade that was not overtly political in nature,[1226] and Portland celebrates the body each year with its World Naked Bike Ride.[1227] Without divine authority, empiricism at least promises some consistency, credibility, and opportunities for well-reasoned debate. Very little attention has been paid to measuring the effects of differences in relevant laws. This is a key missing element in a potentially progressive solution to America's contentious and dysfunctional moral environment.

There are encouraging signs in lower federal court decisions concerning potential use of the scientific method and empirical evidence to support constitutional decisions in moral crimes cases. *Stanley v. Georgia* (2013).[1228] called for empirical evidence of harm to justify obscenity laws. *Lawrence v. Texas* (2003).[1229] posited that majority moral views alone cannot pass constitutional muster regarding private sexual activities. Neither Congress nor the courts have articulated policies to embrace such signposts of moral management.

Professor Goldberg of Columbia Law School argued twenty years ago that the Supreme Court had been trending for a long time away from morals-based lawmaking..[1230] The analysis presented here largely supports her observations but exposes some meandering and countervailing nuances, particularly with respect to indecent exposure, since then. The lack of attribution to Christian authority on moral matters has continued to confound and undermine the credibility and precedential value of judicial decisions based on *custos morum*. Admitting to the source of authority would have created additional constitutional challenges such as those unearthed here. The natural successor to *custos morum* is empiricism. This outcome flows from the last three centuries of social, political, and legal moral development that began with jurisdictional contention between church and state and the rise of rationalist philosophies and scientific methods. The best way for the courts to embrace this transformation is to demand thoughtful, well-constructed empirical arguments from legislators supporting the definition of crimes in statutes, costs to actors and audiences, and implicated state interests.

The trend that Goldberg observed did not continue unabated. Without clear adherence and guidance from the Supreme Court requiring that moral laws must have empirical support, lower federal courts continued to embrace *custos morum*. The Supreme Court denied certiorari in *State v. Lilley* (2019), a case that would have provided a platform to make the point that a change to empiricism is needed.

Dobbs (2022) was another opportunity for the Court to outline an evidence-based approach to assessing claims relating to moral matters. The Court proposed a test for substantive due process claims for alleged rights not listed in the Constitution: "whether the right is "deeply rooted in [our] history and tradition" and whether it is essential to our Nation's "scheme of ordered liberty."[1231] As pointed out earlier, this study's analysis of the original meaning of the Constitution does not support the view that courts can parcel out fundamental rights already belonging to the people. Leaving that aside, the Court did advocate an evidence-based approach to assessment of the issue. It punted tough questions of morality to legislatures, which is a good thing. However, it didn't encourage broader thinking about evidence, experimentation, and scholarly analysis of costs, benefits, and effectiveness. The court could foster further progress by holding that statutes and regulations not backed by findings based on empirical evidence would face strict scrutiny when challenged on constitutional grounds regardless of the nature of the rights involved.

Although the *Dobbs* (2022) opinion directed attention to history, tradition, and the nation's scheme of ordered liberty, it also noted that defenders of *Roe* (1973) "do not claim that any new scientific learning calls for a different answer to the underlying moral question . . . ."[1232] The Court did not indicate what effect such evidence would have on the basic calculus if any of the other factors are missing or unpersuasive. In *Lawrence v Texas* (2003), the Court quoted with approval the statement from Justice Kennedy in *County of Sacramento v. Lewis* (1998) that "[h]istory and tradition are the starting point but not in all cases the ending point of the substantive due process inquiry."[1233] The influence of tradition is ambiguous and reactionary, not an ideal for moral progress.

Areas for further study have been uncovered and illuminated in this study. There has been a great deal of scholarly study of the role of clothing in microcosms like ethno-religious garments,[1234] school uniforms,[1235] occupational dress codes,[1236] and stigmatized youth dress.[1237] The effects of freedom of the body from such restrictions has not engendered similar attention outside the subculture of social nudism. The ontological, epistemological, and political distortions and inequalities generated by or signaled through organizing principles of dress requirements and fashion have been largely ignored by criminologists and other scholars.

Strong messaging from the Supreme Court advocating evidence-based approaches as the preferred analytic method for judicial decision-making would be helpful. Experimentation flowing naturally from local authorities could be used to inspire and inform scientific study and policy decisions in other jurisdictions and mitigate the effects of the obsolescence of *custos morum*. Witnessing progress toward decriminalization of marijuana shows how such a process might work. Although marijuana use is still a crime under federal law, legalization of marijuana under state laws has allowed experimentation to debunk stereotypes and bad assumptions, leading the federal government to suspend prosecution and begin steps toward decriminalization. The "long and winding road" of improvement in LGBTQ rights provides another example of experimentation at the state level informing policymakers and allowing the marketplace of ideas to debunk weak arguments of state interests used to suppress this class of rights.[1238]

Elected leaders and rulers by divine right and/or overwhelming power alike have created the myths that form the moral structure of civilizations. Religion and ruthless demonstrations of power have been the tentpoles of good order throughout history. Beginning a few centuries ago, along with the advent of the scientific method, the rule of reason emerged as a potential alternative source of moral truth. Coincidentally, the common law of England became an organized source of judicial doctrine, America was born, and indecent exposure became a crime.

Advancements in science since then, culminating in the digital technology revolution, foreshadow a possible path for American democracy to accommodate its polytheistic ideals and provide potential paths to moral truth for the religiously unaffiliated. The first step, undertaken here, is to identify relevant precedents, elucidate the role of Christian ideals in shaping legal regulation of bodies, and encourage examination of the costs and benefits of this crime in promotion of good order. Clothing is a critical element in power relations. A better understanding of its effects will facilitate formulation of effective policy.

Myths governing Christian morality cannot be completely reconciled with those of other religions, nor can than they continue to usurp the gestalt of reason and the progress of science and technology. The grip of established religion on political power is weakening here and abroad. According to Pew Research, government restrictions on religion around the world have reached records highs.[1239] The power relations of church and state continue to evolve to greater secular control over moral affairs. The transition to a more pragmatic rule of law regarding regulation of morals is progressing discursively, lacking leadership from a presumptive valid source of authority. It is going to be a hard row to hoe.[1240] On the other hand, it may be an inevitable consequence of the maturing of our constitutional democracy and the expansion of democratic forms of government around the world. Amid these changes, the court's role as *custos morum* will naturally diminish as inconsistent with democratic ideals, returning management of morals to elected officials and respecting their judgments.

The core principles of the framers of the Constitution included accommodation for differences of opinion in religious matters. It may not have occurred to them that the courts would assume the role of *custos morum* and impose a homogenous morality over the states and individuals. This was not even a possibility until adoption of the Fourteenth Amendment, and even then, the focus of the amendment was on post-Civil War reconstruction and unification, not sexual morality. As a matter of constitutional law, resolution of differences of views on public indecency is "best left to the political process and the judgment of ordinary people, not to the judgment of unelected elites in the judiciary."[1241]

The code of moral jurisprudence in America was written in the laws of the colonies, based on the unchallenged truth of Scripture, with that truth protected by blasphemy laws. Modern legal management of morals lacks authority in this sense.[1242] The path to synthesis of major religious doctrine, science, and digital hegemony has not been mapped. In terms of governing structure, local legislative management of the body would, at a minimum, provide robust experimentation generating data analytics to feed policy decisions about how to adapt the regulation of morals to maintain good order. Our educational system would also need to be reformed to reorient students to the new moral authority or pluralistic model. It would be a messy and difficult process. Witness how the clash of competing interests over textbooks to gain hegemony for their representations of moral truth is at a historic high, evidencing profound moral ambiguity.[1243]

The opinion in *Dobbs* (2023) was an important step toward use of factual and statistical information to form a rational basis for laws prohibiting public nakedness. Such a new model of managing morality calls for a better understanding of the practical value of prohibiting nakedness in public. Laws prohibiting public nakedness promote socially acceptable presentations of the self. They promote conformity, order, and productivity. These goals of public indecency laws are legitimate concerns of civil society and could serve as a more principled basis for discussion of the wisdom and constitutionality of such laws, but what of the individual and societal costs of the prohibition? As we have seen, worthy arguments exist on both sides of the issue. Broad-minded research and scholarship concerning the balance of costs and benefits of legal management of bodies is critically needed. Legal repression of the body profoundly shapes individual understanding of reality, including epistemology, ontology, and self-concept. Liberation of the body may or may not contribute to a better civil society. In any case, well-reasoned policy would be served by a better understanding of the implications of criminalization of public nakedness in the transition from Christian moral dominance to a more secular and morally diverse nation..[1244] The nation has been on a rocky road of transition from divine authority over morals without a clear destination in mind.

Epilogue

Indecent exposure laws are one of the tools by which political and religious leaders shape individual epistemology and ontology in the gestalt of civil society. The universality of these laws implies that they may be integral components of broader power structures that govern sexuality and the body in America. Indecent exposure laws create a minimum standard of morally acceptable appearance and conduct in public spaces, contribute to the definition of deviance, and safeguard established religious and social institutions. They establish a strong and intimidating boundary between public and private, observable and hidden dimensions of sexuality, and related matters of intimacy, emotion, and spirituality. The laws fashion actors in a morality play scripted with biblical inspiration. They offer compelling visuals depicting compliance and defiance, obedience and rebellion, normalcy and abnormality, and decency and indecency. They "safeguard" children, where the influences of power are nascent, from the natural state of bodies.

Diminishment and fragmentation of the dominant moral influence is inspiring rebellion by traditionally politically disadvantaged classes against the repressive regime it represents and defends, including a wide range of archetypes represented in the Berkeley scenario outlined in chapter ten. The insurgent voices are varied, often distorted and tentative, and sometimes chaotic. The permissions they extract through political advocacy and constitutional claims move our society down an uncharted course of self-exploration. As Foucault wrote in *The History of Sexuality*, sexuality is not a natural or biological phenomenon.[1245] It is a historical and cultural construct that is shaped by discourses and practices of power. Legal repression of the body does not extinguish sexuality. Instead, it shapes it in powerful ways. Cloaking bodies in fashion imposes subjective realities and alien identity, concealing authentic selves (if there is such a thing) beneath culture's imperatives. This produces what Foucault called "docile bodies," bodies that are disciplined, normalized, and useful for maintenance of good order in society. Institutions such as clothing-optional beaches, strip clubs, R-rated movies, events celebrating LGBTQ+ identity, and pornography subject bodies to a proliferation of discourses and regulations that control, normalize, and classify them. These forces address Locke's concern about indolency of the body, but with decreasing effectiveness.

Our incomplete understanding of these matters is unsettling. America is lurching and stumbling forward toward a new morality. Management of bodies is a foundational element of morality and may be a cornerstone of civil society. There is a need for analytical clarity and well-reasoned strategy to guide policy development. Leadership is lacking. These metaphysical trends beg for scholarship. The recipe for a successful transition, if one is possible, is intricate and possibly incomprehensible. Is there a discoverable natural self at all? What is its agenda? Adam Smith's concept of the invisible hand comes to mind.[1246]

Throughout history, loosening morals have been correlated with the collapse of civilizations. The American model of constitutional democracy plays an important role in global politics. The term "democracy" was coined around 500 BCE in ancient Athens.[1247] Historians count among the oldest democracies the polis of Athens and the Iroquois Nation.[1248] The Iroquois "great league of peace" has been acknowledged as an inspiration for American representative democracy. Neither of these democracies survived. The Iroquois culture was decimated by Europeans settlers, and democracy in Athens succumbed to a complex of many factors "amid a crippling economic downturn, while politicians committed financial misdemeanours [*sic*], sent its army to fight unpopular foreign wars and struggled to cope with a surge in immigration."[1249] The circumstances surrounding the collapse of democracy in Athens are hauntingly similar to the current state of America. Surveys show that as many as three quarters of Americans think America is on the wrong track despite a lack of objective data to support their sense of despair.[1250]

What has this to do with indecent exposure? The American democratic model has shown enviable prowess in managing through crises. To do so, there needs to be a sense of conviction and achievable goals. As the moral direction provided by Christianity fades, without better insights, the changing concepts of decency and other tools for management of bodies are fraught with risk. The halting and meandering changes imposed by the court as *custos morum* obfuscate opportunities for a better model of America's constitutional democracy or its abandonment. Management of bodies may be the obscure bedrock of civil order. Public nakedness is one of the last surviving hallmarks of traditional American decency. This study provides fuel for a broad spectrum of novel and renewed constitutional challenges. This begs the question of the wisdom of change.

Humans are the only mammals that adorn their bodies for social reasons. Strong correlations have been observed between body adornment and civilization.[1251] Clothing's critical role in subcultures has been well-documented. Most people are likely to adorn themselves with clothing or other symbols to create and maintain connections with attractive affinity groups. Careful apolitical study of the consequences of a broadening range of choice in such matters may yield important insights.

What is so wrong with public display of nakedness that it requires the force of law to buttress shame, modesty, and clothing as fashion and indicia of affiliation?

being qua being

Aristotle, *Metaphysics*.[1252]

We won't know unless we allow freedom to experiment, assess, learn, share, and debate. The first few steps have been taken here in exposing and describing the sources and evolution of the laws and their relation to the U.S. Constitution, hopefully opening the door to further reflection, reform, experimentation, and study of the ontology of nakedness. The findings of this comprehensive history raise many questions and fuel novel arguments and more thorough reasoning for assessment of the laws' constitutionality and consequences. A few questions and arguments have been addressed as illustration, inspiration, and starting points for briefs and studies. The Berkeley crowd awaits your informed and well-reasoned judgment.

Bibliography

English Common Law Cases

1 Keb. 526 (1663)
125 1 Sess. Cases 231 (1733)
2 Rolle's Abridgement 78 (1668)
3 Cro. Jac. 421 (1658)
Atwood's Case (1618)
Coggs v. Bernard, 2 Ld. Raymond 911 (1762)
Coram Rege Roll, Mich. 15 Car. 2 (1639)
Dugdale v. The Queen, 1 El. & B. 435 (1853)
Harring v. Walrond, 1681, 1 Russ. Cr. 436 (1681)
Le Roy v. Sir Charles Sedley, 1 Siderfin 168, 83 Eng. Rep. 1146 (1663)
Reg. v. Buyan, 1 Cox C.C. 74 (1844)
Reg. v. Elliot, 1 L. & C. 103 (1861)
Reg. v. Hicklin, L.R. 3 Q. B. 360 (1868)
Reg. v. Holmes, 169 E.R. 697 (1853)
Reg. v. Read, Fortescue 98, 92 Eng. Rep. 777 (1708)
Reg. v. Rowed, 3 Q.B. 180, 2 G. & D. 518, 6 Jur. 396, 11 L.J.M.C. 74 (1842)
Reg. v. Thallman, Leigh & C.C.C. 326, 169 Eng. Rep. 1416 (1863)
Reg. v. Watson, 2 Cox C.C. 376 (1847)
Reg. v. Webb, 2 Car. & K. 933, 175 Eng. Rep. 391 (1848)
Rex v. Crunden, 2 Camp. 89, 170 Eng. Rep. 1091 (1809)
Rex v. Curl, (1 George II.) 2 Strange 788 (1727)
Rex v. Curl, 93 Eng. Rep. 849, 850 (K.B. 1727)
Rex v. Delaval, 1 Black. Rep. 410; 3 Burr. 1434 (1763)
Rex v. Field, 1 Siderfin 69, 1 Keb. 175 (1661)
Rex v. Gallard, 25 Eng. Rep. 547 (1733)
Rex v. Justices of the Town & Country of Newcastle-upon-Tyne, 1 Barn & Ad. 933, 109 Eng. Rep. 1033 (1831)
Rex v. Orchard, 3 Cox C.C. 248 (1848)
Rex v. Tallard, 2 Barn. 328, 345, 94 Eng. Rep. 532 (1733)
Rex v. Taylor, 1 Ven. 293, 3 Keb. 607 (1676)
Rex v. Wheelhorse, Poph. 208 (1627)
Sir Charles Sydlyes Case, 1 Keble 619, 82 Eng. Rep. 1036 (1663)
Sparrow v. Sherwood, Popham's King's Bench Reports (1627)

English Statutes

1 Hen. Stat. at Large 240 (1819-1823)

10 & 11 Vict. (1847)
14 & 15 Vict., c. 100 ss. 24, 25 (1851)
3 Geo. 4 (1822)
31 Stats. Henry VIII, c. 8, s, 1 (1539), amended by 34 and 35 Stats. Henry VIII c. 23 (1542)
5 Geo. 4 ch. 83 (1824)
Acts and Resolves, May the 7th, 1662, in SEVERALL LAWES AND ORDERS MADE AT SEVERALL GENERAL COURTS IN THE YEARS 1661, 1662, 1663 (Library of Cong., microfiche)
An Act for More Effectually Preventing the Sale of Obscene Books, Pictures, Prints, and Other Articles, in A COLLECTION OF THE PUBLIC GENERAL STATUTES: 1857,2
BRYDALL, J., COMPENDIOUS COLLECTION OF THE LAWS OF ENGLAND, TOUCHING MATTERS CRIMINAL (1675)
C.L.C. 153 § 1 (1672)
Statutes of the Realm, 13 Car. 2
Statutes of the Realm, 1819, 14 Car. II, c. 33

Colonial and U.S. Statutes and Regulations

18 U.S.C. § 1461 (1994)
19 U.S.C. § 1305 (2023)
25 C.F.R § 11.408 (2023)
61 P.L. 277, 36 Stat. 825, 61 Cong. Ch. 395 (1910)
BLUE LAWS OF CONNECTICUT (Smucker ed., 1861)
CAL. PENAL CODE § 314 (West 2023)
CAL. PENAL CODE § 318 (West 2012)
CODE OF IOWA § 2709 (1851)
COLO. REV. STAT. ANN. § 18-7-302(1) (West 2023)
COLONIAL LAWS OF MASSACHUSETTS (1889)
CONN. PUB. STAT. LAWS tit. 97 (1808)
Cotton, John, *An Abstract of the Lawes of New England* (1641, 1655); *reprinted in* HUTCHINSON, COLLECTION OF ORIGINAL PAPERS (1769), 3(9) FORCE'S TRACT (1733), and 5 MASS. HIST. SOC. COLLECTION (1st series 1792)
CUSHING, JOHN D., 1ST LAWS OF THE STATE OF CONNECTICUT (1784)
CUSHING, JOHN D., CONNECTICUT
CUSHING, JOHN D., GOVERNOR EATON'S CODE FOR THE NEW HAVEN COLONY T (1784)
CUSHING, JOHN D., MARYLAND (1838)
CUSHING, JOHN D., NEW YORK (1872)
CUSHING, JOHN D., RHODE ISLAND (1798)
CUSHING, JOHN D., THE 1ST LAWS OF THE STATE OF VIRGINIA (1983)
CUSHING, JOHN D., THE LAWS OF THE PILGRIMS (1977)
FIELD, DAVID, DRAFT OF A PENAL CODE FOR THE STATE OF NEW YORK (1864)
HINMAN, ROYAL R., THE BLUE LAWS OF NEW HAVEN COLONY, USUALLY CALLED BLUE LAWS OF CONNECTICUT (1838)
IND. CODE ANN. § 35-45-4-1 (LEXISNEXIS 2023)
IOWA CODE ANN. § 709.9 (West 2023)

KY. REV. STAT. ANN. § 232.021 (West 2023)
LAWS UNDER CONSTITUTION OF 1851 vol. 69 (1862)
MASS. STAT. 1784 ch. 40 § A (1791)
MINN. STAT. § 617.23(a)(3) (1996)
MODEL PENAL CODE § 207.10 cmt. 8 (Tent. Draft No. 6 1957)
N.H. LAWS 1791 ch. 28
N.H. LAWS 1828 ch. 92
NEV. REV. STAT. ANN. § 201.220(1) (West 2023)
NEW HAMPSHIRE LAWS vol. 1 (1679)
Pub. L. No. 103-141, 107 Stat. 1488 (Nov. 16, 1993), codified at 42 U.S.C. § 2000bb through 42 U.S.C. § 2000bb-4
REVISED STATUTES OF THE STATE OF ARKANSAS 182 (1838)
THE COLONIAL LAWS OF MASSACHUSETTS REPRINTED FROM THE EDITION OF 1660 . . . CONTAINING ALSO THE BODY OF LIBERTIES OF 1641 (Fred B. Rothman & Co. 1995) (1889)
THE EARLIEST LAWS OF THE NEW HAVEN AND CONNECTICUT COLONIES, 1639-1673 (John D. Cushing ed., 1784)
The Massachusetts Body of Liberties, HANOVER COLL. DEP'T HIST. (1641), http://history.hanover.edu/texts/masslib.html
THE PENAL CODE OF THE STATE OF TEXAS (1857)
THE REVISED STATUTES OF THE STATE OF NEW HAMPSHIRE PASSED DECEMBER 23, 1842 (1843)
Title VII, 42 U.S.C §§ 2000e - 2000e-17 (2023)
U.S. CODE § 920c, vol. 10, art. 120c(c) (2023)
UTAH CODE ANN. § 76-10-1201(5)(a) (2023)
Ward, N., *The Body of Liberties of 1641*, *in* COLONIAL LAWS OF MASSACHUSETTS 94 (1889)
WHITMORE, WILLIAM H., BOS. CITY COUNCIL, THE COLONIAL LAWS OF MASSACHUSETTS: REPRINTED FROM THE EDITION OF 1672 WITH THE SUPPLEMENTS THROUGH 1686 : CONTAINING ALSO A BIBLIOGRAPHICAL PREFACE AND INTRODUCTION TREATING OF ALL THE PRINTED LAWS FROM 1649 TO 1686 : TOGETHER WITH THE BODY OF LIBERTIES OF 1641, AND THE RECORDS OF THE COURT OF ASSISTANTS, 1641-1644 (1890)

Local Regulations

BERKELEY, CAL., MUNICIPAL CODE tit. 13 (2023)
FORT COLLINS, COLO., MUN. CODE § 17-142(b), (d) (2016)
S.F., CAL., POLICE CODE art. 15.3 § 1071.1 (2011)
S.F., CAL., POLICE CODE art. 2 § 154 (2013)

Treatises

BLACKSTONE, WILLIAM, COMMENTARIES ON THE LAWS OF ENGLAND vol. 4 (1765)
BURN, RICHARD, & JOSEPH GREENLEAF, AN ABRIDGEMENT OF BURN'S JUSTICE OF THE PEACE AND PARISH OFFICER (1773)

BURN, RICHARD, AN ABRIDGEMENT, OR THE AMERICAN JUSTICE (1773)
BURN, RICHARD, AN ABRIDGEMENT, OR THE AMERICAN JUSTICE (1792)
BURN'S JUSTICE (1743)
CARRINGTON, FREDERICK AUGUSTUS, ANDREW VALENTINE KIRWAN, & GREAT BRITAIN CENTRAL CRIMINAL COURT, REPORTS OF CASES ARGUED AND RULED AT NISI PRIUS: IN THE COURTS OF QUEEN'S BENCH, COMMON PLEAS, & EXCHEQUER; TOGETHER WITH CASES TRIED ON THE CIRCUITS, AND IN THE CENTRAL CRIMINAL COURT . . . S. SWEET (1852)
CHITTY, JOSEPH, A PRACTICAL TREATISE ON THE CRIMINAL LAW vol. 2 (1816)
COKE, EDWARD, THE 1ST PART OF THE INSTITUTES OF THE LAWS OF ENGLAND (1628)
COKE, EDWARD, THE THIRD PART OF THE INSTITUTES OF THE LAW OF ENGLAND vol. 3 (5th ed., 1671)
COKE, EDWARD, THE THIRD PART OF THE INSTITUTES OF THE LAW OF ENGLAND vol. 3 (6th ed., 1680)
COOLEY, THOMAS M., A TREATISE ON THE LAW OF TORTS OR THE WRONGS WHICH ARISE INDEPENDENT OF CONTRACT (1879)
DALTON, MICHAEL, THE COUNTREY JUSTICE 10 (1666 ed.)
EAST, EDWARD HYDE, A TREATISE OF THE PLEAS OF THE CROWN vol. 1 (1803)
HALE, WILLIAM H., A SERIES OF PRECEDENTS AND PROCEEDINGS IN CRIMINAL CAUSES, 1475–1640 (1847)
HAWKINS, WILLIAM, A TREATISE OF THE PLEAS OF THE CROWN vol. 1 (1716)
Hudson, William, *A Treatise on the Court of the Star-Chamber*, *in* 2 FRANCIS HARGRAVE, COLLECTANEA JURIDICA (1791)
JOYCE, JOSEPH A., & HOWARD C. JOYCE, TREATISE ON THE LAW GOVERNING NUISANCES (1906)
RUSSELL, WILLIAM O., A TREATISE ON CRIMES AND MISDEMEANORS (1843)
RUSSELL, WILLIAM O., A TREATISE ON CRIMES AND MISDEMEANORS vol. 1 (1819)
SAINT GERMAN, CHRISTOPHER, & WILLIAM MUCHALL, THE DOCTOR AND STUDENT: OR, DIALOGUES BETWEEN A DOCTOR OF DIVINITY AND A STUDENT IN THE LAWS OF ENGLAND: CONTAINING THE GROUNDS OF THOSE LAWS TOGETHER WITH QUESTIONS AND CASES CONCERNING THE EQUITY THEREOF (A. Strahan & W. Woodfall eds., 1787)
STEPHEN CHARLES DENISON, CROWN CASES RESERVED FOR CONSIDERATION AND DECIDED BY THE JUDGES OF ENGLAND, FROM THE YEAR 1844 TO THE YEAR 1850 vol. 1, at 339–45 (1850)
STORY, JOSEPH, COMMENTARIES ON THE CONSTITUTION (1833)
TIEDEMAN, CHRISTOPHER G., A TREATISE ON THE LIMITATIONS OF POLICE POWER IN THE UNITED STATES (1886)
WHARTON, FRANCIS, A TREATISE ON THE CRIMINAL LAW OF THE UNITED STATES (1855)

U.S. State and Local Cases

Abbott v. State, 163 Tenn. 384 (1931)
Ardery v. State, 56 Ind. 328 (1877)
Baines v. Birmingham, 240 So. 2d 689 (Ala. Crim. App. 1970)

Barker v. Commonwealth, 19 Pa. 412 (1852)
Bell v. State, 31 Tenn. 42 (1851)
Britain v. State, 22 Tenn. (3 Hum.) 203 (1842)
Brown v. Pena, 441 F. Supp. 1382 (S.D. Fla. 1977)
Case v. Commonwealth, 231 S.W.2d 86 (Ky. 1950)
Cent. Tex. Nudists v. Cty. of Travis, 2000 Tex. App. LEXIS 8136 (Tex. Ct. App. 2000)
Commonwealth v. Buckley, 86 N.E. 910 (Mass. 1909)
Commonwealth v. Calef, 10 Mass. (9 Tyng) 153 (1813)
Commonwealth v. Catlin, 1 Mass. (Will.) 8 (1804)
Commonwealth v. Haynes, 68 Mass. (2 Gray) 72 (1854)
Commonwealth v. Kneeland, 37 Mass. 206 (1838)
Commonwealth v. Lambert, 94 Mass. 177 (1866)
Commonwealth v. Moniz, 155 N.E.2d 762 (Mass. 1959)
Commonwealth v. Sharpless, 2 Serg. & Rawle 91 (Pa. 1815)
Commonwealth v. Turner, 26 Va. 678 (1827)
Commonwealth v. Wardell, 128 Mass. 52 (1880)
Crownover v. Musick, 509 P.2d 497 (Cal. 1973)
Dameron v. State, 8 Mo. 494 (1844)
Duran v. State, 948 A.2d 139 (2008)
Eckl v. Davis, 51 Cal. App. 3d 831 (Cal. Ct. App. 1975)
Elysium Inst. v. Cty. of L.A., 232 Cal. App. 3d 408 (Cal. App. Dep't Super. Ct. 1991)
Excelsior Pictures Corp. v. Regents of Univ., 144 N.E.2d 31 (N.Y. 1957)
Fowler v. State, 5 Day 81 (Conn. 1811)
Grisham v. State, 10 Tenn. 589 (1831)
Howell v. State, 81 S.E. 247 (Ga. Ct. App. 1914)
In re Dallas W., 102 Cal. Rptr. 2d 493 (Cal. Ct. App. 2000)
In re Davis, 51 Cal. Rptr. 702 (Cal. Ct. App. 1966)
In re Smith, 497 P.2d 807 (Cal. 1972)
Jennings v. State, 16 Ind. 335, 335 (1861)
Kirkorian v. State, 196 A.2d 866 (Md. 1964)
Knowles v. State, 3 Day 103 (Conn. 1808)
McJunkins v. State, 10 Ind. 105 (1858)
Messina v. State, 130 A.2d 578 (Md. 1957)
Miller v. People, 5 Barb. 203 (N.Y. App. Div. 1849)
Morris v. Mun. Ct., 652 P.2d 51 (Cal. 1982)
New York v. Hollman, 500 N.E.2d 297 (N.Y. Ct. App. 1986)
Nolin v. Mayor of Franklin, 12 Tenn. 163 (1833)
People *ex rel.* Campbell v. Bd. of Police Comm'rs, 43 N.Y.S. 118 (N.Y. App. Div. 1897)
People *ex rel.* Lee v. Bixby, 67 Barb. 221 (N.Y. 1875)
People v. Anonymous Female, 539 N.Y.S.2d 868 (Buffalo City Ct. 1989)
People v. Barrus, 232 P.3d 264 (Colo. App. 2009)
People v. Gilbert, 338 N.Y.S.2d 457 (City Crim. Ct. 1972)
People v. Hollman, 500 N.E.2d 297 (N.Y. 1986)
People v. Honan, 111 Cal. Rptr. 3d 351 (Cal. Ct. App. 2010)

People v. Massicot, 118 Cal. Rptr. 2d 705 (Cal. Ct. App. 2002)
People v. Muller, 96 N.Y. 408 (1884)
People v. Ruggles, 8 Johns. 290 (N.Y. Sup. Ct. 1811)
People v. Smith, 147 Cal. Rptr. 3d 314 (Cal. Ct. App. 2012)
People v. Ulman, 258 App Div. 262 (N.Y. App. Div. 1939)
People v. Woody, 394 P.2d 813 (Cal. 1964)
Redd v. State, 67 S.E. 709 (Ga. App. 1910)
Rollins v. State, 181 A.3d 958 (Md. Ct. Spec. App. 2017)
Scopes v. State, 154 Tenn. 105 (1927)
Spears v. State, 175 So. 2d 158 (Miss. 1965)
Spectrum WT v. Wendler, 2023 U.S. Dist. LEXIS 168753 (N.D. Tex. 2023)
State v. Appling, 25 Mo. 315 (1857)
State v. Cagle, 2 Humph. 414 (Tenn. 1841)
State v. Castaneda, 245 P.3d 550 (Nev. 2010)
State v. Ciancanelli, 45 P.3d 451 (Or. Ct. App. 2002)
State v. Crenshaw, 597 P.2d 13 (Haw. 1979)
State v. Duncan, 605 N.W.2d 745 (Minn. Ct. App. 2000)
State v. Fly, 501 S.E.2d 656 (N.C. 1998)
State v. Hanson, 23 Tex. 232 (1859)
State v. Hazle, 20 Ark. 156 (1859)
State v. Isaac, 756 N.W.2d 817 (Iowa 2008)
State v. Juneau, 88 Wis. 180 (1894)
State v. King, 201 S.E.2d 724 (N.C. Ct. App. (1974)
State v. Lilley, 204 A.3d 198 (N.Y. 2019)
State v. Millard, 18 Vt. 574 (1846)
State v. Moore, 31 Tenn. 136 (1851)
State v. Nelson, 178 N.W.2d 434 (Iowa 1970)
State v. Plenty Horse, 741 N.W.2d 763 (S.D. 2007)
State v. Roper, 18 N.C. 208 (1835)
State v. Schramel, 581 N.W.2d 400 (Minn. Ct. App. 1998)
State v. Streath, 327 S.E.2d 240 (N.C. Ct. App. 1985)
State v. Walter, 16 Del. 444 (1895)
State v. Watts, 2021 UT 60 (Utah 2021)
Updegraph v. Commonwealth, 11 Serg. & Rawle 394 (Pa. 1824)
Van Houten v. State, 46 N.J.L. 16 (1884)
Washington v. Thompson, No. 84366-4-I (Wash. Ct. App. Aug. 28, 2023)
Wisneski v. State, 921 A.2d 73 (Md. 2007)
Wittbold v. Miami-Dade Cty., 2013 U.S. Dist. LEXIS 90514 (S.D. Fla. 2013)
Woodlands Pride, Inc. v. Paxton, No. 4:23-cv-02847, 2023 U.S. Dist. LEXIS 171268 (S.D. Tex. 2023)
Young v. State, 692 S.W. 2d 752 (Ark. 1985)

Constitutional Provisions

CAL. CONST. § 4 (1849)
CONST. OF CONN. § 3 (1776)
CONST. OF CONN. § 4 (1776)
DEL. CONST. § 1 (1792)

KAN. CONST. § 7 (1855)
MASS. CONST. (1779)
MD. CONST. art. XXXIII (1776)
MISS. CONST. art. I (1817)
MISS. CONST. art. VII, §§ 5, 14 (1832)
N.Y. CONST. art. I, § XXXVI (1777)
N.Y. CONST. art. XXXVII (1777)
NEV. CONST. art. I (1864)
U.S. CONST. amend. I
U.S. CONST. amend. IX (1971)
U.S. CONST. amend. V
U.S. CONST. amend. X (1971)

U.S. Federal Cases

A Book Named "John Cleland's Memoirs of a Woman of Pleasure" v. Attorney Gen. of Mass., 383 U.S. 413 (1966)
Am. Booksellers Ass'n v. Hudnut, 771 F.2d 323 (7th Cir. 1985)
Animal Legal Def. Fund v. Reynolds, 630 F. Supp. 3d 1105 (S.D. Iowa 2022)
Baker v. Glover, 776 F. Supp. 1511 (M.D. Ala. 1991)
Bakke v. Regents of the Univ. of Cal., 438 U.S. 265 (1978)
Ball v. Bd. of Trs., 584 F.2d 684 (5th Cir. 1978)
Barnes v. Glen Theatre, 501 U.S. 560 (1991)
Bates v. City of Little Rock, 361 U.S. 516 (1960)
Bd. of Trs. of Univ. of Ala. v. Garrett, 531 U.S. 356 (2001)
Beauharnais v. Illinois, 343 U.S. 250 (1952)
Bolling v. Sharpe, 347 U.S. 497 (1954)
Bowers v. Hardwick, 478 U.S. 186 (1986)
Brandenburg v. Ohio, 395 U.S. 444 (1969)
Branzburg v. Hayes, 408 U.S. 665 (1972)
Breen v. Kahl, 419 F.2d 1034 (7th Cir. 1969)
Brown v. Bd. of Educ., 347 U.S. 483 (1954)
Brown v. Dade Christian Sch., Inc., 556 F.2d 310 (5th Cir. 1977)
Brown v. Kemp, 2023 U.S. App. LEXIS 30112 (7th Cir. 2023)
Brown v. Maryland, 25 U.S. 419 (1827)
Buck v. Bell, 274 U.S. 200 (1927)
Buckley v. Valeo, 424 U.S. 1 (1976)
Burstyn v. Wilson, 343 U.S. 495 (1952)
California v. LaRue, 409 U.S. 109 (1972)
Cantwell v. Connecticut, 310 U.S. 296 (1940)
Carey v. Population Servs. Int'l, 431 U.S. 678 (1977)
CBDM Redlands, LLC v. Prieto, 2017 U.S. Dist. LEXIS 59218 (C.D. Cal. 2017)
Chaplinsky v. New Hampshire, 315 U.S. 568 (1942)
Church of the Holy Trinity v. United States, 143 U.S. 457 (1892)
City of Boerne v. Flores, 521 U.S. 507 (1997)
City of Erie v. Pap's A.M., 529 U.S. 277 (2000)

City of L.A. v. Alameda Books, 535 U.S. 425 (2002)
City of Ocala v. Rojas, 143 S. Ct. 764 (2023)
Coates v. Cincinnati, 402 U.S. 611 (1971)
Cohen v. California, 403 U.S. 15 (1971)
Cousins v. Wigoda, 419 U.S. 477 (1975)
Ctr. for Investigative Reporting v. Se. Pa. Transp. Auth., 975 F.3d 300 (3rd Cir. 2020)
Dandridge v. Williams, 397 U.S. 471 (1970)
Davis v. Beason, 133 U.S. 333 (1890)
De Veau v. Braisted, 363 U.S. 144 (1960)
Dease v. City of Anaheim, 826 F. Supp. 336 (C.D. Cal. 1993)
Dobbs v. Jackson Women's Health Org., 142 S. Ct. 2228 (2022)
Dombrowski v. Pfister, 380 U.S. 479 (1965)
Doran v. Salem Inn, Inc., 422 U.S. 922 (1975)
E. Hartford Educ. Ass'n v. Bd. of Educ., 562 F. 2d. 838 (2d. Cir. 1977)
Edge v. City of Everett, 636 F. Supp. 3d 1247 (W.D. Wa. 2022)
Egolf v. Witmer, 421 F. Supp. 2d 858 (E.D. Pa. 2006)
Eisenstadt v. Baird, 405 U.S. 438 (1972)
Eline v. Town of Ocean City, 7 F.4th 214 (4th Cir. 2021)
Emp. Div. v. Smith, 494 U.S. 872 (1990)
Engel v. Vitale, 370 U.S. 421 (1962)
Epperson v. Arkansas, 393 U.S. 97 (1968)
Erznoznik v. Jacksonville, 422 U.S. 205 (1975)
Everson v. Bd. of Educ., 330 U.S. 1 (1947)
Excelsior Pictures Corp. v. Chicago, 182 F. Supp. 400 (N.D. Ill. 1960)
Ferguson v. Skrupa, 372 U.S. 726 (1963)
Ferrel v. Dallas Indep. Sch. Dist., 393 U.S. 856 (1968)
Free Speech Coal., Inc. v. Attorney Gen. U.S., 974 F.3d 408 (3rd Cir. 2020)
Free the Nipple v. City of Springfield, 923 F.3d 508 (8th Cir. 2019)
Free the Nipple-Fort Collins v. City of Fort Collins, 916 F.3d 792 (10th Cir. 2019)
Frontiero v. Richardson, 411 U.S. 677 (1973)
Fry v. United States, 421 U.S. 542 (1975)
Gertz v. Robert Welch, 418 U.S. 323 (1974)
Gfell v. Rickelman, 441 F.2d 444 (6th Cir. 1971)
Ginsberg v. New York, 390 U.S. 629 (1968)
Ginzburg v. United States, 383 U.S. 463 (1966)
Goldfarb v. Va. State Bar, 421 U.S. 773 (1975)
Grayned v. City of Rockford, 408 U.S. 104 (1972)
Griswold v. Connecticut, 381 U.S. 479 (1965)
Harrah Indep. Sch. Dist. v. Martin, 99 S. Ct. 1062 (1979)
Harris v. McRae, 448 U.S. 297 (1980)
Harrison v. NAACP, 360 U.S. 167 (1959)
Hudnut v. Am. Booksellers Ass'n, 475 U.S. 1001 (1986)
Huffman v. Michigan, 549 U.S. 814 (2006)
Iancu v. Brunetti, 139 S. Ct. 2294, 2300 (2019)
Ill. St. Bd. of Elections v. Socialist Workers Party, 440 U.S. 173 (1979)
In re Goalen, 414 U.S. 1148 (1974)

Int'l Soc'y for Krishna Consciousness, Inc. v. Barber, 506 F. Supp. 147 (N.D.N.Y. 1980)
Jacobellis v. Ohio, 378 U.S. 184 (1964)
Jacobson v. Massachusetts, 197 U.S. 11 (1905)
Johnson v. Robison, 415 U.S. 361 (1974)
Jones v. Opelika, 316 U.S. 584 (1942)
Junior Sports Magazines Inc. v. Bonta, 80 F.4th 1109 (9th Cir. 2023)
Kalman v. Cortes, 723 F. Supp. 2d 766 (E.D. Pa. 2010)
Kelley v. Johnson, 425 U.S. 238 (1976)
Kennedy v. Bremerton Sch. Dist., 142 S. Ct. 2407 (2022)
Labine v. Vincent, 401 U.S. 532 (1971)
Late Corp. of Church of Jesus Christ v. United States, 136 U.S. 1 (1890)
Lawrence v. Texas, 539 U.S. 558 (2003)
Lawton v. Steele, 152 U.S. 133 (1894)
Lee v. Weisman, 505 U.S. 577 (1992)
Lefkowitz v. Cunningham, 431 U.S. 801 (1977)
Leisy v. Hardin, 135 U.S. 100 (1890)
Lemon v. Kurtzman, 403 U.S. 602 (1971)
Linn v. United Plant Guard Workers, 383 U.S. 53 (1966)
Lochner v. New York, 198 U.S. 45 (1905)
Lorillard Tobacco Co. v. Reilly, 533 U.S. 525 (2001)
Loving v. Virginia, 388 U.S. 1 (1967)
Lujan v. Defenders of Wildlife, 504 U.S. 555 (1992)
Mackey v. Montrym, 443 U.S. 1 (1979)
Mahanoy Area Sch. Dist. v. B.L., 141 S. Ct. 2038 (2021)
Maher v. Roe, 432 U.S. 464, 472 (1977)
Manigault v. Springs, 199 U.S. 473 (1905)
Matal v. Tam, 582 U.S. 218, 244 (2017)
McCollum v. Bd. of Educ., 333 U.S. 203 (1948)
McCoy v. Town of Pittsfield, 59 F.4th 497 (D.N.H. 2023)
McGowan v. Maryland, 366 U.S. 420 (1961)
McLaughlin v. Florida, 379 U.S. 184 (1964)
Memorandum in Support of Penkoski's Motion, Supported by Plaintiff Sevier, for a Preliminary Injunction and Permanent Injunction, Penkoski v. Bowser, 548 F. Supp. 3d 12 (D.D.C. 2021) (No. 1:20-cv-01519)
Miller v. California, 413 U.S. 15 (1973)
Miller v. Sch. Dist. Number 167, 496 F.2d 658 (7th Cir. 1974)
Miranda v. Arizona, 384 U.S. 436 (1966)
Mitchell v. Helms, 530 U.S. 793 (2000)
Moore v. Sims, 99 S. Ct. 2371 (1979)
Murphy v. Ramsey, 114 U.S. 15 (1885)
Myers v. United States, 272 U.S. 52 (1926)
N.Y. St. Liquor Auth. v. Bellanca, 452 U.S. 714 (1981)
NAACP v. Button, 371 U.S. 415 (1963)
Nat'l Socialist Party v. Skokie, 432 U.S. 43 (1977)
Near v. Minnesota, 283 U.S. 697 (1931)
New York v. United States, 505 U.S. 144 (1992)

Nixon v. Adm'r of Gen. Servs., 433 U.S. 425 (1977)
O'Connor v. Donaldson, 422 U.S. 563 (1975)
Obergefell v. Hodges, 576 U.S. 644, 647 (2015)
Ohralik v. Oh. St. Bar Ass'n, 436 U.S. 447 (1978)
Olmstead v. United States, 277 U.S. 438 (1928)
Paris Adult Theatre I v. Slaton, 413 U.S. 49 (1973)
Parmelee v. United States, 113 F.2d 729 (1940)
Patrick v. LeFevre, 745 F.2d 153 (2d Cir. 1984)
Paul v. Davis, 424 U.S. 693 (1976)
Penkoski v. Bowser, 548 F. Supp. 3d 12 (D.D.C. 2021)
Poe v. Ullman, 367 U.S. 497 (1961)
Prigg v. Pennsylvania, 41 U.S. 539 (1842)
R.A.V. v. St. Paul, 505 U.S. 377 (1992)
Reno v. ACLU, 521 U.S. 844 (1997)
Reynolds v. Sims, 377 U.S. 533 (1963)
Reynolds v. United States, 98 U.S. 145 (1879)
Richards v. Thurston, 424 F.2d 1281 (1st Cir. 1970)
Robins v. County of L.A., 248 Cal. App. 2d 1 (1966)
Roe v. Wade, 410 U.S. 113 (1973)
Rose v. Mitchell, 99 S. Ct. 2993 (1979)
Rosenberg v. LoanDepot.com LLC, 435 F. Supp. 3d 308 (D. Mass. 2020)
Rosenberger v. Rector of Univ. of Va., 515 U.S. 819 (1995)
Rosenblatt v. Baer, 383 U.S. 75 (1966)
Roth v. United States, 354 U.S. 476 (1957)
S. Fla. Free Beaches, Inc. v. Miami, 734 F.2d 608 (11th Cir. 1984)
Sable Commc'ns of Cal. v. FCC, 492 U.S. 115 (1989)
San Antonio Indep. Sch. Dist. v. Rodriguez, 411 U. S. 1 (1973)
San Diego Bldg. Trades Council v. Garmon, 359 U.S. 236 (1959)
Sch. Dist. of Abington Twp. v. Schempp, 374 U.S. 203 (1963)
Selective Draft Law Cases, 245 U.S. 366 (1918)
Sessions v. Morales-Santana, 582 U.S. 47 (2017)
Sherbert v. Verner, 374 U.S. 398 (1963)
Skinner v. Oklahoma, 315 U.S. 789 (1942)
Snyder v. Phelps, 562 U.S. 443 (2011)
Stanley v. Georgia, 394 U.S. 557 (1969)
Stevens v. Georgia, 2013 U.S. Dist. LEXIS 183862 (N.D. Ga. 2013)
Stone v. Mississippi, 101 U.S. 814 (1879)
Storer v. Brown, 415 U.S. 724 (1974)
Taub v. City of S.F., 696 Fed. Appx. 181 (9th Cir. 2017)
Teamsters, Chauffeurs & Helpers Union v. Morton, 377 U.S. 252 (1964)
Theriault v. Carlson, 495 F.2d 390 (5th Cir. 1974)
Tilton v. Richardson, 403 U.S. 672 (1971)
UAW v. Hoosier Cardinal Corp., 383 U.S. 696 (1966)
United States v. 12 200-Ft. Reels of Super 8mm Film, 413 U.S. 123 (1973)
United States v. Alvarez, 567 U.S. 709 (2012)
United States v. Biocic, 928 F.2d 112 (4th Cir. 1991)
United States v. Carolene Prods. Co., 304 U.S. 144 (1938)
United States v. Darby, 312 U.S. 100 (1941)

United States v. Kennerly, 209 Fed. 119 (1913)
United States v. Kuch, 288 F. Supp. 439 (D.D.C. 1968)
United States v. Loftis, 12 F. 671 (D. Or. 1882)
United States v. O'Brien, 391 U.S. 367 (1968)
United States v. Playboy Entm't Grp., 529 U.S. 803 (2000)
United States v. Seeger, 380 U.S. 163 (1965)
United States v. Stevens, 559 U.S. 460 (2010)
Uphaus v. Wyman, 360 U.S. 72 (1959)
Vidal v. Philadelphia, 2 Howard 127 (U.S. 1844)
Virginia v. Black, 538 U.S. 343 (2003)
W. Va. St. Bd. of Educ. v. Barnette, 319 U.S. 624 (1943)
Walz v. Tax Comm'n of N.Y., 397 U.S. 664 (1970)
Ward v. Rock Against Racism, 491 U.S. 781 (1989)
Washington v. Glucksberg, 521 U.S. 702 (1997)
Welsh v. United States, 398 U.S. 333 (1970)
Whalen v. Roe, 429 U.S. 589 (1977)
White Tail Park, Inc. v. Stroube, 413 F.3d 451 (4th Cir. 2005)
Williamson v. Lee Optical of Okla., Inc., 348 U.S. 483 (1955)
Winters v. New York, 333 U.S. 507 (1948)
Wisconsin v. Yoder, 406 U.S. 205 (1972)
Young v. Am. Mini Theatres, 427 U.S. 50 (1976)
Young v. Arkansas, 474 U.S. 1070 (1986)
Zablocki v. Redhail, 434 U.S. 374 (1978)
Zorach v. Clauson, 343 U.S. 306 (1952)

Law Review Articles and Notes

Alisobhani, Nassim, *Female Toplessness: Gender Equality's Next Frontier*, 8 U.C. IRVINE L. REV. 299 (2018)

Alpert, Leo M., *Judicial Censorship of Obscene Literature,* 52 HARV. L. REV. 40 (1938)

B., J.B., *Criminal Law and Procedure: Indecent Exposure: Nudism*, 33 MICH. L. REV. 936 (1935)

Baker, Tyler, Note, Roe *and* Paris*: Does Privacy Have a Principle?*, 26 STAN. L. REV. 1161 (1974) 330

Balkin, J.M., *The Constitution of Status*, 106 YALE L.J. 2313 (1997)

Ballingrud, Gordon, *Obscenity, Hate Speech, and Viewpoint Discrimination: A Formula for Hate Speech as an Unprotected Category*, 20 DARTMOUTH L.J. 6 (2022)

Bennett, Theodore, *State of Undress: Law, Carnival and Mass Public Nudity Events*, 29 GRIFFITH L. REV. 199 (2020)

Berger, Raoul, *The 14th Amendment: The Framers' Design*, 30 S.C. L. REV. 495 (1979)

Clark, J. Morris, *Guidelines for the Free Exercise Clause*, 83 HARV. L. REV. 327 (1969)

Comment, *A Taxonomy of Privacy: Repose, Sanctuary, and Intimate Decision*, 64 CALIF. L. REV. 1446 (1976)

Comment, *Criminal Law and Procedure – Indecent Exposure – Nudism*, 33 MICH. L. REV. 936 (1935)
Finkelman, Paul, *The Bill of Rights in Historical and International Perspective: How an 18th Century Document Illuminates Liberty in the 21st Century Lead Articles*, 46 OH. NORTHERN U. L. REV. 291 (2020)
Fowler, Thomas L., *Of Moons, Thongs, Holdings and Dicta: State v. Fly and the Rule of Law*, 22 CAMPBELL L. REV. 253 (2000)
Friedman, Lawrence M., & Joanna L. Grossman, *A Private Underworld: The Naked Body in Law and Society*, 61 BUFF. L. REV. 169 (2013)
Fuller, P. Brooks, et al., *Porn Wars: Serious Value, Social Harm, and the Burdens of Modern Obscenity Doctrine*, 28 AM. UNIV. J. GENDER, SOC. POL'Y & L. 121 (2020)
Galanter, Marc, *Religious Freedoms in the United States: A Turning Point?*, 1966 WISC. L. REV. 217 (1966)
Garety, Tom, *Redefining Privacy*, 12 HARV. C.R. – C.L. L. REV. 233 (1977)
Gayford, J.J., *Indecent Exposure: A Review of Literature*, 21 MED., SCI. & L. 233 (1981)
Goebel, Julius, & T.R. Naughton, *King's Law and Local Custom in Seventeenth Century New England*, 31 COLUM. L. REV. 417 (1931)
Goldberg, Suzanne B., *Morals-Based Justifications for Lawmaking: Before and After* Lawrence v. Texas, 88 MINN. L. REV. 1233 (2003–2004)
Green, Steven K., *The Fount of Everything Just and Right? The Ten Commandments as a Source of American Law*, 14 J.L. & RELIGION 525, 532 (2000)
Green, Stuart P., *To See and Be Seen: Reconstructing the Law of Voyeurism and Exhibitionism*, 55 AM. CRIM. L. REV. 203 (2018)
Greenberg, Douglas, *Crime, Law Enforcement, and Social Control in Colonial America*, 26 AM. J. LEGAL HIST. 293 (1982)
Hall, Ford W., *The Common Law: An Account of Its Reception in the United States*, 4 VAND. L. REV. 791 (1951)
Haskins, G.L., *Representative Government and the "Bible Commonwealth" in Early Massachusetts*, 9 AKRON L. REV. 2 (1976)
Havighurst, Alfred F., *The Judiciary and Politics in the Reign of Charles II*, LAW Q. REVS. 64 (1950)
Henkin, Louis, *Morals and the Constitution: The Sin of Obscenity*, 63 COLUM. L. REV. 391 (1963)
Holdsworth, W.S., *State and Religious Nonconformity: An Historical Retrospect*, 36 L.Q. REV. 339 (1920)
Jameson, Tyler C., *No Standing, No Backlash: How Federal Courts Use Standing to Avoid Deciding Controversial Cases Involving Religious and Political Displays*, 12 WAKE FOREST J.L. & POL'Y 359 (2022)
Kane, Tiernan, *Right by Precedent, Wrong by RFRA: The "Substantial Burden" Inquiry in* Oklevueha Native American Church of Hawaii, Inc. v. Lynch*, 828 F.3d 1012 (9th Cir. 2016)*, 794 HARV. J.L. & PUB. POL'Y 793 (2017)
Kearns, David, *Sovereignty and Common Law Judicial Office in* Taylor's Case *(1675)*, 37 L. & HIST. REV. 397 (2019)
Leigh, L.H., *Vagrancy, Morality and Decency*, CRIM. L. REV. 381 (1975)
Lupu, Ira C., *The Failure of RFRA*, 20 U. ARK. LITTLE ROCK L. REV. 575 (1998)

Maril, Robin, *Queer Rights After* Dobbs v. Jackson Women's Health Org., 60 SAN DIEGO L. REV. 45 (2023)
Meiklejohn, Alexander, *The 1st Amendment Is an Absolute*, 1961 SUP. CT. REV. 245 (1961)
Michaud, Leonard J., Note, *Decent Exposure: An Inquiry into the Constitutionality of State Statutes Proscribing Expressive Public Nakedness*, 22 LOY. L. REV. 1018 (1976)
Minot, Mark Jordan, *The Irrelevance of Blackstone: Rethinking the Eighteenth-Century Importance of the Commentaries*, 104 VA. L. REV. 1359 (2018)
Monroe, Emily, *A Nude Awakening: Female-Only Toplessness Bans as Unconstitutional Under the Equal Protection Clause Notes*, 30 S. CAL. REV. L. & SOC. JUST. 113 (2021)
Moriber, Danielle, Note, *A Right to Bare All? Female Public Toplessness and Dealing with the Laws That Prohibit*, 8 CARDOZO PUB. L., POL'Y, & ETHICS J. 453 (2010)
Narvil, Jeffrey C., *Revealing the Bare Uncertainties of Indecent Exposure,* 29 COLUM. J.L. & SOC. PROBS. 85 (1995)
Note, *Toward a Constitutional Definition of Religion*, 91 HARV. L. REV. 1056 (1978)
Offences Contra Bonos Mores, 2 J. CRIM. L. 609 (1938)
Piar, Daniel F., *Morality as a Legitimate Government Interest*, 117 PENN ST. L. REV. 117 (2012)
Pound, Roscoe, *Puritanism and the Common Law*, 45 AM. L. REV. 811 (1911)
Rooth, F.G., *Some Historical Notes on Indecent Exposure and Exhibitionism*, 38 MEDICO-LEGAL J. 135 (1970)
Schauer, Frederick, *Towards an Institutional First Amendment*, 89 MINN. L. REV. 1256 (2005)
Schneider, Richard D., *Exhibitionism: An Exclusively Male Deviation?*, 26 INT'L J. OFFENDER THERAPY & COMP. CRIMINOLOGY 173 (1982)
Schneider, Ronna G., *School Matters*, 92 U. CIN. L. REV. 1 (2023)
Schwartz, Louis B., *Morals Offenses and the Model Penal Code Symposium on the Model Penal Code*, 63 COLUM. L. REV. 669 (1963)
Simpson, Robert Mark, *Won't Somebody Please Think of the Children?" Hate Speech, Harm, and Childhood*, 38 LAW & PHIL. 79 (2019)
Stark, Vincent, *Public Morality as a Police Power After* Lawrence v. Texas *and* Gonzales v. Carhart, 10 GEO. J. GENDER L. 165 (2009)
Steffes, James C., *Public Nakedness Is Not Privileged as an Exercise of Free Speech When It Is in Opposition to a Compelling Government Statute*, 20 DRAKE L. REV. 400 (1971)
Stone, Geoffrey R., American Booksellers Association v Hudnut*: "The Government Must Leave to the People the Evaluation of Ideas*," 77 U. CHIC. L. REV. 1219 (2010)
Stone, Geoffrey R., *Free Speech in the Twenty-First Century: Ten Lessons from the Twentieth Century*, 36 PEPP. L. REV. 273, 274 (2009)
Stone, Geoffrey R., *Origins of Obscenity*, 31 N.Y.U. REV. L. & SOC. CHANGE 711 (2007)
Story, Joseph, *Christianity a Part of the Common Law*, 9 AM. JURIST 346 (1833)

Symposium on the Griswold Case and the Right of Privacy, 64 MICH. L. REV. 197 (1965)
Vukovits, Stephen, *Offended-Observer Standing's Last Stand: Kennedy as the Final Nail in a Flawed Doctrine's Coffin*, U. CHI. L. REV. ONLINE 1 (2023)
Warren, Charles, *The New "Liberty" Under the 14th Amendment*, 39 HARV. L. REV. 431 (1926)
Wechsler, Herbert, *Toward Neutral Principles Constitutional Law*, 73 HARV. L. REV. 1 (1959)
Williams, Susan H., *Content Discrimination and the First Amendment*, 139 U. PENN. L. REV. 615 (1991)
Willis, Jaime, *Obscenity Third Annual Review of Gender and Sexuality Law: Part I: Constitutional Law Chapter: Section F.*, 3 GEO J. GENDER & L. 263 (2002)
Yoshino, Kenji, *The New Equal Protection*, 124 HARV. L. REV. 747 (2011)

Other Journal Articles

Billings, Warren M., *Law in the Colonial South*, 73 J.S. HIST. 603 (2007)
Block, Mary R., *Rape Law in 19th-Century America: Some Thoughts and Reflections on the State of the Field*, 7 HIST. COMPASS 1391 (2009)
Bodine, Ann, *School Uniforms, Academic Achievement, and Uses of Research*, 97 J. EDUC. RES. 67 (2003)
Cooper, Davina, *Theorising Nudist Equality: An Encounter Between Political Fantasy and Public Appearance*, 43 ANTIPODE 326 (2011)
David, Joshua T., et al., *Liberty for Us, Limits for Them: Christian Nationalism and Americans' Views on Citizens' Rights*, SOCIO. RELIGION (2023)
De Vries, Bouke, *The Right to Be Publicly Naked: A Defense of Nudism*, 25 RES PUBLICA 407 (2019)
Dellinger, Kirsten, *Wearing Gender and Sexuality "On Your Sleeve": Dress Norms and the Importance of Occupational and Organizational Culture at Work*, GENDER ISSUES, Winter 2002
Feinberg, Paul D., *The Christian and Civil Authorities*, 10 MASTER'S SEMINARY J. 87 (1999)
Fontanille, *Jacques, Figures of the Body and the Semiotics of Imprint: Semiotic Figures of the Body in the Humanities*, 9 CHINESE SEMIOTIC STUD. 37 (2013)
Fortenberry, J. Dennis, & Devon J. Hensel, *Sexual Modesty in Sexual Expression and Experience: A Scoping Review, 2000–2021*, 59 J. SEX RES. 1000 (2022)
Frank, Katherine, *Thinking Critically About Strip Club Research*, 10 SEXUALITIES (2007)
Freedman, Estelle B., *Sexuality in Nineteenth-Century America: Behavior, Ideology, and Politics*, 10 REVS. IN AM. HIST. (1982)
Grant, Jennifer, *Indecent Exposure: A Serious "Nuisance" Offence*, 30 WOMEN'S HIST. REV. 1219 (2021)
Greitemeyer, Tobias, *The Dark and Bright Side of Video Game Consumption: Effects of Violent and Prosocial Video Games*, 46 CURR. OP. IN PSYCH. 101326 (2022)

Harbke, Colin R., & Dana F. Lindemann, *Objectification and Reactions Toward Public Female Toplessness in the United States: Looking Beyond Legal Approval*, 27 SEXUALITY & CULTURE 104 (2023)

Homans, *The Puritans and Clothing Industry in England*, 13 NEW ENG. Q. 519 (1940)

Knipp, Hannah, & Rae Stevenson, *"A Powerful Visual Statement": Race, Class, and Gender in Uniform and Dress Code Policies in New Orleans Public Charter Schools*, 37 AFFILIA (2021), https://doi.org/10.1177/08861099211010026

Lehmberg, Stanford E., *Star Chamber: 1485-1509*, 24 HUNTINGTON LIBR. Q. 24 189 (1961)

Levine, Philippa, *States of Undress: Nakedness and the Colonial Imagination*, 50 VICTORIAN STUD. 189 (2008)

McCreary, Charles P., *Personality Profiles of Persons Convicted of Indecent Exposure*, 31 J. CLINICAL PSYCH. 260 (1975)

Palmer-Hague, Jaime, et al., *Androgen Deprivation Alters Attention to Sexually Provocative Visual Stimuli in Elderly Men*, 5 SEXUAL MED. e245 (2017)

Parkes, Henry B., *Morals & Law Enforcement in Colonial New England*, 5 NEW ENG. Q. 431 (1932)

Romack, Katherine, & Semiotic Society of American, in cooperation with the Philosophy Documentation Center, *"For This Is the Naked Truth": The Early Quakers and Going Naked as a Sign*, 27 AM. J. SEMIOTICS 203 (2011)

Rosenbaum, Betty B., *The Sociological Basis of the Laws Relating to Women Sex Offenders in Massachusetts (1620-1860)*, 28 J. CRIM. L. & CRIMINOLOGY (1931-1951) 815 (1938)

Sandler, Gerald, *Lockean Ideas in Thomas Jefferson's Bill for Establishing Religious Freedom*, 21 J. HIST. IDEAS 110 (1960)

Snaith, Philip, *Exhibitionism: A Clinical Conundrum*, 143 BRIT. J. PSYCHIATRY 231 (1983)

Soylemez, Kerem Kemal, et al., *A Qualitative Insight into the Experiences of Naturists Perceived Stigma of Naturism*, 16 GSC ADVANCED RES. & REVS. 148 (2023)

Story, Marilyn D., *Factors Associated with More Positive Body Self-Concepts in Preschool Children*, 108 J. SOC. PSYCH. 49 (1979)

Visconsi, Elliott, *The Invention of Criminal Blasphemy:* Rex v. Taylor (1676), 103 REPRESENTATIONS 30 (2008)

Wachs, Sebastian, et al., *Associations Between Witnessing and Perpetrating Online Hate Speech Among Adolescents: Testing Moderation Effects of Moral Disengagement and Empathy*, 12 PSYCHOL. VIOLENCE 371 (2022)

West, Keon, & Eliza Kukawska, *Good Nudes and Bad Nudes: How Naturism, Casual Stripping, and Sexting Predict Social Physique Anxiety and Body Appreciation*, 26 SEXUALITY & CULTURE 2151(2022)

West, Keon, *I Feel Better Naked: Communal Naked Activity Increases Body Appreciation by Reducing Social Physique Anxiety*, 58 J. SEX RES. 958 (2021)

West, Keon, *Naked and Unashamed: Investigations and Applications of the Effects of Naturist Activities on Body Image, Self-Esteem, and Life Satisfaction*, 19 J. HAPPINESS STUD. 677 (2018)

West, Keon, *Think of the Children!: Relationships Between Nudity-Related Experiences in Childhood, Body Image, Self-Esteem and Adjustment*, 37 CHILDREN & SOC'Y 1187 (2023)

Other Books and Book Chapters

Adams, John, *Colonial Declaration of Rights: Massachusetts*, *in* THE SEPARATION OF CHURCH AND STATE (2011)

ADAMS, SAMUEL, THE LIFE AND PUBLIC SERVICE OF SAMUEL ADAMS vol. 1 (1865)

ANNALS OF CONG. vol. 1 (1789)

Annotation, CRIMINAL OFFENSE PREDICATED UPON INDECENT EXPOSURE, 94 A.L.R.2D 1353 (2023)

ARCHBOLD, JOHN FREDERICK, THE FORMS OF INDICTMENT: WITH THE EVIDENCE NECESSARY TO SUPPORT THEM : INCLUDING THE STATUTES WHICH MAKE MANY VALUABLE REGULATIONS RELATIVE TO CRIMINAL PROCEEDINGS ; CONTAINING ALSO, A TABLE SHOWING THOSE STATUTES WHICH HAVE BEEN REPEALED (1828)

BACON, FRANCIS, HISTORIE OF THE REIGNE OF KING HENRY THE SEVENTH (1641)

BAINS, PAUL, THE PRIMACY OF SEMIOSIS: AN ONTOLOGY OF RELATIONS (2006)

Baker, J., *The Dark Age of Legal History*, *in* LEGAL HISTORY STUDIES 1972 (Dafydd Jenkins ed., 1975)

BATEMAN, VICTORIA, NAKED FEMINISM: BREAKING THE CULT OF FEMALE MODESTY (2023)

BAUMAN, RICHARD, LET YOUR WORDS BE FEW—SYMBOLISM OF SPEAKING AND SILENCE AMONG SEVENTEENTH CENTURY QUAKERS (1983)

BECKER, ERNEST, THE DENIAL OF DEATH (1973)

Benn, Stanley I., *Privacy, Freedom, and Respect for Persons*, *in* PRIVACY (J.R. Pennock & John W. Chapman eds., XIII NOMOS: Yearbook of the American Society for Political and Legal Philosophy, 1971)

BIOGRAPHIA BRITANNICA vol. 5 (1760)

BIOGRAPHIA BRITANNICA vol. 6-1 (1763)

BIOGRAPHIA BRITANNICUS vol. 6 (1747–66)

Black, Jeremiah S., *Religious Liberty*, *in* JEREMIAH S. BLACK, ESSAYS AND SPEECHES 51 (1886)

BLACKFORD, RUSSELL, FREEDOM OF RELIGION AND THE SECULAR STATE (2012)

BLAKELY, WILLIAM, AMERICAN STATE PAPERS ON FREEDOM OF RELIGION (3d ed. 1943)

BOONE, ISLEY, THE JOYS OF NUDISM (1934)

BOORSTIN, DANIEL J., THE AMERICANS (1958)

BOOTH, A., & A. BOON, EXAMEN LEGUM ANGLIAE: OR, THE LAWS OF ENGLAND EXAMINED, BY SCRIPTURE, ANTIQUITY, AND REASON (1656)

BOURNE, HENRY R.F., 1 ENGLISH NEWSPAPERS (1887)

BRADFORD, WILLIAM, BRADFORD'S HISTORY OF 'PLIMOTH PLANTATION' (2021) (1898)

Bray, Gerald, *Canon Law and the Church of England*, *in* 1 THE OXFORD HISTORY OF ANGLICANISM 168 (2017)

BREYER, STEPHEN, THE AUTHORITY OF THE COURT AND THE PERIL OF POLITICS (2021)

BURNET, GILBERT, BISHOP BURNET'S HISTORY OF HIS OWN TIME: FROM THE RESTORATION OF K. CHARLES II TO THE CONCLUSION OF THE TREATY OF PEACE AT UTRECHT, IN THE REIGN OF QUEEN ANNE. TO WHICH IS PREFIXED, A SUMMARY RECAPITULATION OF AFFAIRS IN CHURCH AND STATE, FROM KING JAMES I. TO THE RESTORATION IN THE YEAR 1660. TOGETHER WITH THE AUTHOR'S LIFE AND SOME EXPLANATORY NOTES vol. 1

BURNET, GILBERT, SOME ACCOUNT OF THE LIFE AND DEATH OF JOHN, EARL OF ROCHESTER, WHO DIED JULY 26, 1680 (1724)

CALENDAR OF STATE PAPERS: DOMESTIC SERIES vol. 3 (1860)

CALVIN, JOHN, COMMENTARIES ON THE FOUR LAST BOOKS OF MOSES vol. 4 (1634)

CAMPBELL, JOHN, LIVES OF THE CHIEF JUSTICES OF ENGLAND vol. 2 (1874)

CAMPBELL, JOHN, LIVES OF THE LORD CHANCELLORS vol. 3 (2d Am. ed., 1851)

CARDOZA, BENJAMIN N., PARADOXES OF LEGAL SCIENCE (1927)

CHAPIN, BRADLEY, CRIMINAL JUSTICE IN COLONIAL AMERICA, 1606-1660 (2010)

CHASE, MARY E., THE BIBLE AND THE COMMON READER (1952)

CIBBER, THEOPHILUS, LIVES OF THE POETS OF GREAT BRITAIN AND IRELAND vol. 3 (1753)

CLARENDON, EDWARD H., THE LIFE OF EDWARD, EARL OF CLARENDON vol. 2 (1759)

COFFEY, JOHN, EXODUS AND LIBERATION: DELIVERANCE POLITICS FROM JOHN CALVIN TO MARTIN LUTHER KING JR. (2014)

COLEMAN, EMILY, & BETTY EDWARDS, BODY LIBERATION: FREEING YOUR BODY FOR GREATER SELF-ACCEPTANCE, HEALTH, AND SEXUAL SATISFACTION (1977)

Commonplace Book, Feb. 10, 1814, *in* 6 H.A. WASHINGTON, THE WRITINGS OF THOMAS JEFFERSON: 1760–1775 (1892)

CORWIN, EDWARD S., THE CONSTITUTION AND WHAT IT MEANS TODAY (14th ed. 1978)

Cotton, John, *A Discourse About Civil Government*, *in* CHURCH AND STATE IN AMERICAN HISTORY 7 (John Wilson & Donald Drakeman eds., 1987)

COUNTESS OF ELIZABETH CHUDLEIGH BRISTOL, THE LAWS RESPECTING WOMEN (1777)

CUSHING, JOHN D., RECORDS OF THE COLONY OF NEW PLYMOUTH (1855-1861) vol. 11

D'EMILIO, JOHN, & ESTELLE B. FREEDMAN, INTIMATE MATTERS: A HISTORY OF SEXUALITY IN AMERICA (1997)

DAVID H. FLAHERTY, ESSAYS IN THE HISTORY OF EARLY AMERICAN LAW (2014)

DE VATTEL, EMER, THE LAW OF NATIONS: OR, PRINCIPLES OF THE LAW OF NATURE, APPLIED TO THE CONDUCT AND AFFAIRS OF NATIONS AND SOVEREIGNS. FROM THE FRENCH OF MONSIEUR DE VATTEL (Joseph Chitty & Edward D. Ingraham eds., 1853)

DEVLIN, PATRICK, THE ENFORCEMENT OF MORALS (1968)

DOBREE, BONAMY, ESSAYS IN BIOGRAPHY 1680-1726 (1925)

Donne, John, *Elegy XIX: To His Mistress Going to Bed*, *in* BROADVIEW ANTHOLOGY OF SEVENTEENTH-CENTURY VERSE AND PROSE 117 (2004)

Drakeman, Donald L., *Why Do We Think the Framers Wanted to Separate Church and State?*, *in* THE PALGRAVE HANDBOOK OF RELIGION AND STATE VOLUME II (Shannon Holzer ed., 2023)

Dussias, Allison M., *Indigenous Religious Rights in the United States*, *in* INTERNATIONAL PERSPECTIVE ON INDIGENOUS RELIGIOUS RIGHTS (2023)

ENCYCLOPEDIA BRITANNICA: MICROPAEDIA vol. 7 (1975)

FANE, FRANCIS, REPORTS ON THE LAWS OF CONNECTICUT (C. Andrews ed., 1915)

Forgues, Emile D., *John Wilmot, Count of Rochester*, *in* ROCHESTER: THE CRITICAL HERITAGE (David Farley-Hills ed., 1972)

FOSS, EDWARD, JUDGES OF ENGLAND vol. 7 (1864)

FOUCAULT, M., THE HISTORY OF SEXUALITY, VOLUME 1: AN INTRODUCTION (1976)

FRANKHAUSER, EDUARD, NUDISM, OBSCENITY AND THE LAW (Alois S. Knapp trans., 1951)

FREUND, ERNST, THE POLICE POWER: PUBLIC POLICY AND CONSTITUTIONAL RIGHTS (1904)

FRIEDMAN, LAWRENCE, CRIME AND PUNISHMENT IN AMERICAN HISTORY (2010)

GARDINER, SAMUEL R., HISTORY OF THE COMMONWEALTH AND THE PROTECTORATE 1649-1660 vol. 2 (1897)

GARTON, STEPHEN, SEXUAL REVOLUTION, IN HISTORIES OF SEXUALITY ANTIQUITY TO SEXUAL REVOLUTION (2004)

GAY, JAN, ON GOING NAKED (1932)

GIGEROFF, ALEX K., SEXUAL DEVIATIONS IN THE CRIMINAL LAW (1968)

GODBEER, RICHARD, SEXUAL REVOLUTION IN EARLY AMERICA (2004)

GRAEBER, DAVID, & DAVID WENGROW, THE DAWN OF EVERYTHING: A NEW HISTORY OF HUMANITY (2021)

GREAT BRITAIN COURT OF KING'S BENCH, CHARLES JAMES GALE, AND SIR HENRY DAVISON. REPORTS OF CASES ARGUED AND DETERMINED IN THE COURT OF QUEEN'S BENCH: AND UPON WRITS OF ERROR FROM THAT COURT TO THE EXCHEQUER CHAMBER, IN EASTER, TRINITY, AND MICHAELMAS TERMS, 1841[-HIL. AND EAST. TERMS, 1843] ... S. SWEET (1843)

GREENAWALT, KENT, INTERPRETING THE CONSTITUTION (2015)

GREENE, GRAHAM, LORD ROCHESTER'S MONKEY (1974)

GREENE, MARIA L., THE DEVELOPMENT OF RELIGIOUS LIBERTY IN CONNECTICUT (1905)

HALL, JEROME, THEFT, LAW, AND SOCIETY (2d ed. 1952)

HALL, MARK D., DID AMERICA HAVE A CHRISTIAN FOUNDING? SEPARATING MODERN MYTH FROM HISTORICAL TRUTH (2019)

HALLER, WILLIAM, THE RISE OF PURITANISM (1938)

HARRIS, BRICE, CHARLES SACKVILLE SIXTH EARL OF DORSET: PATRON AND POET OF THE RESTORATION (1940)

HASKINS, GEORGE L., LAW AND AUTHORITY IN EARLY MASSACHUSETTS (1960)

HEALEY, ROBERT M., JEFFERSON ON RELIGION IN PUBLIC EDUCATION (1926)

Heard, F., *Introduction to R. Compton*, *in* RICHARD COMPTON, STAR CHAMBER CASES (1881)

HENRY, PHILIP, 1 DIARIES AND LETTERS, PHILIP HENRY, M.A. (Matthew H. Lee ed., 1882)

HOFFMAN, BRIAN, NAKED: A CULTURAL HISTORY OF AMERICAN NUDISM (2015)

HOLDSWORTH, W., HISTORY OF ENGLISH LAW vol. 9 (1926)

HOLDSWORTH, WILLIAM S., A HISTORY OF ENGLISH LAW vol. 4 (1924)

HOLDSWORTH, WILLIAM S., A HISTORY OF ENGLISH LAW vol. 5 (1924)

HOLDSWORTH, WILLIAM S., A HISTORY OF ENGLISH LAW vol. 6 (5th ed., 1922–1938)

HUDSON, WINTHROP, RELIGION IN AMERICA (2d ed. 1973)

HUMPHREYS, LAUD, TEAROOM TRADE: IMPERSONAL SEX IN PUBLIC PLACES (2017)

ILFELD, FRED, & ROGER LAUER, SOCIAL NUDISM IN AMERICA (1964)

JEFFERSON, THOMAS, NOTES ON THE STATE OF VIRGINIA (1787)

JEFFERSON, THOMAS, THE COMPLETE JEFFERSON (S. Padover ed., 1943)

JEFFERSON, THOMAS, THE PAPERS OF THOMAS JEFFERSON 1760-1776 vol. 1 (Julian P. Boyd ed., 2018)

JEFFERSON, THOMAS, THE WRITINGS OF THOMAS JEFFERSON vol. 13 (Andrew A. Lipscomb ed., 1903)

JEFFERSON, THOMAS, THE WRITINGS OF THOMAS JEFFERSON: BEING HIS AUTOBIOGRAPHY, CORRESPONDENCE, REPORTS, MESSAGES, ADDRESSES, AND OTHER WRITINGS, OFFICIAL AND PRIVATE vol. VI (H.A. Washington ed., 1861)

JERNEGAN, MARCUS W., THE AMERICAN COLONIES, 1492-1750 (1929)

JOHNSON, SAMUEL, LIVES OF THE ENGLISH POETS vol. 3 (George B. Hill ed., 1905)

JOHNSON, THOMAS H., THE PURITANS (Perry Miller ed., 1938)

JOURNAL OF THE 1ST SESSION OF THE SENATE vol. 1 (1789)

KATZ, JONATHAN NED, THE INVENTION OF HETEROSEXUALITY (1995)

KEEBLE, N.H., THE RESTORATION: ENGLAND IN THE 1660S (2002)

KINNEY, JR., CHARLES B., CHURCH & STATE: THE STRUGGLE FOR SEPARATION IN NEW HAMPSHIRE 1630-1900 (1955)

KOLATCH, ALFRED J., THE SECOND JEWISH BOOK OF WHY (2nd, rev'd ed., 1985)

LAWSON, JOHN D., A CONCORDANCE OF WORDS AND PHRASES CONSTRUED IN THE JUDICIAL REPORTS (1883)

LE NEVE, PETER, 8 LE NEVE'S PEDIGREES OF THE KNIGHTS MADE BY KING CHARLES II, KING JAMES II, KING WILLIAM III, AND QUEEN MARY, KING WILLIAM ALONE AND QUEEN ANNE (George W. Marshall ed., 1873)

Letter to M. Dupont De Nemours, April 24, 1816, *in* 6 H.A. WASHINGTON, THE WRITINGS OF THOMAS JEFFERSON: 1740-1826 (2018)

Letter to Peter Carr, August 10, 1787, *in* 2 H.A. WASHINGTON, THE WRITINGS OF THOMAS JEFFERSON: 1740-1826 (2018)

Letters Patent to Sir Thomas Gates, *in* JOHN D. CUSHING, STATUTES OF VIRGINIA (1609)

Locke, John, *5. John Locke (1632-1704), Letter on Toleration, 1686*, *in* TOLERANCE: THE BEACON OF THE ENLIGHTENMENT 22 (Caroline Warman et al., ed. and trans., Open Book Publishers, 2017), http://books.openedition.org/obp/2954

LOCKE, JOHN, A LETTER CONCERNING TOLERATION (Bobbs-Merrill 2d ed. 1955) (1950)

LOCKE, JOHN, OF CIVIL GOVERNMENT AND TOLERATION (1895)

LOCKE, JOHN, TWO TREATISES OF GOVERNMENT AND A LETTER CONCERNING TOLERATION (Ian Shapiro ed., 2003)

LUDLOW, EDMUND, MEMOIRS OF EDMUND LUDLOW (1751)

LUNCEFORD, BRETT, PUBLIC NUDITY AND THE RHETORIC OF THE BODY (2018)

LUTHER, MARTIN, A COMMENTARY ON ST. PAUL'S EPISTLE TO THE GALATIANS (1860)

LUTTRELL, NARCISSUS, A BRIEF HISTORICAL RELATION OF STATE AFFAIRS FROM SEPTEMBER 1678 TO APRIL 1714 (1857)

MACAULAY, THOMAS B., THE HISTORY OF ENGLAND FROM THE ASCENSION OF JAMES THE SECOND vol. 1 (C. Fifth ed., 1913)

MACDONALD, JOHN M., INDECENT EXPOSURE (1973)

MACK, WILLIAM, & WILLIAM BENJAMIN HALE, CORPUS JURIS: BEING A COMPLETE AND SYSTEMATIC STATEMENT OF THE WHOLE BODY OF THE LAW AS EMBODIED IN AND DEVELOPED BY ALL REPORTED DECISIONS vol. 8 (1917)

MADISON, JAMES, *Memorial and Remonstrance Against Religious Assessments*, in 2 THE WRITINGS OF JAMES MADISON (Gallard Hunt ed., 1901)

MADISON, JAMES, *Notes of Speech Against Assessments for Support of Religion*, *in* 2 THE WRITINGS OF JAMES MADISON (Gallard Hunt ed., 1901)

MALBIN, MICHAEL J., RELIGION AND POLITICS: THE INTENTIONS OF THE AUTHORS OF THE 1ST AMENDMENT (1978)

Masmaliyeva, Tarlan, *Turkish Secularism: How to Raise Its Level of Protection* (European Union and European Union and Its Neighbours in a Globalized World No. 12, 2024)

MAY, GEOFFREY, SOCIAL CONTROL OF SEX EXPRESSION (1931)

MCALLISTER, DAVID, THE NATIONAL REFORM MOVEMENT (1898)

MELVILLE, WILLIAM LAURISTON, A HISTORY OF POLICE IN ENGLAND (1901)

MERRILL, FRANCES, & MASON MERRILL, SOCIAL NUDISM COMES TO AMERICA (1932)

MORGAN, EDMUND, THE PURITAN FAMILY (1944)

MORIARTY, G.A., SOCIAL AND GEOGRAPHIC ORIGINS OF THE FOUNDERS OF MASSACHUSETTS, in COMMONWEALTH HISTORY OF MASSACHUSETTS (Hart ed., 1927–1928)

MORYSON, FYNES, AN ITINERARY vol. 3 (1907)

MORYSON, FYNES, AN ITINERARY vol. 4 (1908)

NELSON, WILLIAM EDWARD, THE COMMON LAW IN COLONIAL AMERICA: THE MIDDLE COLONIES AND THE CAROLINAS, 1660-1730 (2013)

NEW HAVEN COLONY HISTORICAL RECORDS, ANCIENT TOWN RECORDS: NEW HAVEN TOWN RECORDS, 1662-1684 (1919)

NOKES, GERALD D., A HISTORY OF THE CRIME OF BLASPHEMY (1928)
NOVAK, WILLIAM J., THE PEOPLE'S WELFARE: LAW AND REGULATION IN NINETEENTH-CENTURY AMERICA (1996)
OLMSTED, HENRY K., GENEALOGY OF THE OLMSTEAD FAMILY IN AMERICA (1912)
OSBORNE, BERTRAM, JUSTICES OF THE PEACE 1361–1848 (1960)
OSGOOD, HERBERT L., THE AMERICAN COLONIES IN THE SEVENTEENTH CENTURY vol. 1 (1904-1907)
PARMELEE, MAURICE, THE NEW GYMNOSOPHY (1927)
PATTERSON, BENNETT B., THE FORGOTTEN 9TH AMENDMENT (1955)
PEPYS, SAMUEL, THE DIARY OF SAMUEL PEPYS vol. 2 (Robert Latham & William Mathews eds., 1970)
PEPYS, SAMUEL, THE DIARY OF SAMUEL PEPYS vol. 3 (University of California Press, 2000 (1662)
PEPYS, SAMUEL, THE DIARY OF SAMUEL PEPYS, A NEW AND COMPLETE TRANSCRIPTION vol. 9 (Robert Latham & William Mathews eds., 1970)
PEPYS, SAMUEL, THE DIARY OF SAMUEL PEPYS: A NEW AND COMPLETE TRANSCRIPTION vol. 4 (Robert Latham & William Matthews eds., 1970)
PERKINS, WILLIAM, A GOLDEN CHAIN: OR THE DESCRIPTION OF THEOLOGY, CONTAINING THE ORDER OF THE CAUSES OF SALVATION AND DAMNATION, ACCORDING TO GOD'S WORD (2021) (1600)
PFEFFER, LEO, CHURCH, STATE AND FREEDOM (rev. ed. 1967)
PIKE, LUKE O., A HISTORY OF CRIME IN ENGLAND vol. 2 (1876)
PINTO, VIVIAN DE SOLA, SIR CHARLES SEDLEY, 1639-1701: A STUDY IN THE LIFE AND LITERATURE OF THE RESTORATION (1927)
PLYMOUTH COLONY RECORDS vol. 11 (1855–1861)
POWERS, EDWIN, CRIME AND PUNISHMENT IN EARLY MASSACHUSETTS 1620-1692 (1966)
PRACTICING L. INST., PRIVACY (1974)
PRIDEAUX, WILLIAM, 8 NOTES AND QUERIES (9th Series 1901)
PRIESTLEY'S LECTURES ON HISTORY, AND GENERAL POLICY (1791)
PROCEEDING AND DEBATES OF THE NEW YORK CONSTITUTIONAL CONVENTION (1821)
RADZINOWICZ, LEON, A HISTORY OF ENGLISH CRIMINAL LAW (1948)
Records of the Particular Court of Connecticut, 1639-1663, *in* 12 COLLECTION OF THE CONNECTICUT HISTORICAL SOCIETY (1928)
REMBAR, CHARLES, THE END OF OBSCENITY: THE TRIALS OF LADY CHATTERLEY, TROPIC OF CANCER & FANNY HILL BY THE LAWYER WHO DEFENDED THEM (2015)
ROOT, ELIHU, ADDRESSES ON GOVERNMENT AND CITIZENSHIP (Robert Bacon & James B. Scott eds., 1916)
RUBINSTEIN, RUTH, DRESS CODES: MEANINGS AND MESSAGES IN AMERICAN CULTURE (2018)
SANDERS, ANTHONY B., BABY 9TH AMENDMENTS: HOW AMERICANS EMBRACED UNENUMERATED RIGHTS AND WHY IT MATTERS (2023)
SCHILDER, PAUL, THE IMAGE AND APPEARANCE OF THE HUMAN BODY: STUDIES IN THE CONSTRUCTIVE ENERGIES OF THE PSYCHE (1999)

SHTEIR, RACHEL, STRIPTEASE: THE UNTOLD HISTORY OF THE GIRLIE SHOW (2004)
SHURTLEFF, NATHANIEL B., RECORDS OF THE COLONY OF NEW PLYMOUTH IN NEW ENGLAND (1855-1861)
STATE TRIALS vol. 1 (T. Donald ed., 1972)
STEPHEN, JAMES FITZJAMES, A HISTORY OF THE CRIMINAL LAW OF ENGLAND vol. 2 (1883)
STOKES, ANSON P., & LEO PFEFFER, CHURCH AND STATE IN THE UNITED STATES (1964)
STONE, GEOFFREY R., SEX AND THE CONSTITUTION: SEX, RELIGION, AND LAW FROM AMERICA'S ORIGINS TO THE TWENTY-FIRST CENTURY (2017)
STRACHEY, WILLIAM, LAWES DIVINE, MORALL AND MARTIALL, &C (1612)
SUNSTEIN, CASS R., HOW TO INTERPRET THE CONSTITUTION (2023)
SWANCARA, FRANK, THOMAS JEFFERSON VERSUS RELIGIOUS OPPRESSION (1969)
THE LIFE AND TIMES OF ANTHONY WOOD, ANTIQUARY, OF OXFORD, 1632–1695, DESCRIBED BY HIMSELF: COLLECTED FROM HIS DIARIES AND OTHER PAPERS (Andrew Clarke ed., 1892)
THE MEETING OF CIVILIZATIONS: MUSLIM, CHRISTIAN, AND JEWISH (Moshe Ma'oz, ed., 2009)
THE PALGRAVE HANDBOOK OF RELIGION AND STATE VOLUME I: THEORETICAL PERSPECTIVES (Shannon Holzer ed., 2023)
THE PURITAN REVOLUTION: A DOCUMENTARY HISTORY (Stuart E. Prall ed., 1968)
THE SOMERS COLLECTION OF SCARCE AND VALUABLE TRACTS vol. 7 (W. Scott ed., 1812)
TRIBE, LAURENCE H., AMERICAN CONSTITUTIONAL LAW (1978)
TRUMBULL, BENJAMIN, A COMPLETE HISTORY OF CONNECTICUT, CIVIL AND ECCLESIASTICAL vol. 1 (1898)
VER STEEG, CLARENCE L., THE FORMATIVE YEARS, 1607-1763 (1964)
WARD, ADOLPHUS W., & ALFRED R. WALLER, THE CAMBRIDGE HISTORY OF ENGLISH LITERATURE: THE AGE OF DRYDEN (1920)
WEBSTER'S NEW WORLD DICTIONARY (2d college ed. 1970)
Weinberg, Martin S., *The Nudist Management of Respectability*, *in* SEX RESEARCH; STUDIES FROM THE KINSEY INSTITUTE (1976)
WHITMAN, WALT, "Song of Myself," *in* LEAVES OF GRASS (1855)
WHITMAN, WALT, SPECIMEN DAYS IN AMERICA (1887)
WILSON, JOHN H., THE COURT WITS OF THE RESTORATION (1948)
WINTHROP, JOHN, THE JOURNAL OF JOHN WINTHROP, 1630-1649 (James Savage et al. eds., Harv. Univ. Press, 2009)
WOJTYLA, KAROL, LOVE AND RESPONSIBILITY (Grzegorz Ignatik trans., 2013)

Internet Content

2023 WNBR PDX, KEEP PORTLAND WEIRD, https://keep-portland-weird.com/2023-world-naked-bike-ride/
A Proclamation Against Vicious, Debauch'd, and Prophane Persons, PROQUEST,

https://www.proquest.com/docview/2264187817/99870613?accountid=14166&parentSessionId=eGuMzZjBAl50YT%2FU4p3anFblHPBgq%2FiWLeT5grN1WhQ%3D&pq-origsite=primo&sourcetype=Books

About, BLACK LIVES MATTER, https://blacklivesmatter.com/about/

Alund, Natalie N., *White House Says Activist Who Took Top Off at Pride Celebration Won't Be Invited Back*, MSN, https://www.msn.com/en-us/news/us/white-house-says-activist-who-took-top-off-at-pride-celebration-won-t-be-invited-back/ar-AA1cxAUs?ocid=hpmsn&cvid=5a46349628c3498196721f01af0a6c0b&ei=65

AM. ASS'N FOR NUDE RECREATION, https://www.aanr.com/

Aristotle, *Metaphysics* (Book 4), PERSEUS, https://www.perseus.tufts.edu/hopper/text?doc=Perseus%3Atext%3A1999.01.0052%3Abook%3D4 (last visited Jan. 30, 2024)

ArtIII.S1.7.2.1 Historical Background on the Stare Decisis Doctrine, LEGAL INFO. INST.

Associated Press, *Gavin Newsom Signs New Bills to Protect California's LGBTQ Community One Day After Issuing Controversial Veto*, MSN, https://www.msn.com/en-us/news/other/gavin-newsom-signs-new-bills-to-protect-california-s-lgbtq-community-one-day-after-issuing-controversial-veto/ar-AA1hc8JZ

Breastfeeding Laws, NAT'L CONF. ST. LEGISLATURES (updated Aug. 26, 2021), https://www.ncsl.org/health/breastfeeding-state-laws

Bryant, Kenzie, *The Penile Code: What TV's Increase in Full-Frontal Male Nudity Really Means*, VANITY FAIR (Mar. 17, 2022), https://www.vanityfair.com/hollywood/2022/03/minx-euphoria-tvs-increase-in-full-frontal-male-nudity-prosthetics

Buchholz, Katharina, *Where Women's Headscarves Are Regulated* (infographic), STATISTA (Feb. 1, 2021), https://www.statista.com/chart/24065/rules-laws-about-womens-head-coverings

Burtka, Jeff, *Indecent Exposure Laws by State*, FINDLAW (last rev'd May 21, 2017), https://www.findlaw.com/state/criminal-laws/indecent-exposure-laws-by-state.html

CAUGHEY, MILLIE, THE CTR. FOR FAITH, IDENTITY, & GLOBALIZATION, FAITH AND THE LAW: THE EXTENT OF RELIGIOUS FREEDOM IN MODERN AMERICA (Aug. 2023), https://rumiforum.org/wp-content/uploads/2023/11/Faith-and-the-Law.pdf

Chounlamountry, Jade, *Strip Club Laws and the Regulation of Sexually Oriented Business*, FINDLAW (last rev'd Aug. 17, 2023), https://www.findlaw.com/smallbusiness/business-laws-and-regulations/adult-entertainment-law-zoning-and-other-regulations.html

Clothing Laws by State 2023, WORLD POPULATION REV., https://worldpopulationreview.com/state-rankings/clothing-laws-by-state

Const. Rts. Found., *The Second Great Awakening and Reform in the 19th Century*, BILL OF RIGHTS IN ACTION, vol. 32, Winter 2017

Debauched (Adj.), ETYMOLOGY ONLINE, https://www.etymonline.com/word/debauched

Democracy, BRITANNICA (last updated Jan. 24, 2024), https://www.britannica.com/topic/democracy

Diary Entries from July 1663, THE DIARY OF SAMUEL PEPYS https://www.pepysdiary.com/diary/1663/07/

Driesbach, Daniel L., *Thomas Jefferson and the Mammoth Cheese*, ACTON INST. (July 20, 2010), https://www.acton.org/pub/religion-liberty/volume-12-number-3/thomas-jefferson-and-mammoth-cheese

Everyman, BRITANNICA, https://www.britannica.com/topic/Everyman-English-morality-play

Fast Facts: Preventing Child Sexual Abuse, CTRS. FOR DISEASE CONTROL & PREVENTION (Sept. 5, 2023), https://www.cdc.gov/violenceprevention/childsexualabuse/fastfact.html

Force and Arms, LSD, https://www.lsd.law/define/force-and-arms

Friday 23 October 1668, DIARY OF SAMUEL PEPYS, https://www.pepysdiary.com/diary/1668/10/23/

Fritze, John, *Gay Counselor's Firing by Indianapolis Catholic School Permitted by Federal Appeals Court*, MSN, https://www.msn.com/en-us/news/us/federal-appeals-court-rules-catholic-school-was-permitted-to-fire-gay-counselor/ar-AA1dS0PE?ocid=hpmsn&cvid=310afeeada7e4891915e69d79aad9185&ei=26

Fundamental Agreement, or Original Constitution of the Colony of New Haven, June 4, 1639, AVALON PROJ., https://avalon.law.yale.edu/17th_century/ct01.asp

Gangitano, Alex, *Top Five Naked British Protests*, POLITICS (Nov. 23, 2012, 12:00 AM), https://www.politics.co.uk/comment-analysis/2012/11/23/top-five-naked-british-protests/

Gentile, Luke, *Conservatives Bash Seattle Pride Parade After Men Go Full-Frontal in Front of Children*, MSN, https://www.msn.com/en-us/lifestyle/lifestyle-buzz/conservatives-bash-seattle-pride-parade-after-men-go-full-frontal-in-front-of-children/ar-AA1d48M8?ocid=hpmsn&cvid=d04781f13de5437b9b780c4150ed5205&ei=76

Germany Suppresses Nudist Movement as Menace to Morality, CHI. DAILY TRIB., Mar. 8, 1933

Greene, Jamal, COLUM. L. SCH., https://www.law.columbia.edu/faculty/jamal-greene

Grier, W.J., *Calvin Versus the Libertines*, CHRISTIAN LIBRARY, https://www.christianstudylibrary.org/article/calvin-versus-libertines

Grossman, Joanna L., & Lawrence M. Friedman, *The Chosen Few: Polyamory and the Law*, VERDICT (Apr. 6, 2021), https://verdict.justia.com/2021/04/06/the-chosen-few-polyamory-and-the-law

IDLEMAN, CONSTITUTIONAL LAW—FACIAL V. AS-APPLIED CHALLENGES (Spring 2023)

In Their Own Words: How Americans Describe "Christian Nationalism," PEW RES. CTR. (Oct. 27, 2022), https://www.pewresearch.org/religion/2022/10/27/in-their-own-words-how-americans-describe-christian-nationalism/

Indolent, DICTIONARY.COM, https://www.dictionary.com/browse/indolent

Invisible Hand, BRITANNICA (last updated Jan. 24, 2024), https://www.britannica.com/money/topic/invisible-hand

Javaid, Raja Muhammad Mustansar, *Religious Wisdom: Modesty & Modest Dresses in Islam & Christianity*, MEDIUM (blog) (June 9, 2022), https://mustansarjavaid.medium.com/religious-wisdom-modesty-modest-dresses-in-islam-christianity-1474d3545fa5

John Stuart Mill, STANFORD ENCYCLOPEDIA OF PHILOSOPHY, https://plato.stanford.edu/entries/mill/

Johnson, Chip, *How Berkeley's "Naked Guy" Met a Tragic End*, SFGATE (May 19, 2009), https://www.sfgate.com/bayarea/article/How-Berkeley-s-Naked-Guy-met-a-tragic-end-3232119.php

King Charles II, PBS, https://www.pbs.org/empireofthebay/profiles/charles_ii.html

Klein, Christopher, *Why Did the Puritans Come to America?*, HISTORY (Nov. 13, 2020), https://www.history.com/news/why-pilgrims-came-to-america-mayflower

Laboris, Ius, *The Legal Landscape on Employer Dress Code and Appearance Policies: A U.S. and European Perspective*, LEXOLOGY (May 30, 2017), https://www.lexology.com/library/detail.aspx?g=da7fb0a1-172a-45de-9060-12a16cabb9d1

Lakshmeeramya, Malladi, *United States v. Dennett (1930)*, EMBRYO PROJECT ENCYCLOPEDIA (June 23, 2017), https://embryo.asu.edu/pages/united-states-v-dennett-1930

Lascivious (Adj.), ONLINE ETYMOLOGY DICTIONARY, https://www.etymonline.com/word/lascivious

Lasciviousness, BIBLE HUB, https://biblehub.com/dictionary/l/lasciviousness.htm

Laura, *Why Adultery Is Not Considered a Crime in the United States*, LEICESTERSHIRE VILLAGES (Dec. 1, 2021), https://www.leicestershirevillages.com/is-adultery-considered-a-crime-in-the-usa/

Lauria, Lisa M., *Sexual Misconduct in Plymouth Colony*, PLYMOUTH COLONY ARCHIVE PROJECT ch. VIII (1998), http://www.histarch.illinois.edu/plymouth/Lauria1.html#VIII

Lewd (Adj.), ONLINE ETYMOLOGY DICTIONARY, https://www.etymonline.com/search?q=lewd

List of Social Nudity Places in North America, WIKIPEDIA, https://en.wikipedia.org/wiki/List_of_social_nudity_places_in_North_America#United_States

Lollo, Peter, *The Science of Nudity: The Skinny on Showing Skin*, KQED (Feb. 22, 2013), https://www.kqed.org/quest/49966/the-science-of-nudity-the-skinny-on-showing-skin

London, Emily, & Maggie Siddiqi, *Religious Liberty Should Do No Harm*, CTR. FOR AM. PROG. (Apr. 11, 2019), https://www.americanprogress.org/article/religious-liberty-no-harm/

Majumdar, Samirah, *Government Restrictions on Religion Around the World Reached New Record in 2018*, PEW RES. CTR. (blog), https://www.pewresearch.org/short-reads/2020/11/10/government-restrictions-on-religion-around-the-world-reached-new-record-in-2018/

May, Meredith, *Baring Their Anti-War Feelings: Fighting in Iraq Is Indecent, Not Their Nakedness, They Say*, SFGATE (July 1, 2005), https://www.sfgate.com/bayarea/article/san-francisco-baring-their-anti-war-feelings-2658616.php

Murdie, Alan, *The History of the Vagrancy Act 1824*, THE PAVEMENT (June 6, 2010), www.thepavement.org.uk

Naked Protest (Channel 4 (UK) broadcast), CULTURE UNPLUGGED, https://www.cultureunplugged.com/documentary/watch-online/play/5446/naked-protest

Nicholas Olmstead (1612–1684), FAMILYPEDIA, http://familypedia.wikia.com/wiki/Nicholas_Olmstead_(1612-1684)

Nolfi, Joey, *Ts Madison Joins RuPaul's Drag Race Season 15 as Rotating Judge*, ENTERTAINMENT (Dec. 19, 2022)

NSPCC LEARNING, CHILDREN'S EXPERIENCES OF LEGAL BUT HARMFUL CONTENT ONLINE (Feb. 2022), https://learning.nspcc.org.uk/media/2727/legal-but-harmful-content-online-helplines-insight-briefing.pdf

Pam, *The Genesis of G.O.E.*, GARDEN OF EDEN CHURCH, https://gardenofedenchurch.org/about.html

Paul, Jacob, *Michigan Residents Face Five Years in Prison and a $10,000 Fine for Using Wrong Pronouns*, MSN, https://www.msn.com/en-us/news/us/michigan-residents-face-five-years-in-prison-and-a-10-000-fine-for-using-wrong-pronouns/ar-AA1dgKg8?ocid=hpmsn&cvid=90f0f59fc1194955a6d15184553db49a&ei=59

Paulsen, Michael Stokes, *Freedom* for *Religion*, YALE L.J.F., https://www.yalelawjournal.org/pdf/PaulsenYLJForumEssay_tatbqq3s.pdf

Peters, Elliot, *"We Are Founded on Judeo-Christian Principles"—Trump Vows to End Religious Freedom for non-Christians in the United States*, MSN, https://www.msn.com/en-us/news/opinion/we-are-founded-on-judeo-christian-principles-trump-vows-to-end-religious-freedom-for-non-christians-in-the-united-states/ss-AA1jkWDU?ocid=hpmsn&cvid=d027e4e471144a75b5bcbd1ab176eafb&ei=80

Population Estimates, July 1, 2022, U.S. CENSUS, https://www.census.gov/quickfacts/fact/table/US/PST045222

Portman, Janet, *Public Urination Laws and Penalties*, CRIM. DEF. LAWYER (Nov. 18, 2022), https://www.criminaldefenselawyer.com/resources/criminal-defense/sex-crimes/public-urination-law-penalty.htm

Prurient (Adj.), ONLINE ETYMOLOGY DICTIONARY, https://www.etymonline.com/word/prurient

Ritter, Karl, *Why Does Sweden Allow Quran Burnings? Like Much of West, It Has No Blasphemy Laws*, ABC NEWS (July 20, 2023), https://abcnews.go.com/International/wireStory/sweden-quran-burnings-101529405

RuPaul's Drag Race, WIKIPEDIA, https://en.wikipedia.org/wiki/RuPaul%27s_Drag_Race

Smith, Gregory A., et al., *45% of Americans Say U.S. Should Be a "Christian Nation,"* PEW RES. CTR. (Oct. 27, 2022), https://www.pewresearch.org/religion/2022/10/27/45-of-americans-say-u-s-should-be-a-christian-nation/

The Athenians: Another Warning from History?, UNIV. OF CAMBRIDGE (Oct. 2, 2009), https://www.cam.ac.uk/research/news/the-athenians-another-warning-from-history

The Influence of the Field Code: An Introduction to the Critical Issues, KELLEN FUNK (Sept. 1, 2014), https://kellenfunk.org/field-code/the-influence-of-the-field-code-an-introduction/

The NRA (National Reform Association) and the Christian Amendment, CONST. PRINCIPLE: SEPARATION OF CHURCH & ST., https://candst.tripod.com/nra.htm

The World Sees What America Does Not. Fareed Explains, MSN, https://www.msn.com/en-us/health/medical/the-world-sees-what-america-does-not-fareed-explains/vi-AA1mADEs?ocid=msedgntp&cvid=f5157fd2020a4308acd50e9cab44197e&ei=28

Thomas Jefferson and the Virginia Statute for Religious Freedom, VA. HIST., https://virginiahistory.org/learn/thomas-jefferson-and-virginia-statute-religious-freedom#:~:text=The%20Virginia%20Statute%20for%20Religious%20Freedom%20is%20a,of%20the%20first%20amendment%20protections%20for%20religious%20freedom

Timeline of Social Nudity, WIKIPEDIA, https://en.wikipedia.org/wiki/Timeline_of_social_nudity

U.S. Christians Projected to Fall Below 50% of Population If Recent Trends Continue, PEW RES. CTR. (Sept. 8, 2022), https://www.pewresearch.org/religion/2022/09/13/modeling-the-future-of-religion-in-america/pf_2022-09-13_religious-projections_00-01/

U.S. High Court Stops School's Skirt Rule for Girls, MSN, https://www.msn.com/en-us/news/world/us-high-court-stops-school-s-skirt-rule-for-girls/ar-AA1d4qIz?ocid=hpmsn&cvid=94f6ef67da52499cb3f11c1c8250c7dc&ei=29

U.S. Immigrant Population and Share Over Time, 1850-Present, MIGRATION POL'Y INSTIT., https://www.migrationpolicy.org/programs/data-hub/charts/immigrant-population-over-time

UC Berkeley's "Naked Guy" Dies in His Jail Cell, L.A. TIMES (May 21, 2006, 12 AM PT), https://www.latimes.com/archives/la-xpm-2006-may-21-me-naked21-story.html

Van der Kerkhof, Maup, *Lady Godiva: Who Was Lady Godiva and What's the Truth Behind Her Ride*, HIST. COOPERATIVE (Nov. 15, 2023), https://historycooperative.org/lady-godiva/
Views of the U.S. as a "Christian Nation" and Opinions About "Christian Nationalism," PEW RES. CTR'S RELIGION & PUB. LIFE PROJECT (blog) (Oct. 27, 2022), https://www.pewresearch.org/religion/2022/10/27/views-of-the-u-s-as-a-christian-nation-and-opinions-about-christian-nationalism/
Villa, Virginia, *Women in Many Countries Face Harassment for Clothing Deemed Too Religious—or Too Secula*r, PEW RSCH. CTR. (blog). (Dec. 16, 2020), https://www.pewresearch.org/short-reads/2020/12/16/women-in-many-countries-face-harassment-for-clothing-deemed-too-religious-or-too-secular/
Wilson, Sam, *Ukraine's Femen: Topless Protests "Help Feminist Cause,"* BBC (Oct. 24, 2012), https://www.bbc.com/news/world-europe-20028797
Wooten, Claude, *Barack Obama Warns American Christians That Sacred Texts Are Threatened*, MSN, https://www.msn.com/en-us/entertainment/news/barack-obama-warns-american-christians-that-sacred-texts-are-threatened/ar-AA1dYTPp?ocid=hpmsn&cvid=c2d6f7b3a01e481080d2b2cbd92467e4&ei=41

Other

Annotation, *Criminal Offense Predicated Upon Indecent Exposure*, 94 A.L.R.2D 1353 (2023)
Annotation, *Validity of State and Municipal Indecent Exposure Statutes and Ordinances*, 71 A.L.R.6TH 283 (2023)
Annotation, *What Constitutes "Public Place" Within Meaning of State Statute or Local Ordinance Prohibiting Indecency or Commission of Sexual Act in Public Place*, 95 A.L.R.5TH 229 (2023)
Black, Janie, Lascivious Pilgrims: Sexuality and Sexual Laws in British Puritan New England Colonies During the Seventeenth-Century (Dec. 7, 2012) (research paper, Washington State University)
Bowling, Kenneth R., Politics in the 1st Congress, 1789-1791 (1968) (Ph.D. dissertation, University of Wisconsin)
Do You Let Your Kids See You Naked?, TODAY'S PARENT, Feb. 2016
Gal. 5:13-15 (KJV)
Gal. 5:16-26 (NKJV; KJV)
Gal. 5:17 (KJV)
Gal. 5:22-23 (KJV)
GREENAWALT, KENT, LEGAL PROTECTIONS OF PRIVACY: FINAL REPORT TO THE OFFICE OF TELECOMMUNICATIONS POLICY, EXECUTIVE OFFICE OF THE PRESIDENT (1975)
Hall, Robert Dennis, John Locke and Natural Human Rights: An Inconsistency Between His Metaphysical/Epistemological Positions and His Moral/Political Theories (1981) (Ph.D. dissertation, St. John's University)
LL.D., *Memoirs of Sir Charles Sedley*, 6 LONDON MAG. 265 (1822)
Madison, James, Address at debate of June 8, 1789, 1 ANNALS OF CONG. (1789)

Mark 12:17
Novkov, Julie L., Sex and Substantive Due Process: The Gendered Nature of Constitutional Development, 1873-1937 (1998) (unpublished Ph.D. dissertation, University of Michigan), https://www.proquest.com/docview/304474406/abstract/9858C21701D40B6PQ/1
Pouraskari, Neda, Adherence to Islamic Dress Code and Hijabi Muslim Students' Experiences of Belonging, Social Adjustment, and Islamophobia (2020) (D.Ed. dissertation, University of North Carolina at Charlotte), https://www.proquest.com/docview/2385705767/abstract/E8BE207F0A744B2DPQ/1
Rom. 13:1a
Seal, Herb, Family-group Identification with the Nudist Movement of Oregon and Northern California (1960) (master's thesis, San Francisco State College)
Sister Wives (TLC), https://www.tlc.com/shows/sister-wives

Appendices

Appendix A: Transcriptions of Legal Reports of Sedley's Case
A-1: Howell's translation of Thomas Siderfin's report[1253]
A-2: Thomas Siderfin's report
A-3: Joseph Keble's report

A-1: [translation] T. Siderfin, 1. THE REPORTS OF DIVERSE SPECIAL CASES ARGUED & ADUNDICATED IN THE COURT OF KING'S BENCH & COURT OF EXCHEQUER 168 (1683).

Le Roy versus SR. CHARLES SIDLEY, 1 Siderf. 168 (1663)
Fine &C. under indictment for misdemeanors.

Sir Charles was indicted at common law for several misdemeanors against the king's peace, and which were to the great scandal of Christianity; and the cause was, for that he shewed his naked body in a balcony in Covent Garden to a great multitude of people, and there did such things, and spoke such words, &c. (mentioning some particulars of his misbehavior). And this indictment was openly read to him in court; and the justices told him, that notwithstanding there was not then any Star-Chamber, yet they would have him know, that the Court of Kings-bench was the *custos morum* of all the king's subjects; and that it was then high time to punish such profane actions, committed against all modesty, which were as frequent, as if not only Christianity, but morality also had been neglected. After that, he was kept in court by recognizance from Trinity term to the end of Michaelmas term. 15 Car. 2, 1663.

The Court required him to take his trial at bar, but being advised, he submitted himself to the Court, and confessed the indictment. The Court considered what judgment to give; and inasmuch as he was a gentleman; bearing arms for the King, from a very ancient family (residing in the county of Kent) and his estate was encumbered, (not intending his ruin, but his reformation) they fined him only 2000 marks, imprisoned him for a week without bail, and ordered him to provide sureties for his good behavior for 3 years.

A-2: [original version] T. Siderfin, 1 LES REPORTS DES SPECIAL CASES ABGUE & ADJUDGE DEL BANK LE ROY, ET AUXY EN LE CO. BA. & L'EXCHEQUER 168 (1683).

LE ROY versus SR. CHARLES SIDLEY.

Fine &C. sur Indict' pur misdemeanors.

Sr: Ch. S. fuit indict al common ley pur several misdemeanors encounter le peace del Roy & que fueront al grand scandal de Christianity, el le cause fuit qui ail monstre son nude corps in un balcony in Covent Garden al grand multitude de people & la fist tiel choses & parle iel paolls &c. (monstrant ascun particulars de son misbehavior) & cel indictment fuit overtment lie a luy en Court & fuit dit a luy per les justices que coment la ne fuit a cel temps ascun Star-Chamber uncore ils voil fair luy de scaver que cest Court est *Custos morum* de touts les subjects le Roy, et ore haut temps de punnier tiels profane actions fait encounter tour modesty queux sont cy frequent sicome nient solement Christianity. Mes auxy morality ad ester derelinquy, et après que il ad ee continue in Court p recogn del terme de Trin. Al fine del terme de St. Mich.

1 Sid. 168 Mich. 15 Car II.B.R. (1663)

Le Court luy demand daver son trial pur cel al Barr, mes il aiant advise submit luy mesne al Court & confesse l'indictment. Pur que let Court consider quell judgment a doner, et pur cev q il fuit gent' home de trope aunc family (ore del pays de Kent) & son estate incumber (nient intendant son ruine me spur luy reforme) ils fine luy forsque 2000 marks & que serra imprison pur un weeks sans baile & del bone port par 3 ans.

A-3: J. Keble, 1 REPORTS IN THE COURT OF KING'S BENCH AT WESTMINSTER FROM XII TO XXX YEAR OF THE REIGN OF OUR LATE SOVEREIGN LORD KING CHARLES II. 619 (185).

Sir Charles Sydlyes Case. 1 Keb. 620 (1663).

Peace.

He was Fined 2000 marks, committed without Bail for a week, and Bound to his good behavior for a year, on his Confession of Information against him, for shewing himself naked in a Balkony, and throwing down Bottles (pist in) vi & armis among the people in Covent Garden, contra pacem and to the Scandal of the Government.

Appendix B: Transcriptions of Sedley Layperson Reports

B-1: Account of Joshua Hotchkiss to Ralph Eddow, as told by Philip

Henry.
B-2: Account of William Batten as told by Samuel Pepys.
B-3: Account of an undisclosed informant as told by Anthony à Wood.
B-4: Comment by Anthony à Wood on his earlier report.

B-1: P. Henry, 1 DIARIES AND LETTERS, PHILIP HENRY, M.A. 158 (M.H. Lee, ed. 1882).

July 2. this week lord Buckhurst & Sr Chas. Sidley were arrayn'd at ye King's Bench & fined for Debauchery. Being in Covent Garden at a house known by ye name of Oxford Kate's they had six dishes of meat brought in by six naked women, after dinner y^{ei} went forth in their shirts into ye Balcony & there shewing Bottles of wine y^{ei} Proclaym'd, Ho everyone y^{t} thirsteth come yee to ye water - &c. they drank a health to ye salvation of Judas & another to ye Babe of Bethlehem, after all y^{ei} said, come now let us goe in & make laws for ye mation, the one or both being, as y^{ei} say, Parliam^{t} men.

This was written in a letter from Mr. Oshua Hotchkiss to His Brother-in-law Ralph Eddow:

I hear since, only Sr Charles Sidley was arraign'd & fin'd £4000, lord Buckhurst having made an escape. This is that lord Buckhurst who tis said murther d ye Tanner last year upon ye road near london if so evil men wax worse & worse.

B-2: S. Pepys, 4 THE DIARY OF SAMUEL PEPYS. A NEW AND COMPLETE TRANSCRIPTION 209-10 (R. Latham & Wm. Matthews, eds. 19701254F[1254]

July 2, 1663

Mr. Batten telling us of a late triall of Sir Charles Sydly the other day, before Lord Chief Justice Foster and the whole bench – for his debauchery a little while since at Oxford Kate's, coming in open day into the Balcone and showed his nakedness – acting out all postures of lust and buggery that could be imagined, and abusing of scripture and as it were 'rom thence preaching a Mountebank sermon from that pulpitt, saying that there he hath to sell such a pouder as should make all the cunts in town run after him – a thousand people standing underneath to see and hear him.

And that being done he took a glass of wine and washed his prick in it and then drank it off; and then took another and drank to the King's health.

It seems my Lord and the rest of the Judges did all of them round give him a most high reproof—my Lord Chief Justice saying that it was for him, and such wicked wretches as he was, that God's anger and judgments hung over us, calling him "Sirrah" many times. It's said they have bound him to his good behaviour (there being no law against him for it). It being told that my Lord Buckhurst was there, my Lord asked whether it was that Buckhurst that vas lately tried for robbery; and when answered "Yes," he asked whether he had so soon forgot his deliverance at that time, and that it would have more become him to have been at his prayers begging God's forgiveness, than now running into such courses again.

Upon this discourse, Sir J. Mennes, and Mr. Batten both saying that buggery is now almost grown as common among our gallants as in Italy. . . .

B-3: A. Wood, THE LIFE OF ANTHONY à WOOD FROM THE YEAR 1632 to 1672, *Written by Himself, and Published by Mr. Thomas Hearne. Now Continued to the Time of His Death from Authentic Materials. The Whole Illustrated with Notes and the Addition of Several Curious Original Papers Never before Printed.* Oxford: at the Clarendon-Press. M DCC LXXII. Printed for J. and J. Fletcher in the Turl; and J. Pote at Eton, 1772. pp187-188.

https://link.gale.com/apps/doc/CW0125225539/ECCO?sid=bookmark-ECCO&xid=1f27abfa&pg=1.

Sir Charles Sedley, B^{t}, Charles Lord Buckhurst (afterwards Earl of Middlesex) Sir Thom. Ogle, &c. were at a Cook's House at the Sign of the Cock in Bow Street near Covent Garden, within the Liberty of Westminster; and being inflam'd with strong Liquors, they went into the Balcony, joyning to their Chamber-Window, and putting down their Breeches they shit in the Street. Which being done, Sedley stripped himself naked, and with Eloquence preached Blasphemy to the People. Whereupon a Riot being raised, the people became very clamorous, and would have forced the dore, next to the Street open; but being hindred, the Preacher and his Company were pelted into their Rome or Chamber, and the Windows belonging thereunto were broken.

This Frolick being soon spread abroad, especially by the Fanatical Party, who aggravated it to the utmost, by making it the most scandalous thing in nature, and nothing more reproachful to Religion than that; the said Company were summoned to the Court of Justice in Westminster-Hall, where being indicted of a Riot before Sir Rob. Hyde, L. Ch. Just. of the Com. Pleas, were all fined, and Sir Char. Sedley being fined £500, he made Answer, that he thought he was the first Man that paid for Shiting. Sir Rob. Hyde asked him whether he had ever read the Book called The Complete Gentleman, &c. to which Sir Ch. made Answer, that set aside his Lordship, he had read more Books than himself, &c. The day for Payment being appointed, Sir Charles desired Mr. Henry Killegrew and another Gent. to apply themselves to his Majesty, to get it off; but instead of that, they beg'd the said sum of his Majesty, and would not abate Sir Charles two pence of the Money. Afterwards Sr. Charles taking up, and growing very serious, he was chosen a Recruiter for that long Parliament, which began 8 May 1661. and was dissolved in the latter End of 1678.

B-4: A. Wood, 2 THE LIFE AND TIMES OF ANTHONY à WOOD ... COLLECTED FROM HIS DIARIES 335 (A. Clarke, ed. 1891-1900). Jan. 1676

1663 [this slip is a blank leaf from one of Wood's old commonplace books; cut up for its paper; it has the heading 'Navigatio, navis, natuta.] concerning the balcony business mentioned in one of my almanac [i.e. vol. I, p.476] Lord Buckhurst, Sir Charles Sidley of Kent, baronet, Sir Thomas Ogle, etc., being at a cook's house at the signe of the Cock in Bow-street neare Covent Garden, and drunk, went into the balcony looking into the street, put downe their breeches, and shit into the street; stripped themselves naked (they say). Sir Charles Sidley, being the most eager, preached blasphemy to the people. And thereupon a riot raised; people would have forced the dore open, broke the windows, etc. Whereupon being endited of a riot, appeared before (Robert) Hide, Lord Chief Justice, who fin'd Sidley £500 to be paid to the king (the other two being not able to pay such a sum). Sidley therefore answered that he thought he was the first man that paid for shiting.

Endnotes

[1] Louis Henkin, *Morals, and the Constitution: The Sin of Obscenity*, 63 COLUM. L. REV. 391, 401–02 (1963).
[2] Dobbs v. Jackson Women's Health Org., 142 S. Ct. 2228 (2022).
[3] J. Dennis Fortenberry & Devon J. Hensel, *Sexual Modesty in Sexual Expression and Experience: A Scoping Review, 2000–2021*, 59 J. SEX RES. 1000 (2022).
[4] John Donne, *Elegy XIX: To His Mistress Going to Bed*, *in* BROADVIEW ANTHOLOGY OF SEVENTEENTH-CENTURY VERSE AND PROSE 117 (2004).
[5] German politician, military leader and convicted war criminal, commenting on nudism. *Germany Suppresses Nudist Movement as Menace to Morality*, CHI. DAILY TRIB., Mar. 8, 1933, at 7.
[6] Mark 12:17.
[7] Geoffrey R. Stone, *Origins of Obscenity*, 31 N.Y.U. REV. L. & SOC. CHANGE 711, 720 (2007).
[8] *See, e.g.*, Kenzie Bryant, *The Penile Code: What TV's Increase in Full-Frontal Male Nudity Really Means*, VANITY FAIR (Mar. 17, 2022), https://www.vanityfair.com/hollywood/2022/03/minx-euphoria-tvs-increase-in-full-frontal-male-nudity-prosthetics.
[9] *Lewd (Adj.)*, ONLINE ETYMOLOGY DICTIONARY, https://www.etymonline.com/search?q=lewd (last visited Dec. 8, 2023).
[10] *Lascivious (Adj.)*, ONLINE ETYMOLOGY DICTIONARY, https://www.etymonline.com/word/lascivious (last visited Dec. 8, 2023). The word was used several times in the New Testament. *Lasciviousness*, BIBLE HUB, https://biblehub.com/dictionary/l/lasciviousness.htm (last visited Dec. 8, 2023).
[11] *See* note 281, *infra*.
[12] Blackstone is an oft-quoted source in historical studies of English common law. His *Commentaries* (1765) have had substantial influence in the U.S. Supreme Court's quest for original public meaning of the Constitution, having been cited in eight percent of the Court's opinions during the period 1990–2018. Mark Jordan Minot, *The Irrelevance of Blackstone: Rethinking the Eighteenth-Century Importance of the Commentaries*, 104 VA. L. REV. 1359 (2018).
[13] The meaning in the mid-1600s was to "indulge in excess in sensual enjoyment." *Debauched (Adj.)*, ETYMOLOGY ONLINE, https://www.etymonline.com/word/debauched (last visited Dec. 28, 2023).
[14] This case is referred to variously as *Le Roy v. Sedley*, *Rex v. Sedley*, and *Sedley's Case*. The inconsistent case names reflect the language of the legal reports of the trial that are source material for analyses.

[15] *See, e.g.*, Morris v. Mun. Ct., 652 P.2d 51 (Cal. 1982). Health and hygiene and traffic management rationales have not been persuasive.
[16] MILLIE CAUGHEY, THE CTR. FOR FAITH, IDENTITY, & GLOBALIZATION, FAITH AND THE LAW: THE EXTENT OF RELIGIOUS FREEDOM IN MODERN AMERICA (Aug. 2023), https://rumiforum.org/wp-content/uploads/2023/11/Faith-and-the-Law.pdf.
[17] There is a wealth of literature on strip clubs. *See, e.g.*, Katherine Frank, *Thinking Critically About Strip Club Research*, 10 SEXUALITIES (2007), https://doi.org/10.1177/1363460707080989; RACHEL SHTEIR, STRIPTEASE: THE UNTOLD HISTORY OF THE GIRLIE SHOW (2004).
[18] A Book Named "John Cleland's Memoirs of a Woman of Pleasure" v. Attorney Gen. of Mass., 383 U.S. 413 (1966).
[19] *Id.* (Douglas, J., concurring) (citing Leo M. Alpert, *Judicial Censorship of Obscene Literature*, 52 HARV. L. REV. 40, 47 (1938)).
[20] Roth v. United States, 354 U.S. 476 (1957), *reh'g denied*, 355 U.S. 852 (1957).
[21] JEROME HALL, THEFT, LAW, AND SOCIETY (2d ed. 1952).
[22] *Art. III.S1.7.2.1 Historical Background on the Stare Decisis Doctrine*, LEGAL INFO. INST., https://www.law.cornell.edu/constitution-conan/article-3/section-1/historical-background-on-the-stare-decisis-doctrine (last visited Oct. 22, 2023).
[23] *See, e.g.*, CASS R. SUNSTEIN, HOW TO INTERPRET THE CONSTITUTION (2023).
[24] The plurality in *Frontiero* argued for strict scrutiny of gender discrimination. As a plurality opinion, it did not establish precedent. Frontiero v. Richardson, 411 U.S. 677 (1973).
[25] Kennedy v. Bremerton Sch. Dist., 142 S. Ct. 2407 (2022).
[26] Ronna G. Schneider, *School Matters*, 92 U. CIN. L. REV. 1, 4 (2023).
[27] Dobbs v. Jackson Women's Health Org., 142 S. Ct. 2228 (2022).
[28] STEPHEN BREYER, THE AUTHORITY OF THE COURT AND THE PERIL OF POLITICS (2021).
[29] The *Dobbs* decision is highly controversial. It has been criticized for failure to follow precedent, misrepresenting history, embracing specific religious tenets, exercising bare political will, and disrespecting women and pregnant people, especially those who are marginalized and people of color, among other things. Robin Maril, *Queer Rights After* Dobbs v. Jackson Women's Health Org., 60 SAN DIEGO L. REV. 45 (2023).
[30] Richard D. Schneider, *Exhibitionism: An Exclusively Male Deviation?*, 26 INT'L J. OFFENDER THERAPY & COMP. CRIMINOLOGY 173 (1982).
[31] Jennifer Grant, *Indecent Exposure: A Serious "Nuisance" Offence*, 30 WOMEN'S HIST. REV. 1219 (2021).
[32] Lawrence M. Friedman & Joanna L. Grossman, *A Private Underworld: The Naked Body in Law and Society*, 61 BUFF. L. REV. 169 (2013).
[33] *See, e.g.*, GEOFFREY R. STONE, SEX AND THE CONSTITUTION: SEX, RELIGION, AND LAW FROM AMERICA'S ORIGINS TO THE TWENTY-FIRST CENTURY (2017) (containing no mention of indecent exposure or *Sedley's Case*).
[34] ALEX K. GIGEROFF, SEXUAL DEVIATIONS IN THE CRIMINAL LAW (1968). Chapters two and three discuss major cases and statutes in the English common law.

[35] JOHN M. MACDONALD, INDECENT EXPOSURE (1973).
[36] *Id.* at 121–31.
[37] Philip Snaith, *Exhibitionism: A Clinical Conundrum*, 143 BRIT. J. PSYCHIATRY 231 (1983), doi:10.1192/bjp.143.3.231.
[38] *E.g.*, Charles P. McCreary, *Personality Profiles of Persons Convicted of Indecent Exposure*, 31 J. CLINICAL PSYCH. 260 (1975).
[39] Grant, *supra* note 31, at 1222.
[40] *Id.*
[41] F.G. Rooth, *Some Historical Notes on Indecent Exposure and Exhibitionism*, 38 MEDICO-LEGAL J. 135 (1970); *see also* Charles P. McCreary, *supra* note 38 (finding that first offenders had relatively normal psychiatric profiles).
[42] Jeffrey C. Narvil, *Revealing the Bare Uncertainties of Indecent Exposure,* 29 COLUM. J.L. & SOC. PROBS. 85, 113 (1995).
[43] Bouke de Vries, *The Right to Be Publicly Naked: A Defense of Nudism*, 25 RES PUBLICA 407 (2019).; Keon West, *Naked and Unashamed: Investigations and Applications of the Effects of Naturist Activities on Body Image, Self-Esteem, and Life Satisfaction*, 19 J. HAPPINESS STUD. 677 (2018), https://doi.org/10.1007/s10902-017-9846-1.
[44] Fortenberry & Hensel, *supra* note 3.
[45] *E.g.*, J.J. Gayford, *Indecent Exposure: A Review of Literature*, 21 MED., SCI. & L. 233 (1981).
[46] Notable exceptions include Julie L. Novkov, Sex and Substantive Due Process: The Gendered Nature of Constitutional Development, 1873-1937 (1998) (unpublished Ph.D. dissertation, University of Michigan), https://www.proquest.com/docview/304474406/abstract/9858C21701D40B6PQ/1; Mary R. Block, *Rape Law in 19th-Century America: Some Thoughts and Reflections on the State of the Field*, 7 HIST. COMPASS 1391 (2009), https://doi.org/10.1111/j.1478-0542.2009.00623.x; STONE, *supra* note 33; CHARLES REMBAR, THE END OF OBSCENITY: THE TRIALS OF LADY CHATTERLEY, TROPIC OF CANCER & FANNY HILL BY THE LAWYER WHO DEFENDED THEM (2015); Stuart P. Green, *To See and Be Seen: Reconstructing the Law of Voyeurism and Exhibitionism*, 55 AM. CRIM. L. REV. 203 (2018).
[47] Douglas Greenberg, *Crime, Law Enforcement, and Social Control in Colonial America*, 26 AM. J. LEGAL HIST. 293 (1982).
[48] GEORGE L. HASKINS, LAW AND AUTHORITY IN EARLY MASSACHUSETTS ix (1960).
[49] Le Roy v. Sir Charles Sedley, 1 Siderfin 168 (1663); Sir Charles Sydlyes Case, 1 Keble 620 (1663).
[50] Leo M. Alpert, *Judicial Censorship of Obscene Literature*, 52 HARV. L. REV. 40 (1938) (undertaking the most extensive analysis by a legal commentator).
[51] Professor Goldberg thought a trend toward evidence-based assessment of state interests was beginning in the early 2000s, but history since then has been a bit of a meander. Suzanne B. Goldberg, *Morals-Based Justifications for Lawmaking: Before and After* Lawrence v. Texas, 88 MINN. L. REV. 1233 (2003–2004).
[52] *See, e.g.*, WILLIAM HALLER, THE RISE OF PURITANISM (1938); WINTHROP HUDSON, RELIGION IN AMERICA (2D ED. 1973); CHARLES B. KINNEY, JR.,

CHURCH & STATE: THE STRUGGLE FOR SEPARATION IN NEW HAMPSHIRE 1630-1900 (1955); MARCUS W. JERNEGAN, THE AMERICAN COLONIES, 1492-1750 (1929).

[53] *E.g.*, Henry B. Parkes, *Morals & Law Enforcement in Colonial New England*, 5 NEW ENG. Q. 431 (1932); JOHN D'EMILIO & ESTELLE B. FREEDMAN, INTIMATE MATTERS: A HISTORY OF SEXUALITY IN AMERICA (1997).

[54] The most noted study of American colonial law is Haskins's study on the law of Massachusetts. HASKINS, *supra* note 48.

[55] ERNST FREUND, THE POLICE POWER: PUBLIC POLICY AND CONSTITUTIONAL RIGHTS 220 (1904).

[56] Brown v. Maryland, 25 U.S. 419, 443 (1827).

[57] Rooth, *supra* note 41.

[58] Friedman & Grossman, *supra* note 32.

[59] *Id.* at 207–08.

[60] Coggs v. Bernard, 2 Ld. Raymond 911 (1762).

[61] EDWARD COKE, THE 1ST PART OF THE INSTITUTES OF THE LAWS OF ENGLAND § 138 (1628).

[62] Narvil, *supra* note 42, at 91. For current laws, see Jeff Burtka, *Indecent Exposure Laws by State*, FINDLAW (last visited May 17, 2021), https://www.findlaw.com/state/criminal-laws/indecent-exposure-laws-by-state.html.

[63] De Vries, Bouke, *supra* note 43; Narvil, *supra* note 42; Green, *supra* note 46. There is hardly any evidence of deep and lasting psychological harm to victims of indecent exposure. *See also, e.g.*, Fortenberry & Hensel, *supra* note 3; Marilyn D. Story, *Factors Associated with More Positive Body Self-Concepts in Preschool Children*, 108 J. SOC. PSYCH. 49 (1979); Keon West, *Think of the Children!: Relationships Between Nudity-Related Experiences in Childhood, Body Image, Self-Esteem and Adjustment*, 37 CHILDREN & SOC'Y 1187 (2023); *Do You Let Your Kids See You Naked?*, TODAY'S PARENT, Feb. 2016.

[64] Narvil, *supra* note 42, at 111.

[65] De Vries, *supra* note 43.

[66] Green, *supra* note 46.

[67] *E.g.*, ILSLEY BOONE, THE JOYS OF NUDISM (1934); JAN GAY, ON GOING NAKED (1932).

[68] *E.g.*, FRED ILFELD & ROGER LAUER, SOCIAL NUDISM IN AMERICA (1964); MAURICE PARMELEE, THE NEW GYMNOSOPHY (1927); Herb Seal, Family-group Identification with the Nudist Movement of Oregon and Northern California (1960) (master's thesis, San Francisco State College); Martin S. Weinberg, *The Nudist Management of Respectability, in* SEX RESEARCH; STUDIES FROM THE KINSEY INSTITUTE 217 (1976); Davina Cooper, *Theorising Nudist Equality: An Encounter Between Political Fantasy and Public Appearance*, 43 ANTIPODE 326 (2011).

[69] *E.g.*, EDUARD FRANKHAUSER, NUDISM, OBSCENITY AND THE LAW (Alois S. Knapp trans., 1951); Comment, *Criminal Law and Procedure – Indecent Exposure – Nudism*, 33 MICH. L. REV. 936 (1935).

[70] James C. Steffes, *Public Nakedness Is Not Privileged as an Exercise of Free Speech When It Is in Opposition to a Compelling Government Statute*, 20 DRAKE L. REV. 400 (1971); Leonard J. Michaud, Note, *Decent Exposure: An*

Inquiry into the Constitutionality of State Statutes Proscribing Expressive Public Nakedness, 22 LOY. L. REV. 1018 (1976).
[71] Emily Monroe, *A Nude Awakening: Female-Only Toplessness Bans as Unconstitutional Under the Equal Protection Clause Notes*, 30 S. CAL. REV. L. & SOC. JUST. 113 (2021).
[72] KENT GREENAWALT, INTERPRETING THE CONSTITUTION (2015).
[73] Dobbs v. Jackson Women's Health Org., 142 S. Ct. 2228 (2022).
[74] Ford W. Hall, *The Common Law: An Account of Its Reception in the United States*, 4 VAND. L. REV. 791 (1951).
[75] Le Roy v. Sir Charles Sedley, 1 Siderfin 168 (1663) ; Sir Charles Sydlyes Case, 1 Keble 620 (1663).
[76] Leo M. Alpert, *Judicial Censorship of Obscene Literature,* 52 HARV. L. REV. 40 (1938).
[77] *Sir Charles Sydlyes Case*, 1 Keb. 620 (1663). A margin note in Keble's report indicates that Keble probably was not present at the arraignment and relied on Siderfin's report for details of that event.
[78] A good legal precedent is a fully litigated case that provides a well-reasoned guide for future cases, contributes to the consistency and predictability of the law, and stands the test of time and changing societal values. *Sedley's Case* falls short. "A flimsier, more appallingly pointless foundation for the superstructure of law that was later erected could hardly have been deliberately laid." Alpert, *supra* note 76, at 43.
[79] GRAHAM GREENE, LORD ROCHESTER'S MONKEY 189 (1974). The poem was originally published in 1680.
[80] *See generally* VIVIAN DE SOLA PINTO, SIR CHARLES SEDLEY, 1639-1701: A STUDY IN THE LIFE AND LITERATURE OF THE RESTORATION (1927).
[81] Philip Henry, Samuel Pepys, and Anthony à Wood. Other reconstructions of events have been written using the diaries, with varying degrees of literary license. *See, e.g.*, 3 THEOPHILUS CIBBER, LIVES OF THE POETS OF GREAT BRITAIN AND IRELAND 96–97 (1753); 5 BIOGRAPHIA BRITANNICA 3557 (1760); 6-1 BIOGRAPHIA BRITANNICA 3603–04 (1763); 3 SAMUEL JOHNSON, LIVES OF THE ENGLISH POETS 303 (George B. Hill ed., 1905); LL.D., *Memoirs of Sir Charles Sedley*, 6 LONDON MAG. 265 (1822); WILLIAM PRIDEAUX, 8 NOTES AND QUERIES 157–08 (9th Series 1901); BRICE HARRIS, CHARLES SACKVILLE SIXTH EARL OF DORSET: PATRON AND POET OF THE RESTORATION 27–29 (1940).
[82] 4 SAMUEL PEPYS, THE DIARY OF SAMUEL PEPYS: A NEW AND COMPLETE TRANSCRIPTION 209–10 (Robert Latham & William Matthews eds., 1970). Pepys heard the story from William Batten, who also apparently did not witness the event but got his information from witnesses at the hearing. JOHN H. WILSON, THE COURT WITS OF THE RESTORATION 40 (1948).
[83] PHILIP HENRY, 1 DIARIES AND LETTERS, PHILIP HENRY, M.A. 158 (Matthew H. Lee ed., 1882). Philip Henry was not even in London at the time and learned of the case from a letter written by Joshua Hotchkiss to his brother-in-law Ralph Eddon. WILSON, *supra* note 82, at 41.
[84] Though it was not possible to identify a source for Wood's account, a reference in a recollection by Wood of that account to something "they said" about an aspect of the misbehavior implies that the information was secondhand.

THE LIFE AND TIMES OF ANTHONY À WOOD, ANTIQUARY, OF OXFORD, 1632–1695, DESCRIBED BY HIMSELF: COLLECTED FROM HIS DIARIES AND OTHER PAPERS 335 (Andrew Clarke ed., 1892). Prideaux summarized accounts by Pepys and Wood in his *Notes and Queries*. PRIDEAUX, *supra* note 81, at 157–58.

[85] HENRY R.F. BOURNE, 1 ENGLISH NEWSPAPERS 27–35 (1887).

[86] Statutes of the Realm, 1819, 14 Car. II, c. 33; *see also* N.H. KEEBLE, THE RESTORATION: ENGLAND IN THE 1660S 148 (2002).

[87] Emile D. Forgues, *John Wilmot, Count of Rochester*, *in* ROCHESTER: THE CRITICAL HERITAGE 227 (David Farley-Hills ed., 1972).

[88] J. Baker, *The Dark Age of Legal History*, *in* LEGAL HISTORY STUDIES 1972 at 39 (Dafydd Jenkins ed., 1975); *see also* 9 WILLIAM S. HOLDSWORTH, HISTORY OF ENGLISH LAW 232 (1926).

[89] Wood's account was primarily based on events at trial in October. Pepys's entry was dated July 1, and Henry's was dated the next day. PINTO, *supra* note 80, at 61.

[90] WILLIAM LAURISTON MELVILLE, A HISTORY OF POLICE IN ENGLAND 132 (1901).

[91] *King Charles II*, PBS, https://www.pbs.org/empireofthebay/profiles/charles_ii.html (last visited Dec. 30, 2023).

[92] 4 WILLIAM BLACKSTONE, COMMENTARIES ON THE LAWS OF ENGLAND 64 (1765).

[93] 1 THOMAS B. MACAULAY, THE HISTORY OF ENGLAND FROM THE ASCENSION OF JAMES THE SECOND 177 (C. Fifth ed., 1913).

[94] 1 GILBERT BURNET, BISHOP BURNET'S HISTORY OF HIS OWN TIME: FROM THE RESTORATION OF K. CHARLES II TO THE CONCLUSION OF THE TREATY OF PEACE AT UTRECHT, IN THE REIGN OF QUEEN ANNE. TO WHICH IS PREFIXED, A SUMMARY RECAPITULATION OF AFFAIRS IN CHURCH AND STATE, FROM KING JAMES I. TO THE RESTORATION IN THE YEAR 1660. TOGETHER WITH THE AUTHOR'S LIFE AND SOME EXPLANATORY NOTES 128 (1809); 1 GILBERT BRUNET, HISTORY OF HIS OWN TIME 145 (1725).

[95] 7 THE SOMERS COLLECTION OF SCARCE AND VALUABLE TRACTS 424 (W. Scott ed., 1812); *A Proclamation Against Vicious, Debauch'd, and Prophane Persons*, PROQUEST, https://www.proquest.com/docview/2264187817/99870613?accountid=14166&parentSessionId=eGuMzZjBAl50YT%2FU4p3anFblHPBgq%2FiWLeT5grN1WhQ%3D&pq-origsite=primo&sourcetype=Books (last visited Dec. 14, 2023).

[96] 7 THE SOMERS COLLECTION, *supra* note 95 at 425.

[97] KEEBLE, *supra* note 86.

[98] EDMUND LUDLOW, MEMOIRS OF EDMUND LUDLOW 385 (1771).

[99] PINTO, *supra* note 80, at 109.

[100] *Id.* at 55–56.

[101] *Id.*

[102] GEOFFREY MAY, SOCIAL CONTROL OF SEX EXPRESSION 204 (1931).

[103] PINTO, *supra* note 80, at 59.

[104] Sedley was 24; Buckhurst, 18. KEEBLE, *supra* note 86.

[105] Later in life, Ogle became highly respectable as Governor of Chelsea College, where he died in 1702. PETER LE NEVE, 8 LE NEVE'S PEDIGREES OF

THE KNIGHTS MADE BY KING CHARLES II, KING JAMES II, KING WILLIAM III, AND QUEEN MARY, KING WILLIAM ALONE AND QUEEN ANNE 93 (George W. Marshall ed., 1873); NARCISSUS LUTTRELL, A BRIEF HISTORICAL RELATION OF STATE AFFAIRS FROM SEPTEMBER 1678 TO APRIL 1714 (1857).

[106] BRICE HARRIS, CHARLES SACKVILLE, SIXTH EARL OF DORSET, PATRON AND POET OF THE RESTORATION 27, 29 (1940).

[107] HENRY, *supra* note 83 (see App. B-1).

[108] *Id.*

[109] Anthony à Wood, *infra*, App. B-6.

[110] *Id.* The expression "in their shirts" probably should not be taken literally. It was common to use such an expression to describe the public appearance of a gentleman without his coat and waistcoat.

[111] App. B-6, *infra* (Wood).

[112] App. B-1, *infra* (Henry).

[113] "Naked" as used in Sedley's time may not have meant "stark naked." A person wearing underclothes or flimsy dress might be said to be naked. JOHN H. WILSON, THE COURT WITS OF THE RESTORATION 39 (1948); *cf.* 4 FYNES MORYSON, AN ITINERARY 236–38 (1908). Writing in 1617, the author described the Irish practice of going about "naked," but he apparently meant by this that they wore only loose smocks, or "mantles," that provocatively exposed private areas. Yet in other instances, when he says "naked" or "bare," he seems to truly mean it. *E.g.*, 3 FYNES MORYSON, AN ITINERARY (1907); 4 FYNES MORYSON, AN ITINERARY 235 (1908). Pepys once used the term "naked" to describe someone who was not quite fully unclothed. 2 SAMUEL PEPYS, THE DIARY OF SAMUEL PEPYS 44 (Robert Latham & William Mathews eds., 1970) (referring to "a Quaker, came naked through the Hall, only very civilly tied about the privities to avoid scandal").

[114] A summary of court proceedings in the Coram Rege Roll, Mich. 15, Car. 2 (1639), estimated the crowd size at fifty persons, not one thousand as Pepys alleged.

[115] PEPYS, *supra* note 113.

[116] Apps. A-3, B-6, *infra* (Keble and Wood).

[117] App. B-6, *infra* (Wood).

[118] Henry believed that Sedley and Buckhurst had been indicted. Wood reported that all three were indicted and fined. Siderfin, Keble, and Pepys reported only Sedley's indictment.

[119] Sedley was arraigned on "the 1st Saturday following the *Octaves of St. Martin.*" Coram Rege Roll, 15 Mich. 2 (1639).

[120] PINTO, *supra* note 80, at 63.

[121] 2 PEPYS, *supra* note 113.

[122] *Id.* Lord Buckhurst and others killed an innocent tanner, claiming that they mistook him for a robber. They were tried and acquitted. *See* PINTO, *supra* note 80, at 66; 3 SAMUEL PEPYS, THE DIARY OF SAMUEL PEPYS 35–36 (University of California Press, 2000 (1662).

[123] Le Roy v. Sir Charles Sedley, 1 Siderfin 168 (1663). *See* App. A-1, *infra.*

[124] Le Roy v. Sir Charles Sidley, 1 Siderfin 168 (1663) in Appendix; App. A-1, *infra.*

[125] Steven K. Green, *The Fount of Everything Just and Right? The Ten Commandments as a Source of American Law*, 14 J.L. & RELIGION 525, 532 (2000).
[126] WILLIAM H. HALE, A SERIES OF PRECEDENTS AND PROCEEDINGS IN CRIMINAL CAUSES, 1475–1640 *passim* (1847).
[127] Gerald Bray, *Canon Law and the Church of England*, *in* 1 THE OXFORD HISTORY OF ANGLICANISM 168 (2017), https://doi.org/10.1093/acprof:oso/9780199639731.003.0009.
[128] CLARENCE L. VER STEEG, THE FORMATIVE YEARS, 1607-1763, at 10 (1964).
[129] Stats. Henry VIII, vol. 31 c. 8, s, 1 (1539), amended by Stats. Henry VIII, vol. 34 and 35 c. 23 (1542)); *see* 4 WILLIAM S. HOLDSWORTH, A HISTORY OF ENGLISH LAW 99–104 (1924); 5 WILLIAM S. HOLDSWORTH, A HISTORY OF ENGLISH LAW 213–14 (1924).
[130] William Hudson, *A Treatise on the Court of the Star-Chamber*, *in* 2 FRANCIS HARGRAVE, COLLECTANEA JURIDICA 126 (1791). (Hudson's treatise was written circa 1635.)
[131] *Id.* at 107.
[132] FRANCIS BACON, HISTORIE OF THE REIGNE OF KING HENRY THE SEVENTH 64 (1641).
[133] F. Heard, *Introduction to R. Compton*, *in* RICHARD COMPTON, STAR CHAMBER CASES vii n.2 (1881).
[134] Hudson, *supra* note 130, at 108–11.
[135] *Id.* at 112 ("Infinite more are the causes usually punished in this court, for which the law provideth no remedy in any sort or ordinary course . . . .").
[136] THE PURITAN REVOLUTION: A DOCUMENTARY HISTORY xix (Stuart E. Prall ed., 1968).
[137] William S. Holdsworth, *State and Religious Nonconformity: An Historical Retrospect*, 36 L.Q. REV. 339, 341 (1920).
[138] Atwood's Case (1618); 3 Cro. Jac. 421 (1658); 2 Rolle's Abridgement 78 (1668) (first published in 1658 in Croke's Reports temp James 1, Kings Bench and Common Pleas). The case was referred to King's Bench on appeal from a conviction before a justice of the peace for lack of jurisdiction.
[139] Rex v. Taylor, 1 Ven. 293, 3 Keb. 607, 621 (1676).
[140] Atwood's Case (1618); 2 Rolle's Abridgement 78 (1668) (translated from Norman French).
[141] Holdsworth, *supra* note 137.
[142] Atwood's Case (1618) ; 3 Cro. Jac. 421 ; 2 Rolles Abridgement 78 (1668).
[143] 4 WILLIAM BLACKSTONE, COMMENTARIES ON THE LAWS OF ENGLAND 64 (1765).
[144] Sparrow v. Sherwood, Popham's King's Bench Reports 208 (1627).
[145] A nineteenth-century commentator remarked that Blackstone was "neither a profound nor an accurate thinker." 2 JAMES FITZJAMES STEPHEN, A HISTORY OF THE CRIMINAL LAW OF ENGLAND 14 (1883).
[146] 4 WILLIAM BLACKSTONE, COMMENTARIES ON THE LAWS OF ENGLAND 64 (1765).
[147] 3 EDWARD COKE, THE THIRD PART OF THE INSTITUTES OF THE LAW OF ENGLAND 205 (6th ed., 1680). According to Coke, the original purpose of the law against brothels was enforcement of religious principles: "The keeping of

them is against the law of God, on which the common law of England . . . is grounded." *Id.*

148 Young v. Am. Mini Theatres, 427 U.S. 50 (1976).

149 Baker, *supra* note 88, at 32.

150 Thomas Twisden, Charge to the Grand Jury of Middlesex, 1 Keb. 526 (1663).

151 *Id.* at 533–34.

152 In her study of Victorian Britain's views on nakedness, Levine noted "that in Christian Britain the body was central and the need for surveillance and classification of it was essential for orderliness. Dress and discipline were closely related; nakedness figured a chaotic range of anxieties around sin, immorality, desire, and resistance." Philippa Levine, *States of Undress: Nakedness and the Colonial Imagination*, 50 VICTORIAN STUD. 189, 215 (2008).

153 3 CALENDAR OF STATE PAPERS: DOMESTIC SERIES 249–50 (1860).

154 1 Siderfin 168 (1663).

155 Anthony à Wood wrote that the fine was £500. Henry said it was £4000. Keble reported that it was 2000 marks.

156 1 Siderfin 168 (1663). Another reporter, Joseph Keble, was apparently present for the rendering of judgment although he had not been at the arraignment last term. His account differs in particulars from that of Siderfin. It mentions one of the "particulars of his misbehavior," alluded to by Siderfin, that of having thrown down bottles "pist in" among the people in Covent Garden. Rather than characterize the offense as one to the "scandal of Christianity," he referred to it as one to the "scandal of the Government." And he reported the period for which Sedley was ordered to provide sureties for good behavior to be one year rather than three. Sir Charles Sydlyes Case, 1 Keb. 619.

157 2 JOHN CAMPBELL, LIVES OF THE CHIEF JUSTICES OF ENGLAND (1874). Foster died between terms on October 4. Hyde was appointed to replace him on October 19 during the Michaelmas Term. Pinto erroneously concluded that Wood's account was inaccurate in reporting that Hyde presided at trial. Pinto apparently was not aware of the delay between arraignment and trial. Wood's account was written much later than those of Henry and Pepys, which were written shortly after the arraignment. The effect of the difference in dates on the relative accuracy of these accounts is difficult to assess. One the one hand, the influence of rumor may have grown, and the truth was somewhat forgotten, as the months passed; on the other hand, open discussion and possibilities of investigation and speaking with the participants could make Wood's recollection most accurate.

158 Wood, App. B-6, *infra*.

159 In 1674, Killigrew became a groom to the King. WILSON, *supra* note 113, at 53. Pinto incorrectly asserted that Killigrew was a groom of the King's bedchamber at the time of Sedley's trial. PINTO, *supra* note 80, at 65.

160 Wood, App. B-6, *infra*.

161 3 CALENDAR OF STATE PAPERS: DOMESTIC SERIES 576, 583, 634 (1860).

162 PINTO, *supra* note 80, at 66. Fines levied by the court customarily went into the King's privy purse. Quite often they were assigned in payment of his personal debts or as loans or gratuities to friends and other close associates. Proceeds of Sedley's fine were assigned to George Hamilton, brother of one of

the diarists relied upon to reconstruct *Sedley's Case* and close friend and former page of King Charles I.

[163] *Id.* at 65.

[164] Wood, App. B-6, *infra*.

[165] Henry, App. B-1, *infra*; 2 PEPYS, *supra* note 113.

[166] GERALD D. NOKES, A HISTORY OF THE CRIME OF BLASPHEMY 44–45 (1928). Examination of the court rolls led Nokes to believe that the "gist of the offense" was Sedley's actions. However, he pointed out that the words may have been legally relevant as evidence to support the charges against the defendant. If speech was not the point of the offense, then reliance on *Atwood's Case* as a source of *custos morum* authority would be ruled out.

[167] Coram Rege Roll, 15 Mich, Car. 2 (1639).

[168] MICHAEL DALTON, THE COUNTREY JUSTICE (1666 ed.) ("Peace, in effect, is the Amity, Confidence, and Quiet that is between man; and he that breaketh this Amity or Quiet breaketh the Peace.").

[169] *Id.* at 252 ("An unlawful Assembly, Riot, or Rout, is where three or more shall gather together, come, or meet in one place, to do some unlawful act with violence . . . ."). The definition of the offense seems to have originated in the Court of Star Chamber. Stanford E. Lehmberg, *Star Chamber: 1485-1509*, 24 HUNTINGTON LIBR. Q. 24, 189 (1961). Commentators have incorrectly speculated that Sedley was convicted for breach of the peace. *See, e.g.*, Stone, *supra* note 7, at 720 n.65 and authorities cited therein (2007). He entered a plea. The declaration of *custos morum* would not have been necessary to sustain a charge of breach of the peace.

[170] *E.g.*, Rex v. Field, 1 Siderfin 69, 1 Keb. 175, 194, 209, 233 (1661) (involving prosecution for saying "The Government of the Church of England is popish, superstitious, and will worship, . . . (etc.)" under a statute providing for the punishment of anyone who shall "by writing, printing, preaching, or other speaking, express, publish, utter or declare any words, sentences, or other thing or things, to incite or stir up the people to hatred or dislike of the person of his Majesty, or the established government, . . . " Statutes of the Realm, 13 Car. 2, st. 1, c. 1, s. 2; Atwood's Case (1618).

[171] If the force used by the actors on the balcony in throwing down bottles did not constitute an actual assault, it could have been deemed a procurement, or part of the res gestae, of the offense. NOKES, *supra* note 166, at 26. "Hot words" were sufficient cause for a constable to demand that the speaker provide sureties for his good behavior. DALTON, *supra* note 168, at 193, 222.

[172] DALTON, *supra* note 168, at 227.

[173] 7 EDWARD FOSS, JUDGES OF ENGLAND 1003 (1864).

[174] *Id.* at 127; 2 EDWARD H. CLARENDON, THE LIFE OF EDWARD, EARL OF CLARENDON 43 (1759).

[175] 2 CLARENDON, *supra* note 174, at 39.

[176] Alfred F. Havighurst, *The Judiciary and Politics in the Reign of Charles II*, LAW Q. REVS. 64 (1950); 6 WILLIAM S. HOLDSWORTH, A HISTORY OF ENGLISH LAW 500 (5th ed., 1922–1938).

[177] 6 HOLDSWORTH, *supra* note 176, at 500.

[178] *See generally* 7 FOSS, *supra* note 173, at 97–199.

[179] 7 FOSS, *supra* note 173, at 136.

[180] 6 HOLDSWORTH, *supra* note 176, at 501; Havighurst, *supra* note 176, at 62–65.
[181] JOHN CAMPBELL, LIVES OF THE LORD CHANCELLORS vol.3:184 (2d Am. ed., 1851).
[182] 7 FOSS, *supra* note 173, at 128.
[183] *Id.* at 129.
[184] *Id.* at 130.
[185] ADOLPHUS W. WARD & ALFRED R. WALLER, THE CAMBRIDGE HISTORY OF ENGLISH LITERATURE: THE AGE OF DRYDEN 209 (1920).
[186] *E.g.*, J. BRYDALL, COMPENDIOUS COLLECTION OF THE LAWS OF ENGLAND, TOUCHING MATTERS CRIMINAL (1675); 3 EDWARD COKE, THE THIRD PART OF THE INSTITUTES OF THE LAW OF ENGLAND (5th ed., 1671); DALTON, *supra* note 168.
[187] GILBERT BURNET, SOME ACCOUNT OF THE LIFE AND DEATH OF JOHN, EARL OF ROCHESTER, WHO DIED JULY 26, 1680, AT 28 (1724).
[188] WILSON, *supra* note 113, at 39.
[189] BONAMY DOBREE, ESSAYS IN BIOGRAPHY 1680-1726, at 23 (1925); PINTO, *supra* note 80, at 61 n.4.
[190] WILSON, *supra* note 113, at 40. Wilson described other raucous incidents that did not involve public nakedness but are illustrative of the licentious freedom they enjoyed. *Id.* at 37–38.
[191] *Friday 23 October 1668*, DIARY OF SAMUEL PEPYS, https://www.pepysdiary.com/diary/1668/10/23/; WILSON, *supra* note 113, at 36, 38. Wilson noted their "freedom from moral and legal restraints" and refers to a specific case in which "[t]here was much talk that [they] would be charged with responsibility for [one of their companions'] death—talk which, as usual, came to nothing."
[192] 9 SAMUEL PEPYS, THE DIARY OF SAMUEL PEPYS, A NEW AND COMPLETE TRANSCRIPTION (Robert Latham & William Mathews eds., 1970).
[193] *Id.*
[194] BERTRAM OSBORNE, JUSTICES OF THE PEACE 1361–1848, at 125 (1960) (reporting that on a number of occasions, Charles directed constable in the "plainest terms" not to enforce Acts of Parliament regarding religious uniformity).
[195] Charles II often interfered in cases. In private suits, he gave advice to the justices favoring one party over the other. Once, during a treason trial, he wrote to the Lord Chancellor on the subject of putting the accused "out of the way." 2 LUKE O. PIKE, A HISTORY OF CRIME IN ENGLAND 204–05 (1876).
[196] LE NEVE, *supra* note 105, at 93.
[197] 6 BIOGRAPHIA BRITANNICUS 3604 (1747–66). He was selected to the House of Commons in the succeeding reign of James II.
[198] Rex v. Taylor, 1 Ven. 293, 3 Keb. 607, 621 (1676) ; 6 BIOGRAPHIA BRITANNICUS 3604 (1747–66); *see also* Elliott Visconsi, *The Invention of Criminal Blasphemy*: Rex v. Taylor (1676), 103 REPRESENTATIONS 30 (2008), https://doi.org/10.1525/rep.2008.103.1.30 (considered the fountainhead of all subsequent blasphemy jurisprudence).
[199] Visconsi, *supra* note 198.

[200] PRIDEAUX, *supra* note 81, at 158.
[201] David Kearns, *Sovereignty and Common Law Judicial Office in Taylor's Case (1675)*, 37 L. & HIST. REV. 397 (2019); Visconsi, *supra* note 198.
[202] Royal Proclamation, 1 Ven. 293, 3 Keb. 607, 621 (1675).
[203] NOKES, *supra* note 166, at 490.
[204] MAY, *supra* note 102, at 208.
[205] Reg. v. Read, Fortescue 98, 92 Eng. Rep. 777 (1708). It urged prosecution of offenses and published blacklists of persons convicted of crimes involving immorality. NOKES, *supra* note 166, at 126.
[206] There had been other minor prosecutions during the preceding fifteen years. Many are described in 1 STATE TRIALS 132–33 (T. Donald ed., 1972).
[207] *Force and Arms*, LSD, https://www.lsd.law/define/force-and-arms (last visited Jan. 23, 2024).
[208] Fortescue 98, 92 Eng. Rep. 77 (1707).
[209] *Id.* at 99.
[210] *Id.*
[211] *Id.* at 98.
[212] Stone, *supra* note 7, at 722 n.75.
[213] 1 WILLIAM HAWKINS, A TREATISE OF THE PLEAS OF THE CROWN 358 (1716).
[214] *Id.* § 5.
[215] *Id.*
[216] *Id.* at §7.
[217] Rex v. Curl, (1 George II.) 2 Strange 788 (1727).
[218] 1 WILLIAM HAWKINS, A TREATISE OF THE PLEAS OF THE CROWN vol. 1, ch. 5 § 4 (1716). It is noteworthy that this vague description of the offense fairly reflected the event, as it has been reconstructed. It indicates that Sedley was not alone on the balcony and that the exposure was accompanied by the "most abominable circumstances." Hawkins appears to have been aware of facts not contained in the legal reports of the case, but there is no indication of the source of those facts.
[219] Rex v. Curl, 93 Eng. Rep. 849, 850 (K.B. 1727).
[220] 2 Str. 788 (1727).
[221] *Id.* at 790.
[222] Rex v. Gallard, 25 Eng. Rep. 547 (1733).
[223] 1 STATE TRIALS, *supra* note 206, at 134 (citing *Sedley's Case*) (internal citations omitted).
[224] Rex v. Tallard, 2 Barn. 328, 345, 94 Eng. Rep. 532, 543 (1733).
[225] Rex v. Gallard, 125 1 Sess. Cases 231 (1733).
[226] HENRY FIELDING, 13 COMPLETE WORKS OF HENRY FIELDING 214–18 (1957); *see also* LEON RADZINOWICZ, A HISTORY OF ENGLISH CRIMINAL LAW 400 (1948).
[227] Rex v. Delaval, 1 Black. Rep. 410, 439; 3 Burr. 1434 (1763).
[228] According to Coke, the original purpose of the law against brothels was enforcement of religious principles: "Keeping of them is against the Law of God, on which the common law of England . . . is grounded." 3 COKE, *supra* note 147, at 205.
[229] Rex v. Delaval, 97 Eng. Rep. 91, 1 Black. Rep. 410, 439; 3 Burr. 1434, 1439 (1763).

[230] *Id.* at 1438–39 (1763).
[231] 4 WILLIAM BLACKSTONE, COMMENTARIES ON THE LAWS OF ENGLAND 64–65 (1765), citing *Sedley's Case* (1663); Rex v. Wheelhorse, Poph. 208 (1627) (frequenting houses of ill fame).
[232] BLACKSTONE, *supra* note 231 at 41.
[233] RADZINOWICZ, *supra* note 226, at 400.
[234] COUNTESS OF ELIZABETH CHUDLEIGH BRISTOL, THE LAWS RESPECTING WOMEN 299 (1777).
[235] 1 EDWARD HYDE EAST, A TREATISE OF THE PLEAS OF THE CROWN ch. 1, § 1 (1803).
[236] Rex v. Crunden, 2 Camp. 89, 89–91, 170 Eng. Rep. 1091 (1809).
[237] 2 JOSEPH CHITTY, A PRACTICAL TREATISE ON THE CRIMINAL LAW 41 (1816).
[238] 2 Camp. 89, 90; 170 Eng. Rep. 1091 (1809).
[239] *Id.*
[240] *Id.*
[241] *Id.*
[242] CHITTY, *supra* note 237, at 41.
[243] 1 WILLIAM O. RUSSELL, A TREATISE ON CRIMES AND MISDEMEANORS 438 (1819).
[244] L.H. Leigh, *Vagrancy, Morality and Decency*, CRIM. L. REV. 381, 413 (1975) (Apparently, the offenses are no longer considered sufficiently serious to warrant proceeding by way of indictment or information at common law. "Section 4 of the Vagrancy Act of 1824 makes it an offence for any person 'wilfully, openly, lewdly and obscenely to expose his person in any street, road, or public highway, or in view thereof, or in any place or public resort, with the intent to insult any female'. This was amended by The Criminal Justice Act 1925 Section 42, so that the offence was not limited to public places and read thus: 'any person wilfully, openly, lewdly and obscenely, to expose his person with intent to insult any female'. There is a similar offence under Section 28 of the Town Police Clauses Act 1847, that states that 'every person who is in any street, to the annoyance of the residents or passengers wilfully and indecently exposes his person is guilty of an offence punishable summarily.'").
[245] Vagrancy Act of 1822, 3 Geo. 4, c. 40, s. 3 (1822).
[246] Alan Murdie, *The History of the Vagrancy Act 1824*, THE PAVEMENT (June 6, 2010), www.thepavement.org.uk.
[247] Vagrancy Act of 1824, 5 Geo. 5:4 c. 83, s. 4 (1824).
[248] Rooth, *supra* note 41, at 138.
[249] Rex v. Justices of the Town & Country of Newcastle-upon-Tyne, 1 Barn & Ad. 933, 109 Eng. Rep. 1033 (1831).
[250] Unreported case described in Reg. v. Webb, 2 Car. & K. 933, 934, 175 Eng. Rep. 391 (1848).
[251] Reg. v. Rowed, 3 Q.B. 518 (1842); GREAT BRITAIN COURT OF KING'S BENCH, CHARLES JAMES GALE, AND SIR HENRY DAVISON. REPORTS OF CASES ARGUED AND DETERMINED IN THE COURT OF QUEEN'S BENCH: AND UPON WRITS OF ERROR FROM THAT COURT TO THE EXCHEQUER CHAMBER, IN EASTER, TRINITY, AND MICHAELMAS TERMS, 1841-1843. S. SWEET (1843).
[252] Reg. v. Bunyan, 1 Cox C.C. 74 (1844).

[253] Four years later, in Rex v. Orchard, 3 Cox C.C. 248 (1848), the sufficiency of an indictment for sodomitical acts committed in a public urinal was questioned. The Court did not offer a direct response. Rather, it dismissed the indictment on the ground that a urinal is not a public place. It is possible that the dismissal was due in part to uncertainty about inclusion of homosexual acts in the moral offenses, for courts sometimes seize upon the most convenient doctrine to justify a decision to justify a decision motivated by other concerns. There were no indications in the language of the opinion that this was the case here.
[254] Reg. v. Watson, 2 Cox C.C. 376 (1847).
[255] Town Police Clauses Act, 10&11 Vict. c.89 s.28 (1847).
[256] Rex v. Orchard, 3 Cox C.C. 248 (1848).
[257] *Id.* at 251.
[258] Reg. v. Webb, 2 Car. & K. 933, 175 Eng. Rep. 391 (1848).
[259] 1 EAST, *supra* note 235, at 3.
[260] *See* 1 STEPHEN CHARLES DENISON, CROWN CASES RESERVED FOR CONSIDERATION AND DECIDED BY THE JUDGES OF ENGLAND, FROM THE YEAR 1844 TO THE YEAR 1850, at 339–45 (1850).
[261] Dugdale v. The Queen, 1 El. & B. 435 (1853).
[262] Reg. v. Holmes, 169 E.R. 697 (1853).
[263] Criminal Procedure Act 1851, 14 & 15 Vict. c. 100 ss. 24, 25 (1851).
[264] FREDERICK AUGUSTUS CARRINGTON, ANDREW VALENTINE KIRWAN, & GREAT BRITAIN CENTRAL CRIMINAL COURT, REPORTS OF CASES ARGUED AND RULED AT NISI PRIUS: IN THE COURTS OF QUEEN'S BENCH, COMMON PLEAS, & EXCHEQUER; TOGETHER WITH CASES TRIED ON THE CIRCUITS, AND IN THE CENTRAL CRIMINAL COURT . . . S. SWEET 362 (1852).
[265] *Id.* at 363.
[266] Reg. v. Elliot, 1 L. & C. 103 (1861).
[267] Reg. v. Thallman, Leigh & C.C.C. 326, 169 Eng. Rep. 1416 (1863).
[268] Reg. v. Hicklin, L.R. 3 Q. B. 360 (1868).
[269] *An Act for More Effectually Preventing the Sale of Obscene Books, Pictures, Prints, and Other Articles*, *in* A COLLECTION OF THE PUBLIC GENERAL STATUTES 2 (1857), https://books.google.com/books?id=h2BFAAAAcAAJ&pg=PA813#v=onepage&q&f=false. The Act superseded a 1787 Royal Proclamation by George III titled Proclamation for the Discouragement of Vice.
[270] Malladi Lakshmeeramya, *United States v. Dennett (1930)*, EMBRYO PROJECT ENCYCLOPEDIA (June 23, 2017), https://embryo.asu.edu/pages/united-states-v-dennett-1930.
[271] Roth v. United States, 354 U.S. 476 (1957), *reh'g denied*, 355 U.S. 852 (1957).
[272] Reg. v. Hicklin, L.R. 2 Q.B. 360 (1863) (providing a definition of "obscenity" as a matter of statutory construction that became the standard test of obscenity in the United States before Roth v. United States, 354 U.S. 476, *reh'g denied*, 355 U.S. 852 (1957): "whether the tendency of the matter charged as obscenity is to deprave and corrupt those whose minds are open to such immoral influences.").

[273] As recently as the 1960s, Lord Devlin, in *The Enforcement of Morals*, noted that "Christian morals remained embedded in the law" of England. PATRICK DEVLIN, THE ENFORCEMENT OF MORALS 87 (1968).
[274] The southern colonies of North and South Carolina and Georgia did not materially contribute statutory or case law to the modern jurisprudence of indecent exposure. Warren M. Billings, *Law in the Colonial South*, 73 J.S. HIST. 603 (2007). Charles II reversed practices of his predecessors of granting charters to religious dissidents and granted charters to new colonies to confidents, including Edward Hyde and other for the Carolinas. WILLIAM EDWARD NELSON, THE COMMON LAW IN COLONIAL AMERICA: THE MIDDLE COLONIES AND THE CAROLINAS, 1660-1730, at 2 (2013). Flexibility on laws was restricted for colonies established after the Restoration.
[275] Population estimates are generally from Pew Research.
[276] BRADLEY CHAPIN, CRIMINAL JUSTICE IN COLONIAL AMERICA, 1606-1660 (2010). The majority of substantive criminal law in Rhode Island, Virginia, Plymouth, and Maryland was sourced from English common law. Study of colonial statutes will show that a disproportionate share of moral law was biblical.
[277] G.A. Moriarty, *Social and Geographic Origins of the Founders of Massachusetts*, *in* COMMONWEALTH HISTORY OF MASSACHUSETTS 49–63 (Hart ed., 1927–1928).
[278] VER STEEG, *supra* note 128, at 27; Homans, *The Puritans and Clothing Industry in England*, 13 NEW ENG. Q. 519, 528 (1940).
[279] VER STEEG, *supra* note 128, at 194. "Bible Commonwealth" is a term used to describe colonies such as Massachusetts Bay and New Haven during the majority of the early North American Colonial Period. These communities were deeply religious, with laws often citing Scripture.
[280] *See, e.g.*, Christopher Klein, *Why Did the Puritans Come to America?*, HISTORY (Nov. 13, 2020), https://www.history.com/news/why-pilgrims-came-to-america-mayflower.
[281] The term "unclean carriage" typically referred to a person who had contracted a contagious disease or was suspected of carrying an infectious condition that could easily spread to others. During colonial times, infectious diseases were a significant concern, and communities implemented measures to prevent the spread of illnesses. Quarantines were used to isolate individuals who were believed to be infected or had contact with contagious diseases. The term "unclean carriage" was used to identify those individuals and emphasize the need for caution and separation. The concept of an "unclean carriage" can be traced back to European practices, particularly in relation to the management of outbreaks like the bubonic plague. In the American colonies, where populations were densely packed in cities and towns, the fear of epidemics and the importance of maintaining public health led to the use of such terms to identify individuals who posed a potential risk to others.
[282] CHAPIN, *supra* note 276, at 77.
[283] *Id.* at 3.
[284] Population estimates are generally from Pew Research.

[285] TARLAN MASMALIYEVA, TURKISH SECULARISM: HOW TO RAISE ITS LEVEL OF PROTECTION (European Union and European Union and Its Neighbours in a Globalized World No. 12, 2024).
[286] Nelson, *supra* note 274, at 1; Greenberg, *supra* note 47.
[287] *Letters Patent to Sir Thomas Gates*, *in* JOHN D. CUSHING, STATUTES OF VIRGINIA 57 (1609).
[288] JOHN D. CUSHING, 1ST LAWS OF THE STATE OF CONNECTICUT vii (1784).
[289] JERNEGAN, *supra* note 52, at 141–42.
[290] Green, *supra* note 125.
[291] CHAPIN, *supra* note 276, at 5.
[292] *Id.* Common-law cases accounted for more than half of the prosecutions in Virginia and Maryland where royal charters prescribed allegiance to the common law of England.
[293] *Id.* at 14.
[294] PRIESTLEY'S LECTURES ON HISTORY, AND GENERAL POLICY 149 (1791), *quoted in* 1 HENRY, STATUTES AT LARGE (1809).
[295] THOMAS H. JOHNSON, THE PURITANS 1 (Perry Miller ed., 1938).
[296] DANIEL J. BOORSTIN, THE AMERICANS 5 (1958).
[297] G.L. Haskins, *Representative Government and the "Bible Commonwealth" in Early Massachusetts*, 9 AKRON L. REV. 2, art. 1 (1976); *see also* Janie Black, Lascivious Pilgrims: Sexuality and Sexual Laws in British Puritan New England Colonies During the Seventeenth-Century 1 (Dec. 7, 2012) (research paper, Washington State University) ("The beliefs and laws that colonial culture established concerning personal life and sexuality in the seventeenth-century were greatly influential to the formation of subsequent beliefs and laws in later American culture.").
[298] Roscoe Pound, *Puritanism and the Common Law*, 45 AM. L. REV. 811 (1911).
[299] MARIA L. GREENE, THE DEVELOPMENT OF RELIGIOUS LIBERTY IN CONNECTICUT 58 (1905).
[300] 1 NEW HAMPSHIRE LAWS xi (1679).
[301] JOHNSON, *supra* note 295 at 43, 57.
[302] 2 SAMUEL R. GARDINER, HISTORY OF THE COMMONWEALTH AND THE PROTECTORATE 1649-1660, at 265 (1897).
[303] A. BOOTH & A. BOON, EXAMEN LEGUM ANGLIAE: OR, THE LAWS OF ENGLAND EXAMINED, BY SCRIPTURE, ANTIQUITY, AND REASON (1656).
[304] EDMUND MORGAN, THE PURITAN FAMILY 166 (1944).
[305] 1 HERBERT L. OSGOOD, THE AMERICAN COLONIES IN THE SEVENTEENTH CENTURY 201 (1904-1907); BOORSTIN, *supra* note 296, at 6.
[306] MARTIN LUTHER, A COMMENTARY ON ST. PAUL'S EPISTLE TO THE GALATIANS 347 (1860); MARY E. CHASE, THE BIBLE AND THE COMMON READER 358 (1952).
[307] 1 NEW HAMPSHIRE LAWS x1 (1679) (introduction).
[308] LAWRENCE FRIEDMAN, CRIME AND PUNISHMENT IN AMERICAN HISTORY 32 (2010).
[309] WILLIAM STRACHEY, LAWES DIVINE, MORALL AND MARTIALL, &c (1612); *see also* JOHN D. CUSHING, THE 1ST LAWS OF THE STATE OF VIRGINIA (1983).

The extent of enforcement of these laws is not known. The content of later Virginia codes differed.
[310] STRACHEY, *supra* note 309 § 22.
[311] *Id.* § 14.
[312] ROYAL R. HINMAN, THE BLUE LAWS OF NEW HAVEN COLONY, USUALLY CALLED BLUE LAWS OF CONNECTICUT iii (1838); JOHN D. CUSHING, MARYLAND 5 (1838).
[313] *Cf.* Julius Goebel & T.R. Naughton, *King's Law, and Local Custom in Seventeenth Century New England*, 31 COLUM. L. REV. 417, 442 n.50 (1931) (stating that trials for Sabbath breaking, drunkenness, and fornication were three times more prevalent than those for offices against the peace, and twice as common as those for economic offenses).
[314] HINMAN, *supra* note 312, at 131–32. *See* NATHANIEL B. SHURTLEFF, RECORDS OF THE COLONY OF NEW PLYMOUTH IN NEW ENGLAND (1855-1861), for the full text.
[315] SHURTLEFF, *supra* note 314, at 94 (describing order of the Court of Assistants at Boston, October 8, 1631).
[316] Betty B. Rosenbaum, *The Sociological Basis of the Laws Relating to Women Sex Offenders in Massachusetts (1620-1860)*, 28 J. CRIM. L. & CRIMINOLOGY (1931-1951) 815 (1938).
[317] SHURTLEFF, *supra* note 314, at 43.
[318] EDWIN POWERS, CRIME AND PUNISHMENT IN EARLY MASSACHUSETTS 1620-1692, at 412 (1966). As used here, it appears to be broader than being suspected of carrying infectious disease, a common meaning of the term during that period.
[319] RICHARD GODBEER, SEXUAL REVOLUTION IN EARLY AMERICA 63 (2004). Puritans were taught to avoid debauchery of their bodies for the sake of their souls.
[320] Lisa M. Lauria, *Sexual Misconduct in Plymouth Colony*, PLYMOUTH COLONY ARCHIVE PROJECT ch. VIII (1998), http://www.histarch.illinois.edu/plymouth/Lauria1.html#VIII.
[321] JOHN D. CUSHING, THE LAWS OF THE PILGRIMS (1977).
[322] DAVID H. FLAHERTY, ESSAYS IN THE HISTORY OF EARLY AMERICAN LAW 112 (2014).
[323] Green, *supra* note 125.
[324] N. Ward, *The Body of Liberties of 1641*, *in* COLONIAL LAWS OF MASSACHUSETTS 94 et seq. (1889).
[325] John Cotton, *An Abstract of the Lawes of New England* (1641, 1655); *reprinted in* HUTCHINSON, COLLECTION OF ORIGINAL PAPERS (1769), 3(9) FORCE'S TRACT (1733), and 5 MASS. HIST. SOC. COLLECTION (1st series 1792).
[326] COLONIAL LAWS OF MASSACHUSETTS (1889); *see also* BLUE LAWS OF CONNECTICUT 97 (Smucker ed., 1861).
[327] The government of Massachusetts Bay later supplemented Ward's Liberties, making fornication subject to corporal punishment, fine, and the enjoining of marriage. WILLIAM H. WHITMORE, BOS. CITY COUNCIL, THE COLONIAL LAWS OF MASSACHUSETTS: REPRINTED FROM THE EDITION OF 1672 WITH THE SUPPLEMENTS THROUGH 1686 : CONTAINING ALSO A BIBLIOGRAPHICAL

PREFACE AND INTRODUCTION TREATING OF ALL THE PRINTED LAWS FROM 1649 TO 1686 : TOGETHER WITH THE BODY OF LIBERTIES OF 1641, AND THE RECORDS OF THE COURT OF ASSISTANTS, 1641-1644 (1890).

[328] *The Massachusetts Body of Liberties*, HANOVER COLL. DEP'T HIST. (1641), http://history.hanover.edu/texts/masslib.html.

[329] John Cotton, *A Discourse About Civil Government*, *in* CHURCH AND STATE IN AMERICAN HISTORY 7 (John Wilson & Donald Drakeman eds., 1987); JOHN WINTHROP, THE JOURNAL OF JOHN WINTHROP, 1630-1649, at 380 (James Savage et al. eds., Harv. Univ. Press, 2009); THE COLONIAL LAWS OF MASSACHUSETTS REPRINTED FROM THE EDITION OF 1660 . . . CONTAINING ALSO THE BODY OF LIBERTIES OF 1641 (Fred B. Rothman & Co. 1995) (1889).

[330] HEN. STAT. AT LARGE, vol. 1:240 (1819-1823).

[331] *Id.*

[332] CONN. PUB. STAT. LAWS tit. 97, n.1 (1808).

[333] 1 BENJAMIN TRUMBULL, A COMPLETE HISTORY OF CONNECTICUT, CIVIL AND ECCLESIASTICAL 124 (1898).

[334] *Nicholas Olmstead (1612–1684)*, FAMILYPEDIA, http://familypedia.wikia.com/wiki/Nicholas_Olmstead_(1612-1684); https://www.wikitree.com/wiki/Olmstead-32

[335] *Records of the* Particular Court of *Connecticut, 1639-1663*, *in* 12 COLLECTION OF THE CONNECTICUT HISTORICAL SOCIETY 12 (1928).

[336] HENRY K. OLMSTED, GENEALOGY OF THE OLMSTEAD FAMILY IN AMERICA 12 (1912).

[337] *Id.* at 13.

[338] For another example of youthful dalliance transition to mature statesman, see JOHN D'EMILIO & ESTELLE B. FREEDMAN, INTIMATE MATTERS: A HISTORY OF SEXUALITY IN AMERICA 15 (1997).

[339] *See, e.g.*, HINMAN, *supra* note 312, at 129, 180, 197; JOHN D. CUSHING, CONNECTICUT 27, 35, 47, 48 (Connecticut Code of 1650). Cotton's code referenced Scripture for each and every capital offense. These citations were carried over in Governor Eaton's Code in New Haven. *See* THE EARLIEST LAWS OF THE NEW HAVEN AND CONNECTICUT COLONIES, 1639-1673, at vii (John D. Cushing ed., 1784); CUSHING, *supra* note 321.

[340] The code of laws of Rhode Island, in effect from 1647 to 1705, showed more reliance on English laws than any code of the other New England colonies. JOHN D. CUSHING, RHODE ISLAND vii (1798). The crimes enumerated included rebellion, witchcrafts, sodomy, buggery, rape, adultery, fornication, prostitution, lying, and drunkenness. Citations to English statutes appeared in the place of citations to Scripture. Crimes against religion were excluded.

[341] JOHN D. CUSHING, GOVERNOR EATON'S CODE FOR THE NEW HAVEN COLONY viii (1784).

[342] 11 JOHN D. CUSHING, RECORDS OF THE COLONY OF NEW PLYMOUTH xv (1855-1861); *cf.* 4 JOHN CALVIN, COMMENTARIES ON THE FOUR LAST BOOKS OF MOSES chaps. 15–16, 20, 22 (1634).

[343] D'EMILIO & FREEDMAN, *supra* note 338.

[344] HINMAN, *supra* note 312, at 210.

[345] D'EMILIO & FREEDMAN, *supra* note 338.

[346] 11 PLYMOUTH COLONY RECORDS 156 (1855–1861).

[347] NEW HAVEN COLONY HISTORICAL RECORDS, ANCIENT TOWN RECORDS: NEW HAVEN TOWN RECORDS, 1662-1684 (1919).
[348] C.L.C. 153 § 1 (1672).
[349] *Acts and Resolves, May the 7th, 1662*, *in* SEVERALL LAWES AND ORDERS MADE AT SEVERALL GENERAL COURTS IN THE YEARS 1661, 1662, 1663 (Library of Cong., microfiche). Connecticut also had such laws.
[350] *Id.* at 159. Brackets indicate passages that were translated into Latin by Hinman.
[351] New York's *Duke's Law*, which was drawn up in 1664 and became effective throughout Delaware, New Jersey, and Pennsylvania, appears to have been based principally on the code of laws of Rhode Island. JOHN D. CUSHING, NEW YORK vii (1872).
[352] JERNEGAN, *supra* note 52, at 412–14.
[353] Greenberg, *supra* note 47, at 304 et seq.
[354] FRANCIS FANE, REPORTS ON THE LAWS OF CONNECTICUT 97 (C. Andrews ed., 1915).
[355] Green, *supra* note 125.
[356] Two other cases, *Olmstead's Case* (1640) (lascivious carriage) and Sparrow v. Sherwood, Popham's King's Bench Reports 208 (1627) (frequenting a house suspected of being a bawdy-house but also for being a common night-walker) influenced nascent statutes from which modern statutory elaborations and condensations evolved.
[357] RICHARD BURN & JOSEPH GREENLEAF, AN ABRIDGEMENT OF BURN'S JUSTICE OF THE PEACE AND PARISH OFFICER (1773).
[358] RICHARD BURN, AN ABRIDGEMENT, OR THE AMERICAN JUSTICE 294 (1792). The expression may also have been taken from volumes containing it which were published in England prior to 1784, such as 4 WILLIAM BLACKSTONE, COMMENTARIES ON THE LAWS OF ENGLAND 64 (1765); RICHARD BURN, BURN'S JUSTICE (1743), OR 1 WILLIAM HAWKINS' PLEAS OF THE CROWN 797 (1716).
[359] MASS. STAT. 1784 ch. 40 § A (1791). A New Hampshire law that adopted the basic form and language of this statute incorporated an express provision against adultery and was amended in 1828 to include fornication, to provide a comprehensive law against immoral sexual affairs. N.H. LAWS 1791 ch. 28; N.H. LAWS 1828 ch. 92.
[360] 1 WILLIAM HAWKINS, A TREATISE OF THE PLEAS OF THE CROWN Ch. 6 § 4.IV (1716).
[361] RICHARD BURN, AN ABRIDGEMENT, OR THE AMERICAN JUSTICE (1792).
[362] 4 WILLIAM BLACKSTONE, COMMENTARIES ON THE LAWS OF ENGLAND 64 (1765).
[363] Rex v. Crunden, 2 Camp. 89, 170 Eng. Rep. 1091 (1809).
[364] Hall, *supra* note 74, *The Common Law: An Account of Its Reception in the United States*, 4 VAND. L. REV. 791 (1951).
[365] The legal heritage of the American rule against cohabitation is a mystery. The wedding of the prohibitions against cohabitation and against open gross lewdness may have been a consequence of the common theme of publicity implicit in the former and explicit in the latter.

[366] Thomas Jefferson drafted the Declaration, with input from John Adams, Benjamin Franklin, Roger Sherman, and Robert Livingston. John Adams believed that "civil government essentially depends upon piety, religion, and morality." John Adams, *Colonial Declaration of Rights: Massachusetts*, *in* THE SEPARATION OF CHURCH AND STATE 33 (2011).
[367] A committee of delegates drafted the Constitution, with James Madison, Gouverneur Morris, and James Wilson playing key roles.
[368] CAUGHEY, *supra* note 16.
[369] Const. Rts. Found., *The Second Great Awakening and Reform in the 19th Century*, BILL OF RIGHTS IN ACTION, vol. 32, Winter 2017.
[370] Lawrence v. Texas, 539 U.S. 558 (2003) ("The absence of legal prohibitions focusing on homosexual conduct may be explained in part by noting that according to some scholars the concept of the homosexual as a distinct category of person did not emerge until the late 19th century. *See, e.g.*, JONATHAN NED KATZ, THE INVENTION OF HETEROSEXUALITY 10 (1995); D'EMILIO & FREEDMAN, *supra* note 338 ("The modern terms *homosexuality* and *heterosexuality* do not apply to an era that had not yet articulated these distinctions.").
[371] Green, *supra* note 125.
[372] Commonwealth v. Catlin, 1 Mass. (Will.) 8 (1804).
[373] Commonwealth v. Calef, 10 Mass. (9 Tyng) 153 (1813).
[374] Fowler v. State, 5 Day 81 (Conn. 1811).
[375] Knowles v. State, 3 Day 103 (Conn. 1808).
[376] *Id.* ("That no mountebank, tumbler, rope-dancer, master of puppet-shows, or other person or persons, shall exhibit, or cause to be exhibited, on any public stage or place whatsoever, within this state, any games, tricks, plays, shows, tumbling, rope-dancing, puppet-shows, or feats of uncommon dexterity or agility of body, or offer, vend or otherwise dispose of on any such stage, or place, to any persons so collected together, any drugs or medicines recommended to be useful in various disorders.").
[377] The U.S. Supreme Court cited *Fowler* (1811) in *Roth v. United States* in 1957 for the proposition that obscenity was outside the constitutional protections for speech and press, given the occurrence of the case after ratification of the Constitution. Roth v. United States, 354 U.S. 476, 483 (1957).
[378] Commonwealth v. Sharpless, 2 Serg. & Rawle 91 (Pa. 1815).
[379] Rex v. Curl (1 George II.), 2 Strange 788 (1727).
[380] Rex v. Crunden, 2 Camp. 89, 170 Eng. Rep. 1091 (1809).
[381] *Id.*
[382] Grisham v. State, 10 Tenn. 589 (1831).
[383] *Id.*
[384] *Id.*
[385] *Id.* at 596.
[386] *Offences Contra Bonos Mores*, 2 J. CRIM. L. 609 (1938).
[387] Nolin v. Mayor of Franklin, 12 Tenn. 163 (1833).
[388] State v. Roper, 18 N.C. 208, 208 (1835).
[389] Rex v. Crunden, 2 Camp. 89 (1809).
[390] *Roper*, 18 N.C. at 209.
[391] REVISED STATUTES OF THE STATE OF ARKANSAS 182 (1838).

[392] *Fundamental Agreement, or Original Constitution of the Colony of New Haven, June 4, 1639*, AVALON PROJECT., https://avalon.law.yale.edu/17th_century/ct01.asp (last visited Nov. 15, 2023).
[393] State v. Cagle, 2 Humph. 414 (Tenn. 1841).
[394] *Id.*
[395] *Id.*
[396] Britain v. State, 22 Tenn. (3 Hum.) 203, 204 (1842).
[397] THE REVISED STATUTES OF THE STATE OF NEW HAMPSHIRE PASSED DECEMBER 23, 1842, at 221 (1843).
[398] Ward v. Rock Against Racism, 491 U.S. 781 (1989).
[399] WILLIAM O. RUSSELL, A TREATISE ON CRIMES AND MISDEMEANORS 61 (1843).
[400] *Id.* at 60.
[401] *Id.* at 438.
[402] Harring v. Walrond, 1681, 1 Russ. Cr. 436 (1681).
[403] State v. Millard, 18 Vt. 574 (1846).
[404] *Id.*
[405] Miller v. People, 5 Barb. 203 (N.Y. App. Div. 1849).
[406] *Id.*
[407] Commonwealth v. Haynes, 68 Mass. (2 Gray) 72 (1854).
[408] EMER DE VATTEL, THE LAW OF NATIONS: OR PRINCIPLES OF THE LAW OF NATURE, APPLIED TO THE CONDUCT AND AFFAIRS OF NATIONS AND SOVEREIGNS. FROM THE FRENCH OF MONSIEUR DE VATTEL (Joseph Chitty & Edward D. Ingraham eds., 1853).
[409] JOHN FREDERICK ARCHBOLD, THE FORMS OF INDICTMENT: WITH THE EVIDENCE NECESSARY TO SUPPORT THEM : INCLUDING THE STATUTES WHICH MAKE MANY VALUABLE REGULATIONS RELATIVE TO CRIMINAL PROCEEDINGS ; CONTAINING ALSO, A TABLE SHOWING THOSE STATUTES WHICH HAVE BEEN REPEALED 317 (1828).
[410] State v. Moore, 31 Tenn. 136 (1851).
[411] State v. Cagle, 2 Humph. 414 (Tenn. 1841).
[412] Bell v. State, 31 Tenn. 42 (1851).
[413] *Cagle*, 2 Hum. 414.
[414] Bell, 31 Tenn. at 46.
[415] Barker v. Commonwealth, 19 Pa. 412 (1852).
[416] State v. Appling, 25 Mo. 315 (1857).
[417] Matal v. Tam, 582 U.S. 218 (2017).
[418] FRANCIS WHARTON, A TREATISE ON THE CRIMINAL LAW OF THE UNITED STATES 1919 et seq. (1855).
[419] McJunkins v. State, 10 Ind. 105 (1858).
[420] *Id.* at 109.
[421] *Id.*
[422] State v. Hazle, 20 Ark. 156 (1859).
[423] State v. Hanson, 23 Tex. 232 (1859).
[424] Jennings v. State, 16 Ind. 335, 335 (1861).
[425] THE PENAL CODE OF THE STATE OF TEXAS. ch. IV. art. 399 (1857).
[426] CODE OF IOWA § 2709 (1851).

[427] 69 LAWS UNDER CONSTITUTION OF 1851, at 352 (1862).
[428] 5 Geo. 4 ch. 83 (1824).
[429] DAVID FIELD, DRAFT OF A PENAL CODE FOR THE STATE OF NEW YORK (1864).
[430] Reg. v. Watson, 2 Cox C.C. 376 (1847).
[431] Reg. v. Webb, 2 Car. & K. 933, 175 Eng. Rep. 391 (1848).
[432] Rex v. Orchard, 3 Cox C.C. 248 (1848).
[433] Reg. v. Holmes, 169 E.R. 697 (1853).
[434] *Id.*
[435] *Id.* tit. III.
[436] *See generally The Influence of the Field Code: An Introduction to the Critical Issues*, KELLEN FUNK (Sept. 1, 2014), https://kellenfunk.org/field-code/the-influence-of-the-field-code-an-introduction/.
[437] *Id.*
[438] People *ex rel.* Campbell v. Bd. of Police Comm'rs, 43 N.Y.S. 118 (N.Y. App. Div. 1897), *app. dismissed*, 47 N.E. 1110 (1897).
[439] Commonwealth v. Lambert, 94 Mass. 177 (1866) (keeping of bawdy house).
[440] Commonwealth v. Wardell, 128 Mass. 52 (1880).
[441] State v. Juneau, 88 Wis. 180 (1894).
[442] Dameron v. State, 8 Mo. 494 (1844).
[443] People *ex rel.* Lee v. Bixby, 67 Barb. 221 (N.Y. 1875).
[444] State v. Ciancanelli, 45 P.3d 451 (Or. Ct. App. 2002), provided a good overview of nineteenth-century public indecency case law and statutes.
[445] Van Houten v. State, 46 N.J.L. 16 (1884).
[446] State v. Walter, 16 Del. 444 (1895).
[447] Block, *supra* note 46.
[448] FIELD, *supra* note 429.
[449] Estelle B. Freedman, *Sexuality in Nineteenth-Century America: Behavior, Ideology, and Politics*, 10 REVS. IN AM. HIST. 196 (1982).
[450] WILLIAM J. NOVAK, THE PEOPLE'S WELFARE: LAW AND REGULATION IN NINETEENTH-CENTURY AMERICA 189 (1996).
[451] *U.S. Immigrant Population and Share Over Time, 1850-Present*, MIGRATION POL'Y INST., https://www.migrationpolicy.org/programs/data-hub/charts/immigrant-population-over-time (last visited Dec. 8, 2023).
[452] Brown v. Bd. of Educ., 347 U.S. 483 (1954).
[453] Reynolds v. Sims, 377 U.S. 533 (1963).
[454] Miranda v. Arizona, 384 U.S. 436 (1966).
[455] *Id.*
[456] Loving v. Virginia, 388 U.S. 1 (1967)
[457] *In re* Davis, 51 Cal. Rptr. 702 (Cal. Ct. App. 1966).
[458] *Id.* at 667.
[459] "Indecent exposure" in CAL. PENAL CODE § 314 (West 2023) is still defined vaguely as follows:
Every person who willfully and lewdly, either:
1. Exposes his person, or the private parts thereof, in any public place, or in any place where there are present other persons to be offended or annoyed thereby; or,

2. Procures, counsels, or assists any person so to expose himself or take part in any model artist exhibition, or to make any other exhibition of himself to public view, or the view of any number of persons, such as is offensive to decency, or is adapted to excite to vicious or lewd thoughts or acts, is guilty of a misdemeanor.

The element of intent was added, requiring a showing of sexual motivation. Thus, a juvenile engaged in "mooning" was seeking to "affront" the audience and not guilty of indecent exposure. *In re* Smith, 497 P.2d 807 (Cal. 1972). The North Carolina Supreme Court reached a contrary conclusion in 1998 while protecting G-strings and thong bikinis, noting that the mooner in that case exposed his anus, genitals, or both while "mooning," even if no one saw them, where his conduct was intended to offend an unwilling audience. State v. Fly, 501 S.E.2d 656 (N.C. 1998). *See* Thomas L. Fowler, *Of Moons, Thongs, Holdings and Dicta: State v. Fly and the Rule of Law*, 22 CAMPBELL L. REV. 253 (2000). Theatrical performances (e.g., strip clubs) also were not prohibited by the North Carolina statute. *In re Smith*, 497 P.2d at 1972.

[460] Cotton, *supra* note 325. The New Haven colony enacted a specific prohibition of "unclean carriages" in 1642.

[461] Laura, *Why Adultery Is Not Considered a Crime in the United States*, LEICESTERSHIRE VILLAGES (Dec. 1, 2021), https://www.leicestershirevillages.com/is-adultery-considered-a-crime-in-the-usa/.

[462] *See, e.g.*, People v. Massicot, 118 Cal. Rptr. 2d 705 (Cal. Ct. App. 2002). Indecent exposure remains a common-law offense in some jurisdictions. Wisneski v. State, 921 A.2d 73 (Md. 2007); Kirkorian v. State, 196 A.2d 866 (Md. 1964); Duran v. State, 948 A.2d 139, *judgment aff'd*, 967 A.2d 184 (2009) (Md. Ct. Spec. App. 2008).

[463] See Appendix C for a brief description of each state's laws.

[464] Grant, *supra* note 31.

[465] Narvil, *supra* note 42, at 91.

[466] *Indecent Exposure*, 25 C.F.R. § 11.408 (2017) ("A person commits a misdemeanor if he or she exposes his or her genitals under circumstances in which he or she knows his or her conduct is likely to cause affront or alarm.").

[467] Other Sexual Misconduct, 10 U.S. CODE § 920c art. 120c sec. (c) (2023) ("Any person subject to this chapter who intentionally exposes, in an indecent manner, the genitalia, anus, buttocks, or female areola or nipple is guilty of indecent exposure and shall by punished as a court-martial may direct.").

[468] Jeff Burtka, *Indecent Exposure Laws by State*, FINDLAW (last rev'd May 17, 2021), https://www.findlaw.com/state/criminal-laws/indecent-exposure-laws-by-state.html. For an extensive table of statutes, list of modern case-law precedent, and index of terms, see Annotation, *Criminal Offense Predicated upon Indecent Exposure*, 94 A.L.R.2D 1353 (2023).

[469] *UC Berkeley's "Naked Guy" Dies in His Jail Cell*, L.A. TIMES (May 21, 2006, 12 AM PT), https://www.latimes.com/archives/la-xpm-2006-may-21-me-naked21-story.html.

[470] Alex Gangitano, *Top Five Naked British Protests*, POLITICS (Nov. 23, 2012, 12:00 AM), https://www.politics.co.uk/comment-analysis/2012/11/23/top-five-

naked-british-protests/. The British cases are interesting but beyond the scope of this study. *See, e.g.*, *Naked Protest* (Channel 4 (UK) broadcast), CULTURE UNPLUGGED, https://www.cultureunplugged.com/documentary/watch-online/play/5446/naked-protest (last visited Jan. 23, 2024).
[471] *Clothing Laws by State 2023*, WORLD POPULATION REV., https://worldpopulationreview.com/state-rankings/clothing-laws-by-state (last visited Dec. 9, 2023).
[472] Eline v. Town of Ocean City, 7 F.4th 214 (4th Cir. 2021). For further discussion of cases assessing statutes targeting exposure of female breasts, see Colin R. Harbke & Dana F. Lindemann, *Objectification and Reactions Toward Public Female Toplessness in the United States: Looking Beyond Legal Approval*, 27 SEXUALITY & CULTURE 104, 106 (2023).
[473] *Breastfeeding Laws*, NAT'L CONF. ST. LEGISLATURES (updated Aug. 26, 2021), https://www.ncsl.org/health/breastfeeding-state-laws.
[474] Duran v. State, 948 A.2d 139 (2008), *judgment aff'd*, 967 A.2d 184 (2009).
[475] Annotation, *Criminal Offense Predicated Upon Indecent Exposure*, *supra* note 468 ; People v. Ulman, 258 App Div. 262 (N.Y. App. Div. 1939).
[476] State v. Watts, 2021 UT 60 (Utah 2021).
[477] The statute was revised to remove this element. It was a carryover expression from Roth v. United States, 354 U.S. 476 (1957). Only Louisiana and Virginia statutes currently use this term.
[478] Rollins v. State, 181 A.3d 958 (Md. Ct. Spec. App. 2017).
[479] *Id.*
[480] Wisneski v. State, 921 A.2d 73 (Md. 2007).
[481] Messina v. State, 130 A.2d 578 (Md. 1957).
[482] People v. Smith, 147 Cal. Rptr. 3d 314 (Cal. Ct. App. 2012) (interpreting CAL. PENAL CODE § 314, subd. 1).
[483] Annotation, *What Constitutes "Public Place" Within Meaning of State Statute or Local Ordinance Prohibiting Indecency or Commission of Sexual Act in Public Place*, 95 A.L.R.5TH 229 (2023).
[484] Abbott v. State, 163 Tenn. 384 (1931).
[485] *Id.*
[486] Grisham v. State, 10 Tenn. 589 (1831).
[487] *See, e.g.*, cases cited in Annotation, *Criminal Offense Predicated Upon Indecent Exposure*, *supra* note 468; J.B. B., *Criminal Law and Procedure: Indecent Exposure: Nudism*, 33 MICH. L. REV. 936 (1935).
[488] Theodore Bennett, *State of Undress: Law, Carnival and Mass Public Nudity Events*, 29 GRIFFITH L. REV. 199 (2020).
[489] Washington v. Thompson, No. 84366-4-I (Wash. Ct. App. Aug. 28, 2023).
[490] Woodlands Pride, Inc. v. Paxton, No. 4:23-cv-02847, 2023 U.S. Dist. LEXIS 171268 (S.D. Tex. 2023).
[491] *See also* People v. Massicot, 118 Cal. Rptr. 2d 705 (2002) (finding that a man showing off wearing women's lingerie under a robe to a female hotel clerk had not exposed his "person").
[492] State v. Plenty Horse, 741 N.W.2d 763, 764 (S.D. 2007).
[493] State v. Streath, 327 S.E.2d 240, 244 (N.C. Ct. App. 1985), *cert. denied*, 329 S.E.2d 402 (N.C. 1985). *Cf.* People v. Anonymous Female, 539 N.Y.S.2d 868, 871 (Buffalo City Ct. 1989).

[494] Case v. Commonwealth, 231 S.W.2d 86 (Ky. 1950).
[495] Mainly public bathroom exposures.
[496] *See, e.g.*, S.F., CAL., POLICE CODE art. 2 § 154 (2013) ("Prohibiting Public Nudity"), https://codelibrary.amlegal.com/codes/san_francisco/latest/sf_police/0-0-0-9618.
[497] *See, e.g.*, CAL. PENAL CODE § 314 (West 2023) ; People v. Honan, 111 Cal. Rptr. 3d 351 (Cal. Ct. App. 2010), *rev. denied* (Oct. 13, 2010).
[498] Annotation, *Criminal Offense Predicated upon Indecent Exposure*, *supra* note 468. Indecent exposure does not require visual observation of the exposure by others. NEV. REV. STAT. ANN. § 201.220(1) (West 2023); State v. Castaneda, 245 P.3d 550 (Nev. 2010), *opinion modified on denial of reh'g*, State v. Castaneda, 2010 WL 5559401 (Nev. 2010). Contrary view: Indecent exposure is essentially a visual-assault crime. The state needs to produce a victim who saw the defendant's genitals. IOWA CODE ANN. § 709.9 (West 2023); State v. Isaac, 756 N.W.2d 817 (Iowa 2008).
[499] Not always true. "As female breasts are not private parts or genitalia, exposure thereof, without more, is not lewd act within meaning of open lewdness statute." State v. Crenshaw, 597 P.2d 13 (Haw. 1979).
[500] Not always true. In State v. King, 201 S.E.2d 724 (N.C. Ct. App. 1974), the North Carolina Supreme Court rejected the notion that the audience must be annoyed or offended by the exposure in a case against strippers in a paid admission adult entertainment venue.
[501] Annotation, *Criminal Offense Predicated upon Indecent Exposure*, *supra* note 468. Where defendant removed her bathing suit on public beach and was nude as she played ball, waved at passing boat, slowly applied suntan lotion to frontal portion of her body and sunbathed with knees approximately twelve to eighteen inches apart, evidence did not establish beyond reasonable doubt crime of public lewdness. People v. Gilbert, 338 N.Y.S.2d 457 (City Crim. Ct. 1972).
[502] State v. Schramel, 581 N.W.2d 400 (Minn. Ct. App. 1998).
[503] Annotation, *Criminal Offense Predicated upon Indecent Exposure*, *supra* note 468. Evidence that defendants, while patrons of nude dancing bar, paid for, encouraged, or otherwise directly involved themselves in obscene behavior of dancers employed by the bar was sufficient to support conviction for lewd and lascivious behavior in violation of indecent exposure statute. MINN. STAT. § 617.23(a)(3) (1996); State v. Duncan, 605 N.W.2d 745 (Minn. Ct. App. 2000).
[504] Indecent exposure statute requires proof that the defendant's conduct would tend to cause offense or fear to a reasonable person. COLO. REV. STAT. ANN. § 18-7-302(1) (West 2023); People v. Barrus, 232 P.3d 264 (Colo. App. 2009), *as modified on denial of reh'g* (Mar. 4, 2010) and *cert. denied*, 2010 WL 2582827 (Colo. 2010).
[505] If the actor's intent is not immoral, there may be no offense. For instance, in *In re* Dallas W., 102 Cal. Rptr. 2d 493 (Cal. Ct. App. 2000), *as modified on denial of reh'g* (Jan. 17, 2001), the defendant juvenile who bared his buttocks to oncoming traffic was not guilty of indecent exposure because he did not do so to arouse his or his audience's sexual desire or for his or his audience's gratification.

[506] For instance, Professor Schwart evidenced no awareness of history in her critique of the open lewdness provision in the Model Penal Code. Louis B. Schwartz, *Morals Offenses and the Model Penal Code Symposium on the Model Penal Code*, 63 COLUM: L. REV. 669, 675–76 (1963).
[507] *E.g.*, Stone, *supra* note 7, at 720 (commenting on *Sedley's Case* (1663): "This was a conviction for breach of the peace (contra pacem) for causing the mob to become unruly, rather than for expression as such.").
[508] *See generally* Annotation, *Validity of State and Municipal Indecent Exposure Statutes and Ordinances*, 71 A.L.R.6TH 283 (2023).
[509] Dobbs v. Jackson Women's Health Org., 142 S. Ct. 2228 (2022).
[510] Miller v. California, 413 U.S. 15, 34 (1973); P. Brooks Fuller et al., *Porn Wars: Serious Value, Social Harm, and the Burdens of Modern Obscenity Doctrine*, 28 AM. UNIV. J. GENDER, SOC. POL'Y & L. 121, 128 (2020) ("The obscenity doctrine focuses solely on sex. The doctrine excludes whole swaths of explicit, non-sexual material from the *Miller* obscenity definition. Although their literary, artistic, political, or scientific value is not presumed, depictions of excretory activities, depictions of gore and violence, and misogynist or racist language do not implicate *Miller*.").
[511] Labine v. Vincent, 401 U.S. 532 (1971).
[512] BENJAMIN N. CARDOZA, PARADOXES OF LEGAL SCIENCE 37 (1927).
[513] Commonwealth v. Turner, 26 Va. 678 (1827).
[514] Henkin, *supra* note 1.
[515] Title VII, 42 U.S.C §§ 2000e - 2000e-17 (2023). There is no distinction between theistic and nontheistic religions.
[516] Lawrence v. Texas, 539 U.S. 558 (2003) (overruling Bowers v. Hardwick, 478 U.S. 186 (1986)) (citing, with approval, *Bowers* (Stevens, J., dissenting)).
[517] Dobbs v. Jackson Women's Health Org., 142 S. Ct. 2228, 2306 (2022).
[518] Roe v. Commonwealth, 405 S.W.2d 25 (1966). Establishment Clause and free-exercise objections were raised but not addressed by the court in declaring a statute regulating nudist societies an unreasonable exercise of police power due to the economic burdens it imposed. The statute was revised to remove the objectionable provisions. KY. REV. STAT. ANN. § 232.021 (West 2023).
[519] MARK D. HALL, DID AMERICA HAVE A CHRISTIAN FOUNDING? SEPARATING MODERN MYTH FROM HISTORICAL TRUTH (2019).
[520] *In Their Own Words: How Americans Describe "Christian Nationalism,"* PEW RES. CTR. (Oct. 27, 2022), https://www.pewresearch.org/religion/2022/10/27/in-their-own-words-how-americans-describe-christian-nationalism/.
[521] For a basic explanation of these types of challenges, see, e.g., IDLEMAN, CONSTITUTIONAL LAW—FACIAL V. AS-APPLIED CHALLENGES (Spring 2023), https://law.marquette.edu/sites/default/files/Facial%20v.%20As-Applied%20Challenges.pdf.
[522] The focus here is the effect of the law generally, not the consequences of a specific criminal act and experience.
[523] *See* Dobbs v. Jackson Women's Health Org., 142 S. Ct. 2228 (2022).
[524] BREYER, *supra* note 28.
[525] There is an enormous body of scholarly literature debating the meaning of these clauses that is beyond the scope of this publication.

[526] Cantwell v. Connecticut, 310 U.S. 296, 303 (1940).
[527] MICHAEL J. MALBIN, RELIGION AND POLITICS: THE INTENTIONS OF THE AUTHORS OF THE 1ST AMENDMENT 3 (1978).
[528] 1 ANNALS OF CONG. 434 (1789).
[529] *Id.* at 436.
[530] *Id.* at 730.
[531] *Id.*
[532] *Id.*
[533] *Id.* at 732.
[534] MALBIN, *supra* note 527, at 10–11.
[535] 1 ANNALS OF CONG. 766 (1789).
[536] 1 JOURNAL OF THE 1ST SESSION OF THE SENATE 77 (1789).
[537] MALBIN, *supra* note 527, at 13.
[538] *Id.* at 14.
[539] Michael Stokes Paulsen, *Freedom for Religion*, YALE L.J.F. (Dec. 4, 2023). https://www.yalelawjournal.org/pdf/PaulsenYLJForumEssay_tatbqq3s.pdf. (last visited Dec. 7, 2023). Paulsen makes a strong argument that the Religion Clauses were meant to promote religion, not to divorce the government from it.
[540] MALBIN, *supra* note 527.
[541] Kenneth R. Bowling, Politics in the 1st Congress, 1789-1791 (1968) (Ph.D. dissertation, University of Wisconsin).
[542] Allison M. Dussias, *Indigenous Religious Rights in the United States*, *in* INTERNATIONAL PERSPECTIVE ON INDIGENOUS RELIGIOUS RIGHTS 140–60 (2023).
[543] 1 ANNALS OF CONG. 766 (1789).
[544] MALBIN, *supra* note 527, at 11.
[545] *Thomas Jefferson and the Virginia Statute for Religious Freedom*, VA. HIST., https://virginiahistory.org/learn/thomas-jefferson-and-virginia-statute-religious-freedom#:~:text=The%20Virginia%20Statute%20for%20Religious%20Freedom%20is%20a,of%20the%20first%20amendment%20protections%20for%20religious%20freedom (last visited Dec. 9, 2023).
[546] MALBIN, *supra* note 527, at 23.
[547] *Id.* at 21–22 (citing Gallard Hunt, *James Madison and Religious Liberty*, *in* 1 Annual Report of the American Historical Association, H.R. Doc. No. 702, 57th Cong., 1st Sess. 163, 166–67 (1901).) Madison's proposal reiterated much of an earlier proposal by George Mason but substituted "free exercise" for "fullest toleration in the exercise."
[548] *Id.* at 22.
[549] *Id.* (quoting Gallard Hunt, *James Madison and Religious Liberty*, *in* 1 Annual Report of the American Historical Association, H.R. Doc. No. 702, 57th Cong., 1st Sess. 163, 167 (1901).)
[550] Madison was a Princeton graduate and well-schooled in Greek and Roman literature.
[551] JAMES MADISON, *Notes of Speech Against Assessments for Support of Religion*, *in* 2 THE WRITINGS OF JAMES MADISON 88 (Gallard Hunt ed., 1901).

[552] JAMES MADISON, *Memorial and Remonstrance Against Religious Assessments*, in 2 THE WRITINGS OF JAMES MADISON 186 (Gallard Hunt ed., 1901).
[553] *Id.* at 5.
[554] *Id.*
[555] *Id.* at 187; *see also* FRANK SWANCARA, THOMAS JEFFERSON VERSUS RELIGIOUS OPPRESSION 72–73 (1969) (discussing letter from Madison to Robert Smith, written in 1819, denying the necessity of an established religion to survival of civil government).
[556] JOHN LOCKE, A LETTER CONCERNING TOLERATION 15 (Bobbs-Merrill 2d ed. 1955); *see* Gerald Sandler, *Lockean Ideas in Thomas Jefferson's Bill for Establishing Religious Freedom*, 21 J. HIST. IDEAS 110 (1960).
[557] LOCKE, *supra* note 556.
[558] *Id.* at 17.
[559]*Id.* at 17, 18, 29, 39.
[560] *Id.* at 19.
[561] *Id.* at 24.
[562] *Id.*
[563] JOHN LOCKE, OF CIVIL GOVERNMENT AND TOLERATION 176 (1895). This concern had been a reality in contention between the church and state in England and may have played a role in *Sedley's Case* (1663).
[564] *Id.* at 169.
[565] *Indolent*, DICTIONARY.COM, https://www.dictionary.com/browse/indolent (defining "indolent" as "having or showing a disposition to avoid exertion; slothful").
[566] LOCKE, *supra* note 563, at 176.
[567] *Id.* at 172.
[568] *Id.* at 182.
[569] *Id.* at 187.
[570] *Id.* at 160.
[571] *Id.* at 180. Locke believed in a discoverable natural law resulting from intuition, careful reason, or divine revelation. THE PALGRAVE HANDBOOK OF RELIGION AND STATE VOLUME I: THEORETICAL PERSPECTIVES 92 (Shannon Holzer ed., 2023).
[572] LOCKE, *supra* note 563.
[573] Robert Dennis Hall, John Locke and Natural Human Rights: An Inconsistency Between His Metaphysical/Epistemological Positions and His Moral/Political Theories (1981) (Ph.D. dissertation, St. John's University), https://www.proquest.com/docview/303136521/abstract/44FF13CCE82B4D4CPQ/1. Hall engages in an extensive discussion of Locke's ambivalence about the roles of rationalism and hedonism in natural rights theory.
[574] Gal. 5:13-15 (KJV).
[575] Gal. 5:16-26 (NKJV; KJV).
[576] Gal. 5:17 (KJV).
[577] Gal. 5:22-23 (KJV).
[578] Rom. 13:1a; Paul D. Feinberg, *The Christian and Civil Authorities*, 10 MASTER'S SEMINARY J. 87 (1999).

[579] John Locke, *5. John Locke (1632-1704), Letter on Toleration, 1686*, *in* TOLERANCE: THE BEACON OF THE ENLIGHTENMENT 22–23 (Caroline Warman et al., ed. and trans., Open Book Publishers, 2017), http://books.openedition.org/obp/2954.
[580] LOCKE, *supra* note 563, at 176.
[581] *Id.*
[582] *Id.* at 186.
[583] Feinberg, *supra* note 578, at 87.
[584] *Commonplace Book, Feb. 10, 1814*, *in* 6 H.A. WASHINGTON, THE WRITINGS OF THOMAS JEFFERSON: 1760–1775, at 315 (1892); VI THOMAS JEFFERSON, THE WRITINGS OF THOMAS JEFFERSON: BEING HIS AUTOBIOGRAPHY, CORRESPONDENCE, REPORTS, MESSAGES, ADDRESSES, AND OTHER WRITINGS, OFFICIAL AND PRIVATE (H.A. Washington ed., 1861), https://www.gutenberg.org/files/55075/55075-h/55075-h.htm. Jefferson was critical of *Blackstone's Commentaries*, writing in a letter from Thomas Jefferson to Judge John Tyler (June 17, 1812), 13 THOMAS JEFFERSON, THE WRITINGS OF THOMAS JEFFERSON 165, 165–67 (Andrew A. Lipscomb ed., 1903), that he would be pleased to see circumstances "uncanonize Blackstone whose book although the most elegant and best digested of our law catalogue has been perverted more than all others to the degeneracy of legal science. A student finds there a smattering of everything and his indolence easily persuades him that if he understands that book he is master of the whole body of the law."
[585] *Letter to Peter Carr, August 10, 1787*, *in* 2 H.A. WASHINGTON, THE WRITINGS OF THOMAS JEFFERSON: 1740-1826, at 239 (2018), at 239 (2018).
[586] *Letter to M. Dupont De Nemours, April 24, 1816*, *in* 6 H.A. WASHINGTON, THE WRITINGS OF THOMAS JEFFERSON: 1740-1826, at 592 (2018).
[587] THOMAS JEFFERSON, THE COMPLETE JEFFERSON 355 (S. Padover ed., 1943).
[588] *Id.* at 675.
[589] *Id.* at 676.
[590] 1 THOMAS JEFFERSON, THE PAPERS OF THOMAS JEFFERSON: 1760-1776, at 549 (Julian P. Boyd ed., 2018) (in his notes on Locke).
[591] ROBERT M. HEALEY, JEFFERSON ON RELIGION IN PUBLIC EDUCATION 26 (1926) (letter to Charles Thomson dated Jan. 9, 1816); *see also id.* (letter to Benjamin Rush dated Apr. 21, 1803 ("I am a Christian, in the only sense in which he wished any one to be; sincerely attached to his doctrines, in preference to all others; ascribing to himself every human excellence; and believing he never claimed any other. At the short intervals since these conversations, when I could justifiably abstract my mind from public affairs, the subject has been under my contemplation.").
[592] *Id.*
[593] *Id.* (from a letter to Ezra Stiles, June 25, 1819).
[594] CONST. OF CONN. § 4 (1776).
[595] MD. CONST. art. XXXIII (1776).
[596] N.Y. CONST. art. I, § XXXVI (1777) ("And whereas we are required, by the benevolent principles of rational liberty, not only to expel civil tyranny, but also to guard against that spiritual oppression and intolerance wherewith the bigotry and ambition of weak and wicked priests and princes have scourged mankind,

this convention doth further, in the name and by the authority of the good people of this State, ordain, determine, and declare, that the free exercise and enjoyment of religious profession and worship, without discrimination or preference, shall forever hereafter be allowed, within this State, to all mankind: Provided, That the liberty of conscience, hereby granted, shall not be so construed as to excuse acts of licentiousness, or justify practices inconsistent with the peace or safety of this State.").

[597] *E.g.*, MASS. CONST. (1779); DEL. CONST. § 1 (1792); MISS. CONST. art. VII, §§ 5, 14 (1832); KAN. CONST. § 7 (1855).

[598] CONST. OF CONN. § 3 (1776); MD. CONST. art. XXXIII (1776); N.Y. CONST. art. XXXVII (1777); MISS. CONST. art. I § 3 (1817); CAL. CONST. § 4 (1849); NEV. CONST. art. I § 4 (1864).

[599] PROCEEDING AND DEBATES OF THE NEW YORK CONSTITUTIONAL CONVENTION 462 et seq. (1821).

[600] People v. Ruggles, 8 Johns. 290 (N.Y. Sup. Ct. 1811).

[601] PROCEEDING AND DEBATES, *supra* note 599 at 462, 463 (1821).

[602] *Id.* at 463.

[603] *Id.*

[604] *Ruggles*, 8 Johns. at 292.

[605] *Id.*

[606] *Id.* at 295.

[607] *Id.* at 294–95.

[608] *Id.* at 293 (quoting Rex v. Woolston, 2 Str. 834 (1729).

[609] In some jurisdictions, even dispassionate, rational, verbal criticism of Christianity was not tolerated. *See, e.g.*, Updegraph v. Commonwealth, 11 Serg. & Rawle 394 (Pa. 1824) (involving prosecution of debate society member for saying "Holy Scriptures were a mere fable: . . . a contradiction . . ., although they contained a number of good things, yet they contained a great many lies").

[610] PROCEEDING AND DEBATES OF THE NEW YORK CONSTITUTIONAL CONVENTION 463 (1821).

[611] 8 WILLIAM MACK & WILLIAM BENJAMIN HALE, CORPUS JURIS: BEING A COMPLETE AND SYSTEMATIC STATEMENT OF THE WHOLE BODY OF THE LAW AS EMBODIED IN AND DEVELOPED BY ALL REPORTED DECISIONS 1117 (1917).

[612] Commonwealth v. Kneeland, 37 Mass. 206 (1838).

[613] *Id.* at 219.

[614] DAVID MCALLISTER, THE NATIONAL REFORM MOVEMENT 16 (1898), *quoted in* ANSON P. STOKES & LEO PFEFFER, CHURCH AND STATE IN THE UNITED STATES 241 (1964).

[615] *The NRA (National Reform Association) and the Christian Amendment*, CONST. PRINCIPLE: SEPARATION OF CHURCH & ST., https://candst.tripod.com/nra.htm (last visited Jan. 26, 2024).

[616] ANSON P. STOKES & LEO PFEFFER, CHURCH AND STATE IN THE UNITED STATES 242 (1964).

[617] *Id.*

[618] *Id.* at 243.

[619] *Id.*

[620] Gregory A. Smith et al., *45% of Americans Say U.S. Should Be a "Christian Nation,"* PEW RES. CTR. (Oct. 27, 2022),

https://www.pewresearch.org/religion/2022/10/27/45-of-americans-say-u-s-should-be-a-christian-nation/. See this study for more detailed views on the subject.
[620] *Views of the U.S. as a "Christian Nation" and Opinions About "Christian Nationalism,"* PEW RES. CTR'S RELIGION & PUB. LIFE PROJECT (blog) (Oct. 27, 2022), https://www.pewresearch.org/religion/2022/10/27/views-of-the-u-s-as-a-christian-nation-and-opinions-about-christian-nationalism/.
[621] *Id.*
[622] Meaning "Muslim."
[623] PFEFFER, *supra* note 619, at 243.
[624] *Id.*
[625] Vidal v. Philadelphia, 2 Howard 127 (U.S. 1844).
[626] PFEFFER, *supra* note 619, at 245.
[627] *Id.* Story had authored an article previously, arguing that Christianity was a part of the common law. Joseph Story, *Christianity a Part of the Common Law*, 9 AM. JURIST 346 (1833).
[628] Reynolds v. United States, 98 U.S. 145 (1879); Donald L. Drakeman, *Why Do We Think the Framers Wanted to Separate Church and State?*, *in* THE PALGRAVE HANDBOOK OF RELIGION AND STATE VOLUME II, at 635 (Shannon Holzer ed., 2023), https://doi.org/10.1007/978-3-031-35609-4_26.
[629] Drakeman, *supra* note 628, at 637.
[630] *See, e.g.*, Daniel L. Driesbach, *Thomas Jefferson and the Mammoth Cheese*, ACTON INST. (July 20, 2010), https://www.acton.org/pub/religion-liberty/volume-12-number-3/thomas-jefferson-and-mammoth-cheese.
[631] *Id.* Jefferson's verbatim statement: "Believing with you that religion is a matter which lies solely between Man & his God, that he owes account to none other for his faith or his worship, that the legitimate powers of government reach actions only, & not opinions, I contemplate with sovereign reverence that act of the whole American people which declared that their legislature should 'make no law respecting an establishment of religion, or prohibiting the free exercise thereof,' thus building a wall of separation between Church & State."
[632] JOSEPH STORY, COMMENTARIES ON THE CONSTITUTION 462 (1833).
[633] The Virginia Statute for Religious Freedom was drafted by Thomas Jefferson and passed by the Virginia General Assembly on January 16, 1786. It declared that no one can be compelled to support any religious worship or ministry, and that all people have the right to choose their own religious beliefs without interference from the government.
[634] Reynolds v. United States, 98 U.S. 145, 165 (1879).
[635] As to Justice Waite's concern that polygamy leads to patriarchy, the long-running reality TV show *Sister Wives* provides evidence to the contrary. *Sister Wives* (TLC), https://www.tlc.com/shows/sister-wives.
[636] Joanna L. Grossman & Lawrence M. Friedman, *The Chosen Few: Polyamory and the Law*, VERDICT (Apr. 6, 2021), https://verdict.justia.com/2021/04/06/the-chosen-few-polyamory-and-the-law.
[637] Murphy v. Ramsey, 114 U.S. 15 (1885).
[638] *Id.* at 45.

[639] Davis v. Beason, 133 U.S. 333, 341 (1890), *overruled by* Romer v. Evans, 517 U.S. 620 (1996); *see also* arguments of counsel for appellant and opinion, *id.* at 342.
[640] Late Corp. of Church of Jesus Christ v. United States, 136 U.S. 1, 49 (1890) (Bradley, J.).
[641] *Id.*
[642] *Beason*, 133 U.S. at 341.
[643] *Id.* at 343.
[644] PFEFFER, *supra* note 619, at 645.
[645] Reynolds v. United States, 98 U.S. 145, 166 (1879); *Davis*, 133 U.S. at 342; *see, e.g.*, Late Corp. of Church of Jesus Christ, 136 U.S. at 50 (1890).
[646] *Beason*, 133 U.S. at 342.
[647] CHRISTOPHER G. TIEDEMAN, A TREATISE ON THE LIMITATIONS OF POLICE POWER IN THE UNITED STATES 167 (1886).
[648] WILLIAM PERKINS, A GOLDEN *Chain:* OR THE DESCRIPTION OF *Theologie,* CONTAINING THE ORDER OF THE CAUSES OF *Salvation* AND DAMNATION, ACCORDING TO GOD'S WORD (2021) (1600). Perkins was one of the leaders of the Puritan movement. Chapter 30 is entitled "Christian Warfare." (2021).
[649] *Id.* at 85.
[650] *Id.* at 129.
[651] Vincent Stark, *Public Morality as a Police Power After* Lawrence v. Texas *and* Gonzales v. Carhart, 10 GEO. J. GENDER L. 165 (2009), https://heinonline.org/HOL/P?h=hein.journals/grggenl10&i=167.
[652] 4 WILLIAM BLACKSTONE, BLACKSTONE'S COMMENTARIES 162 (1765).
[653] Prigg v. Pennsylvania, 41 U.S. 539 (1842).
[654] *Id.* at 625.
[655] Lawton v. Steele, 152 U.S. 133, 136 (1894); *accord* Lochner v. New York, 198 U.S. 45, 53 (1905); Near v. Minnesota, 283 U.S. 697 (1931) (stating that the authority of the State to enact laws to protect the morals of its people is "necessarily admitted").
[656] Leisy v. Hardin, 135 U.S. 100 (1890) (citing cases), *superseded by statute as stated in* Granholm v. Heald, 544 U.S. 460 (2005).
[657] Stone v. Mississippi, 101 U.S. 814, 819 (1879); *cf.* Manigault v. Springs, 199 U.S. 473, 480 (1905) (stating that sovereign right of government to protect the morals of the people is paramount to any rights under contracts between individuals).
[658] The validity of *Reynolds* was questioned in Patrick v. LeFevre, 745 F.2d 153 (2d Cir. 1984), in which the Second Circuit observed that courts had "jettisoned the objective, content-based approach previously employed to define religious belief . . . in favor of a more subjective definition of religion, which examines an individual's inward attitudes towards a particular belief system." *Id.* at 157 (citations omitted).
[659] Winters v. New York, 333 U.S. 507, 515 (1948).
[660] Poe v. Ullman, 367 U.S. 497, 539 (1961) (Harlan, J., dissenting).
[661] Church of the Holy Trinity v. United States, 143 U.S. 457, 465 (1892).
[662] Everson v. Bd. of Educ., 330 U.S. 1 (1947).
[663] *Id.* at 8.
[664] *Id.* at 16–17.

[665] *See, e.g.*, STEPHEN GARTON, SEXUAL REVOLUTION, IN HISTORIES OF SEXUALITY ANTIQUITY TO SEXUAL REVOLUTION 210–28 (2004).
[666] Lemon v. Kurtzman, 403 U.S. 602 (1971).
[667] Kennedy v. Bremerton Sch. Dist., 142 S. Ct. 2407 (2022).
[668] Epperson v. Arkansas, 393 U.S. 97, 103–04 (1968).
[669] Tilton v. Richardson, 403 U.S. 672, 678 (1971) (opinion by Chief Justice Berger in which Justices Harlan, Stewart, and Blackman concurred); *cf.* Gillette v. United States, 401 U.S. 437, 450 (1971) (opinion by Justice Marshall joined by Justice Blackman and others) ("the Establishment Clause stands at least for the proposition that when government activities touch on the religious sphere, they must be secular in purpose, evenhanded in operation, and neutral in primary impact."); Mitchell v. Helms, 530 U.S. 793 (2000) (holding that law providing government aid to both public and private schools that did not result in religious indoctrination by the government nor define its recipients by reference to religion did not advance religion in violation of the Establishment Clause).
[670] *Kennedy*, 142 S. Ct. at 2421.
[671] City of Ocala v. Rojas, 143 S. Ct. 764 (2023).
[672] CHRISTOPHER SAINT GERMAN & WILLIAM MUCHALL, THE DOCTOR AND STUDENT: OR, DIALOGUES BETWEEN A DOCTOR OF DIVINITY AND A STUDENT IN THE LAWS OF ENGLAND: CONTAINING THE GROUNDS OF THOSE LAWS TOGETHER WITH QUESTIONS AND CASES CONCERNING THE EQUITY THEREOF 10 (1787). This treatise was available to students of the law during the colonial period.
[673] Epperson v. Arkansas, 393 U.S. 97, 103–04 (1968).
[674] *Id.* at 103.
[675] *Id.* at 107–08 (Douglas, J., dissenting) (quoting Robert Leflar, *Legal Liability for the Exercise of Free Speech*, 10 ARK. L. REV. 155, 158 (1956)). The same can be said for obscenity laws. *See* United States v. 12 200-Ft. Reels of Super 8mm Film, 413 U.S. 123, 131 (1973) (Douglas, J., dissenting) (stating that nineteenth-century punishment of obscene libels was a "retention by the States of vestiges of established religious after the enactment of the Establishment and Free Exercise Clauses . . . .").
[676] Scopes v. State, 154 Tenn. 105 (1927).
[677] *Epperson*, 393 U.S. at 109.
[678] Burstyn v. Wilson, 343 U.S. 495, 505 (1952) (opinion by Justice Clark) (lifting ban on sacrilegious film *The Miracle*).
[679] McGowan v. Maryland, 366 U.S. 420 (1961).
[680] *Id.* at 434, 442, 450 et seq.
[681] Myers v. United States, 272 U.S. 52, 175–76 (1926), *cited with approval in* Brennan v. U.S. Postal Serv., 439 U.S. 1345, 1347 (1978).
[682] BRIAN HOFFMAN, NAKED: A CULTURAL HISTORY OF AMERICAN NUDISM (2015).
[683] *See, e.g.*, White Tail Park, Inc. v. Stroube, 413 F.3d 451 (4th Cir. 2005); Elysium Inst. v. Cty. of L.A., 232 Cal. App. 3d 408 (Cal. App. Dep't Super. Ct. 1991).

[684] *List of Social Nudity Places in North America*, WIKIPEDIA, https://en.wikipedia.org/wiki/List_of_social_nudity_places_in_North_America#United_States (last visited Dec. 9, 2023).
[685] Torcaso v. Watkins, 367 U.S. 488, 495 (1961); *accord* Everson v. Bd. of Educ., 330 U.S. 1, 15 (1947).
[686] WEBSTER'S NEW WORLD DICTIONARY 1134 (2d college ed. 1970).
[687] Raja Muhammad Mustansar Javaid, *Religious Wisdom: Modesty & Modest Dresses in Islam & Christianity*, MEDIUM (blog) (June 9, 2022), https://mustansarjavaid.medium.com/religious-wisdom-modesty-modest-dresses-in-islam-christianity-1474d3545fa5.
[688] Virginia Villa, *Women in Many Countries Face Harassment for Clothing Deemed Too Religious—or Too Secular*, PEW RSCH. CTR. (blog). (Dec. 16, 2020), https://www.pewresearch.org/short-reads/2020/12/16/women-in-many-countries-face-harassment-for-clothing-deemed-too-religious-or-too-secular/.
[689] Katharina Buchholz, *Where Women's Headscarves Are Regulated* (infographic), STATISTA (Feb. 1, 2021), https://www.statista.com/chart/24065/rules-laws-about-womens-head-coverings.
[690] Sch. Dist. of Abington Twp. v. Schempp, 374 U.S. 203, 225 (1963).
[691] *Id.* at 215, 226; *accord* Walz v. Tax Comm'n of N.Y., 397 U.S. 664, 694 (1970) (separate opinion of Justice Harlan); Welsh v. United States, 398 U.S. 333 (1970) (Harlan, J., concurring).
[692] Church of the Holy Trinity v. United States, 143 U.S. 457 (1892).
[693] Zorach v. Clauson, 343 U.S. 306, 313–14 (1952) (Jackson, J., Frankfurter, and Black, JJ., dissenting).
[694] WILLIAM BLAKELY, AMERICAN STATE PAPERS ON FREEDOM OF RELIGION 183 (3d ed. 1943).
[695] Engel v. Vitale, 370 U.S. 421 (1962).
[696] *Zorach*, 343 U.S. at 314.
[697] Harris v. McRae, 448 U.S. 297 (1980).
[698] *Id.* at 319.
[699] Jeremiah S. Black, *Religious Liberty*, *in* JEREMIAH S. BLACK, ESSAYS AND SPEECHES 51, 53 (1886), *quoted in* McCollum v. Bd. of Educ., 333 U.S. 203, 219 (1948) (Frankfurter, J., concurring); *cf.* ELIHU ROOT, ADDRESSES ON GOVERNMENT AND CITIZENSHIP 137, 140 (Robert Bacon & James B. Scott eds., 1916) (referring to "the great American principle of eternal separation" between church and state), *quoted in McCollum*, 333 U.S. at 219.
[700] Lemon v. Kurtzman, 403 U.S. 602, 614 (1971) (involving state aid to church-related elementary and secondary schools).
[701] United States v. Seeger, 380 U.S. 163 (1965) (Douglas, J., concurring in a separate opinion).
[702] Note, *Toward a Constitutional Definition of Religion*, 91 HARV. L. REV. 1056, 1064 n.56 (1978).
[703] Selective Draft Law Cases, 245 U.S. 366, 389–90 (1918).
[704] *Seeger*, 380 U.S. at 172.
[705] *Id.* at 174.
[706] *Id.* at 186–87.
[707] *Id.* at 176.
[708] Welsh v. United States, 398 U.S. 333 (1970).

[709] *Id.* at 339.
[710] *Id.* at 341.
[711] *Id.*
[712] *Id.* at 356.
[713] *Id.*
[714] Walz v. Tax Comm'n of N.Y., 397 U.S. 664, 695 (1970).
[715] Wisconsin v. Yoder, 406 U.S. 205, 210–11 (1972).
[716] *Id.* at 215.
[717] *Id.* at 216.
[718] Brown v. Dade Christian Sch., Inc., 556 F.2d 310, 324 (5th Cir. 1977).
[719] Brown v. Pena, 441 F. Supp. 1382, 1384 (S.D. Fla. 1977).
[720] Theriault v. Carlson, 495 F.2d 390 (5th Cir.), *cert. denied*, 419 U.S. 1003 (1974); *see also Brown*, 441 F. Supp. 1382.
[721] Marc Galanter, *Religious Freedoms in the United States: A Turning Point?*, 1966 WISC. L. REV. 217, 270 (1966).
[722] *Brown*, 556 F.2d at 324.
[723] United States v. Kuch, 288 F. Supp. 439 (D.D.C. 1968)). The court held that the First Amendment protects the right to have and to express beliefs but has not given protection to acts done in the name of or under the impetus of religion.
[724] People v. Woody, 394 P.2d 813 (Cal. 1964).
[725] *Kuch*, 288 F. Supp. at 449–50.
[726] *Id.* at 446.
[727] Sherbert v. Verner, 374 U.S. 398 (1963).
[728] *Id.* at 403 (quoting NAACP v. Button, 371 U.S. 415, 438 (1963)).
[729] *Id.*
[730] Jones v. Opelika, 316 U.S. 584, 594 (1942). The propriety of time, place, and manner restrictions was affirmed in Int'l Soc'y for Krishna Consciousness, Inc. v. Barber, 506 F. Supp. 147 (N.D.N.Y. 1980).
[731] Emp. Div. v. Smith, 494 U.S. 872 (1990).
[732] *Id.* at 901.
[733] Pub. L. No. 103-141, 107 Stat. 1488 (Nov. 16, 1993), codified at 42 U.S.C. § 2000bb through 42 U.S.C. § 2000bb-4.
[734] Ira C. Lupu, *The Failure of RFRA*, 20 U. ARK. LITTLE ROCK L. REV. 575, 588 (1998).
[735] Tiernan Kane, *Right by Precedent, Wrong by RFRA: The "Substantial Burden" Inquiry in* Oklevueha Native Am. Church of Hawaii, Inc. v. Lynch, 828 F.3d 1012 (9th Cir. 2016), 794 HARV. J.L. & PUB. POL'Y 793 (2017).
[736] City of Boerne v. Flores, 521 U.S. 507 (1997).
[737] Emily London & Maggie Siddiqi, *Religious Liberty Should Do No Harm*, CTR. FOR AM. PROG. (Apr. 11, 2019), https://www.americanprogress.org/article/religious-liberty-no-harm/.
[738] The criterion that the beliefs be held "with the strength of traditional religious convictions" is so vague that it cannot be taken to mean more than that the profession of the belief must be sincere. Those who travel long distances or risk fine or imprisonment to do so in a social atmosphere at the beach must be impelled by strong motivations. There is perfidy in the suggestion that the sincerity of a religious belief ought to be judged by the degree of suffering its

holder is willing to bear to express it. *Cf.* J. Morris Clark, *Guidelines for the Free Exercise Clause*, 83 HARV. L. REV. 327, 338 (1969) (stating that "many churches, like most political groups, have memberships whose dedication ranges from near-fanatical to insouciant").

[739] Pam, *The Genesis of G.O.E.*, GARDEN OF EDEN CHURCH, https://gardenofedenchurch.org/about.html (last visited Nov. 18, 2023).

[740] Lee v. Weisman, 505 U.S. 577 (1992).

[741] *Timeline of Social Nudity*, WIKIPEDIA, https://en.wikipedia.org/wiki/Timeline_of_social_nudity, last visited Mar. 10, 2024.

[742] The American Association for Nude Recreation has over 30,000 members. AM. ASS'N FOR NUDE RECREATION, https://www.aanr.com/ (last visited Nov. 18, 2023). This is a subset of nudist organizations and adherents.

[743] 7 ENCYCLOPEDIA BRITANNICA: MICROPAEDIA 436 (1975).

[744] FRANCES MERRILL & MASON MERRILL, SOCIAL NUDISM COMES TO AMERICA 56 (1932).

[745] Wisconsin v. Yoder, 406 U.S. 205, 216 (1972).

[746] Only one state, Kentucky, has statewide regulation of social nudism. KY. REV. STAT. ANN. § 232.021 (West 2023).

[747] Friedman & Grossman, *supra* note 32.

[748] EMILY COLEMAN & BETTY EDWARDS, BODY LIBERATION: FREEING YOUR BODY FOR GREATER SELF-ACCEPTANCE, HEALTH, AND SEXUAL SATISFACTION 205 (1977).

[749] *Id.*

[750] Note, *Toward a Constitutional Definition of Religion*, *supra* note 702, at 1073.

[751] W. Va. St. Bd. of Educ. v. Barnette, 319 U.S. 624 (1943).

[752] *Id.* at 631.

[753] *Id.* at 634–35 (holding that promoting national unity was not a sufficient state interest to justify the infringement of liberty involved in this case).

[754] *Id.* at 638.

[755] *Id.* at 639.

[756] Population estimates are generally from Pew Research.

[757] Kenji Yoshino, *The New Equal Protection*, 124 HARV. L. REV. 747 (2011).

[758] Joshua T. Davis et al., *Liberty for Us, Limits for Them: Christian Nationalism and Americans' Views on Citizens' Rights*, SOCIO. RELIGION (2023), https://doi.org/10.1093/socrel/srac044.

[759] "Society itself is a codified hero system, which means that society everywhere is a living myth of the significance of human life, a defiant creature of meaning. Every society thus is a 'religion.'" ERNEST BECKER, THE DENIAL OF DEATH (1973).

[760] Smith et al., *supra* note 620.

[761] ALFRED J. KOLATCH, THE SECOND JEWISH BOOK OF WHY (2nd, rev'd ed., 1985); THE MEETING OF CIVILIZATIONS: MUSLIM, CHRISTIAN, AND JEWISH 220–29 (Moshe Ma'oz, ed., 2009).

[762] KAROL WOJTYLA, LOVE AND RESPONSIBILITY (Grzegorz Ignatik trans., 2013).

[763] Commonwealth v. Kneeland, 37 Mass. 206 (1838).

[764] Baines v. Birmingham, 240 So. 2d 689 (Ala. Crim. App. 1970) (finding that use of profanity in public is indecent conduct, a constructive breach of peace, and not protected speech).
[765] Burstyn v. Wilson, 343 U.S. 495 (1952).
[766] Kalman v. Cortes, 723 F. Supp. 2d 766 (E.D. Pa. 2010).
[767] Penkoski v. Bowser, 548 F. Supp. 3d 12 (D.D.C. 2021).
[768] Memorandum in Support of Penkoski's Motion, Supported by Plaintiff Sevier, for a Preliminary Injunction and Permanent Injunction, Penkoski v. Bowser, 548 F. Supp. 3d 12 (D.D.C. 2021) (No. 1:20-cv-01519).
[769] Penkoski, 548 F. Supp. at 24 n.15 (D.D.C. 2021).
[770] Stephen Vukovits, *Offended-Observer Standing's Last Stand: Kennedy as the Final Nail in a Flawed Doctrine's Coffin*, U. CHI. L. REV. ONLINE 1 (2023), https://heinonline.org/HOL/Page?handle=hein.journals/uchidial91&collection=journals&id=9&startid=&endid=15.
[771] City of Ocala v. Rojas, 143 S. Ct. 764 (2023).
[772] Lujan v. Defenders of Wildlife, 504 U.S. 555, 560–61 (1992).
[773] *About*, BLACK LIVES MATTER, https://blacklivesmatter.com/about/.
[774] Memorandum in Support of Penkoski's Motion, Supported by Plaintiff Sevier, for a Preliminary Injunction and Permanent Injunction 8, Penkoski v. Bowser, 548 F. Supp. 3d 12 (D.D.C. 2021) (No. 1:20-cv-01519)
[775] *Id.* at 9.
[776] JOHN LOCKE, TWO TREATISES OF GOVERNMENT AND A LETTER CONCERNING TOLERATION 246 (Ian Shapiro ed., 2003).
[777] Tyler C. Jameson, *No Standing, No Backlash: How Federal Courts Use Standing to Avoid Deciding Controversial Cases Involving Religious and Political Displays*, 12 WAKE FOREST J.L. & POL'Y 359 (2022).
[778] Geoffrey R. Stone, *Free Speech in the Twenty-First Century: Ten Lessons from the Twentieth Century*, 36 PEPP. L. REV. 273, 274 (2009).
[779] Frederick Schauer, *Towards an Institutional First Amendment*, 89 MINN. L. REV. 1256 (2005).
[780] Susan H. Williams, *Content Discrimination and the First Amendment*, 139 U. PENN. L. REV. 615 (1991).
[781] Parmelee v. United States, 113 F.2d 729 (1940).
[782] United States v. Kennerly, 209 Fed. 119 (1913).
[783] *Parmelee*, 113 F.2d at 732.
[784] Roth v. United States, 354 U.S. 476 (1957).
[785] *Id.* at 476.
[786] Reg. v. Hicklin, L. R. 3 Q. B. 360 (1868).
[787] *Roth*, 354 U.S. at 487.
[788] *Id.* at 715 (quoting Thornhill v. Alabama, 310 U.S. 88 (1940).
[789] People v. Muller, 96 N.Y. 408 (1884).
[790] *Roth*, 354 U.S. at 487 n.20.
[791] *Id.* at 477.
[792] *Prurient (Adj.)*, ONLINE ETYMOLOGY DICTIONARY, https://www.etymonline.com/word/prurient (last visited Dec. 9, 2023) ("'having an itching desire for something,' especially 'lasciviousness, inclined to lewd thoughts'").

-

[793] 18 U.S.C. § 1461 (1994).
[794] *Roth*, 354 U.S. at 491.
[795] *Id.* at 485.
[796] *Id.* at 489.
[797] *Everyman*, BRITANNICA, https://www.britannica.com/topic/Everyman-English-morality-play (last visited Dec. 9, 2023).
[798] Ginsberg v. New York, 390 U.S. 629 (1968).
[799] *Id.* at 641.
[800] Stanley v. Georgia, 394 U.S. 557 (1969).
[801] Cohen v. California, 403 U.S. 15 (1971).
[802] *Id.* at 20.
[803] Miller v. California, 413 U.S. 15, 24 (1973) (citation omitted).
[804] *Population Estimates, July 1, 2022*, U.S. CENSUS, https://www.census.gov/quickfacts/fact/table/US/PST045222
[805] Jaime Willis, *Obscenity Third Annual Review of Gender and Sexuality Law: Part I: Constitutional Law Chapter: Section F.*, 3 GEO J. GENDER & L. 263 (2002)
[806] Ginzburg v. United States, 383 U.S. 463, 469 (1966) (continuing value as precedent questioned in United States v. Williams, 444 F.3d 1286, 1301 (2006)).
[807] Paris Adult Theatre I v. Slaton, 413 U.S. 49 (1973).
[808] *See, e.g.*, Robins v. County of L.A., 248 Cal. App. 2d 1, 13 (1966) (applying some nuance in upholding a county ordinance requiring a license for topless entertainment: "The County may not apply its ordinance in a prohibitive manner on the presumption that the display of bare breasts will be conducted in a manner calculated to deliberately emphasize sexual provocation. In the absence of contrary evidence, it must be assumed that such publication will be addressed only to those who freely and voluntarily elect the so-called pleasure and will not be imposed upon those whose sense of propriety might be injured or their annoyance or disgust be aroused, since they are equally free to avoid exposure.").
[809] *Paris Adult Theatre I*, 413 U.S. at 57.
[810] *Id.* at 63–64.
[811] *Id.* at 59 (citing Jacobellis v. Ohio, 378 U.S. 187, 199 (1964) (Warren, C.J., dissenting).
[812] *Id.*
[813] *Id.* at 67.
[814] Carey v. Population Servs. Int'l, 431 U.S. 678 (1977).
[815] State v. Nelson, 178 N.W.2d 434 (Iowa 1970).
[816] *Id.* at 436.
[817] *Id.* at 441.
[818] *Id.* at 438.
[819] Steffes, *supra* note 70; Michaud, *supra* note 70.
[820] Steffes, *supra* note 70, at 401.
[821] He mischaracterized the court's findings regarding obscenity.
[822] Erznoznik v. Jacksonville, 422 U.S. 205 (1975).
[823] *Id.* at 210.
[824] *Id.* at 215 (quoting Police Dep't of Chicago v. Mosley, 408 U.S. 92, 95 (1972)).

[825] *Erznoznik*, 422 U.S. at 223 (Burger, C.J. & Rehnquist, J., dissenting).
[826] *Id.* at 224 (White, J., dissenting).
[827] Excelsior Pictures Corp. v. Chicago, 182 F. Supp. 400 (N.D. Ill. 1960); Commonwealth v. Moniz, 155 N.E.2d 762 (Mass. 1959); *cf.* MODEL PENAL CODE § 207.10. comment 8 (Tent. Draft No. 6 1957).
[828] Cohen v. California, 403 U.S. 15, 26 (1971).
[829] *Erznoznik*, 422 U.S. at 213 n.10 (quoting Cohen v. California, 403 U.S. 15 (1971)).
[830] *See, e.g.*, United States v. Playboy Entm't Grp., 529 U.S. 803 (2000).
[831] Michaud, *supra* note 70, at 1030.
[832] *Erznoznik*, 422 U.S. at 214 (1975).
[833] West, *supra* note 43.
[834] Peter Lollo, *The Science of Nudity: The Skinny on Showing Skin*, KQED (Feb. 22, 2013), https://www.kqed.org/quest/49966/the-science-of-nudity-the-skinny-on-showing-skin; *see also* studies cited in DeVries, *supra* note 43, at 413; West, *supra* note 63; Keon West & Eliza Kukawska, *Good Nudes and Bad Nudes: How Naturism, Casual Stripping, and Sexting Predict Social Physique Anxiety and Body Appreciation*, 26 SEXUALITY & CULTURE 2151 (2022).
[835] Lollo, *supra* note 834.
[836] *Fast Facts: Preventing Child Sexual Abuse*, CTRS. FOR DISEASE CONTROL & PREVENTION (Sept. 5, 2023), https://www.cdc.gov/violenceprevention/childsexualabuse/fastfact.html.
[837] Robert Mark Simpson, *"Won't Somebody Please Think of the Children?" Hate Speech, Harm, and Childhood*, 38 LAW & PHIL. 79 (2019); Sebastian Wachs et al., *Associations Between Witnessing and Perpetrating Online Hate Speech Among Adolescents: Testing Moderation Effects of Moral Disengagement and Empathy*, 12 PSYCHOL. VIOLENCE 371 (2022); *see also* Gordon Ballingrud, *Obscenity, Hate Speech, and Viewpoint Discrimination: A Formula for Hate Speech as an Unprotected Category*, 20 DARTMOUTH L.J. 6 (2022).
[838] Tobias Greitemeyer, *The Dark and Bright Side of Video Game Consumption: Effects of Violent and Prosocial Video Games*, 46 CURR. OP. IN PSYCH. 101326 (2022).
[839] Story, *supra* note 63.
[840] Doran v. Salem Inn, Inc., 422 U.S. 922 (1975).
[841] California v. LaRue, 409 U.S. 109, 118 (1972).
[842] *Doran*, 422 U.S. at 932.
[843] Am. Booksellers Ass'n v. Hudnut, 771 F.2d 323 (7th Cir. 1985).
[844] *Id.* at 328.
[845] *Id.* at 329.
[846] *Id.*
[847] *Id.*
[848] Hudnut v. Am. Booksellers Ass'n, 475 U.S. 1001 (1986).
[849] *John Stuart Mill*, STANFORD ENCYCLOPEDIA OF PHILOSOPHY, https://plato.stanford.edu/entries/mill/ (last visited Dec. 26, 2023).
[850] ROBERT M. HEALEY, JEFFERSON ON RELIGION IN PUBLIC EDUCATION 26 (1926) (letter to Charles Thomson dated Jan. 9, 1816).

[851] *John Stuart Mill*, STANFORD ENCYCLOPEDIA OF PHILOSOPHY, https://plato.stanford.edu/entries/mill/ (last visited Dec. 26, 2023).
[852] Daniel F. Piar, *Morality as a Legitimate Government Interest*, 117 PENN ST. L. REV. 117, 139, 149 et seq. (2012).
[853] Young v. Arkansas, 474 U.S. 1070 (1986); Young v. State, 692 S.W. 2d 752 (Ark. 1985); *see also* Huffman v. Michigan, 549 U.S. 814 (2006) (denying petition for writ of certiorari) (conviction for three-minute public access TV show with flaccid penis marked with facial features).
[854] *Id.* at 1072 (White & Brennan, JJ, dissenting).
[855] *Id.* Neither justice is still on the bench.
[856] The Twenty-first Amendment has been held to allow reasonable regulation of such establishments, including restrictions on nude dancing. *See* California v. LaRue, 409 U.S. 109 (1972).
[857] *Young*, 474 U.S. at 1072 (White & Brennan, JJ, dissenting)
[858] N.Y. St. Liquor Auth. v. Bellanca, 452 U.S. 714 (1981).
[859] *Young*, 474 U.S. at 1072 (White & Brennan, JJ, dissenting).
[860] *Bellanca*, 452 U.S. at 723 (Stevens, J., dissenting).
[861] U.S. CONST. amend. I.
[862] S. Fla. Free Beaches, Inc. v. Miami, 734 F.2d 608 (11th Cir. 1984).
[863] *Id.* at 610 (citing Chapin v. Southampton, 457 F. Supp. 1170 (1978), and Erznoznik v. City of Jacksonville, 422 U.S. 205 (1975), for the proposition that nude sunbathing or swimming is not First Amendment expression (*Chapin* relied on nuisance theory to address privacy claims)).
[864] *Id.*
[865] People v. Hollman, 68 N.Y.2d 202 (1986).
[866] *Id.* at 206.
[867] *Id.* at 207.
[868] Egolf v. Witmer, 421 F. Supp. 2d 858, 878 (E.D. Pa. 2006) (citing SOB, Inc. v. Cty. of Benton, 317 F.3d 856 (8th Cir. 2003); People v. Hollman, 500 N.E.2d 297 (N.Y. 1986); State v. Nelson, 178 N.W.2d 434 (Iowa 1970).
[869] *Egolf*, 421 F. Supp. 2d at 868.
[870] Barnes v. Glen Theatre, 501 U.S. 560 (1991).
[871] *Id.* at 566.
[872] United States v. O'Brien, 391 U.S. 367 (1968).
[873] *Barnes*, 501 U.S. at 567.
[874] *Id.* at 569.
[875] Winters v. New York, 333 U.S. 507 (1948).
[876] *Barnes*, 501 U.S. at 568.
[877] *Id.*
[878] *Id.*
[879] IND. CODE ANN. § 35-45-4-1 (LEXISNEXIS 2023).
[880] *Barnes*, 501 U.S. at 575 (Scalia, J., concurring).
[881] *Id.* at 580–81 (Scalia, J., concurring).
[882] *Id.* at 581 (Souter, J., concurring).
[883] *Id.* at 577.
[884] *Id.*
[885] *Id.* at 573 (Scalia, J., concurring).
[886] City of Erie v. Pap's A.M., 529 U.S. 277 (2000).

[887] *Id.* at 290.
[888] City of L.A. v. Alameda Books, 535 U.S. 425 (2002); *see also* Lorillard Tobacco Co. v. Reilly, 533 U.S. 525 (2001).
[889] Sable Commc'ns of Cal. v. FCC, 492 U.S. 115 (1989).
[890] *Id.* at 125 ("Sexual expression which is indecent but not obscene is protected by the 1st Amendment . . . .").
[891] Reno v. ACLU, 521 U.S. 844, 899 (1997).
[892] *See, e.g.*, United States v. Playboy Entm't Grp., 529 U.S. 803 (2000).
[893] United States v. Stevens, 559 U.S. 460 (2010).
[894] *Id.* at 468.
[895] *Id.* at 460.
[896] See early American and English cases holding that exhibition of a deformed fetus constitutes indecent exposure. Harring v. Walrond, 1681, 1 Russ. Cr. 436 (1681); Knowles v. State, 3 Day 103 (Conn. 1808).
[897] *Stevens*, 559 U.S. 460.
[898] Taub v. City of S.F., 696 Fed. Appx. 181 (9th Cir. 2017).
[899] *Id.*
[900] *Id.* (citing City of Erie v. Pap's A.M., 529 U.S. 277, 296 (2000) (O'Connor, J.) (plurality opinion).
[901] *Id.* (quoting S.F., CAL., POLICE CODE art. 2 § 154(a)).
[902] *Id.*
[903] *Id.* (quoting United States v. O'Brien, 391 U.S. 367, 377 (1968)).
[904] Chaplinsky v. New Hampshire, 315 U.S. 568 (1942), *superseded by statute as stated in* Fallin v. City of Huntsville, 865 So. 2d 473 (Ala. Crim. App. 2003).
[905] Meredith May, *Baring Their Anti-War Feelings: Fighting in Iraq Is Indecent, Not Their Nakedness, They Say*, SFGATE (July 1, 2005), https://www.sfgate.com/bayarea/article/san-francisco-baring-their-anti-war-feelings-2658616.php.
[906] Maup van der Kerkhof, *Lady Godiva: Who Was Lady Godiva and What's the Truth Behind Her Ride*, HIST. COOPERATIVE (Nov. 15, 2023), https://historycooperative.org/lady-godiva/.
[907] Free the Nipple-Fort Collins v. City of Fort Collins, 916 F.3d 792 (10th Cir. 2019).
[908] FORT COLLINS, COLO., MUN. CODE § 17-142(b), (d) (2016) ("No female who is ten (10) years of age or older shall knowingly appear in any public place with her breast exposed below the top of the areola and nipple while located: (1) In a public right-of-way, in a natural area, recreation area or trail, or recreation center, in a public building, in a public square, or while located in any other public place; or (2) On private property if the person is in a place that can be viewed from the ground level by another who is located on public property and who does not take extraordinary steps, such as climbing a ladder or peering over a screening fence, in order to achieve a point of vantage. . . . The prohibition [on female toplessness] does not extend to women breastfeeding in places they are legally entitled to be.").
[909] *Free the Nipple-Fort Collins*, 916 F.3d at 799 (quoting J.E.B. v. Alabama *ex rel.* T.B., 511 U.S. 127, 136 (1994)).
[910] *Id.* at 801 (quoting United States v. Virginia, 518 U.S. 515, 550 (1996)).

[911] *Id.* at 803 (quoting Nevada Dep't H.R. v. Hibbs, 538 U.S. 721, 736 (2003)).
[912] *Id.* at 804 (citing, by way of comparison, People v. Santorelli, 600 N.E.2d 232, 236 (N.Y. 1992) (Titone, J., concurring)).
[913] *Id.*
[914] *Id.* at 803.
[915] Jaime L. Palmer-Hague et al., *Androgen Deprivation Alters Attention to Sexually Provocative Visual Stimuli in Elderly Men*, 5 SEXUAL MED. e245 (2017).
[916] *Free the Nipple-Fort Collins*, 916 F.3d at 804.
[917] Lochner v. New York, 198 U.S. 45 (1905), *superseded by statute as stated in* Imars v. Contractors Mfg. Servs., 1998 U.S. App. LEXIS 21073 (1998).
[918] Eline v. Town of Ocean City, 2018 U.S. Dist. LEXIS 143951 (2018) (citing cases).
[919] *See, e.g.*, Free the Nipple v. City of Springfield, 923 F.3d 508, 510 (8th Cir. 2019); Cent. Tex. Nudists v. Cty. of Travis, 2000 Tex. App. LEXIS 8136 (Tex. Ct. App. 2000).
[920] *Id.* at 804.
[921] State v. Lilley, 204 A.3d 198 (N.Y. 2019), *cert. denied*, 140 S. Ct. 858 (2020).
[922] *Id.* at 208.
[923] *Id.* at 213.
[924] Mahanoy Area Sch. Dist. v. B.L., 141 S. Ct. 2038 (2021).
[925] *Id.* at 2046.
[926] *Id.*
[927] *Id.* at 2046–47.
[928] *Id.* at 2048 (quoting Tinker v. Des Moines Indep. Cmty. Sch. Dist., 393 U.S. 503, 508 (1969)).
[929] *Id.*
[930] *Id.* at 2061 (Thomas, J., dissenting).
[931] UTAH CODE ANN. § 76-10-1201(5)(a) (2023).
[932] Baker v. Glover, 776 F. Supp. 1511, 1515 (M.D. Ala. 1991).
[933] *Id.*
[934] *Id.*
[935] *Id.* at 1516–17.
[936] *Id.* at 1514–15.
[937] *See, e.g.*, State v. Nelson, 178 N.W.2d 434 (Iowa 1970); Danielle Moriber, Note, *A Right to Bare All? Female Public Toplessness and Dealing with the Laws That Prohibit*, 8 CARDOZO PUB. L., POL'Y, & ETHICS J. 453, 468 (2010).
[938] South Fla. Free Beaches, Inc. v. Miami, 734 F.2d 608 (11th Cir. 1984) (cited with approval U.S.by Barnes v. Glen Theatre, 501 U.S. 560, 576 (1991)). This case is discussed later in this chapter.
[939] De Vries, *supra* note 43, at 407, 414.
[940] *See, e.g.*, Sam Wilson, *Ukraine's Femen: Topless Protests "Help Feminist Cause,"* BBC (Oct. 24, 2012), https://www.bbc.com/news/world-europe-20028797.
[941] Jacques Fontanille, *Figures of the Body, and the Semiotics of Imprint: Semiotic Figures of the Body in the Humanities*, 9 CHINESE SEMIOTIC STUD. 37 (2013).

[942] PAUL BAINS, THE PRIMACY OF SEMIOSIS: AN ONTOLOGY OF RELATIONS (2006).
[943] Crownover v. Musick, 509 P.2d 497 (Cal. 1973).
[944] Note, *Criminal Law and Procedure – Indecent Exposure, Nudism*, *supra* note 69, at 937. Such offenses "in derogation of public morals and decency" are *malum in se* and traditionally classified as a form of public nuisance. *See, e.g.*, JOSEPH A. JOYCE & HOWARD C. JOYCE, TREATISE ON THE LAW GOVERNING NUISANCES ch. 2 § 15 (1906).
[945] Jacobellis v. Ohio, 378 U.S. 184, 199 (1964) (Warren, C.J., dissenting); Paris Adult Theatre I v. Slaton, 413 U.S. 49, 59–60 (1973); *cf.* McGowan v. Maryland, 366 U.S. 420 (1961) (stating government has a legitimate interest in promoting and protecting the "moral well-being of society").
[946] Brandenburg v. Ohio, 395 U.S. 444 (1969); Nat'l Socialist Party v. Skokie, 432 U.S. 43 (1977); R.A.V. v. St. Paul, 505 U.S. 377 (1992); Virginia v. Black, 538 U.S. 343 (2003); Snyder v. Phelps, 562 U.S. 443 (2011).
[947] Excelsior Pictures Corp. v. Regents of Univ., 144 N.E.2d 31, 35 (N.Y. 1957); United States v. Loftis, 12 F. 671, 672 (D. Or. 1882) (stating that indecency is "more than indelicate and less than immodest;" it is "something unfit for the eye or ear"); *id.* at 672 (stating that obscenity "includes on the one hand what is merely inauspicious, foul, or indecent, and on the other what is immodest and calculated to excite impure emotions or desires").
[948] Howell v. State, 81 S.E. 247 (Ga. Ct. App. 1914) (quoting STANDARD DICTIONARY 1247 (1913)).
[949] Commonwealth v. Buckley, 86 N.E. 910, 911 (Mass. 1909).
[950] Redd v. State, 67 S.E. 709 (Ga. App. 1910).
[951] *Buckley*, 86 N.E. at 911.
[952] Ardery v. State, 56 Ind. 328, 329–30 (1877), *quoted or cited with approval in, e.g.*, *Redd*, 67 S.E. 709; JOHN D. LAWSON, A CONCORDANCE OF WORDS AND PHRASES CONSTRUED IN THE JUDICIAL REPORTS (1883).
[953] WALT WHITMAN, SPECIMEN DAYS IN AMERICA (1887).
[954] Spears v. State, 175 So. 2d 158, 162 (Miss. 1965).
[955] Woodlands Pride, Inc. v. Paxton, No. 4:23-cv-02847, 2023 U.S. Dist. LEXIS 171268 (S.D. Tex. 2023).
[956] Guess they have MTV in Texas? *RuPaul's Drag Race* is in its sixteenth season. Joey Nolfi, *Ts Madison Joins RuPaul's Drag Race Season 15 as Rotating Judge*, ENTERTAINMENT (Dec. 19, 2022); *RuPaul's Drag Race*, WIKIPEDIA, https://en.wikipedia.org/wiki/RuPaul%27s_Drag_Race (last visited Dec. 28, 2023).
[957] *Woodlands Pride*, No. 4:23-cv-02847, 2023 U.S. Dist. LEXIS 171268 (S.D. Tex. 2023) (internal citations omitted).
[958] *Id.*
[959] *Id.*
[960] *Id.*
[961] *Id.*
[962] Rosenberger v. Rector of Univ. of Va., 515 U.S. 819, 829 (1995).
[963] *Woodlands Pride*, No. 4:23-cv-02847, 2023 U.S. Dist. LEXIS 171268 (S.D. Tex. 2023) (internal citations omitted).

[964] Miller v. California, 413 U.S. 15 (1973).
[965] Sable Commc'ns of Cal. v. FCC, 492 U.S. 115, 126 (1989).
[966] *Id.*
[967] *Woodlands Pride*, No. 4:23-cv-02847, 2023 U.S. Dist. LEXIS 171268 (S.D. Tex. 2023).
[968] *Id.*
[969] Spectrum WT v. Wendler, 2023 U.S. Dist. LEXIS 168753 (N.D. Tex. 2023).
[970] United States v. Stevens, 559 U.S. 460 (2010).
[971] Coates v. Cincinnati, 402 U.S. 611 (1971).
[972] Burtka, *supra* note 62.
[973] McCoy v. Town of Pittsfield, 59 F.4th 497 (D.N.H. 2023); Barnes v. Glen Theatre, 501 U.S. 560 (1991); Dease v. City of Anaheim, 826 F. Supp. 336 (C.D. Cal. 1993); Ctr. for Investigative Reporting v. Se. Pa. Transp. Auth., 975 F.3d 300 (3rd Cir. 2020).
[974] BRETT LUNCEFORD, PUBLIC NUDITY AND THE RHETORIC OF THE BODY 19–40 (2018).
[975] Beauharnais v. Illinois, 343 U.S. 250, 254 (1952).
[976] Brandenburg v. Ohio, 395 U.S. 444 (1969); Nat'l Socialist Party v. Skokie, 432 U.S. 43 (1977); R.A.V. v. St. Paul, 505 U.S. 377 (1992); Virginia v. Black, 538 U.S. 343 (2003); Snyder v. Phelps, 562 U.S. 443 (2011).
[977] Ballingrud, *supra* note 837 (proposing to treat hate speech like obscenity by modifying the *Miller* test; alternatively, he suggests providing First Amendment protection for obscenity. He does not evidence any knowledge of the historical basis for constitutional treatment of sexual expression.).
[978] Matal v. Tam, 582 U.S. 218, 244 (2017).
[979] Iancu v. Brunetti, 139 S. Ct. 2294, 2300 (2019). The *Matal* case had involved disparaging trademarks. This case addressed "immoral" trademarks.
[980] *Id.* at 2299.
[981] Mahanoy Area Sch. Dist. v. B.L., 141 S. Ct. 2038, 2056 (2021).
[982] A Book Named "John Cleland's Memoirs of a Woman of Pleasure" v. Attorney Gen. of Mass., 383 U.S. 413, 430 (1966) (Douglas, J., concurring).
[983] Woodlands Pride, Inc. v. Paxton, No. 4:23-cv-02847, 2023 U.S. Dist. LEXIS 171268 (S.D. Tex. 2023).
[984] Rosenberg v. LoanDepot.com LLC, 435 F. Supp. 3d 308 (D. Mass. 2020).
[985] Junior Sports Mags. Inc. v. Bonta, 80 F.4th 1109 (9th Cir. 2023).
[986] Animal Legal Def. Fund v. Reynolds, 630 F. Supp. 3d 1105 (S.D. Iowa 2022).
[987] Free Speech Coal., Inc. v. Attorney Gen. U.S., 974 F.3d 408 (3rd Cir. 2020).
[988] Brown v. Kemp, 2023 U.S. App. LEXIS 30112 (7th Cir. 2023).
[989] United States v. Alvarez, 567 U.S. 709, 717 (2012).
[990] Woodlands Pride, Inc. v. Paxton, No. 4:23-cv-02847, 2023 U.S. Dist. LEXIS 171268 (S.D. Tex. 2023) ; Am. Booksellers Ass'n v. Hudnut, 771 F.2d 323 (7th Cir. 1985); United States v. Playboy Entm't Grp., 529 U.S. 803 (2000).
[991] W.J. Grier, *Calvin Versus the Libertines*, CHRISTIAN LIBRARY, https://www.christianstudylibrary.org/article/calvin-versus-libertines (last visited Jan. 5, 2024); JOHN COFFEY, EXODUS AND LIBERATION: DELIVERANCE POLITICS FROM JOHN CALVIN TO MARTIN LUTHER KING JR. (2014).
[992] Edge v. City of Everett, 636 F. Supp. 3d 1247 (W.D. WA. 2022).

[993] *Id.* at 1252.
[994] *Id.* at 1253.
[995] *Id.* at 1251.
[996] GREENAWALT, *supra* note 72.
[997] Green, *supra* note 46, at 241.
[998] Geoffrey R. Stone, American Booksellers Association v Hudnut*: "The Government Must Leave to the People the Evaluation of Ideas,"* 77 U. CHIC. L. REV. 1219 (2010).
[999] Woodlands Pride, Inc. v. Paxton, No. 4:23-cv-02847, 2023 U.S. Dist. LEXIS 171268 (S.D. Tex. 2023).
[1000] S.F., CAL., POLICE CODE art. 2 § 154 (2013) ("Prohibiting Public Nudity"), https://codelibrary.amlegal.com/codes/san_francisco/latest/sf_police/0-0-0-9618.
[1001] S.F., CAL., POLICE CODE art. 15.3 § 1071.1 (2011) ("Regulating Public Nudity in Restaurants and Public Seating Areas"), https://codelibrary.amlegal.com/codes/san_francisco/latest/sf_police/0-0-0-3893.
[1002] Theodore Bennett, *State of Undress: Law, Carnival and Mass Public Nudity Events*, 29 GRIFFITH L. REV. 199 (2020).
[1003] Tom Garety, *Redefining Privacy*, 12 HARV. C.R. – C.L. L. REV. 233, 266 (1977).
[1004] Ius Laboris, *The Legal Landscape on Employer Dress Code and Appearance Policies: A U.S. and European Perspective*, LEXOLOGY (May 30, 2017), https://www.lexology.com/library/detail.aspx?g=da7fb0a1-172a-45de-9060-12a16cabb9d1. Title VII of the Civil Rights Act of 1964 (Title VII) is the federal law impacting employer dress codes.
[1005] U.S. CONST. amend. V.
[1006] Poe v. Ullman, 367 U.S. 497, 543 (1961) (Harlan, J., dissenting).
[1007] Dobbs v. Jackson Women's Health Org., 142 S. Ct. 2228, 2300–17 (2022).
[1008] Carey v. Population Servs. Int'l, 431 U.S. 678, 685 (1977) (citing cases); *see also* Paris Adult Theatre I v. Slaton, 413 U.S. 49, 65 (1973). A constitutional right to marriage was recognized in Zablocki v. Redhail, 434 U.S. 374 (1978).
[1009] Griswold v. Connecticut, 381 U.S. 479, 502–07 (1965) (White, J., concurring).
[1010] *Id.* at 484–85 (majority opinion by Douglas, J.) (hereinafter referred to as the "penumbra theory").
[1011] *Id.* at 486–99 (concurring opinion by Goldberg, J.). Three other theories have been suggested: (1) Fourth Amendment—suppression of evidence to remedy invasions in criminal investigations; (2) First Amendment—freedom of speech implies right to remain silent; and (3) Fourteenth Amendment—due process bars use in prosecutions of fruits of invasions of privacy. *See* PRACTICING L. INST., PRIVACY 12 (1974). These possibilities are not discussed because they pertain to an aspect of privacy, the right to withhold information, that is not related to the constitutionality of indecent exposure laws.
[1012] Whalen v. Roe, 429 U.S. 589, 599–600 (1977).
[1013] Comment, *A Taxonomy of Privacy: Repose, Sanctuary, and Intimate Decision*, 64 CALIF. L. REV. 1446 (1976).

[1014] *See, e.g.*, Breen v. Kahl, 419 F.2d 1034 (7th Cir. 1969), *cert. denied*, 398 U.S. 937 (1970) (local regulation of hair length of high school students held unconstitutional as violation of right of privacy). Whether hairstyle is a fundamental right was questioned in Gfell v. Rickelman, 441 F.2d 444 (6th Cir. 1971).
[1015] *See* KENT GREENAWALT, LEGAL PROTECTIONS OF PRIVACY: FINAL REPORT TO THE OFFICE OF TELECOMMUNICATIONS POLICY, EXECUTIVE OFFICE OF THE PRESIDENT 5 (1975).
[1016] *See, e.g.*, Paris Adult Theatre I v. Slaton, 413 U.S. 49, 65 (1973); Roe v. Wade, 410 U.S. 113, 152 (1973) (stating that "only personal rights that can be deemed 'fundamental' or 'implicit in the concept of ordered liberty' . . . are included in this guarantee of personal privacy" (quoting Palko v. Connecticut, 302 U.S. 319, 325 (1970), *overruled on other grounds by* Benton v. Maryland, 395 U.S. 784 (1969))).
[1017] *See, e.g.*, McLaughlin v. Florida, 379 U.S. 184, 196 (1964); Bates v. City of Little Rock, 361 U.S. 516, 524 (1960).
[1018] *See, e.g.*, Williamson v. Lee Optical of Okla., Inc., 348 U.S. 483 (1955).
[1019] THOMAS M. COOLEY, A TREATISE ON THE LAW OF TORTS OR THE WRONGS WHICH ARISE INDEPENDENT OF CONTRACT 29 (1879).
[1020] Olmstead v. United States, 277 U.S. 438, 478 (1928) (Brandeis, J., dissenting).
[1021] Tyler Baker, Note, Roe *and* Paris*: Does Privacy Have a Principle?*, 26 STAN. L. REV. 1161, 1175 et seq. (1974).
[1022] Eisenstadt v. Baird, 405 U.S. 438 (1972).
[1023] Roe v. Wade, 410 U.S. 113 (1973).
[1024] Paris Adult Theatre I v. Slaton, 413 U.S. 49 (1973).
[1025] Baker, *supra* note 1021, at 1176–77.
[1026] *Id.* at 1180.
[1027] Tyler suggests that the order of importance of these factors in relation to access to abortion and obscenity is subject to empirical examination, but he sees a problem in the development of such societal utilitarian calculus: a tendency toward enforcement of a majoritarian ethic.
[1028] Griswold v. Connecticut, 381 U.S. 479, 498 (1965) (Goldberg, J., concurring); *see also* Baker, *supra* note 1021, at 1182.
[1029] Dobbs v. Jackson Women's Health Org., 142 S. Ct. 2228 (2022).
[1030] *See generally* Herbert Wechsler, *Toward Neutral Principles Constitutional Law*, 73 HARV. L. REV. 1 (1959).
[1031] Garety, *supra* note 1003, at 266.
[1032] LAURENCE H. TRIBE, AMERICAN CONSTITUTIONAL LAW 913 (1978).
[1033] *Cf.* Alexander Meiklejohn, *The 1st Amendment Is an Absolute*, 1961 SUP. CT. REV. 245, 254 (1961), *quoted in* Branzburg v. Hayes, 408 U.S. 665, 713 (1972) (Douglas, J., dissenting) ("For the understanding of these principles it is essential to maintain crucial difference between 'the rights' of the governed and the 'powers' of the governors.").
[1034] *See also* Comment, A Taxonomy of Privacy: Repose, Sanctuary, and Intimate Decision, 64 CALIF. L. REV. 1447, 1472 (1976) ("This pattern recurs in many bodily integrity cases. The individual's decision, although seeming to be

quite intimate on its face, is so bound up with a collective interest that it is within the public realm.").
[1035] *Id.* at 914.
[1036] "Bodily integrity" is Professor's Tribe's expression, but rather than affirm it as a general principle, he presents it piecemeal. *See generally* TRIBE, *supra* note 1032, at 15–19 et seq. (1978). This may be a result of the conceptual confusion discussed above. *See also* Garety, *supra* note 1003, at 274–75 n.153. The term "bodily autonomy" is more appropriate because it connotes individual sovereignty (an active concept) rather than simply immunity from intrusion (a passive one).
[1037] Stanley I. Benn, *Privacy, Freedom, and Respect for Persons*, *in* PRIVACY 1 (J.R. Pennock & John W. Chapman eds., XIII NOMOS: Yearbook of the American Society for Political and Legal Philosophy, 1971).
[1038] *Id.* at 15–16.
[1039] Roe v. Wade, 410 U.S. 113, 154 (1973). Justices White and Rehnquist dissented, finding that no privacy right whatsoever was involved. *Id.* at 172–73, 222–23.
[1040] *See* Paris Adult Theatre I v. Slaton, 413 U.S. 49, 65–67, 66 n.13 (1973).
[1041] Stanley v. Georgia, 394 U.S. 557, 564–65 (1969) (*validity questioned by* United States v. Palladino, 475 F.2d 65 (1st Cir. 1973)).
[1042] Baker, *supra* note 1021, at 1186 nn.135, 136.
[1043] *Id.* at 1187.
[1044] *Paris Adult Theatre I*, 413 U.S. at 66.
[1045] Baker, *supra* note 1021 (citing cases).
[1046] Oddly, the basis for distinguishing private use of obscenity in the home from other criminal activities that might occur there appears to be concern for the "right to information and ideas . . . regardless of their social worth." Stanley v. Georgia, 394 U.S. 557, 564 (1969). How can obscenity, which, by definition, is worthless, be worthy of the effort necessary to create a new constitutional principle?
[1047] Benn, *supra* note 1036.
[1048] *Paris Adult Theatre I*, 413 U.S. at 66. *Cf.* Griswold v. Connecticut, 381 U.S. 479 (1965), which could be characterized as defining a right to buy contraceptives which is a public act.
[1049] Jacobson v. Massachusetts, 197 U.S. 11 (1905).
[1050] Buck v. Bell, 274 U.S. 200 (1927). *But see* Skinner v. Oklahoma, 315 U.S. 789, 541 (1942) (applying strict scrutiny of state discrimination affecting procreation because childbearing is "fundamental to the very existence and survival of the race").
[1051] *Jacobson*, 197 U.S. 11.
[1052] *Buck*, 274 U.S. 200.
[1053] *Griswold*, 381 U.S. at 484.
[1054] *Griswold* recognized the right of married persons to have access to contraceptives. Single persons were guaranteed no government interference with access in Eisenstadt v. Baird, 405 U.S. 438 (1972).
[1055] *E.g.*, *Symposium on the Griswold Case and the Right of Privacy*, 64 MICH. L. REV. 197 (1965).

[1056] U.S. CONST. amend. IX (1971).
[1057] *Id.* amend. X (1791).
[1058] *But see* Raoul Berger, *The 14th Amendment: The Framers' Design*, 30 S.C. L. REV. 495, 505–06 (1979); *cf.* Charles Warren, *The New "Liberty" Under the 14th Amendment*, 39 HARV. L. REV. 431 (1926). The concept of substantive due process developed in this chapter is much narrower than the judicial practice historically associated with the term "Lochnerizing." *See, e.g.*, Lochner v. New York, 198 U.S. 45 (1905). There will be no suggestion that the Court sit as a "superlegislature," *see* Ferguson v. Skrupa, 372 U.S. 726, 731 (1963), only that it enforce fundamental Constitutional principles, specifically, those embodied in the Ninth and Tenth Amendments. *See* BENNETT B. PATTERSON, THE FORGOTTEN 9TH AMENDMENT 36–43 (1955) (arguing that the Ninth Amendment is applicable to the states). There is no doubt that "liberty" in the Fourteenth Amendment includes some substantive aspects; the only questions relate to the nature and extent of that substance. *See, e.g.*, Harrah Indep. Sch. Dist. v. Martin, 99 S. Ct. 1062, 1063–64 (1979) (per curium).
[1059] PATTERSON, *supra* note 1058.
[1060] *See, e.g.*, EDWARD S. CORWIN, THE CONSTITUTION AND WHAT IT MEANS TODAY 442–48 (14th ed. 1978).
[1061] PATTERSON, *supra* note 1058, at 4, 26.
[1062] Griswold v. Connecticut, 381 U.S. 479, 486 (1965). Goldberg makes a curious argument, *id.* at 494, that he does not mean to imply that the Ninth Amendment is to be applied against the states through the Fourteenth Amendment or that it is an independent source of individual civil rights; it only shows that it is evidence that the Framers recognized the existence of certain fundamental rights not expressly provided for in the Constitution. There seem to be no practical consequences of distinguishing between the Ninth Amendment being evidence of the meaning of "liberty" in the Fourteenth Amendment, *id.* at 493, and being incorporated in it.
[1063] *Id.* at 495.
[1064] STORY, *supra* note 632.
[1065] United States v. Darby, 312 U.S. 100, 124 (1941); *see also* Fry v. United States, 421 U.S. 542, 547 n.7 (1975) (stating that the Tenth Amendment "is not without significance. The Amendment expressly declares the constitutional policy that Congress may not exercise power in a fashion that impairs the States' integrity or their ability to function effectively in a federal system."). Doesn't the language of the amendment likewise imply that Congress may not exercise power in a fashion that impairs the integrity or effective functioning of the people? Does the Fourteenth Amendment imply an analogous restriction on State action? Is the end result a fundamental and undifferentiated right of the people "to be let alone"? The Court has on occasion noted that the meaning of "liberty" must be broad indeed, *see e.g.*, Paul v. Davis, 424 U.S. 693, 722 (1976) (Brennan, J., dissenting) (quoting Bd. of Regents v. Roth, 408 U.S. 564, 572 (1972)), but has always done so within the context of the process of double balancing described above. *See also* Bolling v. Sharpe, 347 U.S. 497, 499 (1954) ("Liberty under the law extends to the full range of conduct which an individual is free to pursue.").
[1066] New York v. United States, 505 U.S. 144 (1992).

[1067] Paul Finkelman, *The Bill of Rights in Historical and International Perspective: How an 18th Century Document Illuminates Liberty in the 21st Century Lead Articles*, 46 OH. NORTHERN U. L. REV. 291 (2020).
[1068] *Id.* at 294.
[1069] Rosenblatt v. Baer, 383 U.S. 75, 92 (1966) (Stewart, J., concurring), *quoted in* Gertz v. Robert Welch, 418 U.S. 323, 341 (1974).
[1070] Numerous models of the original meaning of the Ninth Amendment have been offered. Extended discussion of these theories is beyond the scope of this study. Evidence of the original intent of the Bill of Rights included concern that the enumeration of individual rights in the Bill of Rights was considered to be exclusive. The fear was well-founded. Minimally, there should be a balancing the costs and benefits of government actions infringing on individual pursuit of Constitutional ideals of the "blessings of liberty." In matters of morality, it should not be acceptable to ignore costs of enforcement in individual liberty. This express balancing is evident in many Court decisions of the last generation but has not been applied to indecent exposure. ANTHONY B. SANDERS, BABY 9TH AMENDMENTS: HOW AMERICANS EMBRACED UNENUMERATED RIGHTS AND WHY IT MATTERS (2023).
[1071] Bates v. City of Little Rock, 361 U.S. 516, 524 (1960), *cited with approval in* Justice Goldberg's concurring opinion in Griswold v. Connecticut, 381 U.S. 479, 497 (1965).
[1072] McLaughlin v. Florida, 379 U.S. 184, 196 (1964).
[1073] *E.g.*, De Veau v. Braisted, 363 U.S. 144, 155 (1960) (citing Hill v. Florida, 325 U.S. 538 (1945)).
[1074] *E.g.*, UAW v. Hoosier Cardinal Corp., 383 U.S. 696, 721 (1966); Teamsters, Chauffeurs & Helpers Union v. Morton, 377 U.S. 252, 257 (1964).
[1075] *E.g.*, Ohralik v. Oh. St. Bar Ass'n, 436 U.S. 447, 462 (1978).
[1076] *E.g.*, Mackey v. Montrym, 443 U.S. 1 (1979).
[1077] *E.g.*, Maher v. Roe, 432 U.S. 464, 472 (1977); Roe v. Wade, 410 U.S. 113, 162–64 (1973).
[1078] *E.g.*, Moore v. Sims, 99 S. Ct. 2371, 2383 (1979).
[1079] *E.g.*, Linn v. United Plant Guard Workers, 383 U.S. 53, 62 (1966); San Diego Bldg. Trades Council v. Garmon, 359 U.S. 236, 247 (1959).
[1080] *E.g.*, Uphaus v. Wyman, 360 U.S. 72, 81 (1959).
[1081] *E.g.*, Nixon v. Adm'r of Gen. Servs., 433 U.S. 425, 467–68 (1977).
[1082] *E.g.*, Buckley v. Valeo, 424 U.S. 1, 29, 36 (1976), *superseded by statute as stated in* Ams. for Prosperity v. Grewal 2019 U.S. Dist. LEXIS 170793, 2019 WL 485585 3 (D.N.J. 2019); Cousins v. Wigoda, 419 U.S. 477, 489, 491, 974 (1975); Storer v. Brown, 415 U.S. 724, 736 (1974).
[1083] *E.g.*, Grayned v. City of Rockford, 408 U.S. 104, 119 (1972).
[1084] *See, e.g.*, Goldfarb v. Va. St. Bar, 421 U.S. 773 (1975); NAACP v. Button, 371 U.S. 415, 439 (1963).
[1085] *E.g.*, Rose v. Mitchell, 99 S. Ct. 2993, 3011 (1979) (Stewart, J., concurring); Bakke v. Regents of the Univ. of Cal., 438 U.S. 265, 266 (1978).
[1086] *E.g.*, Zablocki v. Redhail, 434 U.S. 374 (1978); *cf. In re* Goalen, 414 U.S. 1148 (1974) (Stevens., J., dissenting from denial of certiorari).

[1087] The characterization of individual rights as compelling interests is a very recent innovation. It is too soon to discern the full implications of this approach, but it is probably a dangerous invention in that it seems to sanction a greater government involvement in the liberty reposed in individuals.
[1088] STORY, *supra* note 632.
[1089] *E.g.*, Sherbert v. Verner, 374 U.S. 398, 407 (1963), *quoted in* Johnson v. Robison, 415 U.S. 361, 387 (1974) (Douglas, J., dissenting), *superseded by statute as stated in* Lewis v. Norton, 2009 U.S. Dist. LEXIS 33146 (E.D. Wis. 2009).
[1090] *See, e.g.*, Harrison v. NAACP, 360 U.S. 167, 175 (1959).
[1091] *See, e.g.*, NAACP v. Button, 371 U.S. 415, 439 (1963).
[1092] *E.g.*, Lefkowitz v. Cunningham, 431 U.S. 801, 809 (1977).
[1093] Ill. St. Bd. of Elections v. Socialist Workers Party, 440 U.S. 173, 187 (1979).
[1094] TRIBE, *supra* note 1032 (quoting Richards v. Thurston, 424 F.2d 1281, 1284–85 (1st Cir. 1970)).
[1095] For historical background, see Finkelman, *supra* note 1067.
[1096] Richards v. Thurston, 424 F.2d 1281, 1284 (1st Cir. 1970), *criticized in* Betts v. McCaughtry, 827 F. Supp. 1400, 1407 (1993)).
[1097] PAUL SCHILDER, THE IMAGE AND APPEARANCE OF THE HUMAN BODY: STUDIES IN THE CONSTRUCTIVE ENERGIES OF THE PSYCHE (1999).
[1098] Kelley v. Johnson, 425 U.S. 238 (1976).
[1099] James Madison, Address at debate of June 8, 1789, 1 ANNALS OF CONG. 456 (1789).
[1100] *Kelley*, 425 U.S. at 250–51; *cf.* Ferrel v. Dallas Indep. Sch. Dist., 393 U.S. 856 (1968) (Douglas, J., dissenting from denial of cert.) ("I suppose that a nation bent on turning out robots might insist that every male have a crew cut and every female wear pigtails. But the ideas of 'life, liberty, and the pursuit of happiness,' expressed in the Declaration of Independence, later found specific definition in the Constitution itself, including of course freedom of expression and a wide zone of privacy. I had supposed those guarantees permitted idiosyncrasies to flourish, especially when they concern the image of one's personality and his philosophy towards government and his fellow men.").
[1101] *Kelley*, 425 U.S. at 244 (Marshall, J., dissenting).
[1102] *Id.* at 247.
[1103] The tradition began with Justice Stone's famous footnote in United States v. Carolene Prods. Co., 304 U.S. 144, 152–53 n.4 (1938), and, until this case, has closely reflected the principles described there.
[1104] Although Marshall also apparently subscribes to the judicial judgment of the personal significance of individual decisions, his conclusion that the right of personal appearance is fundamental gives the remainder of his analysis the proper premise.
[1105] Cohen v. California, 403 U.S. 15, 25 (1971).
[1106] Ball v. Bd. of Trustees., 584 F.2d 684, 685 (5th Cir. 1978).
[1107] *Id.*
[1108] E. Hartford Educ. Ass'n v. Bd. of Educ., 562 F. 2d. 838, 844 (2d. Cir. 1977).
[1109] *Id.* at 844–45.
[1110] *Id.* at 841–42.

[1111] Miller v. Sch. Dist. Number 167, 496 F.2d 658, 664 (7th Cir. 1974) ("The word 'liberty' is not demeaned by construing it to include a right to appear as one pleases.") (Stevens, J.).
[1112] *Id.*
[1113] W. Va. St. Bd. of Educ. v. Barnette, 319 U.S. 624 (1943).
[1114] Cohen v. California, 403 U.S. 15 (1971).
[1115] Mahanoy Area Sch. Dist. v. B.L., 141 S. Ct. 2038 (2021).
[1116] *Id.* at 2043.
[1117] *Id.*
[1118] Miller v. Sch. Dist. Number 167, 496 F.2d 658, 664 n.22 (7th Cir. 1974).
[1119] O'Connor v. Donaldson, 422 U.S. 563, 575 (1975).
[1120] *Id.*
[1121] *Id.*
[1122] TRIBE, *supra* note 1032, at 982–83 (citing Cohen v. California, 403 U.S. 15 (1971).
[1123] Jacobellis v. Ohio, 378 U.S. 184, 199 (1964) (Warren, C.J., dissenting) ("Specifically, we are called upon to reconcile the right of the Nation and of the States to maintain a decent society and, on the other hand, the right of individuals to express themselves freely in accordance with the guarantees of the 1st and 14th Amendments.").
[1124] Bowers v. Hardwick, 478 U.S. 186 (1986), *overruled by* Lawrence v. Texas, 539 U.S. 558 (2003).
[1125] Lawrence v. Texas, 539 U.S. 558 (2003).
[1126] *Id.* at 562.
[1127] *Id.*
[1128] *Id.* at 574 (quoting Planned Parenthood of Se. Pa. v. Casey, 505 U.S. 833, 851 (1992), *overruled by* Dobbs v. Jackson Women's Health Org., 142 S. Ct. 2228 (2022)).
[1129] *Id.* at 577–78 (quoting Bowers v. Hardwick, 478 U.S. 186, 216 (1986) (Stevens, J., dissenting).
[1130] *See, e.g.*, Stark, *supra* note 651.
[1131] *Lawrence*, 539 U.S. at 579 (O'Connor, J., concurring).
[1132] *Id.* at 581 (O'Connor, J., concurring).
[1133] *Id.* at 583 (O'Connor, J., concurring) (quoting Dep't of Agriculture v. Moreno, 413 U.S. 528, 633 (1973)).
[1134] *Id.* at 584 (O'Connor, J., concurring).
[1135] *See* Appendix C: State by State Indecent Exposure Law Summaries, *infra*.
[1136] Green, *supra* note 46, at 241, and sources cited therein.
[1137] Barnes v. Glen Theatre, 501 U.S. 560 (1991)
[1138] California v. LaRue, 409 U.S. 109 (1972).
[1139] CBDM Redlands, LLC v. Prieto, 2017 U.S. Dist. LEXIS 59218 (C.D. Cal. 2017).
[1140] Jade Chounlamountry, *Strip Club Laws and the Regulation of Sexually Oriented Business*, FINDLAW (last rev'd Aug. 17, 2023), https://www.findlaw.com/smallbusiness/business-laws-and-regulations/adult-entertainment-law-zoning-and-other-regulations.html.
[1141] Edge v. City of Everett, 636 F. Supp. 3d 1247 (W.D. Wash. 2022).

[1142] Free the Nipple-Fort Collins v. City of Fort Collins, 916 F.3d 792 (10th Cir. 2019).
[1143] *Id.*
[1144] *Id.* at 804 (citing, by way of comparison, People v. Santorelli, 600 N.E.2d 232, 236 (N.Y. 1992) (Titone, J., concurring)).
[1145] *Id.*
[1146] Eline v. Town of Ocean City, 2018 U.S. Dist. LEXIS 143951 (2018) (citing cases).
[1147] *See, e.g.*, Free the Nipple v. City of Springfield, 923 F.3d 508, 510 (8th Cir. 2019); Cent. Tex. Nudists v. Cty. of Travis, 2000 Tex. App. LEXIS 8136 (Tex. Ct. App. 2000).
[1148] *Id.*
[1149] Sessions v. Morales-Santana, 582 U.S. 47 (2017).
[1150] *Free the Nipple*, 923 F.3d 508. The court cited several cases as precedent.
[1151] State v. Lilley, 204 A.3d 198 (N.H. 2019); *cert. denied*, 140 S. Ct. 858 (2020).
[1152] *Id.* at 208.
[1153] *Id.* at 213.
[1154] *Id.* at 208.
[1155] *Id.* at 224. (Bassett and Hicks, JJ, dissenting).
[1156] *Id.* at 210.
[1157] Eline v. Town of Ocean City, 7 F.4th 214 (4th Cir. 2021). For further discussion of cases assessing statutes targeting exposure of female breasts, see Colin R. Harbke & Dana F. Lindemann, *Objectification and Reactions Toward Public Female Toplessness in the United States: Looking Beyond Legal Approval*, 27 SEXUALITY & CULTURE 104, 106 (2023).
[1158] *Eline*, 7 F.4th at 221.
[1159] *Id.* at 217.
[1160] *Id.*
[1161] United States v. Biocic, 928 F.2d 112 (4th Cir. 1991), and cases cited therein.
[1162] *Id.* at 115.
[1163] *Id.* at 115–16.
[1164] Janet Portman, *Public Urination Laws and Penalties*, CRIM. DEF. LAWYER (Nov. 18, 2022), https://www.criminaldefenselawyer.com/resources/criminal-defense/sex-crimes/public-urination-law-penalty.htm. It is a crime at common law as well. *See, e.g.*, Van Houten v. State, 46 N.J.L. 16 (1884).
[1165] Kerem Kemal Soylemez et al., *A Qualitative Insight into the Experiences of Naturists Perceived Stigma of Naturism*, 16 GSC ADVANCED RES. & REVS. 148 (2023).
[1166] De Vries, *supra* note 43, at 413.
[1167] Cooper, *supra* note 68.
[1168] State v. Lilley, 204 A.3d 198 (N.Y. 2019), *cert. denied*, 140 S. Ct. 858 (2020).
[1169] VICTORIA BATEMAN, NAKED FEMINISM: BREAKING THE CULT OF FEMALE MODESTY (2023).
[1170] Piar, *supra* note 852, at 164.

[1171] Nassim Alisobhani, *Female Toplessness: Gender Equality's Next Frontier*, 8 U.C. IRVINE L. REV. 299 (2018).
[1172] Elliot Peters, *"We Are Founded on Judeo-Christian Principles"—Trump Vows to End Religious Freedom for non-Christians in the United States*, MSN, https://www.msn.com/en-us/news/opinion/we-are-founded-on-judeo-christian-principles-trump-vows-to-end-religious-freedom-for-non-christians-in-the-united-states/ss-AA1jkWDU?ocid=hpmsn&cvid=d027e4e471144a75b5bcbd1ab176eafb&ei=80 (11/3/23).
[1173] Amy Lewis, *"Christianity Will Be the Law": High-Profile Advocate for Ending the Separation of Church and State Is Well Acquainted with Speaker Mike Johnson*, MSN, https://www.msn.com/en-us/news/opinion/christianity-will-be-the-law-high-profile-advocate-for-ending-the-separation-of-church-and-state-is-well-acquainted-with-speaker-mike-johnson/ss-AA1jtx1y?ocid=hpmsn&cvid=93418160845d4817b2483fce83ea2995&ei=31 (`11/6/23).
[1174] 1 SAMUEL ADAMS, THE LIFE AND PUBLIC SERVICE OF SAMUEL ADAMS 22–23 (1865).
[1175] Obergefell v. Hodges, 576 U.S. 644, 647 (2015).
[1176] *See, e.g.*, West & Kukawska, *supra* note 834; Keon West, *I Feel Better Naked: Communal Naked Activity Increases Body Appreciation by Reducing Social Physique Anxiety*, 58 J. SEX RES. 958 (2021); Keon West, *Think of the Children!: Relationships Between Nudity-Related Experiences in Childhood, Body Image, Self-Esteem and Adjustment*, 37 CHILDREN & SOC'Y 1187 (2023).
[1177] DeVries, *supra* note 43.
[1178] *See, e.g.*, NSPCC LEARNING, CHILDREN'S EXPERIENCES OF LEGAL BUT HARMFUL CONTENT ONLINE (Feb. 2022), https://learning.nspcc.org.uk/media/2727/legal-but-harmful-content-online-helplines-insight-briefing.pdf.
[1179] Eckl v. Davis, 51 Cal. App. 3d 831 (Cal. Ct. App. 1975). A state law preemption challenge was dismissed because the state statute required a showing of lewd intent. *See In re* Smith, 497 P.2d 807 (Cal. 1972), where the court observed that the state statute required a showing of lewd intent and the local ordinance did not.
[1180] Crownover v. Musick, 509 P.2d 497 (1973), *overruled by* Morris v. Mun. Ct., 652 P.2d 51 (Cal. 1982).
[1181] *Id.* at 500.
[1182] *Id.* at 505.
[1183] Morris v. Mun. Ct., 652 P.2d 51 (Cal. 1982)).
[1184] *Id.* at 55.
[1185] Eckl v. Davis, 51 Cal. App. 3d 831. The court addressed the four factors set forth in *O'Brien* (1968), as follows: (1) The ordinance falls within traditional police powers, citing *Pap's A.M.*; (2) it furthers important and substantial interests in protecting individuals "who are unwillingly or unexpectedly exposed" to the nakedness and avoids secondary effects of distractions, obstructions and crowds that might interfere with safety and free flow of pedestrian and vehicular traffic; (3) the prohibition "is unrelated to the

suppression of free expression, because the ordinance regulates public nakedness whether or not it is expressive"; and (4) "the incidental restriction on alleged 1st Amendment freedoms is no greater than is essential to the furtherance of that interest."

[1186] *Id.* at 848.

[1187] Wittbold v. Miami-Dade Cty., 2013 U.S. Dist. LEXIS 90514 (S.D. Fla. 2013).

[1188] Woodlands Pride, Inc. v. Paxton, No. 4:23-cv-02847, 2023 U.S. Dist. LEXIS 171268 (S.D. Tex. 2023).

[1189] The jurisdiction is chosen for illustration. Choice of jurisdiction would be an important element of strategy in actual litigation.

[1190] Dombrowski v. Pfister, 380 U.S. 479 (1965). The abstention doctrine is inappropriate for cases where statutes are justifiably attacked on their face as abridging free expression, or as applied for the purpose of discouraging protected activities.

[1191] BERKELEY, CAL., MUNICIPAL CODE tit. 13 (2023), https://berkeley.municipal.codes/BMC/13.32.

[1192] CAL. PENAL CODE § 314 (West 2023).

[1193] Lee v. Weisman, 505 U.S. 577 (1992); *see supra* note 742.

[1194] Pam, *The Genesis of G.O.E.*, GARDEN OF EDEN CHURCH, https://gardenofedenchurch.org/about.html (last visited Nov. 18, 2023).

[1195] *See supra* note 5.

[1196] WALT WHITMAN, "Song of Myself," *in* LEAVES OF GRASS 31 (1855) (1931), *quoted in* ILSLEY BOONE, THE JOYS OF NUDISM 59 (1934).

[1197] Katherine Romack & Semiotic Society of American, in cooperation with the Philosophy Documentation Center, *"For This Is the Naked Truth": The Early Quakers and Going Naked as a Sign*, 27 AM. J. SEMIOTICS 203, 210 (2011), https://doi.org/10.5840/ajs2011271/48; *see also* RICHARD BAUMAN, LET YOUR WORDS BE FEW—SYMBOLISM OF SPEAKING AND SILENCE AMONG SEVENTEENTH CENTURY QUAKERS 84–94 (1983).

[1198] *See* Barnes v. Glen Theatre, 501 U.S. 560 (1991) (Scalia, J., concurring) ("The purpose of [the Indiana statute] forbidding people to appear nude in parks, beaches, hot dog stands, and like public places is to protect others from offense.").

[1199] See Humphreys' groundbreaking work, LAUD HUMPHREYS, TEAROOM TRADE: IMPERSONAL SEX IN PUBLIC PLACES (2017).

[1200] Chip Johnson, *How Berkeley's "Naked Guy" Met a Tragic End*, SFGATE (May 19, 2009), https://www.sfgate.com/bayarea/article/How-Berkeley-s-Naked-Guy-met-a-tragic-end-3232119.php.

[1201] California has not enacted a law imposing RFRA provisions on its municipalities, which leaves open the question of the appropriate standard of review for the religious claims.

[1202] Green, *supra* note 46, at 240 et seq. Green argues for legalization of exhibitionism.

[1203] WILLIAM BRADFORD, BRADFORD'S HISTORY OF 'PLIMOTH PLANTATION' (2021) (1898), http://www.gutenberg.org/cache/epub/24950/pg24950.txt (eBook).

[1204] WHITMAN, *supra* note 1196.

[1205] Ironically, Thomas Hobbes was a teacher and friend of King Charles II.
[1206] See, for example, the writings of Professor Jamal Greene at Columbia Law School. *Jamal Greene*, COLUM. L. SCH., https://www.law.columbia.edu/faculty/jamal-greene (last visited Oct. 18, 2023).
[1207] Dobbs v. Jackson Women's Health Org., 142 S. Ct. 2228 (2022).
[1208] *Id.* at 2265.
[1209] THOMAS JEFFERSON, NOTES ON THE STATE OF VIRGINIA 267 (1787).
[1210] *Dobbs*,142 S. Ct. at 2246.
[1211] *Roe* was decided during a sexual revolution inspired by introduction of contraceptive pills and a rising tide of feminism. Access to abortion became more important in this context. Further study may connect the dots between these cultural phenomena and the opinions of SOTUS justices who supported the decision.
[1212] *Id.* at 2265.
[1213] *Id.* at 2258.
[1214] Roth v. United States, 354 U.S. 476, 512 (1957).
[1215] *Id.* at 502 (Harlan, concurring).
[1216] City of L.A. v. Alameda Books, 535 U.S. 425 (2002).
[1217] *Dobbs*, 142 S. Ct. at 2239.
[1218] *Id.*
[1219] *Id.* at 2243 (quoting Planned Parenthood of Se. Pa. v. Casey, 505 U.S. 833, 851 (1992), *overruled by* Dobbs v. Jackson Women's Health Org., 142 S. Ct. 2228 (2022)) (Scalia, J., concurring in judgment in part and dissenting in part).
[1220] *Id.* at 2283–84 ("It follows that the States may regulate abortion for legitimate reasons, and when such regulations are challenged under the Constitution, courts cannot 'substitute their social and economic beliefs for the judgment of legislative bodies.' Ferguson v. Skrupa, 372 U.S. 726, 729–30 (1963); *see also* Dandridge v. Williams, 397 U.S. 471, 484–86 (1970); United States v. Carolene Products Co., 304 U.S. 144, 152 (1938). That respect for a legislature's judgment applies even when the laws at issue concern matters of great social significance and moral substance. *See, e.g.*, Bd. of Trustees of Univ. of Ala. v. Garrett, 531 U.S. 356 (2001) ("treatment of the disabled"); Washington v. Glucksberg, 521 U.S. 702, 728 (1997) ("assisted suicide"); San Antonio Indep. Sch. Dist. v. Rodriguez, 411 U. S. 1 (1973) ("financing public education").
[1221] Piar, *supra* note 852, at 164.
[1222] 61 P.L. 277, 36 Stat. 825, 61 Cong. Ch. 395 (1910).
[1223] 19 U.S.C. § 1305 (2023).
[1224] *E.g.*, GEOFFREY R. STONE, SEX AND THE CONSTITUTION: SEX, RELIGION, AND LAW FROM AMERICA'S ORIGINS TO THE TWENTY-FIRST CENTURY (2017).
[1225] CAL. PENAL CODE § 318 (West 2012).
[1226] Taub v. City of S.F., 696 Fed. Appx. 181 (9th Cir. 2017); Luke Gentile, *Conservatives Bash Seattle Pride Parade After Men Go Full-Frontal in Front of Children*, MSN, https://www.msn.com/en-us/lifestyle/lifestyle-buzz/conservatives-bash-seattle-pride-parade-after-men-go-full-frontal-in-front-of-children/ar-AA1d48M8?ocid=hpmsn&cvid=d04781f13de5437b9b780c4150ed5205&ei=76

(last visited Oct. 18, 2023); Natalie N. Alund, *White House Says Activist Who Took Top Off at Pride Celebration Won't Be Invited Back*, MSN, https://www.msn.com/en-us/news/us/white-house-says-activist-who-took-top-off-at-pride-celebration-won-t-be-invited-back/ar-AA1cxAUs?ocid=hpmsn&cvid=5a46349628c3498196721f01af0a6c0b&ei=65 (last visited Oct. 18, 2023).

[1227] *2023 WNBR PDX*, KEEP PORTLAND WEIRD, https://keep-portland-weird.com/2023-world-naked-bike-ride/ (last visited Nov. 18, 2023).

[1228] Stevens v. Georgia, 2013 U.S. Dist. LEXIS 183862 (N.D. Ga. 2013).

[1229] Lawrence v. Texas, 539 U.S. 558 (2003).

[1230] Goldberg, *supra* note 51.

[1231] Dobbs v. Jackson Women's Health Org., 142 S. Ct. 2228, 2246 (2022).

[1232] *Id.* at 2259.

[1233] Lawrence v. Texas, 539 U.S. 558, 572 (2003).

[1234] *E.g.*, Neda Pouraskari, Adherence to Islamic Dress Code and Hijabi Muslim Students' Experiences of Belonging, Social Adjustment, and Islamophobia (2020) (D.Ed. dissertation, University of North Carolina at Charlotte), https://www.proquest.com/docview/2385705767/abstract/E8BE207F0A744B2DPQ/1.

[1235] *E.g.*, Ann Bodine, *School Uniforms, Academic Achievement, and Uses of Research*, 97 J. EDUC. RES. 67 (2003).

[1236] *E.g.*, Kirsten Dellinger, *Wearing Gender and Sexuality "On Your Sleeve": Dress Norms and the Importance of Occupational and Organizational Culture at Work*, GENDER ISSUES, Winter 2002, at 3.

[1237] *E.g.*, Hannah Knipp & Rae Stevenson, *"A Powerful Visual Statement": Race, Class, and Gender in Uniform and Dress Code Policies in New Orleans Public Charter Schools*, 37 AFFILIA (2021), https://doi.org/10.1177/08861099211010026.

[1238] Maril, *supra* note 29, at 66–67.

[1239] Samirah Majumdar, *Government Restrictions on Religion Around the World Reached New Record in 2018*, PEW RES. CTR. (blog), https://www.pewresearch.org/short-reads/2020/11/10/government-restrictions-on-religion-around-the-world-reached-new-record-in-2018/ (last visited Jan. 6, 2024).

[1240] *E.g.*, John Fritze, *Gay Counselor's Firing by Indianapolis Catholic School Permitted by Federal Appeals Court*, MSN, https://www.msn.com/en-us/news/us/federal-appeals-court-rules-catholic-school-was-permitted-to-fire-gay-counselor/ar-AA1dS0PE?ocid=hpmsn&cvid=310afeeada7e4891915e69d79aad9185&ei=26 (last visited Oct. 18, 2023); Jacob Paul, *Michigan Residents Face Five Years in Prison and a $10,000 Fine for Using Wrong Pronouns*, MSN, https://www.msn.com/en-us/news/us/michigan-residents-face-five-years-in-prison-and-a-10-000-fine-for-using-wrong-pronouns/ar-AA1dgKg8?ocid=hpmsn&cvid=90f0f59fc1194955a6d15184553db49a&ei=59 (last visited Sept. 24, 2023); *U.S. High Court Stops School's Skirt Rule for Girls*, MSN, https://www.msn.com/en-us/news/world/us-high-court-stops-school-s-skirt-rule-for-girls/ar-AA1d4qIz?ocid=hpmsn&cvid=94f6ef67da52499cb3f11c1c8250c7dc&ei=29

(last visited Oct. 18, 2023); Gentile, *supra* note 1226; Associated Press, *Gavin Newsom Signs New Bills to Protect California's LGBTQ Community One Day After Issuing Controversial Veto*, MSN, https://www.msn.com/en-us/news/other/gavin-newsom-signs-new-bills-to-protect-california-s-lgbtq-community-one-day-after-issuing-controversial-veto/ar-AA1hc8JZ (last visited Oct. 18, 2023).
[1241] J.M. Balkin, *The Constitution of Status*, 106 YALE L.J. 2313 (1997) (paraphrasing Justice Scalia in *Romer* dissent).
[1242] *E.g.*, Karl Ritter, *Why Does Sweden Allow Quran Burnings? Like Much of West, It Has No Blasphemy Laws*, ABC NEWS (July 20, 2023), https://abcnews.go.com/International/wireStory/sweden-quran-burnings-101529405.
[1243] Claude Wooten, *Barack Obama Warns American Christians That Sacred Texts Are Threatened*, MSN, https://www.msn.com/en-us/entertainment/news/barack-obama-warns-american-christians-that-sacred-texts-are-threatened/ar-AA1dYTPp?ocid=hpmsn&cvid=c2d6f7b3a01e481080d2b2cbd92467e4&ei=41 (last visited Oct. 18, 2023).
[1244] *See, e.g.*, RUSSELL BLACKFORD, FREEDOM OF RELIGION AND THE SECULAR STATE (2012); Masmaliyeva, *supra* note 285.
[1245] M. FOUCAULT, THE HISTORY OF SEXUALITY, VOLUME 1: AN INTRODUCTION (1976).
[1246] *Invisible Hand*, BRITANNICA (last updated Jan. 24, 2024), https://www.britannica.com/money/topic/invisible-hand.
[1247] *Democracy*, BRITANNICA (last updated Jan. 24, 2024), https://www.britannica.com/topic/democracy.
[1248] DAVID GRAEBER & DAVID WENGROW, THE DAWN OF EVERYTHING: A NEW HISTORY OF HUMANITY (2021). For discussion of the views of Wendat statesman Kandiaronk on European religion and politics, see *id.* at 48–56.
[1249] *The Athenians: Another Warning from History?*, UNIV. OF CAMBRIDGE (Oct. 2, 2009), https://www.cam.ac.uk/research/news/the-athenians-another-warning-from-history.
[1250] *The World Sees What America Does Not. Fareed Explains*, MSN, https://www.msn.com/en-us/health/medical/the-world-sees-what-america-does-not-fareed-explains/vi-AA1mADEs?ocid=msedgntp&cvid=f5157fd2020a4308acd50e9cab44197e&ei=28 (last visited Jan. 7, 2024).
[1251] RUTH RUBINSTEIN, DRESS CODES: MEANINGS AND MESSAGES IN AMERICAN CULTURE (2018) (providing an overview of theories of clothing).
[1252] Aristotle, *Metaphysics* (Book 4), PERSEUS, https://www.perseus.tufts.edu/hopper/text?doc=Perseus%3Atext%3A1999.01.0052%3Abook%3D4 (last visited Jan. 30, 2024).
[1253] T.B. HOWELL, 17 STATE TRIALS 155f (1809-1826).
[1254] Also available: *Diary Entries from July 1663*, THE DIARY OF SAMUEL PEPYS, https://www.pepysdiary.com/diary/1663/07/ (last visited Dec. 13, 2023).

Index

Made in the USA
Monee, IL
12 November 2026

7ce07a5f-bea7-4b96-ad9c-90843d537395R01